The Art of the Book

— Its Place in Medieval Worship —

The Art of the Book

— Its Place in Medieval Worship —

EDITED BY

Margaret M. Manion

AND

Bernard J. Muir

UNIVERSITY
of
EXETER
PRESS

First published in 1998 by
University of Exeter Press
Reed Hall, Streatham Drive
Exeter, Devon EX4 4QR
UK

© University of Exeter Press 1998

British Library Cataloguing in Publication Data
A catalogue record of this book is available
from the British Library

ISBN: 0 85989 566 1

Typeset in Palatino by Bernard J. Muir

Printed in Great Britain by Redwood Press, Trowbridge

CONTENTS

ACKNOWLEDGEMENTS	vii
ABBREVIATIONS	viii
LIST OF PLATES AND FIGURES	ix

Introduction
Margaret M. Manion 1

1 *The Early Insular Prayer Book Tradition and the Development of the Book of Hours*
Bernard J. Muir 9

2 *Women, Art and Devotion: Three French Fourteenth-Century Royal Prayer Books*
Margaret M. Manion 21

3 *Books for a Dominican Nuns' Choir: Illustrated Liturgical Manuscripts at Saint-Louis de Poissy, c.1330–1350*
Joan Naughton 67

4 *The Illustrated Office of the Passion in Italian Books of Hours*
Bronwyn C. Stocks 111

5 *An Unusual Image of the Assumption in a Fourteenth-Century Dominican Choir-Book*
Margaret M. Manion 153

6 *The Dominican Liturgy of the Assumption: Texts and Music for the Divine Office*
John Stinson   163

7 *A Centre for Devotional and Liturgical Manuscript Illumination in Fifteenth-Century Besançon*
Vera F. Vines   195

8 *The Master of Jacques de Besançon and a Fifteenth-Century Parisian Missal*
Hilary Maddocks   225

9 *Marginalized Jewels: The Depiction of Jewellery in the Borders of Flemish Devotional Manuscripts*
Kate Challis   253

10 *Devotional Objects in Book Format: Diptychs in the Collection of Margaret of Austria and her Family*
Dagmar Eichberger   291

LIST OF CONTRIBUTORS   325

INDEX   327

ACKNOWLEDGEMENTS

PICTURE CREDITS

Adelaide, State Library of South Australia: Pl. 4, Figs 31–32, 34–36, 40–41
Antwerp, Koninklijk Museum voor Schone Kunsten; copyright IRPA-KIK, Brussels: Figs 91–92
Auckland, Central City Library, Special Collections: Pl. 5, Figs 42–49, 53
Besançon, Bibliothèque Municipale: Figs 50–51, 54–55
Brussels, Bibliothèque Royale; copyright IRPA-KIK, Brussels: Figs 87–89
Ghent, Museum voor Schone Kunsten; copyright IRPA-KIK, Brussels: Figs 93–94
Kremsmünster, Stiftsbibliothek: Fig. 38
London, by permission of the British Library: Pls 3, 7, Figs 26, 33, 37, 39, 69–70, 76, 79–80
London, By courtesy of the Trustees of The National Gallery, London: Figs 85–86
London, Collection of the Earl of Yarborough: Fig. 97
London, The Conway Library, Courtauld Institute of Art: Figs 21, 29–30
Melbourne, State Library of Victoria: Fig. 22
New Haven, Beinecke Rare Book and Manuscript Library, Yale University: Figs 1, 5, 13
New York, The Metropolitan Museum of Art. The Cloisters Collection: Figs 2, 14–15
New York, The Metropolitan Museum of Art. The Jack and Belle Linsky Collection: Fig. 96
New York, The Pierpont Morgan Library: Figs 52, 72
Oxford, Bodleian Library, University of Oxford: Figs 73–74
Paris, Bibliothèque de l'Arsenal: Figs 19–20, 24, 27–28
Paris, Bibliothèque Mazarine: Pl. 6, Figs 56–59, 61–66
Paris, Bibliothèque Nationale: Pl. 1, Figs 3–4, 6–12, 16, 25, 60, 67–68. Clichés Bibliothèque Nationale de France, Paris
Perugia, Biblioteca Comunale Augusta: Pl. 2
Philadelphia, Philadelphia Museum of Art: Fig. 17
Vienna, Österreichische Nationalbibliothek: Pl. 8, Figs 71, 75, 77–78, 81–84, 90
    (Negativs aus dem Bildarchiv der Österreichischen Nationalbibliothek, Wien)
Washington, National Gallery of Art. Ailsa Mellon Bruce Fund: Figs 95, 98
Zurich, Schweizerisches Landesmuseum: Fig. 23

Publication of this work was assisted by a special publications grant from The University of Melbourne. The editors gratefully acknowledge the consultation and assistance of Simon Baker (Publisher) and the production staff of University of Exeter Press in the preparation of this work.

ABBREVIATIONS

Add.	Additional (collection, British Library)
Bay. Staatsbibl.	Bayerische Staatsbibliothek (Munich)
Bibl. de l'Arsenal	Bibliothèque de l'Arsenal (Paris)
Bibl. Mazarine	Bibliothèque Mazarine (Paris)
Bibl. mun.	Bibliothèque municipale
Bibl. Roy.	Bibliothèque Royale (Brussels)
Bibl. Laurenziana	Biblioteca Laurenziana (Florence)
Bibl. Marciana	Biblioteca Marciana (Venice)
BL	British Library (London)
BN	Bibliothèque Nationale (Paris)
Bodl.	Bodleian Library (Oxford)
B.A.V.	Biblioteca Apostolica Vaticana (Vatican City)
Mazarine	Bibliothèque Mazarine (Paris)
Morgan	Pierpont Morgan Library (New York)
n.a.	nouvelle acquisition
ON	Österreichische Nationalbibliothek (Vienna)
s.n.	series nova

Reference to manuscripts in all collections and all languages has been standardized to MS(S).

PLATES and FIGURES

COLOUR PLATES (following p. xvi)

1. Instruction of St Louis. *Hours of Jeanne of Navarre*. Paris, Bibliothèque Nationale, MS n.a. lat. 3145, f. 85v.

2. Assumption. Antiphonal. Perugia, Biblioteca Comunale Augusta, MS 2785, f. 91v.

3. Easter Sunday. Missal. London, British Library, Egerton MS 3037, f. 104.

4. Flagellation. Book of Hours. Adelaide, State Library of South Australia, f. 26.

5. Invention of St Stephen's relics. Missal. Auckland, Central City Library, Special Collections, Med. MS G. 139, f. 194.

6. Advent. Missal. Paris, Bibliothèque Mazarine, MS 412, f. 1.

7. Mary Magdalen. Book of Hours. London, British Library, Add. MS 35313, f. 231v.

8. Philip the Good and Charles the Bold praying in front of a diptych. *Prayer Book of Philip the Good*. Vienna, Österreichische Nationalbibliothek, MS 1800, ff. 1v–2.

BLACK & WHITE FIGURES

1. Blanche of Savoy kneeling before the Trinity. *Savoy Hours*. New Haven, Yale University, Beinecke Rare Book and Manuscript Library, MS 390, f. 2.   51

2. Christ addresses Bonne of Luxembourg and Jean le Bon from the Cross. *Psalter of Bonne of Luxembourg*. New York, The Metropolitan Museum of Art. The Cloisters Collection (69.86), f. 329.   52

3. Vision of Isaiah. *Hours of Jeanne of Navarre*. Paris, Bibliothèque Nationale, MS n.a. lat. 3145, f. 25.   53

4. St John the Baptist. *Petites Heures*. Paris, Bibliothèque Nationale, MS lat. 18014, f. 208. 54

5. Blanche of Savoy at prayer. *Savoy Hours*. New Haven, Yale University, Beinecke Rare Book and Manuscript Library, MS 390, f. 25v. 55

6. Annunciation. *Hours of Jeanne of Navarre*. Paris, Bibliothèque Nationale, MS n.a. lat. 3145, f. 39. 56

7. Entombment. *Hours of Jeanne of Navarre*. Paris, Bibliothèque Nationale, MS n.a. lat. 3145, f. 115. 57

8. Anointing of St Louis. *Hours of Jeanne of Navarre*. Paris, Bibliothèque Nationale, MS n.a. lat. 3145, f. 99. 58

9. The preaching of the Crusade. *Hours of Jeanne of Navarre*. Paris, Bibliothèque Nationale, MS n.a. lat. 3145, f. 106v. 59

10. Jeanne de Navarre with her guardian angel gives alms to the poor. *Hours of Jeanne of Navarre*. Paris, Bibliothèque Nationale, MS n.a. lat. 3145, f. 123v. 60

11. Jeanne de Navarre kneels before the Virgin and Child. *Hours of Jeanne of Navarre*. Paris, Bibliothèque Nationale, MS n.a. lat. 3145, f. 118v. 61

12. Jeanne de Navarre kneels before the Virgin and Child. *Hours of Jeanne of Navarre*. Paris, Bibliothèque Nationale, MS n.a. lat. 3145, f. 151v. 62

13. King Charles V kneels before St Anthony. *Savoy Hours*. New Haven, Yale University, Beinecke Rare Book and Manuscript Library, MS 390, f. 4 (upper). 63

14. The wound of Christ and the instruments of the Passion. *Psalter of Bonne of Luxembourg*. New York, The Metropolitan Museum of Art. The Cloisters Collection (69.86), f. 331. 64

15. The degrees of charity. *Psalter of Bonne of Luxembourg*. New York, The Metropolitan Museum of Art. The Cloisters Collection (69.86), f. 315. 65

16. Jean de Berry and his guardian angel. *Petites Heures*. Paris, Bibliothèque Nationale, MS lat. 18014, f. 199. 66

17. Trinity Sunday. Gradual. Philadelphia, Museum of Art, MS 45-65-7, ff. 162v–163.   97

18. Feast of the Translation of St Dominic. Breviary. London, Private Collection, ff. 367v–368.   98

19. Feast of the Eleven Thousand Virgins. Breviary. Paris, Bibliothèque de l'Arsenal, MS 603, f. 378.   99

20. Feast of All Saints. Breviary. Paris, Bibliothèque de l'Arsenal, MS 603, f. 387.   100

21. Feast of St Louis. Breviary. London, Private Collection, f. 422.   101

22. Feast of St Dominic. Antiphonal. Melbourne, State Library of Victoria, MS *096 1/R66A, f. 294v.   102

23. Feast of St Dominic. Gradual. Zurich, Schweizerisches Landesmuseum, MS LM 26117, f. 261v.   103

24. Feast of the Translation of St Dominic. Breviary. Paris, Bibliothèque de l'Arsenal, MS 107, f. 388v.   104

25. Feast of St Dominic. *Belleville Breviary*. Paris, Bibliothèque Nationale, MS lat. 10484, f. 272.   105

26. Feast of Corpus Christi. Missal. London, British Library, Egerton MS 3037, f. 127.   106

27. Feast of Corpus Christi. Breviary. Paris, Bibliothèque de l'Arsenal, MS 603, f. 93.   107

28. Feast of the Nativity. Breviary. Paris, Bibliothèque de l'Arsenal, MS 602, f. 122v.   108

29. Feast of the Eleven Thousand Virgins. Breviary. London, Private Collection, f. 461.   109

30. Psalm 97, *Cantate Domino*. Breviary. London, Private Collection, f. 58.   110

31. Betrayal of Christ. Book of Hours. Adelaide, State Library of South Australia, f. 15.   142

32. Christ before Pilate. Book of Hours. Adelaide, State Library of South Australia, f. 21v.   143

33. Mocking and Buffeting of Christ. Book of Hours. London, British Library, Add. MS 15265, f. 102.   144

34. Carrying of the Cross. Book of Hours. Adelaide, State Library of South Australia, f. 29.   145

35. Christ crucified, offered vinegar to drink. Book of Hours. Adelaide, State Library of South Australia, f. 34.   146

36. Christ dead on the Cross. Book of Hours. Adelaide, State Library of South Australia, f. 39v.   147

37. Christ is nailed to the Cross. Book of Hours. London, British Library, Add. MS 34247, f. 125.   148

38. Crucifixion. Book of Hours. Kremsmünster, Stiftsbibliothek, MS Cim.4, f. 150.   149

39. Crucifixion, with Mass and Baptism. Bolognese Book of Hours. London, British Library, Add. MS 34247, f. 127.   150

40. Deposition. Book of Hours. Adelaide, State Library of South Australia, f. 45v.   151

41. Entombment. Book of Hours. Adelaide, State Library of South Australia, f. 49.   152

42. St Antidius rides to Rome on the back of a devil. Missal. Auckland, Central City Library, Special Collections, Med. MS G. 139, f. 157.   210

43. Meeting of the Magi. Missal. Auckland, Central City Library, Special Collections, Med. MS G. 138, f. 22.   211

44. Stoning of St Stephen. Missal. Auckland, Central City Library, Special Collections, Med. MS G. 138, f. 15v.   212

45. Dedication of the altar of St Stephen. Missal. Auckland, Central City Library, Special Collections, Med. MS G. 139, f. 242.   213

46. Translation of the relics of St Nicholas. Missal. Auckland, Central City Library, Special Collections, Med. MS G. 139, f. 146.   214

47. Feast of All Saints. Missal. Auckland, Central City Library, Special Collections, Med. MS G. 139, f. 253.   215

48. Holy Saturday *Exultet*. Missal. Auckland, Central City Library, Special Collections, Med. MS G. 138, f. 125v.   216

49. Pentecost *Exultet*. Missal. Auckland, Central City Library, Special Collections, Med. MS G. 139, f. 25.   217

50. Ordination to the subdiaconate. Pontifical. Besançon, Bibliothèque municipale, MS 115, f. 14.   218

51. Ordination to the diaconate. Pontifical. Besançon, Bibliothèque municipale, MS 157, f. 34.   219

52. Visitation. Book of Hours. New York, Pierpont Morgan Library, MS M. 28, f. 40.   220

53. Visitation. Missal. Auckland, City Central Library, Special Collections, Med. MS G. 139, f. 170.   221

54. Presentation in the Temple. Book of Hours. Besançon, Bibliothèque municipale, MS 125, f. 40.   222

55. Crucifixion. Missal. Besançon, Bibliothèque municipale, MS 77, f. 233v.   223

56. Nativity of the Virgin. Missal. Paris, Bibliothèque Mazarine, MS 412, f. 333v.   239

57. St Genevieve meets St Germanus. Missal. Paris, Bibliothèque Mazarine, MS 412, f. 315.   240

58. Martyrdom of St Eustace. Missal. Paris, Bibliothèque Mazarine, MS 412, f. 364.   241

59. Burial service. Missal. Paris, Bibliothèque Mazarine, MS 412, f. 410.   242

60. Burial service. Psalter and Vigils of the Dead. Paris, Bibliothèque Nationale, MS Smith-Lesouëf 9, p. 349.   243

61. Feast of the Trinity. Missal. Paris, Bibliothèque Mazarine, MS 412, f. 194v.   244

62. Last Supper and Crucifixion. Missal. Paris, Bibliothèque Mazarine, MS 412, f. 8.   245

63. Crucifixion and Passion scenes. Missal. Paris, Bibliothèque Mazarine, MS 412, f. 6v.   246

64. *Maiestas*. Missal. Paris, Bibliothèque Mazarine, MS 412, f. 7.   247

65. Feast of Christmas. Missal. Paris, Bibliothèque Mazarine, MS 412, f. 17. 248

66. Easter Sunday. Missal. Paris, Bibliothèque Mazarine, MS 412, f. 151. 249

67. Feast of the Annunciation. *Légende dorée*. Paris, Bibliothèque Nationale, MS fr. 244, f. 107. 250

68. Advent Season. *Légende dorée*. Paris, Bibliothèque Nationale, MS fr. 244, f. 4. 251

69. St George and the dragon. Book of Hours. London, British Library, Add. MS 35313, f. 223v. 274

70. Border decoration. *Hours of Joanna of Castile*. London, British Library, Add. MS 18852, f. 243. 275

71. Border decoration. Book of Hours. Vienna, Österreichische Nationalbibliothek, MS 1979, f. 88. 276

72. St Agnes. *Hours of Catherine of Cleves*. New York, Pierpont Morgan Library, MS M.917, p. 300. 277

73. Coronation of the Virgin. Book of Hours. Oxford, Bodleian Library, MS Douce 256, f. 101v. 278

74. St Luke painting the Virgin. Book of Hours. Oxford, Bodleian Library, MS Douce 256, f. 15. 279

75. Border decoration. *Hours of James of Scotland*. Vienna, Österreichische Nationalbibliothek, MS 1897, f. 16v. 280

76. Last Supper. *Hours of Joanna of Ghistelles*. London, British Library, Egerton MS 2125, ff. 142v–143. 281

77. Annunciation. *Rothschild Hours*. Vienna, Österreichische Nationalbibliothek, MS Ser. n. 2844, f. 84v. 282

78. Border decoration. *Rothschild Hours*. Vienna, Österreichische Nationalbibliothek, MS Ser. n. 2844, f. 85. 283

79. Border decoration. *Hours of Joanna of Castile*. London, British Library, Add. MS 18852, f. 319. 284

80. Border decoration. Book of Hours. London, British Library, Add. MS 35313, f. 224. 285

PLATES AND FIGURES

81. Resurrection. *Hours of James of Scotland*. Vienna, Österreichische National-bibliothek, MS 1897, f. 183v. — 286

82. Crucifixion. *Hours of James of Scotland*. Vienna, Österreichische National-bibliothek, MS 1897, f. 241v. — 287

83. St George and the dragon. *Seelengärtlein*. Vienna, Österreichische Nationalbibliothek, MS 2706, f. 250v. — 288

84. St George and the dragon. *Rothschild Hours*. Vienna, Österreichische Nationalbibliothek, MS Ser. n. 2844, f. 204. — 289

Diptych (Figs 85–86)

85. King Richard II praying to the Virgin and Child (left panel). *Wilton Diptych*. The National Gallery, London. — 310

86. King Richard II praying to the Virgin and Child (right panel). *Wilton Diptych*. The National Gallery, London. — 311

87. Jean, Duc de Berry, praying to the Virgin and Child (left page). *Très Belles Heures*. Brussels, Bibliothèque Royale, MS 11060–11061, p. 10. — 312

88. Jean, Duc de Berry, praying to the Virgin and Child (right page). *Très Belles Heures*. Brussels, Bibliothèque Royale, MS 11060–11061, p. 11. — 313

89. Philip the Good in his private prayer tent. *Traité sur l'oraison dominicale*. Brussels, Bibliothèque Royale, MS 9092, f. 9. — 314

90. Philip the Good praying to the Virgin. Diptych and book. Vienna, Österreichische Nationalbibliothek, MS 1800, ff. 13v–14. — 315

Diptych (Figs 91–92)

91. Master of 1499. *Virgin in the Church* (left panel). Antwerp, Koninklijk Museum voor Schone Kunsten. — 316

92. Master of 1499. *Christiaan de Hondt praying* (right panel). Antwerp, Koninklijk Museum voor Schone Kunsten. — 317

Diptych (Figs 93–94)

93. Anonymous Master. *Virgin and Child* (left panel). Ghent, Museum voor Schone Kunsten. 318

94. Anonymous Master. *Margaret of Austria praying* (right panel). Ghent, Museum voor Schone Kunsten. 319

95. Juan de Flandes. *The Temptation of Christ*. Washington, National Gallery of Art, Ailsa Mellon Bruce Fund. 320

96. Juan de Flandes. *The Marriage Feast at Cana*. New York, Metropolitan Museum of Art, The Jack and Belle Linsky Collection. 321

97. Michiel Sittow. *The Ascension of Christ*. Collection of the Earl of Yarborough. 322

98. Michiel Sittow. *The Assumption of the Virgin*. Washington, National Gallery of Art, Ailsa Mellon Bruce Fund. 323

Plate 1. Instruction of St Louis. *Hours of Jeanne of Navarre*. Paris, Bibliothèque Nationale, MS n.a. lat. 3145, f. 85v. 180×135mm.

Plate 2. Assumption. Antiphonal. Perugia, Biblioteca Comunale Augusta, MS 2785, f. 91v. 620×430 mm (detail).

Plate 3. Easter Sunday. Missal. London, British Library, Egerton MS 3037, f. 104. 211 × 138 mm.

Plate 4. Flagellation. Book of Hours. Adelaide, State Library of South Australia, f. 26. 102×79mm.

Plate 5. Invention of St Stephen's relics. Missal. Auckland, City Central Library, Special Collections, Med. MS G. 139, f. 194. 318×238 mm.

Plate 6. Advent. Missal. Paris, Bibliothèque Mazarine, MS 412, f. 1. 455×320 mm.

Plate 7. Mary Magdalen. Book of Hours. London, British Library, Add. MS 35313, f. 231v. 237 × 152 mm.

Plate 8. Philip the Good and Charles the Bold praying in front of a diptych. *Prayer Book of Philip the Good*. Vienna, Österreichische Nationalbibliothek, MS 1800, ff. 1v–2. 185×130 mm (each page).

INTRODUCTION

THE ESSAYS IN THIS COLLECTION result from individual projects carried out by a group of scholars, based in Melbourne, whose research focuses on medieval books—often elaborately decorated or illustrated—that were designed for use in Christian worship, either public or private. Some of the writers have been engaged in this field for many years and the particular questions and problems they address here grow naturally out of earlier studies. Others have recently completed or are carrying out doctoral projects in the area. They all approach the medieval prayer book, of whatever genre—missal, breviary, choir-book or book of hours—as a potentially interactive site where many elements relate to and energize one another, and where the textual and visual traditions from which such books derive are constantly revised and modified by the makers of manuscripts, their patrons and commissioners. The writers also share the belief that the analysis of individual books or texts, including the nature of their commissioning, production and function, is a necessary condition for the accurate delineation of the broader contours of medieval religious culture which is attracting increasing attention today. While various connections have emerged in the course of research on these discrete topics, some of which are discussed below, it should be emphasized that there is no intention of presenting here an integrated study of a particular cultural phenomenon; rather the objective is to make known specific findings relating to certain manuscripts, texts, patrons, etc., of interest and value in themselves, findings on which, it is hoped, others may build.

Each essay addresses the medieval religious book from a particular perspective, and examples are drawn from French, Italian and Netherlandish works of the fourteenth to the early sixteenth centuries, with the opening study by Bernard Muir providing a prologue to the focus on the late medieval period. Since most of the contributors are art historians a strong interest is evident in the way in which the visual aspects of the medieval book relate to its literary content; but this is not exclusively the case. Bernard Muir, for example, is a specialist in Anglo-Saxon and early medieval Latin literature, and his exposition of how English devotional manuals of the eighth to the eleventh centuries anticipated the later medieval phenomenon of the book of hours provides a valuable historical dimension to the studies that follow.

In highlighting the continuity of the tradition of Christian worship Muir demonstrates how a deep-seated need for personal communication with God gave rise at a very early period to prayers that, while stimulated by the liturgy and the Sacred Scriptures, nevertheless clearly belong to the category of personal devotion. His study also helps to illustrate the way in which certain themes were integral to Christian spirituality throughout the Middle Ages. Prominent among these is devotion to the Passion and death of Christ. Muir shows that this is already present in the insular prayer book, while another contributor, Bronwyn Stocks, gives detailed attention to this subject in her analysis of the Office of the Passion and its illustration in fourteenth and early fifteenth-century Italian books of hours.

The Anglo-Saxon prayer books also bring home the fact that, although the tradition of the richly illuminated liturgical or biblical book can be traced back to the early centuries of the Christian era, devotional manuals with detailed illustrative narrative cycles are a phenomenon whose origins, as Jeffrey Hamburger has argued, are associated with prayer books made for religious women in the twelfth century.[1] The contrast between the largely unadorned Anglo-Saxon texts and the elaborately ornamented and illustrated prayer books made for both men and women in the later Middle Ages testifies to the influence of social and cultural factors on the relationship between text and image in Christian worship.

John Stinson expands the scope of the study of the medieval religious book into the realm of music. 'He who sings prays twice', St Augustine is alleged to have said; certainly, since very early times, the solemn celebration of both the Divine Office and the Mass has involved the singing or chanting of many of their texts. Stinson's sustained research on medieval music has included a detailed study of the chants in Dominican choir-books. He presents here an edition of the chants for the Office of the feast of the Assumption, which stems from a collaborative study of the text, music and illustration of a set of fourteenth-century graduals and antiphonals now in the Biblioteca Comunale Augusta, Perugia. The edition of the chants for this particular Office complements the essay by Margaret Manion on the significance of the historiated initial for the feast of the Assumption in the same Perugian choir-book. It also resonates with other studies in this collection. Joan Naughton's analysis of the books commissioned for the Dominican monastery of St Louis de Poissy c.1332–46, for example, shows how their use by the nuns for the chanting of appropriate parts of the Office and the Mass was one of the major factors in the determination of their physical lay-out and illustration.

Liturgical music is also an important element in the missal (now in the Auckland Central City Library, Special Collections) around which Vera Vines reconstructs a centre for manuscript production in mid to late fifteenth-century Besançon. Not only does the rare text and chant of its

---

[1] J. Hamburger, 'A *Liber Precum* in Sélestat and the development of the illustrated prayer book in Germany', *Art Bulletin* 68 (1991), 209–36, esp. 226–34.

Pentecost *Exultet* associate this splendidly illuminated two-volume work with one of the city's two cathedrals, but it also points to scribes familiar with the copying of music as well as text. This, together with Besançon's distinguished reputation for the performance of church music, makes it probable that choir-books also issued from the cathedral centre. Furthermore, extant books of hours, illuminated by the same group of artists responsible for the missal and related liturgical manuscripts, indicate that this centre was responsible for the production of a broad range of religious books for devotional as well as liturgical use.

The manifestly functional breviaries commissioned for the choir of St Louis de Poissy that have been researched by Joan Naughton contrast quite markedly with the famous *Belleville Breviary*, which also found its way to this monastery. It, too, is of Dominican use and was produced in Paris a decade earlier for a female patron. The *Belleville Breviary* is much more lavishly ornamented, however, than the Poissy breviaries, and its programme of illustration has a strongly didactic and theological emphasis. Naughton shows how the fact that this book was not explicitly designed for ease of use in the liturgy is borne out by its subsequent history, when it was owned successively by individual members of the Poissy community.

Visually the *Belleville Breviary* is more closely related to the illuminated prayer books produced a little later in Paris for women of the French royal court, which are discussed by Margaret Manion. Not only are these books more lavishly decorated than those for the choir of St Louis de Poissy; but there is a also a marked difference in the nature of the relationship between their text and illustration. Here the images are often an integral part of the prayer itself, and they provide the opportunity for more expansive contemplation on a particular Christian mystery, or act as a vehicle for detailed theological and spiritual instruction.

These books also indicate the variety of devotional manuals available at the period. Many of the prayers in the psalter-hours of Blanche of Burgundy are in the form of short Offices or suffrages, patterns based on liturgical worship, so that the book in its original state must have been like a customised breviary. On the other hand in the fully developed book of hours of Jeanne of Navarre prayers of a more individual nature, culled from a variety of sources, are mingled with those of liturgical origin, while vernacular rubrics often indicate the appropriateness of a particular prayer for a special need or circumstance. The psalter, one of the most ancient and enduringly influential elements in the formulation of Christian prayer, still holds pride of place in the prayer book of Bonne of Luxembourg, but here it is accompanied by a distinctive collection of prayers and extracts from moral and spiritual treatises in the vernacular, all of which have their own specifically designed illustrations.

Over and above their individual illustrative programmes, the appearance of these prayer books is indicative of their nature and function. Their mannered elegance, the mingling of playful and secular decorative elements with explicitly religious themes, together with frequent references to the patron, by way of portraits and heraldic insignia, show that in late medieval France the visual language of courtly and chivalric idealism was a strong shaping force in the realm of female spirituality. It is interesting also to observe that while these books seem to have been designed by men for the women of the royal household, they were to have a significant influence in the next generation on devotional manuals made for male members of the family.

To date researchers have tended to concentrate on the development of the personal prayer book north of the Alps. Bronwyn Stocks draws attention to the early Italian book of hours and in particular to the relationship between text and imagery in one of the most popular devotions to the Passion at this time, the Office of the Passion and Cross. Her study documents for some twenty-five manuscripts variations in the text and illustration of this Office. At the same time she shows how the literary and visual components of this devotion reinforce once another, based as they both are on the chronological commemoration of the events of Christ's Passion. The location of this particular devotion in the wider context of contemporary spiritual writing and the highlighting of certain Italian characteristics in the visual treatment of the Passion scenes are further instances of the ways in which a close study of individual manuscripts may throw light on the broader issue of popular devotion and regional distinctions. The nature of the visual presentation of the Italian book of hours in the fourteenth and early fifteenth centuries which Stocks also opens up here by examining in detail the illustrations of one particular Passion cycle, that of the *Adelaide Hours*, *c*.1375, further expands the horizons of medieval manuscript studies.

One of the most important of the books used in the Christian liturgy is the Mass book or missal, which contains all the texts for the celebration of the Mass or Eucharist throughout the year. By contrast to the Divine Office whose full and regular performance is confined largely to monastic congregations and clerics, participation in the Mass, the commemoration of Christ's redemptive sacrifice and the Church's official prayer of thanksgiving for this act of salvation, is incumbent on all Christians. The principal celebrant, however, must always be an ordained priest and medieval missals were made almost exclusively for his use. Often they were elaborately ornamented and illustrated. The two studies of fifteenth-century missals presented here by Vera Vines and Hilary Maddocks demonstrate the effect of individual patronage on their production.

That the missal for the use of Besançon already referred to was commissioned for Charles de Neufchâtel, Archbishop of Besançon *c*.1471 is evident from the presence of his coat-of-arms and episcopal insignia throughout. Vines shows how certain illustrations which reflect specifically local Besançon traditions may in some cases have had special significance for the archbishop. While the missal that is the chief object of Maddocks' study (Paris, Bibliothèque Mazarine, MS 412) contains no direct reference to a particular clerical patron, she presents persuasive evidence that it was designed for use at the Cathedral of Notre Dame, and was possibly a royal commission *c*.1492

Both works have in common the fact that they issued from flourishing centres of manuscript production and while each commission must have been under authoritative clerical direction, there was nevertheless scope for innovative contribution on the part of the artists. The Master of Jacques de Besançon, the artist of the Paris missal, was *chef d'atelier* of a flourishing Parisian workshop which had been active for more than half a century. Earlier programmes executed by his predecessors in the workshop were obviously available to him, and his adaptation for missal illustration of certain distinctive iconographical and compositional motifs, developed originally for large-scale narrative and allegorical works, provides a telling example of the variety of influences that might be involved in the production of even the most traditional of liturgical books.

The books of hours that are the subject of Kate Challis' research are the product of artists working in Bruges and Ghent in the late fifteenth and early sixteenth centuries. Their full-page miniatures often simulate panel paintings in frames that illusionistically display a wide range of motifs taken from nature and contemporary life, and Challis' particular interest is in the representation of jewels in these border frames. These Netherlandish manuscripts are a reminder that in the course of the fifteenth century the illuminated prayer book had come to flourish in many different countries and regions, and that its contents and appearance were continuously adapted to the demands of an expanding and varied clientele. The method and nature of the contribution of artist-illuminators also underwent changes. Recently, Jonathan Alexander has questioned the wisdom of assuming that the workshop or atelier was the norm for the production of late medieval manuscripts.[2] Evidence, nevertheless, points to highly developed systems of manuscript production in the late fifteenth century not only in long-established centres such as Paris, but also in prosperous burgher towns like Bruges and Ghent. Here books of hours were not only custom made: there were, it seems, also a few examples kept 'on the shelf' to attract the potential customer or to respond promptly to orders of clients at a distance. As the textual contents of these prayer books became more uniform, so, too, did their illustrative programmes, with miniatures often being prepared on

---

[2] J.J. Alexander, *Medieval Illuminators and their Methods of Work* (New Haven and London, 1992), 127–28.

separate folios by specialist artists for 'tipping in' to the completed book. At the same time a flexibility was maintained that enabled the adding of particular devotions or visual embellishments to meet the wishes of individual patrons.

In this context the jewelled border emerges as a significant element in a carefully coordinated artistic industry. Its combination of acute naturalistic observation with technical precision provides a fresh dimension to the simulated panel which it surrounds. This method of framing sacred subjects was clearly popular with patrons, who, as Challis points out, would have been attracted to such decoration both for aesthetic reasons and because of the association of gems and their luminous properties with the splendour of the divine.

By the fifteenth century, the image of an opened book of hours had become a familiar invitation to prayer and a symbol of engaged devotion. While miniaturists strove to capture the semblance of panel paintings on their pages, we find panels themselves—in particular small two-panel devotional paintings or diptychs—being likened to books of hours. These diptychs often represent patrons at prayer, with an open book of hours before them, and the object of their devotion—Christ, Mary or one of the saints—on the opposite panel. Dagmar Eichberger's analysis of the relationship between prayer book and devotional panel painting, with special reference to the Burgundian-Hapsburg dynasty, demonstrates how private domains, such as the bedroom and study, were equipped with panels and books for personal prayer. In such a setting, the meaning of word and image becomes interwoven, the panels needing to be 'read' in the light of the regular devotions performed before them, while the prayer books communicate their message through words expanded and expounded in ornamentation and imagery. Eichberger is presently engaged in a detailed study of the patronage of Margaret of Austria. In this particular essay the way in which books and panel paintings served Margaret's private devotional life is presented against the backdrop of her public acts of patronage which extended to the foundation and endowment of religious institutions and churches. Margaret was no stranger to solemn church ceremonial and the generous provision for liturgical vestments and objects was part of her largesse.

For the Christian, public and private prayer were intimately related and a close examination of individual manuscripts designed for one type of worship or the other invariably reveals this connection. Nowhere perhaps is the creative force of this interactive relationship more evident than in the decoration and illustration of prayer manuals. It is often through these means that allusions are made to the alternative or complementary tradition, thus enriching the import of a particular ritual or devotion. It is in this way, too, that individual interests and emphases find their expression against a backdrop of received custom. The specialist input of all those involved in the production of the medieval religious book—clerical advisers, scribes, illuminators, artists and patrons—could be combined in almost endless variety. The essays in this collection explore some aspects of this interaction and, it is hoped, point the way for further fruitful investigation.

August, 1997 M.M.M.

ONE

The Early Insular Prayer Book Tradition and the Development of the Book of Hours

Bernard J. Muir

ECGBERT, ARCHBISHOP OF YORK (died 766) once observed that each priest before his ordination ought to be equipped with a psalter, a lectionary, an antiphonal, a missal, a baptismal order and a martyrology.[1] It has been remarked that if this was a realistic rather than an ideal expectation, then there has been a massive and regrettable loss of manuscript books from this golden age of intellectual and ecclesiastical life, since only a small number of liturgical manuscripts survives today from Anglo-Saxon England.[2] Among the best known of such works dating

---

[1] 'Nunc ergo, O fratres, qui voluerit sacerdotalem auctoritatem accipere, inprimitus pro deo cogitet et preparet arma ejus, antequem manus Episcopi tangat caput, id est psalterium, lectionarium, antefonarium, missalem, baptisterium, martyrologium, in anno circulo ad predicationem cum bonis operibus, et compotum et ciclo, hoc est jus sacerdotum, post autem suum penitentialem, qui hoc ordine secundum auctoritatem canonum ordinatur, ut discretiones omnium causarum in vestigiis primitus, sine quibus rectum judicium non potest stare, quia scriptum est: In nulla re appareas indiscretus, sed distingue, quid, ubi, quamdiu, quando, qualiter debeas facere.' A.W. Haddan & W. Stubbs, eds, *Councils and Ecclesiastical Documents relating to Great Britain and Ireland, edited after Spelman and Wilkins* (1869; repr. 1964), III, 417.

[2] P. Sims-Williams, *Religion and Literature in Western England 600–800*, Cambridge Studies in Anglo-Saxon England 3 (Cambridge, 1990), 273.

from before 1100 are *The Benedictional of Saint Æthelwold* (London, BL Add. MS 49598), *The Eadui Gospels* (Hanover, Kestner Museum MS WM xxia 36), *The Cotton Troper* (London, BL Cotton MS Caligula A.XIV) and *The Arenberg Gospels* (New York, Morgan MS M.869). These manuscripts were produced either during the tenth-century monastic revival or soon afterwards under its influence; because of their rich illumination and often detailed illustrative programmes they regularly receive scholarly attention. In addition to these well-known liturgical books, however, there is a smaller, less often discussed group of early English manuscripts that is of considerable significance for the history of Christian medieval worship. They contain prayers for individual and private use, often extracted from a formal liturgical context. Though they are neither richly embellished nor illustrated, they bear witness to the long-standing tradition of personal devotion that lies behind the often sumptuously illuminated books of hours which first appeared in the late thirteenth century and became so popular with the laity in England, France, the Netherlands and certain parts of Italy.[3] In order to determine the significance of the early insular prayer books for these later developments it is necessary first to recall the context in which patterns of prayer were shaped in the West and the central role played by monasticism in the formulation of expressions of Christian worship, both public and private.

St Benedict of Nursia (c.480–550), the most influential figure in the development of Western monasticisim, elevated the words of the psalmist, 'Seven times a day do I praise thee because of thy righteous judgements' (Ps. 119: 164), to the status of an injunction with these words from Chapter 16 of his *Rule:*

> This sacred number seven will be observed by us, if we fulfil the duties of our service in the early morning and the first, third, sixth and ninth hours, in the evening and the close of the day . . . Of the Night Watches the same prophet says: At midnight I arose to give thee praise.[4]

The Benedictine *Rule* was enormously successful in Western Europe, eventually regulating the majority of those dedicated to religious life, whether male or female, while the observance of a ritualistically structured day became the cornerstone of western monasticism. In

---

[3] For the book of hours see V. Leroquais, *Les Livres d'Heures manuscrits de la Bibliothèque Nationale* (Paris, 1927); and *Supplément* (Mâcon, 1943); J. Harthan, *Books of Hours* (London, 1977); and R.S. Wieck *et al., Time Sanctified* (New York, 1988).

[4] *The Rule of Saint Benedict for Monasteries,* trans. Dom B.B. Bolton O.S.B. (Newport, Gwent, 1969); the biblical verses referred to here are Ps. 118:164 and Ps. 118:62. Matins and lauds were originally considered as one hour; later they are often treated in the literature as two, and the number of the canonical hours for prayer is consequently referred to as eight.

addition, participation in the public worship of the Church at the canonical hours—matins, lauds, prime, terce, sext, none, vespers and compline—that resulted from this structuring became a formal obligation for all clerics, while the devotional practices of people not living according to a religious rule (especially it would seem members of the royalty and nobility) were also profoundly influenced.[5]

The book which by the early eleventh century provided a compendium of the various texts used for the recitation of the Divine Office at these canonical hours was the breviary.[6] Since the Divine Office is based on the psalms, which are distributed over the hours of the day and the days of the week so that the whole psalter is recited weekly, a liturgical psalter, reflecting this arrangment and usually including the canticles and hymns also recited in the Office, is an essential element of the breviary. Other basic components are a calendar, the Proper of Time, that is the texts for liturgical feasts and seasons—Advent, Christmas, Lent, Easter etc.; the Proper of the Saints; and the Common of the Saints for various categories of saints such as Apostles, martyrs, virgins, etc.[7] In time, however, further texts were incorporated into the breviary, largely as a result of particular devotions developed in the monasteries. Thus a short service for the Blessed Virgin known as the *Officium parvum beate Marie Virginis* ('Little Office of the Virgin'), whose origins go back to the tenth century, was later added.[8] Modelled on the format of the Divine Office, though much abbreviated, it encompasses all the canonical hours and consists of a selection of psalms, interspersed with short readings, hymns and prayers in honour of the Virgin.[9] The Little Office or Hours of the Virgin, as it came to be known, acquired immense popularity with both religious and laity. It was often appended to the psalter and later became one of the distinctive texts of the book of hours; indeed it is from this devotion that the prayer book so favoured by the laity takes its name.

The relationship of the book of hours to both the breviary and the psalter has long been acknowledged. The basic elements of a book of hours—a calendar, the Little Office or Hours of the Virgin, the Office or Vigils of the Dead, the seven penitential psalms, the litany of the saints and the suffrages in honour of the saints—are all devotions that occurred first in the breviary or are modelled on breviary texts. The psalter also developed certain accretions, so that when it was produced as an

---

[5] See, for example, M.M. Manion (Chapter 2 below).

[6] See V. Leroquais, *Les Bréviaires manuscrits des Bibliothèques publiques de France*, 5 vols (Paris, 1934); R.G. Calkins, *Illuminated Books of the Middle Ages* (Ithaca, New York, 1983), 226–24; A. Hughes, *Medieval Manuscripts for Mass and Office*, (Toronto, 1962).

[7] Harthan, *Books of Hours*, 12–13.

[8] Harthan, *Books of Hours*, 13.

[9] For the development of the book of hours see references cited in n. 4.

independent book it often included the canticles from the Old and New Testaments, together with the *Pater Noster, Credo* and *Gloria*, the litany of the saints and a liturgical calendar. Sometimes it had additional prayers appended to it, many of which were preceded by ancient rubrics attributing them to notable saints and Fathers of the Church, such as Augustine, Jerome and Gregory. For a considerable period, too, there flourished a composite prayer book, the psalter-hours, in which versions of the new compendium were presented with the psalter.

Despite, however, its close relationship with the breviary and the psalter, the book of hours is distinguished from them by its greater emphasis on individual and personal prayer. This is expressed in a variety of ways. The book of hours often includes, for example, prayers and devotions, in either Latin or the vernacular, compiled from a greater variety of sources than either the breviary or the psalter. Such selections may be expressly chosen for inclusion by the patron or a spiritual adviser to honour certain saints or to foster particular devotions. Elaborate and sometimes highly innovative programmes of illumination and illustration were another means through which books of hours involved their readers at a very intimate level. This personal aspect of Christian spirituality existed well before the book of hours, and one must look beyond the breviary and the psalter for some of the most cogent examples of its expression. A study of the early insular prayer book helps to illustrate the deep-seated nature of this tradition and its enduring contribution to medieval piety.

The following English manuscript prayer books, dating from the eighth to the eleventh centuries, survive:

London, BL MS Royal 2.A.XX (second half of the eighth century; hereafter, the Royal prayer book).[10]

London, BL MS Harl. 7633 (formerly BL Add. MS 5004; a fragment, late eighth or early ninth century; the Harley fragment).[11]

London, BL MS Harl. 2965 (eighth or ninth century; *The Book of Nunnaminster*).[12]

Cambridge, University Library MS Ll.I.10 (ninth century; *The Book of Cerne*).[13]

---

[10] The prayers from this manuscript are printed as an appendix to A.B. Kuypers, *The Book of Cerne* (Cambridge, 1902), 200–25.

[11] This fragment has not yet been edited.

[12] W. de Gray Birch, ed., *An Ancient Manuscript of the Eighth or Ninth Century: Formerly Belonging to St. Mary's Abbey* (London, 1889).

[13] Kuypers, *Cerne*.

London, BL Cotton MSS Nero A.II and Galba A.XIV (early eleventh century; the Galba prayer book).¹⁴

The Royal prayer book and the Harley fragment are the oldest surviving examples of this kind of book from Europe. The earliest prayer books sometimes have texts in common with one or more of the others in the group, though there are a large number of divergent readings and variant passages; taken together this suggests that these manuscripts represent a thriving tradition of manuals for private devotion. Further testimony to the vitality of this tradition is provided by the Galba prayer book which has many texts in common with the other manuscripts, though it was compiled nearly a century and a half later. Manuscript evidence suggests that this particular genre, whose features are outlined below, developed in England and spread to the continent during the Carolingian period—it should be recalled that it was an Englishman, Alcuin, who was invited by Charlemagne to plan and inculcate the revival of learning in his empire, and that the programme largely achieved its aims.

A small number of *libelli precum* or *livrets* (as they are sometimes called) survives from the Carolingian period,¹⁵ but were compiled after the earliest surviving English prayer books. The continental examples are small collections containing devotional prayers only (that is, they do not contain types of texts such as litanies, collects, psalms, etc.); interestingly, a number of prayers in them also feature in the insular tradition—all the Carolingian *libelli* have texts in common, for example with the Galba prayer book.¹⁶ Another similar manuscript is the so-called 'Fleury prayer book', written in Bavaria some time between 815 and 840¹⁷; it has four prayers in common with the Galba prayer book.¹⁸ One other continental prayer book survives from this early period; now known as Orléans, Bibl. mun. MS 116, it probably originated in St Benoît-sur-Loire (c.850). Among the prayers in this manuscript, which are assembled in a *livret* comprising folios 21v–28, there are three items which are also found in the Galba prayer book.¹⁹

It should be noted that all of these prayer books are compilations, drawing their texts from a variety of sources. The individual, creative

---

14 B.J. Muir, ed., *A Pre-Conquest English Prayerbook*, Henry Bradshaw Society, vol. CIII (Bury St Edmunds, 1988).

15 Four of these interrelated collections have been published in a single volume by A. Wilmart, *Precum libelli quattuor aeui karolini* (Rome, 1940).

16 Wilmart's no. i contains items 24 and 26 of the Galba prayer book; no. ii has 23 and 68; no. iii has 26; and no. iv has 26 and 69.

17 J.-P. Migne, ed., *Patrologia Latina*, 221 vols (Paris, 1844–64), 101.509–612.

18 Muir, *A Pre-Conquest Prayerbook*, nos 24, 26, 31 and 67.

19 Muir, *A Pre-Conquest Prayerbook*, nos 16, 23 and 24.

impulse is accordingly observable more in how the anthologies are designed or have evolved than in the composition of new material, for this period, often called the Age of Faith, was one in which respect and recognition of authority (*auctoritas*) was paramount—the notion of the model and its imitation was of major importance. Many texts which became popular in devotional literature were composed by St Augustine and other Church Fathers; others that were not are sometimes accompanied in these books by rubrics which misleadingly claim that they *were* written by one of the Fathers, thus attesting to their authority and to the belief that curative powers were innate in words formulated by saints.[20]

The structure and contexts of these prayer books tell us a great deal about the beliefs, habits, desires and fears of the people who compiled and used them. They indicate that the psalms, in particular, were central to the development of private devotion—approximately one half of the biblical allusions or citations in the Galba prayer book are from the psalms. They also demonstrate a dependence on the liturgy; for example, individual collects are often wrested from their liturgical context and take on a new, independent existence as short, personal prayers; alternatively, a prayer will be modelled on a liturgical form such as the litany.[21]

The Book of Cerne begins with fragmentary instructions in Old English that provide a structure for private daily devotions (f. 2a). These instructions are paralleled in collections produced outside England, but are absent in the other English manuals. However, the English books sometimes contain one or more prayers which are clearly meant to be recited at particular times of the day or in particular places, usually within the monastery. One prayer for the early morning which begins, *Domine Ihesu Christe, mane cum surrexero intende ad me . . .* ['Lord Jesus Christ, in the morning when I rise . . .'], is found (in divergent forms) in the Royal prayer book, *The Book of Cerne* and the Galba prayer book. In the last of these there is also a group of prayers to be recited in various rooms of the monastery—in the kitchen, cellar, furnace room, refectory, dormitory, etc. Monks would recite a specified psalm, appropriate for the occasion or place, which was accompanied by a brief prayer or collect. This, for example, is the prayer to be said in the furnace room:

> O eternal Lord and God whose wisdom has so taught mankind that this house may at certain times be devoid of coldness because of the presence of fire, we beseech you that all those either living or gathering together here will

---

[20] See Muir, *A Pre-Conquest Prayerbook*, 42 (n. 1) and 70 (n. 1); the following is a typical rubric: 'In quacumque die cantauerit homo hanc orationem nec diabolus nec ullus homo impedimentum ei facere pot-erit, et quod petierit dabitur ei' (Muir, 61).

[21] See, for example, Muir *A Pre-Conquest Prayerbook*, no. 31.

lack the coldness of infidelity in their hearts through the warmth of the fire of the Holy Spirit . . .[22]

The three surviving complete manuscripts from Mercia in the eighth and ninth centuries (*The Book of Nunnaminster, The Book of Cerne* and the Royal prayer book) have a discernible plan or structure. On the other hand, if the compilers of the later Galba prayer book intended it to be structured, their intention escapes us today; all that can be observed about its composition is that the long prayers are clustered in its first half. *The Book of Cerne* is developed around the theme of the Passion. It contains the Passion narratives from the four Gospels, seventy-four prayers and hymns, a defective breviate psalter, and a narrative of the 'Harrowing of Hell'. *The Book of Nunnaminster* also begins with the Passion narratives (though there is none for Matthew and only part of Mark); most of the other prayers and hymns in this book are concerned with the life of Christ and focus on his sufferings, which suggests that the Passion was intended to be the theme of this collection also. The Royal prayer book seems to be developed around the theme of Christ as healer.[23]

Certain early English liturgical books also contain collections of prayers, usually gathered together as a type of appendix. Representative of this type of manuscript is Cambridge, Corpus Christi College MS 391 (Worcester, c.1065); it has seventeen items in common with the Galba prayer book.[24] There are, as well, a considerable number of extant psalters that contain gatherings of non-biblical private devotions (likewise usually positioned at the end of the manuscript). A typical example is London, BL Arundel MS 155 (Canterbury, 11c.), where the psalter is followed by a litany; in turn this is followed by an extensive collection of Latin prayers, many of which have interlinear glosses in Old English. Arundel MS 155 has seven texts in common with the Galba prayer book.[25] London, BL Harl. MS 863, an eleventh-century psalter from Exeter, has only one text in common with the Galba prayer book, but is noteworthy for the present discussion in that it contains a calendar, hymns, the psalms and canticles, the *Pater noster, Credo* (in two versions), *Gloria* and a litany.

---

[22] 'Domine sempiterne deus cuius sapientia hominem docuit ut domus hec careret aliquando frigore a uicinitate ignis, te quesumus ut omnes habitantes uel conuenientes in ea careant in corde infidelitatis frigore a feruore ignis spiritus sancti ...'. Muir, *A Pre-Conquest Prayerbook*, no. 81.

[23] M. Brown, *Anglo-Saxon Manuscripts* (The British Library, 1991), 40; Brown, however, believes that the *Book of Cerne* is developed largely around the Communion of Saints.

[24] Muir, *A Pre-Conquest Prayerbook*, nos 16, 17, 25, 31, 33, 45, 56, 67, 68, 69, 71, 73, 77, 81, 89, 92 and 95. The Cambridge manuscript has been edited by A. Hughes, *The Portiforium of St. Wulstan*, Henry Bradshaw Society, vols LXXXIX and XC (London, 1958).

[25] Muir, *A Pre-Conquest Prayerbook*, nos 16, 17, 19, 24–26 and 68.

A number of the texts in these early prayer books subsequently feature in books of hours or are related to them. Moreover, prayer books sometimes begin with excerpts from the Gospels (the Passion naratives), as do some books of hours; among the manuscripts under consideration, *The Book of Cerne* and the Royal prayer book have this structure.[26] Though the Galba prayer book differs in not including Gospel passages, it resembles books of hours in having a calendar, two litanies and two series of prayers fashioned around the penitential psalms—the psalter collects (no. 28) and the Good Friday veneration of the cross ceremony taken from the *Regularis Concordia* (no. 68, the *Adoro te* petitions in Latin and Old English).

Indeed, of the surviving early English manuscripts it is the eleventh-century Galba prayer book from Winchester that most closely anticipates later medieval devotional manuscripts, and I would suggest that its compilers were already feeling their way towards a compendium resembling what is today recognized generically as a book of hours; they had a sense of the kinds of things a personal book of private devotion ought to contain, which they apparently handed on to later generations. Moreover, the Galba prayer book differs in significant ways from earlier English prayer books and Carolingian *libelli precum*, as I shall show; it is very much a transitional book.

Of the early manuscripts the Royal prayer book most resembles the Galba collection, though it has only three texts in common with it. It begins with selections from the Gospels, followed by Abgarus' letter, a series of prayers, the canticles, hymns, including an abecedary poem, a short litany, the *Gloria* and *Creed* and lastly, two more alphabetical poems. With the exception of the Gospel selections, the Galba prayer book also contains examples of these devotional genres.

But the Galba prayer book is a unique compilation. I have argued elsewhere that it was first created as a blank book,[27] and I have yet to discover another early manuscript compiled in this way. Because its contents were assembled over a considerable period, they probably reflect a communal notion of what should be collected in a book of private devotional material. The work is also remarkable in that it was written in an institution which housed both men and women; authors or scribes of both genders copied out or composed its texts. Texts that originally had masculine endings are sometimes glossed with feminine inflections, and vice versa. The texts are also in numerous hands, some more skilled than others.

---

[26] For a discussion of the use of Gospel extracts in books of hours, see Wieck, *Time Sanctified*, 158–59.

[27] Muir, *A Pre-Conquest Prayerbook*, xvi–xvii.

The leaves now bound at the front of BL Cotton MS Nero A.II (ff. 3–13), but once part of the Galba prayer book, open with a calendar which contains the feasts of several local Celtic and English saints. This is followed by a number of computational charts used for calculating concurrences and the age of the moon, which were essential for determining the date of Easter and the structure of the liturgical year. Next there follows a badly corrupted poem to King Æthelstan (924–39).[28] This in turn is followed by a prayer to God the Father and two others addressed to the English saints Dunstan and Æthelberht.

Both the Nero and the Galba manuscript sections of this prayer book contain a blend of Celtic and English (or Roman) elements; this is characteristic of early English prayer books. Kuypers, who gives a detailed analysis of the various styles of the prayers in *The Book of Cerne*, sums up the situation thus:

> The instances that have been cited suggest the conclusion that in the *Book of Cerne* we are in the presence of two currents of influence, issuing in two types of prayer: the Roman type which, while keeping in check devotional feeling, manifests a high quality of thought, art, and liturgical culture; and the Irish, which is predominantly an outpouring of feeling and devotion. The question is not whether the individual prayers were composed in Ireland, in Rome, or in England; but whether they were composed under the twofold inspiration of Rome and Ireland. If we look at the matter from the historical standpoint, that is what might *a priori* have been expected; for the two great influences at work in the formation of the Anglo-Saxon Church were the Roman missionaries in the South and the Irish in the North. These two currents of influence were poured out over the whole country; thus we find Roman influence at Wearmouth and Jarrow in the North; while in the South, S. Aldhelm's first teacher at Malmesbury was Irish. The complete fusion of the two influences was effected in the great English school at York.[29]

The collects of the Roman liturgy—and many of them are included in the early prayer books—are characterized by rhythm and balance, often with attention to the *cursus* of classical Latin. The same moderate tone and style also appears in many of the longer private devotional texts of the prayer books. This is, however, in strong contrast to the effusive and unrestrained tone and language of many other prayers, which are known to represent the Irish devotional tradition. Item 31 in the Galba prayer book, *Domine deus meus omnipotens ego humiliter te adoro* ['O Lord, my God omnipotent, I humbly adore you'], is one such prayer. This seems to have been quite popular, since it also occurs in *The Book of Cerne, The Book of*

---

[28] This has been reconstructed by M. Lapidge from a comparison with a Carolingian generic analogue; see Muir, *A Pre-Conquest Prayerbook*, 18–20.

[29] Kuypers, *Cerne*, xxix.

Nunnaminster, The Portiforium of Wulstan and in Basle, MS A.VII.3, a ninth-century Greek psalter with an interlinear Latin gloss, which has a few hymns and prayers added in Irish script. Another version of the text is found in *The Irish Liber Hymnorum*.[30] After a long invocation the confessional aspect of the prayer begins in earnest: the supplicant catalogues the *places where* he has sinned (heaven and earth); those *before whom* he has sinned (God, the angels and saints); *which sins* he has committed (the seven deadly sins are almost lost in this extensive list); and, his real *tour de force*, the *parts of the body* with which he has sinned (eyes, ears, nostrils, tongue, throat, neck, chest, heart, thoughts, hands, feet, bones, flesh, marrow, kidneys, spirit, body). Finally, he asks forgiveness and to be defended against the darts of attacking devils. Another example of this Irish type of prayer is no. 26, *Deus inestimabilis misericordie et inmense. . .* ['O Lord of inestimable mercy and immeasurable. . .']. There are also two alphabetical poems in the 'Hisperic' style (nos. 14 and 15) in the Galba prayer book which are traditionally associated with Saint Columba.[31] Further Irish influence is seen in the inclusion of the 'Celtic Capitella' (no. 54), and a considerable number of Irish saints appear in the calendar and the litanies.

A number of features confirm that the Galba prayer book is a product of the tenth-century monastic reform. The *Regularis Concordia*, a Rule composed *c*.970 under strong Benedictine influence to serve the particular needs of the English Church, outlines in detail the programme of worship to be followed throughout the year in all English monasteries and nunneries, and stresses the interdependence of the Church and state. In keeping with the spirit of the *Regularis Concordia*, the Galba prayer book contains several prayers for the repose of the souls of English kings (Æthelstan: no. 5, Æthelred: no. 60, Edmund: nos 95 & 96, Edward: no. 98), and other prayers for the souls of the reforming bishops Dunstan: nos 7 & 99 and Æthelwold: no. 77. At the height of the reform many monastic and liturgical texts were translated into the vernacular, and poetic versions of the *Pater noster, Credo* and *Gloria* were composed in Old English to teach the basic elements of the faith to those with little knowledge of Latin.[32] In the Galba prayer book a number of Latin prayers are translated into Old English (e.g. no. 12 is a translation of 11); the collection also includes—in a

---

[30] This has been edited by J.H. Bernard and R. Atkinson, *The Irish Liber Hymnorum*, Henry Bradshaw Society, vols XIII and XIV (London, 1898); XIV, 213–16.

[31] See B.J. Muir, 'Two Latin poems by Colum Cille (Columba)', *Revue du moyen âge latin* 39 (1983), 205–16.

[32] These texts are published in B.J. Muir, *The Exeter Anthology of Old English Poetry*. 2 vols (Exeter, 1994) I, 352; and E. Van Kirk Dobbie, ed., *The Anglo-Saxon Minor Poems*. Anglo-Saxon Poetic Records VI (New York, 1942), 70–79 and 94.

cluster, which is probably significant—texts of the *Confiteor, Benedicite* and *Athanasian Creed* (nos 74–76, in Latin). It also contains a large part of the Good Friday ceremony for the veneration of the cross which appears in the *Regularis Concordia*. And reference has already been made to the prayers to be said in various locations throughout the monastery.

Of course, these early prayer books lack one of the fundamental structural elements of the later book of hours, namely the group of texts to be said at particular times of the day by the lay person seeking to emulate the life of a religious, such as the Hours of the Virgin, and the Office of the Dead, etc. But in the Galba prayer book there is a set of prayers in the vernacular to be recited at the canonical hours (no. 65); that these prayers are presented in an unofficial context indicates an attempt by their transcribers to create a personal devotional ritual based upon formal monastic observance. And it is this, taken together with the other evidence rehearsed here, which suggests to me that in this humble manuscript, unillustrated and badly burnt in the Ashburnham House fire of 1731, we can see the book of hours in embryonic form.

The following translation of one of the vernacular texts from the Galba prayer book demonstrates both the humility and the piety of its author, together with the individual's deep personal need for communication with his or her Maker. It is the traditional expression of this need in ways which were nourished by the Church's liturgical and official forms of worship—but which are nevertheless distinct from them—that stands behind the development of the book of hours:

> My Lord Jesus Christ, you who were suspended on the cross, you received the criminal who believed in you into the joy of paradise and let him accompany you—you were a mighty King, even though you hung on the cross; I humbly confess my sins to you and beseech you on account of your great mercy to permit me to enter through the gates of paradise after my journey from this life.[33]

---

[33] This prayer was to be said at none (Muir, *A Pre-Conquest Prayerbook*, 139).

TWO

Women, Art and Devotion: Three French Fourteenth-Century Royal Prayer Books

Margaret M. Manion

AMONG THE MANUSCRIPTS PRODUCED in Paris in the second quarter of the fourteenth century are three prayer books for women of the French royal family[1]: the psalter-hours of Blanche of Burgundy or the *Savoy Hours*,[2] the *Hours of Jeanne of Navarre*[3] and the *Psalter of Bonne of Luxembourg*.[4] All three testify to the continuing tradition of the great Parisian book illuminator, Jean Pucelle, who died in 1334, and are splendid products of artists working in his style, with access to his

---

[1] This study is part of a larger project funded by the Australian Research Council which seeks to plot in detail the varied relationships between text and imagery in fourteenth- and early fifteenth-century prayer books made for members of the French royal family.

[2] The fragment that remains of the *Savoy Hours* is New Haven, Yale University, Beinecke Rare Book and Manuscript Library, MS 390. Vellum, 201x147 mm, 26 folios, 24 of which belong to the original manuscript; two folios belong to the additions of Charles V.

[3] Paris, BN MS n.a. lat. 3145. Vellum, 180x135 mm, 270 folios. This essay follows the foliation marked on the manuscript which includes f. 121, now missing.

[4] New York, The Metropolitan Museum of Art, The Cloisters Collection (69.86). Vellum, 125x91 mm, 333 folios.

compositions and patterns.⁵ With reference, however, to the spiritual life of the laity in the Middle Ages, these richly illustrated prayer books provide an insight into the ways in which forms of prayer, originally developed for liturgical worship, were adapted for private use. They also demonstrate how the interweaving of text and visual imagery in such manuals was consciously directed towards the fostering of personal prayer. This essay presents a comparative analysis of the structure and devotional emphases of the *Savoy Hours* and the *Hours of Jeanne of Navarre*, books which testify to the interests of their immediate patrons, and to the importance of family custom. They reveal, moreover, that illustrated devotions and prayer books, originally designed for women, later came to be used by the men of the family. In this connection it is also appropriate to discuss the *Psalter of Bonne of Luxembourg*.

The psalter-hours of Blanche of Burgundy, hereafter called the *Savoy Hours*, is possibly the earliest of these three books.⁶ In the course of its history it has undergone various vicissitudes and only a fragment of the original work survives. It must have been a very bulky book originally. Probably measuring about 250x170 mm. before later trimming, it comprised a calendar and psalter, together with numerous short Offices and suffrages as well as other devotions. It was abundantly illustrated and originally must have contained over 200 miniatures framed by tricolour

---

⁵ For Jean Pucelle and his followers, see K. Morand, *Jean Pucelle* (Oxford, 1962); M. Meiss, *French Painting in the Time of Jean de Berry. The Late XIV Century and the Patronage of the Duke*, 2 vols (New York, 1969), I, 19–20, 160–69; F. Avril, *Fourteenth Century Manuscript Painting at the Court of France* (Paris, 1978), 12–20, 44–65; Paris, Galeries nationales du Grand Palais, *Les Fastes du Gothique: le siècle de Charles V* (Paris, 1981), F. Avril, 279–80; and nos 235–43, 245–49, 254, 261, 265–70, 272, 286–87 and 297; and C. Sterling, *La Peinture médiévale à Paris 1300–1500*, 2 vols (Paris, 1987–90), I, 67–139.

⁶ See L. Delisle, *Recherches sur la Librairie de Charles V* (Paris, 1907), I, 208–13; II, no. 247 (43–44); H.Y. Thompson, ed., with a notice by Dom P. Blanchard, *Les Heures de Savoie, Facsimile of Fifty-Two Pages from the Hours executed for Blanche of Burgundy, being all that is known to survive of a famous Fourteenth-century MS., which was burnt at Turin in 1904* (London, 1910); P. Durrieu, 'Notice d'un des plus importants livres des prières du roi Charles V. Les Heures de Savoie', *Bibliothèque de L'Ecole des Chartes* 72 (1911), 500–55; *Idem*, 'Les aventures de deux splendides livres d'Heures ayant appartenu au duc Jean de Berry', *Revue de l'art ancien et moderne* 30 (1911), 5–16; R. S. Wieck *et al.*, *Time Sanctified.* (New York, 1986), 31, and no. 11 (176–78); B.A. Shailor, *Catalogue of Medieval and Renaissance Manuscripts in the Beinecke Rare Book and Manuscript Library, Yale University*, 2 vols (Binghampton, 1984–87), II, 254–57; C. de Hamel, 'Les Heures de Blanche de Bourgogne, comtesse de Savoie' in A.P. Bagliani, ed., *Les Manuscrits enluminés des comtes et ducs de Savoie* (Turin, 1990), 89–91, and Bagliani, no. 31 (199); and R. Wieck, 'The Savoy Hours and Its Impact on Jean, duc de Berry', Beinecke Studies in Early Manuscripts.*Yale University Library Gazette* Supplement 66 (1991), 159–80.

quatrefoils.[7] There were also one or more historiated initials, together with numerous smaller painted initials, of both decorative and figurative design; several of these featured coats of arms and others contained human heads. Bar borders, with ivy leaf extensions, featured consistently throughout the manuscript. These varied from simple one-sided bars, to the three-sided frames which marked the major divisions of the book and Offices. The margins of these pages were sometimes ornamented with birds, butterflies and insects, together with figures both fantastic and human (Fig. 1). It is not possible to establish whether Jean le Noir, the chief successor to Pucelle, had any part in this illumination, particularly since the cycles illustrating the Hours of the Virgin and the Hours of the Passion—sections which in the *Hours of Jeanne of Navarre* are by his hand— have now been destroyed; and it is prudent simply to state that the book is the product of artists working in the manner of Jean Pucelle in the second quarter of the fourteenth century.[8]

The psalter section must have been detached from this manuscript relatively early, and we only know of its existence from the note made when the work entered Jean de Berry's collection in 1409.[9] By that time the book had come to be called the *Savoy Hours*, and since the late nine-teenth century there has been general agreement that the coat-of-arms of the house of Savoy, alternating or combined with the blazons of France and Burgundy, together with the portraits of a female donor, that appeared throughout its pages, indicate that it was made for Blanche of Burgundy, daughter of Robert II Duke of Burgundy and granddaughter—through her mother, Agnes of France—of St Louis. Blanche married Edward of Savoy in 1307 and became Countess of Savoy in 1323. She was widowed in 1329 and died in 1348. Since she is represented in the miniatures unaccompanied by her husband, it has been concluded that the book was produced after his death, that is, between 1329 and Blanche's own demise in 1348. Stylistically, it has been dated c.1335–40.

In the 1370s the *Savoy Hours* was acquired by Charles V, perhaps through his wife Jeanne de Bourbon, who had family connections with

---

[7] The description of the manuscript in this paragraph is based on Durrieu, 'Notice'. My focus is on the book commissioned for Blanche, not on the additions for Charles V. Calculations vary as to the exact number of folios and miniatures in the original manuscript. See also de Hamel, 'Les Heures de Savoie', 90. For a detailed reconstruction of the book's original textual and illustrative contents, see the Appendix below.

[8] It has been argued that the extant miniatures reveal the hand of the illuminator responsible for the cycle of St Louis in the *Hours of Jeanne of Navarre* (see Shailor, *Catalogue*, 255); François Avril, however, is not persuaded that this is the case.

[9] Jean Flamel, who acted as librarian for Jean de Berry, entered a detailed list of contents at the end of the volume as well as recording that it was a gift from Charles VI. This was sighted by Durrieu before the Turin fire; see Durrieu, 'Notice', 503.

the house of Savoy.[10] It was at this time that a number of supplementary devotions, also illustrated, were added to the manuscript; two of these folios survive.[11] Later the book came into the possession of Charles VI, who presented it to his brother Jean de Berry on 7 July 1409. Nothing is known about subsequent owners and it was not until the late nineteenth century that the manuscript was brought to light (minus the psalter) in the National Library of Turin, notably by the researches of Leopold Delisle and Paul Durrieu.[12]

The *Savoy Hours* was burnt in a fire that destroyed the Turin Library in 1904. Two factors, however, mitigate this sad loss. As well as the removal of the psalter, twenty-six leaves had been detached from the prayer book before the fire. These were discovered in the Episcopal Library of Portsmouth Cathedral in 1910.[13] After undergoing certain hazardous adventures this portion was acquired by the Beinecke Library, Yale University, in 1969 (MS 390). It is also fortunate that the section destroyed in the fire had been subjected previously to the scrutiny of Durrieu and that he published a detailed description of its contents in 1911.[14]

The *Hours of Jeanne of Navarre* was probably executed around the same time as the *Savoy Hours*.[15] It, too, is a compendious book and abundantly illustrated (Pl. 1). In addition to its illustrated calendar, it originally had some sixty-eight large miniatures and thirty-seven historiated initials. Several hundred smaller initials are filled with decorative and figurative motifs which include coats-of-arms, human heads, animals and hybrids.[16] All but nine of the extant miniatures are framed by tricolour quatrefoils

---

[10] See de Hamel, 'Les Heures de Blanche de Bourgogne', 89.

[11] Again, calculations vary as to the precise number of folios and miniatures that were added. Durrieu's reconstruction indicates that the additions comprised some sixty folios and approximately seventy miniatures, with several folios having two miniatures to a page.

[12] L. Delisle, *Les Livres d'Heures du duc de Berry* (Paris, 1884), 19; and Durrieu, 'Notice'.

[13] Blanchard, *Les Heures de Savoie*.

[14] Durrieu, 'Notice'.

[15] See H. Yates Thompson, *Thirty-Two Miniatures from the Book of Hours of Joan II, Queen of Navarre* (London, 1899); S.C. Cockerell, *A Descriptive Catalogue of the Second Series of Fifty Manuscripts in the Collection of Henry Yates Thompson* (Cambridge, 1902); and, *The Book of Hours of Yolande of Flanders* (London, 1905); K. Morand, *Pucelle*, 20–21, 48–49, Pls XVIIc, XVIII, XXVa, XXXe; Meiss, *French Painting*, I, 120, 139, 161–63, Figs 341, 345–48, 350, 544, and 601; M. Thomas, 'L'iconographie de saint Louis dans les Heures de Jeanne de Navarre', in *Septième centenaire de la mort de saint Louis. Actes du colloque de Royaumont et de Paris (21–27 mai 1970)*, (Paris, 1976), 209–31; F. Avril, *Bibliothèque Nationale. Nouvelles Acquisitions Latines et Français du Département des Manuscrits pendant les Années 1969–1971.* (Paris, 1973), no. 3145 (33–34); *Manuscript Painting*, 20–22, Pls 15–17; and *Fastes du Gothique*, no. 265 (312–13).

[16] A few folios are now missing; see the Appendix for details.

similar to those in the *Savoy Hours*, and most pages have bar borders with ivy-leaf extensions; the margins, too, are inhabited by small figures, birds, insects, grotesques and drolleries and there are occasional subsidiary scenes. Four artists have been distinguished as responsible for this extensive programme; chief among these was Jean le Noir.

The arms of Navarre, d'Evreux and Burgundy which appear throughout this book, together with numerous depictions of a young queen, identify its owner as Jeanne II of Navarre, niece of Blanche of Burgundy. One of the prayers also explicitly refers to her by name.[17] Jeanne, who was born in 1311, was the only child of Louis X and Margaret of Burgundy. She was denied the right to the throne of France, however, on the grounds of gender, although the Valois king, Philip VI, subsequently recognized her claim to the kingdom of Navarre, and she was crowned Queen of Navarre in 1329.[18] At the age of seven Jeanne had married her cousin, Philip, Comte d'Evreux; she survived him six years, dying in 1349. Since the arms in her prayer book contain no reference to Champagne whose jurisdiction Jeanne ceded to the King of France in 1336, it is thought that this work was produced after that event, *c.*1336–40.

The *Psalter of Bonne of Luxembourg* bears the combined arms of Valois and Luxembourg, indicating that it was produced for Bonne, the first wife of Jean le Bon, and mother of Jean de Berry (Fig. 2).[19] Jean le Noir, with a group of artists from the Pucelle circle, was responsible for its illumination and since Bonne died in 1349, shortly before her husband's accession to the throne, the book has been dated on historical and stylistic grounds to *c.*1345–49. In addition to the psalter and a liturgical calendar, this manuscript contains a number of illustrated vernacular texts, which make it a highly personalized commission. As well as calendar illustrations, it has fourteen half-page miniatures and, like the two books already mentioned, it is characterized by elegant bar and ivy-leaf borders and margins inhabited by finely drawn birds, animals and grotesques, together with a mix of serious and playful *bas-de-page* scenes. Particularly distinctive is the use of a grisaille technique for the figures of the main miniatures.

Let us now turn to examine some of the ways in which these books reflect the interests and needs of the clientele for which they were produced.

---

[17] Folio 151v; this is discussed further on p. 34.

[18] See E. Hallson, *Capetian France 987–1328* (London, 1980), 284.

[19] See Avril, *Fastes du Gothique*, nos 267 (315–16), and *Manuscript Painting*, 74; see also Sterling, *Peinture médiévale*, 109–13 and F. Deuchler, 'Looking at Bonne of Luxembourg's prayer book', *The Metropolitan Museum of Art Bulletin* (Feb. 1971), 267–78.

Durrieu's description of the *Savoy Hours* indicates that it was designed as a kind of lay breviary with the calendar and psalter components being complemented by a series of short Offices or hours, an extensive cycle of suffrages in honour of the saints and the major feasts of the Church year, and a sequence of prayers for various classes of people in the Church and lay society. This latter devotion is based on the intercessory prayer of the faithful or the prone which preceded the offertory of the Mass in the Middle Ages and which survives today in the Good Friday liturgy and in the bidding prayers of the Sunday or public Mass.[20] Within this format, so strongly influenced by the ritualized prayer of the Church, the gradual psalms, the penitential psalms and the litany of the saints find a logical place, since these devotions had long been used as public expressions of penitence and in times of communal need such as war or pestilence. They were regular supplements of the Divine Office in the breviary and from there found their way into prayer books designed for lay use.

Devotions of a more personal nature seem to have been the exception in the *Savoy Hours*.[21] Since, however, its psalter was detached relatively early, this manuscript has been almost invariably discussed in the context of the fully developed book of hours. Indeed the genre 'psalter-hours' is seldom referred to in its own right, being customarily regarded as a transitional phase in the development of the book of hours. Recent research, however, on the variety of devotional manuals in the thirteenth and fourteenth centuries, has indicated that psalter-hours often had quite distinctive emphases, both as to text and illustration, and that they merit explicit attention.[22]

Textually, the most distinctive feature of the *Savoy Hours* is its large number of hours or short Offices and the comprehensive and ordered nature of its suffrages and prone prayers. There are eleven Offices in all. Of these the Little Office or Hours of the Virgin, the Hours of the Passion or of the Cross, the Hours of the Holy Spirit and the Office or Vigils of the

---

[20] See N. Beriou, J. Berlioz and J. Longère, eds, *Prier au Moyen Age. Pratiques et Experiences (Ve–XVe siècles)* (Brussels, 1991), 71–73. The word 'prone' derives ultimately from the Latin *praeconium*, 'proclamation'.

[21] A group of prayers in honour of the Virgin followed the Hours of the Angels. Prayers or commemorations of the Trinity, the angels and all saints occurred both before the Vigils of the Dead and after the prone supplications. A prayer in honour of the Passion prefaced the first group, while a prayer for peace concluded the second. Blanche's prayer book seems to have terminated with the only two unillustrated devotions in the book: a prayer in honour of St Peter Martyr and the 'Five Joys of the Virgin'.

[22] See, for example, J. H. Oliver, *Gothic Manuscript Illumination in the Diocese of Liège (1250–c.1330)* 2 vols (Louvain, 1988); and M. Manion, L. Knowles and J. Payne, 'The Aspremont psalter-hours: the making of a manuscript', *Art Bulletin of Victoria* 34 (1994), 25–34.

Dead were by this time regular inclusions in a book of hours.[23] The Hours of the Trinity and the Hours of St John the Baptist appear less frequently, although we already find instances of them in thirteenth-century English books of hours and they recur from time to time.[24] The Hours of St Louis, King of France, had appeared a decade earlier in the prayer book of Queen Jeanne d'Evreux.[25] The Hours of the Angels, of St John the Evangelist, St Louis of Marseilles and St Mary Magdalen are unusual texts which occur only in scattered instances throughout the fourteenth and fifteenth centuries[26] What is particularly noteworthy is the concentration of a group of such hours or Offices within the one book, giving the impression of a kind of breviary.

The principal series of suffrages in the *Savoy Hours* is headed by the rubric 'Commemorations of God, Our Lady, the Apostles, several martyrs, confessors and virgins'. Presumably, these prayers all followed the same format of antiphon, versicle, response and collect, which again derives from the liturgy, being used in both the Divine Office and the Mass. The suffrages are arranged according to the Church's calendar, beginning with the seasonal feasts of Advent, Christmas, Epiphany, Holy Week, Easter, Ascension, Pentecost and the Assumption; and followed by the commemoration of the saints. This section, however, is not ordered according to the dates of the sanctoral cycle, but follows the categories of the *communale*—Apostles, martyrs, confessors and virgins—a system which was also familiar from the litany of the saints.

This basic liturgical format was modified and enriched substantially by the nature and the abundance of the book's illustration. Every calendar page and every canonical hour of the Offices was illustrated, together with virtually every suffrage and particular devotion. Such wealth of illustration distinguishes the *Savoy Hours* from its liturgical models. Cycles of illustrations, composed usually of eight miniatures or historiated initials, one for each of the canonical hours, had already been developed for the Little Office or Hours of the Virgin. These usually comprised events relating to the incarnation, birth and infancy of Christ—in which of course Mary figured prominently—and ended with her death,

---

[23] See Wieck, *Time Sanctified*, 89–93.

[24] See C. Donovan, *The de Brailes Hours*, (London, 1991), 139, for examples of these hours in English books of hours, and Leroquais, *Livres d'Heures*, II, Index, for examples in the Bibliothèque Nationale.

[25] New York, The Metropolitan Museum of Art, The Cloisters Collection, 1954 (54.1.2). See J.J. Rorimer, *The Hours of Jeanne d'Evreux, Queen of France at the Cloisters* (New York, 1957), Pls 22–45; F. Avril, *Manuscript Painting*, 44–59; and Sterling, *Peinture Médiévale*, I, 88–99.

[26] See Leroquais, *Livres d'Heures*, II, Index, for examples of these hours in the Bibliothèque Nationale.

assumption or coronation.[27] This series was sometimes complemented by scenes from the Passion of Christ, or, alternatively, was replaced by them, since the canonical hours of prayer were by tradition associated with the Passion.[28] The only other hours which were regularly accompanied by a full series of images were those of the Passion or the shorter Hours of the Cross and, somewhat less often, the Hours of the Holy Spirit.[29]

In a breviary it was normally only matins or the first page of an Office that attracted major illustration, and the idea of having a series of images to mark the beginning of each of the canonical hours seems only to have developed when particular devotions were presented independently of the liturgical Office book. Such illustrative cycles created a new dynamic. These images rarely relate directly to the section of the Office which they accompany.[30] Instead, they prompt one to contemplate a particular aspect of the Christian faith or of the lives of Christ, Mary and the saints, while reciting psalms, antiphons, hymns and prayers etc. arranged in their honour. This punctuation of the text by substantial pictorial material is clearly more appropriate for private than liturgical prayer, since the latter requires that the reading or chanting of the text proceed at a regular pace as part of a ritualistic celebration.

In the *Savoy Hours* systematic illustrative cycles accompanied all the Offices.[31] Those in honour of the saints consisted of a series of chronological events based on popular and sometimes legendary accounts of their lives. Those for the Hours of the Trinity, the Holy Spirit, the Angels and St John the Baptist drew largely on the Scriptures and early Apocrypha.

The cycle for the Hours of the Trinity was the most sophisticated of these visual programmes, as far as doctrinal content is concerned. Durrieu's description reveals that the series of images used here was the same as that for the *Hours of Jeanne of Navarre* and the later *Petites Heures* of Jean de Berry.[32] The presentation of the mystery of the triune God by way

---

[27] Wieck, *Time Sanctified*, 60–66.

[28] Wieck, *Time Sanctified*, 66–71.

[29] Wieck, *Time Sanctified*, 90–92.

[30] Except for the Hours of the Cross or Passion; see B. Stocks (Chapter 4 below).

[31] With the exception of the Office or Vigils of the Dead, which is distinguished from other devotional Offices in that it consists of only three canonical hours: vespers, matins and lauds. In the *Savoy Hours* it was illustrated with only one—presumably introductory—miniature (Durrieu, 'Notice', 543). For a detailed description of the illustrative cycles for the Offices in the *Savoy Hours* see the Appendix below and Durrieu, 'Notice', 535–36, 537, 539–40, 541–43.

[32] Paris, BN MS lat. 18014. See M.M. Manion, 'Illustrated Hours of the Trinity', in P.R. Monks and D.D.R. Owen, eds, *Medieval Codicology, Iconography, Literature and Translation. Studies for Keith Val Sinclair* (Leiden, 1994), 120–33.

of a chronological sequence of scenes based on the Old and New Testament predicates a considerable knowledge of the commentaries of the Fathers of the Church and of the teachings of such theologians as St Thomas Aquinas. At lauds, for example, two identical divine figures were shown creating Adam. This is an allusion to Genesis 1:26, 'Let us make man to our own likeness', a text which was interpreted as indicating the plurality of persons in God.[33] The apparition of the three angels to Abraham at the tree of Mambre was shown at prime. Again, this is an event which the Fathers interpreted as foreshadowing the mystery of the Trinity, since Abraham addressed the heavenly messengers as 'My Lord'. 'Abraham,' they observed, 'saw three, but adored one.'[34] The Lord enthroned above seraphim at terce is a particularly striking example of the erudition behind this visual programme, as the corresponding image in the *Hours of Jeanne of Navarre* demonstrates (Fig. 3). It is based on the vision of the prophet Isaiah (6:1–3) in which angels salute the divine manifestation with the *trisagion* or triple 'Holy, Holy, Holy', a text which was subsumed into the Mass as the *Sanctus* chant to proclaim the majesty and power of the triune God.[35] Since there is no reference to these texts or to their trinitarian interpretation in the words of the Office, the theological significance of such an image would have required explanation.

The cycle illustrating the Hours of the Holy Spirit also functioned as a means of inculcating precise matters of doctrine, in this case the role of the Holy Spirit in the birth of the Church and in the spread of Christianity through the preaching of the Apostles. Thus after depictions of the baptism of Christ, Pentecost and the Trinity, scenes traditionally associated with the revelation of the Holy Spirit, there followed those of St Peter preaching (based on the Acts of the Apostles), his guiding the converted to the doors of the Church, his administering baptism with St Paul, and his celebrating Mass. The cycle concluded with a representation of St Gregory the Great dictating under the inspiration of the Holy Spirit. This image, familiar from Gothic cathedral sculpture, signified the continuation of the apostolic tradition through the power of the Spirit.[36]

---

[33] Augustine, *De Genesi ad litteram*, XIX, 26–27 in J.-P. Migne, ed., *Patrologia Latina*, 221 vols (Paris, 1844–64), 34.291.

[34] Augustine, *Contra Maximinum Arianum Episcopum* (Migne, PL 42.809).

[35] This text from Isaiah is used for the first lesson at matins for the feast of the Trinity in the Roman breviary; and the eighth lesson comments on its trinitarian significance.

[36] Various Hours or Offices of the Holy Spirit are to be found in books of hours. The version in the *Savoy Hours* was probably the same as that in the *Petites Heures* of Jean de Berry, since the latter has the same illustrative cycle consisting of eight scenes that correspond to eight canonical hours. This cycle was also used for the *Grandes Heures* of Jean de Berry (Paris, BN, MS lat. 919). A shorter version consisted of seven hours (omitting lauds).

Certain illustrations of the hours in honour of the saints may also have incorporated quite specific literary sources. The cycle for the Hours of St John the Baptist appears to have been the same as that in the later *Petites Heures*. There the miniature for terce shows a youthful John the Baptist seated at the entrance of a rocky cave, where he is surrounded by an array of animals and birds (Fig. 4). All of these creatures are rendered docile by his presence, but none more so than the lion he caresses. This rare depiction of the Baptist as an Orpheus-type figure possibly derives from the life of the saint by Domenico Cavalca O.P. *c*.1320–40, who elaborating on an ancient Byzantine apocryphal tradition pictures him as a hermit, living in harmony with nature and embracing 'the lions and the great wild beasts that he met in the desert'.[37]

Durrieu's description also indicates that the cycle for the Hours of King Louis of France was similar, though not identical, to that which appeared in the tiny prayer book of Queen Jeanne d'Evreux.[38] Both sequences focused on the sanctity of Louis, and by emphasizing his austerities and good deeds presented him as a model to be revered and emulated. Scholars have also observed that illustrated Hours of St Louis seem to have been devised expressly for prayer books of female descendants of the sainted king.[39] The introductory rubric in the *Savoy Hours* made explicit reference to this family connection: 'Here begins the Hours of my Lord Saint Louis, King of France, appropriate to be said daily by those who have particular devotion to him, especially those who are of his holy and very noble line of France.'[40]

Whether they adverted to such solemn mysteries of the Christian faith as the Trinity, the shaping power of the Holy Spirit in the early Church,

---

[37] 'Così s'abbracciava coi lioni e colle bestie grandi salvatiche che trovava nel diserto' (D. Cavalca, 'La Vita di San Giovanni Battista' in D.M. Manni and A. Cesari, eds, *Biblioteca scelta di opere italiane, antiche e moderne*, CCXLIV, *Volgarissimento delle vite de' Santi Padri*. 6 vols (Milan, 1829), vol. IV, 290. This is cited in M.A. Lavin 'Giovannino Battista: A Study in Renaissance Symbolism', *Art Bulletin* 37 (June, 1955), 85–101. See also Meiss, *French Painting*, 164; and F. Avril, *Les Petites Heures de Jean, duc de Berry. Introduction and Facsimile of BN ms lat. 18014*, 2 vols (Paris, 1989), I, 339–42.

[38] See Rorimer, *The Hours of Jeanne d'Evreux*, Pls 22–45; J.M. Hoffeld, 'An image of Saint Louis and the structuring of Devotion', *Metropolitan Museum of Art Bulletin* (Feb. 1971), 261–66; Avril, *Manuscript Painting*, 44–59, especially Pls 8–10; and, *Fastes du Gothique*, no. 239 (292–93); and also Sterling, *Peinture médiévale*, 88–99, Figs 47–49. For the *Savoy Hours* see Durrieu, 'Notice', 541–42.

[39] See A. Saulnier-Pinsard, 'Le Livre d'Heures de Marie de Navarre', in E. Sesti, ed., *La Miniatura Italiana tra Gotico e Rinascimento. Atti del II congresso di Storia della Miniatura Italiana, Cortona 24–26 settembre 1982*, 2 vols (Florence, 1985) I, 46–49.

[40] 'Ci commencent les heures Monseigneur saint Loys, roy de France, convenables à dire tous les jours à ceulz qui ont especial devotion à lui, memement à personnes qui sont de si sainte et de si très noble lignié comme est celle de France.' (Durrieu, 'Notice', 510).

the memory of Christ's Passion, or the heartening presence of Mary, the angels and the saints, the illustrations of these short Offices were presented as rhythmic cycles which emphasized the theme of steadfast and continuous prayer throughout the day and throughout the Church year, in keeping with the spirit of the Divine Office performed by clergy and religious. Considered as a group, they reflect devotions fostered by both the Franciscan and Dominican orders.[41] Several of these devotions also came to be especially associated with the French royal family. Cockerell for example, pointed out that the Franciscan saint, Louis of Marseille (or Toulouse), who was canonized in 1317, 'was specially dear to Philippe VI of Valois, as it was to him that he attributed the cure of his son Jean, afterwards King of France, whose life had been despaired of by the physicians. Philippe afterwards made a pilgrimage to his shrine in company with the King of Navarre and others, and left great offerings there.'[42] The Sainte Chapelle, the seat of worship for the royal family, also housed some of his relics. Sts John the Baptist and John the Evangelist were consistently honoured by French royalty, with members of the family both male and female being named after them. Since confessors and chaplains for the French royal court and related establishments were regularly chosen from the friars, it is highly likely that this book, together with its visual programme, was designed by one such friar chaplain.[43] Blanche herself was buried in the church of the Poor Clares in Dijon.

In the suffrages section, the wealth of illustration again energised the text, every individual petition having its visual counterpart. In the commemorations of the main feasts of the Church year, the accompanying scenes encapsulated the life of Christ and his mother, ending with the descent of the Holy Spirit and the feast of the Assumption.

The illustrations for the suffrages of the saints reflected the blend of the generic and the particular contained in the text, with representations of groups of Apostles, martyrs, confessors and virgins being followed by depictions of particular individuals within these categories. The saints were drawn mainly from the Parisian calendar and were much more numerous than those celebrated in the Offices. Durrieu's descriptions and the surviving folios of the *Savoy Hours* indicate that they were depicted,

---

[41] The Franciscans were promoters of devotion to the angels, while the Dominicans had intensified veneration for St Mary Magdalen. See J. Naughton, *Manuscripts from the Dominican Monastery of Saint Louis de Poissy* (Diss., Melbourne, 1995; 2 vols), 1, 63. and n. 112.

[42] Cited in Yates Thompson, *Miniatures*, 17.

[43] For an example of the intermingling of Franciscan and Dominican influences in contemporary devotions see C. Heck, 'L'iconographie de l'ascension spirituelle et la devotion des laics: le Trone de charité dans le Psautier de Bonne de Luxembourg et les Petites Heures du duc de Berry', *Revue de l'Art* 110 (1995) 9–22.

according to established convention, as statuesque figures holding an identifying attribute, or in more dramatic scenes alluding either to notable events in their lives or to their martyrdom and glorification. They were also sometimes shown as the agents of miraculous deeds wrought on behalf of their supplicants.[44] Illustrations for the prone or intercessory prayers represented the various categories for whom supplication was to be offered; this, too, involved a mix of hierarchical depictions with more innovative compositions of groups engaged in various activities.[45]

It is in the suffrages and intercessory prayers that one encounters particularly numerous images of Blanche kneeling in prayer before the object of her devotion. Indeed this has been remarked on as being one of the most distinctive features of the book.[46] Recent research on thirteenth- and early fourteenth-century prayer books, however, reveals that it was not unusual to portray the donor thus.[47] That Blanche appeared so many times in her prayer book was probably because of the large number of prayers illustrated. It should be noted, too, that what at first seems a very personal devotion, labelled 'Prayer for myself', is one of the concluding invocations of the wide ranging prone prayers, and that the focus on the individual is set within the broader context of Church and society. Moreover, the accompanying miniature which shows Blanche kneeling before a sculptured Calvary group (Fig. 5) is a variation on the preceding one in this sequence for family and friends.

The *Savoy Hours* is thus a striking example of an early fourteenth-century prayer book in which liturgical models have been adapted for lay use, a significant element of this adaptation being the visual imagery designed to accompany the text.

The contemporary *Hours of Jeanne of Navarre* provides an interesting comparison and contrast to the *Savoy Hours*. Here the format of a lay breviary has been replaced by that of the fully developed book of hours. This genre which made its first appearance in the second half of the thirteenth

---

[44] See Appendix for examples.

[45] See, for example, the illustration for the prayer for 'les laboureurs', Yale, Beinecke Rare Book Library, MS 390, f. 23v, which shows three peasants at work in the fields (reproduced in Blanchard, *Les Heures*. Pl. XLVI).

[46] Wieck, 'The Savoy Hours and Its Impact on Jean, duc de Berry', 163–66.

[47] See, for example, A. Bennett, 'A Thirteenth-Century French Book of Hours for Marie', *The Journal of the Walters Art Gallery* 54 (1996), 21–49. In this book 'sixteen out of twenty-one historiated initials portray women, either in supplication as in the Office of the Holy Spirit, or actively involved with religious and family life from childhood to death as in the Office of the Virgin and in the Office of the dead'(21). See, too, the *Aspremont Psalter-Hours*, c.1290–1310, where the patrons appear repeatedly in prayer before the object of their devotion. (M.M. Manion and V.F. Vines, *Medieval and Renaissance Illuminated Manuscripts in Australian Collections* (London, 1984), no. 70 (173–76).

century became increasingly popular with the laity in succeeding centuries.[48] In addition to the regular components of a book of hours—a calendar, the Hours of the Virgin, the penitential psalms and the litany of the saints, the Hours of the Cross, suffrages, and two popular prayers in honour of the Virgin, the *Obsecro Te* and the *O Intemerata*—the *Hours of Jeanne of Navarre* contains a generous selection of more personal devotions including prayers to be said at particular times or for special needs.[49] Moreover, several of these prayers are in French. But also included are two of the unusual hours or Offices of the *Savoy Hours*, namely the Hours of the Trinity and the Hours of St Louis, King of France, while the calendar, which is Franciscan in emphasis, is illustrated with a version of the didactic programme first executed by Jean Pucelle for the Dominican *Belleville Breviary*.[50]

As was customary by this time, the Hours of the Virgin received the major decorative emphasis, with the miniatures in this section being by the hand of Jean le Noir himself (Fig. 6).[51] The emotional and dramatic focus on the events of the Passion in the cycle accompanying the Hours of the Cross, also the work of the chief illuminator, is indicative of the growing tendency in the spirituality of this period to emphasize the human dimension of Christ's sufferings and the virtue of compassion (Fig. 7). More unusual, however, is the fact that the Hours of the Virgin are written out in full three times, to incorporate seasonal variations. Each version, moreover, is illustrated with identical subject-matter.[52]

---

[48] See J. Harthan, *Books of Hours* (London, 1977); Wieck, *Time Sanctified*; R.G. Calkins, *Illuminated Books of the Middle Ages* (London, 1983), 243–82; J. Backhouse, *Books of Hours* (London, 1985); and C. de Hamel, *A History of Illuminated Manuscripts* (Oxford, 1986), 168–99.

[49] Later books of hours also typically contain four Gospel lessons and the short Hours of the Holy Spirit. Gospel extracts are interspersed among various personal prayers in the *Hours of Jeanne of Navarre*, but they are not in the format which was later to become more or less standardized. The Hours of the Holy Spirit have also been added by a later hand. This general description is provided to establish the basic distinctions between the *Hours of Jeanne of Navarre* and the *Savoy Hours*. See Appendix for a full list of the book's contents.

[50] For the *Belleville Breviary* (Paris, BN, MSS lat. 10483–4), see Avril, *Manuscript Painting*, 16, 18–19, 35; 'Fastes du Gothique', no. 240 (293–96); *Les Petites Heures*, 207–22; Sterling, *Peinture Médiévale*, I, 71–87; P. Cockshaw, 'Le Bréviaire de Belleville (Paris, Bibliothèque Nationale, MSS lat. 10483–4): Problèmes textuels et iconographiques', in Monks and Owen, 94–109. See also J. Naughton (Chapter 3 below, 87–89).

[51] For an analysis of the four hands in this manuscript see Cockerell, *Descriptive Catalogue*, 163–66.

[52] One of the most skilled associates of Jean le Noir was responsible for the second and third versions, each of which is introduced by a quatrefoil framed miniature at matins, with the scenes for the remaining hours being presented in a series of smaller historiated initials.

The cycle for the Hours of St Louis in Jeanne's prayer book is more chronological in emphasis than that of either the *Savoy Hours* or the *Hours of Jeanne d'Evreux*. It focuses on the saint's early life, the ritual of his anointing and coronation and on the events leading to his embarking on crusade (Pl. 1; Figs 8–9). Not only are aspects of this selection particularly appropriate for such a youthful royal owner, but Marcel Thomas has suggested that it also reflects the contemporary political interests of the Valois king, Philip VI, who in 1333 commissioned the preaching of a crusade and took the cross in a public ceremony, along with a group of royal and noble leaders that included Jeanne's husband, the King of Navarre.[53]

While the liturgical model from which the suffrages derive is still discernible, the arrangement of these prayers is more flexible and the selection more individual than for the *Savoy Hours*. At the same time the two prayer books display certain common emphases. In Jeanne's book, for example, a prayer to one's guardian angel replaces the Hours of the Angels. It is introduced, moreover by a splendidly imaginative composition which shows the queen attended by her heavenly companion as she distributes alms (Fig. 10). There is also a suffrage and accompanying miniature in honour of St Louis of Toulouse (Marseille), while an extract from the life of St Margaret, patron saint of childbirth, here substitutes for a suffrage in her honour.

In addition to the display of her coat-of-arms in borders and initials, Jeanne's book is personalized by numerous images of a young queen at prayer. She is shown gazing towards the sacred events or personages from a discrete border or initial space and occasionally she is made to play an integral role in the main composition (Fig. 11). As with Blanche in the *Savoy Hours* personal reference is also made to her in the body of the text: On folio 151v a prayer to the Virgin is headed by the rubric, 'A very special prayer in honour of Our Lady'. It has been made special both through the depiction in the introductory initial of a young queen kneeling before an image of the crowned Virgin and Christ child (Fig. 12) and by the insertion of Jeanne's name in the text, which reads:

> I beg you O Lady, most holy Mary, mother of the Lord Jesus Christ, most full of pity, daughter of the most high king, most glorious mother, mother of orphans, consolation of the desolate . . . that you intercede for me your handmaid, *Jeanne of Navarre, queen*, in the sight of your son so that through his blessed mercy and your holy intercession he will grant me that before the time of my death I may be cleansed of my sins through confession and true

---

[53] Thomas, 'L'iconographie de Saint Louis', 229–30.

penitence and that after death I may have eternal life and rest with his saints and elect.[54]

Several of the prayers also contain feminine endings such as *peccatrix*, *peccatrici* or the French *pecheresse* for 'sinner'.[55]

Although the complete psalter is not included in Jeanne's prayer book, the psalms remain one of the most fundamental sources for the fashioning of its particular devotions. In addition to their use in the Offices and the hallowed selections of the penitential and gradual psalms, a prayer for one's friends on folios 131v–132v consists of a psalm and several collects, while on folios 141–43v a devotion in honour of the Virgin is based on five psalms and antiphons that begin with the five letters of her name, 'Maria'. The psalter of St Jerome, which is composed of a selection of verses from different psalms, appears towards the end of the book (ff. 247–55).

Despite its more flexible structure, another feature which this prayer book shares in common with the *Savoy Hours* is a detailed system of rubrics and explanatory titles. Written in French, and at times quite expansive, these guide the reader through the more complex Offices or hours, point to the selection of prayers for particular occasions and encourage appropriate devotional sentiments. While most of the prayers in both the *Savoy Hours* and the *Hours of Jeanne of Navarre* are in Latin these lucid explanations in the vernacular are a reminder of the limited access that the lay Christian had to the official language of the Church. Men and women of the court must have been taught prayers in Latin from an early age and they would have become familiar with the texts of the Mass and to a lesser extent those of the Divine Office by regular attendance at such services. Like many modern Catholics before Vatican II, however, they relied on communication in their native tongue for precise instruction.

The Hours of the Virgin in Jeanne's prayer book are for the use of Rome, not Paris, and the rubric on folio 43v is at pains to point out a significant difference in this rite at the end of matins: 'You need to know that according to the usage of the court of Rome *Te Deum laudamus* is not said before lauds each day as is the custom in other uses; but after the

---

[54] 'O precor te Domina sanctissima maria, mater domini nostri ihesu christi, pietate plenissima, summi regis filia, mater gloriosissima, mater orphanorum, consolatio desolatorum . . . ut intercedas pro me ancilla tua, Johanna navarre regina, ante conspectum filii tui ut per sanctam suam misericordiam et tuam sanctam intercessionem michi concedat ante tempus mortis mee puram de peccatis meis confessionem, et veram penitenciam, et post mortem cum sanctis et electis suis vitam et requiem sempiternam.'

[55] See, for example, the prayer which calls on God's protection and that of the archangels Michael, Gabriel and Raphael: 'Deus propicius esto michi peccatrici . . .' (f. 116v), and a prayer in French to the Virgin: 'Je poure (sic) pecheresse vous fais hommage et servage' (f. 119).

third response, the versicle and *Gloria Patri* and its repetition, as set out above, lauds begins.'⁵⁶ Other rubrics indicate when and for what purpose particular prayers should be said. The prayer to one's guardian angel (f. 123v), for example, is to be recited daily on rising and on going to bed against the perils of the night.⁵⁷ The careful phrasing of the rubric which introduces a prayer in honour of St Apollonia (f. 130v) for the relief of toothache, distinguishes between calling for heavenly assistance in one's daily difficulties and superstitious credulity. 'Whoever has the toothache and says devoutly, in firm hope, the following antiphon, versicle and prayer in memory of the passion of St Apollonia, will be cured, with the help of God.'⁵⁸ Certain rubrics also make explicit reference to the close connection between text and image as in the introductory note on folio 182v: 'After (this) commence several suffrages and the images which belong to them.'⁵⁹

Long ago Sidney Cockerell located the *Hours of Jeanne of Navarre* within the context of a number of prayer books executed by Pucelle and his followers for women of the extended royal family.⁶⁰ There are links, for example, with a book of hours (Paris, Musée Jacquemart André, MS 1, *c*.1325–30) made for Jeanne's cousin, another Jeanne, of the house of Savoy, with a Franciscan breviary (Chantilly, Musée Condé, MS 51, *c*.1330) belonging to her sister-in-law, Jeanne d'Evreux, and with a diminutive book of hours made for her daughter-in-law, Yolande of Flanders (London, BL Yates Thompson MS 27, *c*.1353–55).⁶¹ These books testify to a milieu strongly influenced by Franciscan and Dominican spirituality, in which the same group of highly skilled illuminators were consistently commissioned over a quarter of a century to execute visual progammes

---

56 'Vous devez savoir que selone lusage de la court de rome len ne dit une "Te deum laudamus" es heures de notre dame a chascun iour devant laudes si comme l'en fait en autres usages, mes tantost apres le tiers respons, le vers et Gloria patri et la reprise si comme il sont ici devant sont commencees les laudes.'

57 'Ci apres commencent iv biaus vers et une oroison du propre bon ange qui garde chascune persone cretiene et les doit on dire au lever et au coucher chascun iour contre tous perils de nuit.'

58 'Quiconques aura mal et dolour en ses denz. Si die devotement et par ferme esperance lantienne le verset et loroison qui sensuient en la remembrance de la passion sainte apolline, et il en garira a laide de dieu.'

59 'Ci apres commencent pluseurs [sic] suffrages et les ymages qui y apartienent.'

60 Cockerell, *Descriptive Catalogue*, 179–82.

61 For the *Hours of Jeanne of Savoy*, see Avril, *Fastes du Gothique*, no. 235 (289–90); for a virtually identical miniature of unusual subject matter for the Vigils of the Dead in the *Hours of Jeanne of Savoy*, see Bagliani, ed., *Manuscrits enluminés*, Pl. XLVI; for the Chantilly breviary, see Meiss, *French Painting*, 20, 107, 152–54, 182, 188 and Figs 343, 358, 541, 600, 604–06; for the *Hours of Yolande of Flanders*, see Cockerell, *Book of Hours*, and Sterling, *Peinture Médiévale*, I, 115–16, Figs 59–60.

which, while often quite erudite, were invariably realized with lucidity and elegance.

No less striking than the links between these works, however, is the distinctive, indeed unique nature of each of them, both as to text and illustration. It is this individuality which highlights the extraordinarily rich and varied devotional life available to the recipients of such prayer books. In the case of the *Hours of Jeanne of Navarre*, the particular needs and interests of the young queen would seem to be reflected in the unusually detailed and elaborate presentation of the Hours of the Virgin and their seasonal variations, which ensured both an informed knowledge of the Office itself and a familiarity with the visual sequence most often associated with it. Again the mix of formal and more personal prayers gives this book a special liveliness and vigour which is echoed both in the main miniatures and in the border decoration. Indeed this is still a book that invites and delights the reader.

After Jeanne's death the *Hours of Jeanne of Navarre* does not seem to have stayed for long within the royal family.[62] Blanche's book, on the other hand, became a treasured family possession. When King Charles V owned it, he had it updated for his own use with additional prayers and illustrations. Not only was his wife, Jeanne de Bourbon, depicted at prayer in similar fashion to the original female owner, but Charles, too, was shown kneeling before the object of his devotion (Fig. 13). The king also had a costly jewelled cover made for the book which he kept among his personal belongings in the royal apartments at Vincennes.[63]

This is not the only example of a book originally designed for a woman that subsequently influenced the devotional life of a male descendant. The *Psalter of Bonne of Luxembourg* draws on certain themes developed in the Pucelle atelier. Its calendar vignettes, for example, derive from the *Belleville Breviary*, while the scene of Christ's arrest that introduces a commentary on the Passion is closely modelled on a composition in

---

[62] The fact that the arms of Navarre were painted over and those of Evreux transformed into the arms of France indicates that a member of the royal house of France probably owned it for some time after Jeanne's death. By the beginning of the fifteenth century it belonged to an English woman, who is depicted kneeling before the Trinity and the Virgin and Child on the last of a group of three leaves added at the front of the book. Towards the end of the same century, however, it was back in France, this time in the convent of the Poor Clares in the Rue de Lourcines, Paris, which did have royal connections, having been founded by Margaret of Provence, widow of St Louis. A now barely legible *ex libris* states that at this time it belonged to '*seur anne belline*'. It was still at the convent in 1621, being examined there by the scholar M. de Peiresc (Cockerell, *Descriptive Catalogue*, 158–59).

[63] See de Hamel, 'Heures de Blanche de Bourgogne', 89–90.

Jeanne de Savoie's prayer book.[64] However, several of the texts appended to the psalter in this manuscript confronted their illuminators with new challenges.

Five of these focus on the sufferings of Christ; one is an allegorical treatise and another an extract from the popular legend of 'The Three Living and the Three Dead'.[65] It has long been acknowledged that these devotions probably reflect the special interests of the patron; but only recently has any detailed attention been given to their nature and origins.[66] In the present context it is appropriate to comment on the following aspects. The Passion devotions are distinguished by their mix of the visionary and mystical with the earthy and the tangible. A lamentation on the sufferings of Christ is presented through the eyes of the Virgin; in the 'Complaint of the Crucified', it is Christ himself who speaks of the extent and meaning of his sufferings; while the prayer that follows, addressed to his wounds, may be interpreted as an affective response to this plea.[67] These prayers are French in origin and they may be associated with the growing importance paid to the relics of the Passion housed at the Sainte Chapelle.[68] It is also true, however, that devotion to the wounds of Christ was early nurtured in northern European convents. One of the first illustrations of a life-size wound occurs in a fourteenth-century devotional collection made for Kunigunde, the abbess of the Benedictine nunnery of St George's, Prague.[69] Both text and illustration in this book also represent the figure on the cross come to life and addressing the devotee, while the wound in Christ's side is not simply a reminder of his physical suffering, but a symbol of mystical union. Kunigunde was Bonne's great aunt, so it may not be purely coincidental that a life-size wound was depicted in her psalter (Fig. 14), particularly since this is one of the earliest representations of the subject to appear in France and to be associated with a member of the laity.[70] This connection may also explain the miniature illustrating the 'Complaint of the Crucified' which shows the Saviour, his arm freed from the cross, pointing to the wound in his

---

[64] Avril, *Fastes du Gothique*, 290.

[65] For a detailed listing of these texts, see Avril, *Les Petites Heures*, 81–83; and Heck, 'L'iconographie', 19, n. 6.

[66] See Heck, 'L'iconographie'; and F. Lewis, 'The wound in Christ's side and the instruments of the Passion: Gendered experience and response', in L. Smith and J.H.M. Taylor, eds, *Women and The Book* (London, 1997), 204–29.

[67] Lewis, 'The wound in Christ's side', 211–12.

[68] See F. Lewis, 'Devotional images in the book of hours' in *Iconographie Médiévale* (Paris, 1990), 38.

[69] Lewis, 'The wound in Christ's side', 204.

[70] Lewis, 'The wound in Christ's side', 206.

side as he addresses the kneeling Bonne and her husband, 'Ah ! man and woman, see how much I suffer for you' (Fig. 2).[71]

The Six Degrees of Charity describes the soul's ascent to the perfect love of God through a series of steps or degrees. Christian Heck has recently established that this text is a fourteenth-century French paraphrase of part of a treatise on prayer by St Bonaventure, *De tripilici via* c.1260–70. The miniature in Bonne's psalter (Fig. 15) seems to have been specially designed to accompany this text and it is further evidence of the influence of the friars on the development of lay piety at the French court and on the creation of new images.[72] By contrast, the lively narrative style of the illustration of the legend of the three living and the three dead reveals Jean le Noir's contact with Italian art and his probable knowledge of the fourteenth-century frescoes in the Campo Santo, Pisa, devoted to this subject.[73]

While many of the picture prayer books of the early fourteenth century were designed with the needs of royal and noble women in mind, within a generation these very manuals or similar compilations had been adopted by the men of the family. Mention has already been made of the fact that Charles V updated the *Savoy Hours* for his own use. Around the same time (c.1375), the *Petites Heures* was commisioned for the king's brother, Jean de Berry. This work stands out among the duke's prayer books for the number of distinctive devotional texts and images that were copied from books made for older members of the family.[74] Three of the unusual Offices in the *Savoy Hours* recur here, and two of them, the Hours of the Trinity and the Hours of St John the Baptist, have the same unusual cycles.[75] Like Jeanne of Navarre, Jean de Berry, too, is shown accompanied by his guardian angel (Fig. 16). The *Petites Heures* also contained in identical order the vernacular texts of Bonne's psalter. The fact, however, that they were differently illustrated suggests that in this case only the scribe had access to the earlier manuscript.[76]

The three books examined here indicate that the women for whom they were made were trained in a number of different kinds of prayer; and were expected to devote considerable time to its practice. In this context the treatise *Speculum dominarum* written for Jeanne I of Navarre (died 1305)

---

[71] 'Ha homme & fame voi que sueffre pur toi.'

[72] See Heck, 'L'iconographie', 9–22.

[73] Folios 321v and 322; reproduced in Avril, *Manuscript Painting*, Pl. 18B; and Sterling, *Peinture médiévale*, 1, Fig. 54.

[74] See Avril, *Introduction to the Facsimile of the Petites Heures*, 83–87.

[75] Meiss, *French Painting*, Figs 152–61, 164–71; and Avril, *Facsimile of the Petites Heures*.

[76] See Avril, *Introduction to the Facsimile of the Petites Heures*, 353–54; and Heck, 'L'iconographie', 9–22.

by her Franciscan confessor, Durand de Champagne (and also translated into French for her as the *Miroir des Dames*)[77] provides an interesting contrast to the more popular *Miroir des Princes*. Geneviève Hasenohr has pointed out that whereas the latter, which was addressed to men destined to rule, exhorted its readers to lead an active life of high moral principle, the ideal held out to their female counterparts was one of commitment to a more prayerful and contemplative existence.[78]

Women in the early fourteenth century seem also to have played an important role in the shaping of court and family life around regular daily prayer. We know, too, that not only were the children of royal and noble households taught from an early age how to pray but that they often learnt to read and write from their prayer books. Women were involved in these activites, and the illustration of Queen Blanche presiding over the lesson of her young son, in the prayer book of Jeanne of Navarre (Pl. 1) may draw on contemporary experience as well as on pictorial and literary sources.

Champagne comments that three kinds of attention are required for vocal prayer. Firstly one should pay attention to the words so that they are recited correctly, secondly one must attend to the sense of what one is saying; and the third and best sort of attention, which is accessible even to the ignorant and unlettered, is to think on the object of one's prayer, namely God, and of what one seeks from God in prayer. Champagne concedes that it is impossible to attend perfectly in these three ways all the time, and that for prayer to be meritorious it is sufficient to concentrate on its object.[79] Many of the visual aspects of these three devotional manuals reinforce these principles, not least the frequent depiction of the donors shown consistently attentive before the object of their devotion.

---

[77] See G. Hasenohr, 'La Prière des Femmes' in Bériou *et al.*, eds, *Prier au Moyen Age*, 239–40. For a fourteenth-century copy of the French version see London, BL Add. MS 29986.

[78] Hasenohr, 'Prière', 240.

[79] Hasenohr, 'Prière', 240–41.

Appendix

Text and illustration 1: *The Savoy Hours* [80]

1–12
Calendar, use of Paris, with 24 quatrefoil vignettes, two to a page, of the labours of the months and the signs of the zodiac.

Psalter [missing, with eight miniatures marking liturgical divisions?].

13–64
Hours of the Trinity with miniatures for matins: Trinity (p. 13); lauds: Creation of Adam (p. 33); prime: Appearance of three angels to Abraham (p. 42); terce: Vision of Isaiah (p. 45); sext: Baptism of Christ (p. 49); none: Transfiguration (p. 52); vespers: Christ preaching (p. 55); compline: God in Majesty worshipped by the elders of the Apocalypse.

65–90
Hours of the Holy Spirit, with miniatures for matins: Baptism of Christ (p. 65); lauds: Pentecost (p. 71); prime: Trinity (p. 74); terce: St Peter preaching (p. 77); sext: St Peter leading people into the church (p. 79); none: Sts Peter and Paul baptizing (p. 82); vespers: St Peter saying Mass (p. 84); compline: St Gregory writing under the inspiration of the Holy Spirit (p. 87).

One folio inserted at the time of Charles V with pseudo-Greek prayers.

93–134
Hours of the Virgin, use of Paris, with miniatures for matins: Annunciation (p. 93); lauds: Visitation (p. 106); prime: Nativity (p. 113); terce: Annunciation to the Shepherds (p. 117); sext: Adoration of the Magi (p. 120); none: Presentation in the Temple (p. 123); vespers: Flight into Egypt (p. 126); compline: Coronation of the Virgin (p. 131).

135–36
One folio inserted at the time of Charles V with pseudo-Greek prayers.

137–70
Hours of the Passion, with miniatures for matins: Arrest of Christ (p. 137); lauds: Christ before Pilate (p. 144); prime: Scourging (p. 148); terce: Carrying of the Cross (p. 151); sext: Crucifixion (p. 155); none: Descent from the Cross (p. 159); vespers: Entombment (p. 163); compline: Resurrection (p. 165).

---

[80] Numbers throughout refer to the old pagination cited by Durrieu 'Notice', 500–55. An asterisk [*] indicates extant folios in the Beinecke Library, Yale University. For a reconstruction of the additions of Charles V, see Durrieu, 'Notice', 550–55; and Wieck, *Time Sanctified*, 177–78.

171–98
Hours of St John the Baptist, with miniatures for matins: Zachary in the Temple (p. 171); lauds: Visitation (p. 173); prime: Nativity of St John the Baptist (p. 183); terce: St John in the desert (p. 185); sext: Baptism of Christ (p. 187); none: Arrest of St John the Baptist (p. 189); vespers: Dance of Salome (p. 191); compline: Head of the Baptist presented to Herod (p. 194).

199–229, and *folios 5 and 12
Hours of the Angels, with miniatures for matins: St Michael conquering Satan (p. 199); lauds: Angel weighing souls (p. 208); prime: Apparition of two angels to Abraham (p. 214); terce: Jacob wrestles with an angel (p. 216); sext: [missing]; none: *Angels protecting equestrian soldiers? (f. 5); vespers: *Angels ministering to Christ in the desert (f. 12v); compline: St Matthew writing with evangelist symbol of angel (p. 227). [The order from lauds to sext is problematical.]

230–38
Prayers in honour of the Virgin, with miniature: Blanche in prayer before the Virgin (p. 230); and historiated initial: Bust of the Virgin (p. 232).

239–62
Hours of St John the Evangelist, with miniatures for matins: St John writing (p. 239); lauds: St John plunged in boiling oil (p. 216); prime: St John in exile? (p. 246); terce: St John raising Drusiana to life? (p. 248); sext: St John and the poisoned chalice (p. 251); none: [subject uncertain]; vespers: [missing]; compline: St John, half buried in the ground and surrounded by flames adores the Host.

263–94
Hours of St Louis, with miniatures for matins: St Louis enthroned in glory with angels; in the margin his anointing (p. 263); lauds: St Louis receiving the discipline (p. 271); prime: St Louis carrying relics of crown of thorns (p. 279); terce: St Louis, while ill, takes the crusader cross (p. 281); sext: St Louis on the seas in crusading armour (p. 284); none: St Louis in prison receives his breviary from an angel (p. 286); vespers: St Louis buries the bones of Christians of Sayette (p. 288); compline: St Louis serves a leper at table (p. 291).

295–318
Hours of St Louis of Marseille (Toulouse), with miniatures for matins: St Louis gives his crown to the pope (p. 295); lauds: St Louis takes the Franciscan habit (p. 301); prime: St Louis serves the poor at table (p. 306); terce: St Louis revives the dead (p. 308); sext: St Louis on horseback gives his cloak to a beggar (p. 310); none: Burial of St Louis (p. 312); vespers: Miraculous cure of a child (p. 314); compline: Miraculous deliverance of a woman from demonic possession (p. 315).

319–36
Hours of Mary Magdalen, with miniatures for matins: Mary Magdalen at the feet of Christ (p. 319); lauds: Risen Christ appears to Mary Magdalen (p. 323); prime and terce: [missing]; sext: Mary Magdalen drives out demons (p. 328); none: a priest witnesses Mary Magdalen borne aloft (p. 330); vespers: Mary Magdalen receives communion from Bishop Maximinus (p. 332); compline: During Mass Bishop Maximinus witnesses the ascent of the saint's soul to heaven (p. 334).

337–50
Suffrages for the Passion, the Angels, All Saints and the Trinity with miniatures: Calvary (p. 337); Group of standing angels (p. 340); Group of kneeling angels (p. 343); All Saints (p. 348); Trinity: Mercy Seat (p. 348).

351–82
Vigils of the Dead, with miniature for vespers: Funeral service (p. 351).

383–98
Penitential Psalms and litany of the saints, with miniature: Christ in majesty with four evangelist symbols (p. 383).

399–406
Gradual Psalms, with miniature: Blanche kneeling before gilded Calvary group in the sky (p. 399).

407–38 and *folios 3, 6–9, 11, 13–22
Suffrages to God, Our Lady, the Apostles, several martyrs, confessors and virgins, with miniatures for temporal: Annunciation (p. 407); Nativity (p. 408); Epiphany (p. 409); Presentation in the Temple (p. 410); Christ among the doctors (p. 411); Palm Sunday (entry into Jerusalem?) (p. 412); Last Supper (p. 413); Christ in the Garden of Olives (p. 414); Scourging (p. 415); Christ lead to death (Carrying of the Cross?) (p. 416); Crucifixion (p. 417); Descent from the Cross (p. 418); Entombment (p. 419); Resurrection (p. 420); another image of the Resurrection (p. 421); Holy women at the sepulchre (p. 422); Ascension (p. 423); Pentecost (p. 424); Assumption (p. 435); with miniatures for sanctoral/communal; Apostles: Group of Apostles (p. 436); *Group of Apostles (f. 11); *Blanche kneeling before St John the Evangelist (f. 11v); *Blanche kneeling before St Andrew (f. 6); *Blanche kneeling before St James the Greater (f. 6v); Martyrs: St Maurice on horseback (p. 425); St Nicaise (p. 426); St Stephen (p. 427); Blanche kneeling before St Lambert (p. 428); Blanche kneeling before St Christopher (p. 429); St Laurence (p. 430); St George on horseback (p. 431); Martyrdom of St Thomas à Becket (p. 432); St Vincent (p. 433); St Clement (p. 434); *Execution of three martyrs (f. 3); Confessors: *Blanche kneeling before St Louis of France (f. 3v); St Ligier (p. 437), Blanche kneeling before St Dominic (p. 438); *Blanche kneeling before St Silvester (f. 13); *Blanche kneeling before St Augustine (f. 13v); *St Martin giving away his cloak (f. 14); *Blanche kneeling before St Remy (f. 14v); *Blanche kneeling before St Eloi (f. 15); *Blanche kneeling before St Anthony, abbot (f. 15v); *St Leonard venerated by two captives whose chains he holds (f. 16); *Blanche kneeling before St Gregory (f. 16v); *Blanche kneeling before St Benedict (f. 7); *group of confessors (f. 7v); *Blanche kneeling before St Romaricus (f. 17); Virgins: *Death of St Agnes (f. 17v); *Martyrdom of St Agatha (f. 18); *Coronation of Sts Cecilia and Valerian in heaven (f. 18v); *Blanche kneeling before St Lucy (f. 19); *Blanche kneeling before St Lucy (f. 19v); *St Elizabeth receiving visit of the Virgin (Visitation) (f. 20); *Blanche kneeling before St Genevieve (f. 20v); *Blanche kneeling before St Gertrude (f. 21); *Blanche kneeling before St Barbara (f. 21v); *Blanche kneeling before St Mary Magdalen (f. 8); *Blanche kneeling before St Katherine (f. 8v); *St Margaret in prison (f. 9); *Group of virgins (f. 9v); Blanche kneeling before St Clare (f. 22).

*folios 22–25
Intercessory or prone prayers, with miniatures for the pope and members of the Church: *Seated pope surrounded by ranks of the clergy (f. 22); for kings and

princes of the earth: *Group of standing kings and lords (f. 23); for those that work the land: *Three peasants pruning, hoeing and delving (f. 23v); for those in mortal sin: [missing]; for those in peril at sea: [missing]; for prisoners: [missing]; for those who give alms: *Two people distributing alms to the poor (f. 24); for relatives and friends: *Blanche kneeling before altar with sculpted Calvary (f. 24v): for oneself: *Blanche kneeling before altar with sculpted Calvary (f. 25); for those in purgatory: *Angels rescuing nude figures from flames of purgatory (f. 25v).

*folios 2 and 10
Commemorations of the Trinity and several saints, with miniatures for the Trinity: *Blanche kneeling before the Trinity (f. 2); for the angels: *Group of angels (f. 2v); for All Saints: *Group of standing saints (f. 10); for peace: *Blanche at Mass, priest with *Pax* (f. 10v).

f. 26
Prayer in honour of St Peter Martyr (f. 26); Five Joys of Our Lady (f. 26–26v).

Text and illustration 2: *The Hours of Jeanne of Navarre* [81]

1–3v
Fifteenth century additions comprising: suffrages for St Sebastian and St Luppo; prayer beginning *Domine Ihesu Christe qui hanc sacratissmam carnem,* suffrage for St Martin with miniature (English): Kneeling donor before Trinity and Virgin and Child (f. 3v).

4–9v
Calendar, Franciscan use, with illustrative programme for each page. *Bas-de-page:* a prophet removes a stone from a building symbolizing the synagogue, which by the last month of December is shown in ruins; on his left stands an Apostle grasping part of the prophet's mantle as though unveiling his book and prophetic scroll and translating their message into the article of the creed inscribed on his own scroll. Top margin: the gates of Jerusalem or Paradise; Mary appears above the battlements with a pennant displaying the scene referred to in the article of the creed below; on the left, Conversion of St Paul, followed in later months by his preaching on the creed articles; in front of the gate and under the archway: Sign of the zodiac for each month and a landscape indicating the changing seasons with a figure cutting down trees in December.

11–38
Hours of the Trinity, with miniatures for matins: Seated Trinity (f. 11); lauds: Creation of Adam (f. 17); prime: Appearance of three angels to Abraham (f. 23); terce: Vision of Isaiah (f. 25); sext: Baptism of Christ (f. 27v); none: Transfiguration (f. 29v); vespers: Christ preaching (f. 32); compline: God in Majesty worshipped by the elders of the Apocalypse (f. 36).

39–72
Hours of the Virgin, with miniatures for matins: Annunciation (f. 39); lauds: Visitation (f. 44); prime: Nativity (f. 50); terce: Annunciation to the Shepherds (f. 53); sext: Adoration of the Magi (f. 55v); none: Presentation in the Temple (f. 58); vespers: Flight into Egypt (f. 61); compline: Coronation of the Virgin (f. 65v); nocturn variations with historiated initial: Kneeling donor before Virgin and Child (f. 68).

72v–74
O Intemerata with miniature: Seated Virgin and Child and St John (f. 72v).

74–75
Veni Creator with miniature: Pentecost (f. 74).

75–85
Penitential Psalms and litany of the Saints with miniature: Christ in Majesty (f. 75); and Christ and the Saints (f. 81v).

---

[81] Numbers refer to the old foliation which includes f. 121, now missing. One folio is also missing after each of ff. 145 and 152, and three folios after f. 193. Folios 3, 10r-v, 38v and 246v are blank. Only marginal scenes clearly relevant to the text are listed here. For fuller descriptions see Cockerell, *Descriptive Catalogue,* 151–83.

85v–105v
Hours of Saint Louis, with miniatures for matins: St Louis learning to read (f. 85v); lauds: St Louis attending Mass (f. 91v); prime: St Louis en route to Rheims for his anointing (f. 97); terce: Anointing of St Louis (f. 99); sext: Coronation of St Louis (f. 100v); none: Carrying of the relics of the crown of thorns to the Sainte Chapelle (f. 102); vespers: St Louis, ill, takes the crusader's cross (f. 102); compline: Preaching of the crusade (f. 106v).

109–16
Hours of the Cross, with miniatures for matins: Arrest of Christ (f. 109); prime: Mocking of Christ (f. 110); terce: Carrying of the Cross (f. 111); sext: Christ on the Cross (f. 112); none: Christ dies on the Cross (f. 113); vespers: Deposition (f. 114); compline: Entombment of Christ (f. 115).

116v–117
Prayer in honour of the archangels Michael, Gabriel and Raphael, *Deus propicius esto michi peccatrici*, with four-line historiated initial: Three archangels (f. 116v).

117v–118
Prayer to the holy Cross, *Sainte vraie croix*, with miniature: Crucifixion, with Mary and St John (f. 117v).

118
Six verses in honour of Our Lady, *Mater digna dei*.

118v–119
Prayer to the Virgin, *Douce debonnaire, vierge*, with miniature: Kneeling donor before standing Virgin and Child (f. 118v).

119v–120v
Seven Joys of Our Lady (ends abruptly in fifth joy), with miniature: Coronation of the Virgin (f. 119v).

122–22v
Prayer to the Virgin, *Tres douce dame sus toutes honneuree*, with four-line decorated initial (f. 122).

122v–123
Special prayer to the Virgin, *Belle tres douce vierge dame*, with seven-line historiated initial: Kneeling donor before seated Virgin and Child (f. 122v).

123v–124
Prayer to one's guardian angel, *Angele qui meus es custos*, with miniature: Queen accompanied by angel gives alms (f. 123v).

124–24v
Prayer in honour of five feasts of Our Lady, *Deus qui nos beate*, with four-line decorated initial (f. 124).

125
Commemoration of the Trinity, with four-line decorated initial.

125v–126
Prayer to God the Son *Sire de toutes creatures*, with miniature: Donor kneeling before Christ being scourged (f. 125v).

126–26v
Prayer to God the Father, *Ha douz cher pere*, with miniature: Lord in Majesty (f. 126).

127–27v
Prayer to God the Holy Spirit, *Saint esperit urai dieu*, with miniature: Pentecost (f. 127).

127v–129
Prayer for the seven gifts of the Holy Spirit, *Donnez moi siue se il vous plaist*.

129–29v
Prayer to the Holy Trinity, *Sainte Trinite un seul dieu tout puissant*, with miniature: Trinity (f. 129).

130–30v
Prayer to Our Lady against the seven deadly sins, *Douce vierge Marie en qui humanite*, with four-line historiated initial: Kneeling donor before seated Virgin and Child (f. 129).

131–31v
Prayer in honour of St Apollonia against toothache, *Veni sponsa Christi*, with miniature: Torture of St Apollonia (f. 131; rubric on f. 130v).

131v–132v
Prayer for one's friends, *Levavi oculos meos in montes* (Psalm 120) and Latin collects.

132v
Prayer at elevation of the Host, *Ave verum corpus*.

133–34v
Life of St Margaret (French) with miniature: St Margaret issuing from the dragon (f. 133).

134v–135
Prayers at elevation of the Host *Ave Ihesu Christe verbum patris*.

135–36
Beginning of Gospel of St John with miniature: St John writing (f. 135).

136
Prayer in honour of Our Lady, *Precor te sancta Maria virgo perpetua*, with seven-line historiated initial: Kneeling donor before seated Virgin and Child (f. 136).

136v
Prayer in honour of Our Lady, *Sancta Maria mater domini*, with four-line historiated initial: Kneeling donor before seated Virgin and Child (f. 136v).

136v–137
Prayer in honour of Our Lady, *Tres certainne esperance*, with four-line historiated initial: Kneeling donor before seated Virgin and Child (f. 136v).

137
New *Intemerata, Tres douce dame vierge Marie*, with miniature: Kneeling donor before seated Virgin and Child (f. 137v).

140v–141
Five Joys of Our Lady, with eight-line historiated initial: Seated Virgin and Child (f. 140v).

141–43v
Five psalms and antiphons commencing with the five letters of 'Maria'.

143v–145
Fifteen verses beginning with the letters of the words 'Marie Roine Merci'.

145v–150v
Suffrages for the Nativity, St Anne (page with miniature removed), St Nicaise, St Martin, St Giles, St Josse of Ponthieu and the relics of all martyrs, with miniatures: Nativity, *bas-de-page:* Annunciation to the Shepherds (f. 145v); Martyrdom of St Nicaise, *bas-de-page:* saint with head in his hands, supported by angels, four-line historiated initial: Kneeling donor (f. 146v); St Martin gives away his cloak, Christ, attended by angels, displays cloak in heaven above, *bas-de-page:* St Martin supervises almsgiving, four-line historiated initial: St Martin drinks with a poor man (f. 147v); St Giles protects a hind from a huntsman with bow, *bas-de-page:* huntsman pursues rabbits (f. 148v); St Josse feeds fish (upper left), feeds birds (upper right), feeds four deer (below) (f. 149); four-line historiated initial: Seated youth (f. 149v); worship of relics by royal family at Sainte Chapelle, six-line initial (I): Standing Christ (f. 150).

150v–151
Devotions for Communion, *Domine non sum dignus*, with four-line historiated initial: Donor receiving the Host (f. 152).

151
The Gospel of Our Lady (sic) according to St Luke, *Loquente Ihesu ad turbas*.

151v–152
A very special prayer in honour of Our Lady, *Deprecor te O domina sanctissima Marie (mentions Johanna navarre regina)*, with four-line historiated initial: Kneeling donor before standing Virgin and Child (f. 151v).

152
The circumcision of Christ according to St Luke, *Postquam consummati sunt dies octo*.

152–52v
Sequence in honour of Our Lady, *Tibi cordis in altare decet*, with four-line historiated initial: Seated Virgin and Child.

152v–158v
Gradual Psalms.

158v–182v
Vigils of the Dead, with miniature for vespers: Funeral service (f. 159); and four-line historiated initial for matins: Angel seated on tomb (f. 163).

183–93v
Suffrages for the holy Cross, St Michael, All Angels, St John the Baptist, St John the Evangelist, St Peter, Three kings of Cologne, St Leonard, St Louis of Toulouse, St Denis and companions and St Nicholas, with miniatures: St Helena and the finding of the true Cross, *bas-de-page*: St Helena with Cross, and man touching with Cross shrouded woman who rises from the tomb, four-line historiated initial: Angel playing organ (f. 183); St Michael slaying dragon and weighing souls, *bas-de-page*: legend of St Michael *in monte Gargano*, on left, Man shoots at bull; on right, Michael reports to bishop in bed, four-line historiated initial: Young man and woman [subject not clear] (f. 184); Nine choirs of angels, *bas-de-page:* Five music making angels (f. 185); Birth of St John the Baptist, *bas-de-page:* Kneeling donor queen and Visitation (f. 186); St John the Evangelist in boiling oil, *bas-de-page:* Raising of Drusiana and St John and the poisoned chalice (f. 187); St Peter and Nero, St Peter goes to prison, *bas-de-page*: Crucifixion of St Peter, four-line historiated initial: Youth talking to an ape (f. 188); Magi before Herod, *bas-de-page*: Massacre of innocents (f. 189); St Leonard and two captives, *bas-de-page*: a saint helps to move the wheel of a horse-drawn cart, the cartier brandishes a stick (f. 190); St Louis of Toulouse feeds four poor men at table, *bas-de-page*: St Louis saves drowning children, four-line historiated initial: Kneeling donor before image of St Louis (f. 191); Martyrdom of St Denis and companions (f. 192); St Nicholas delivers three princes from prison, *bas-de-page*: on left, St Nicholas throws gold coins through a window to old man in bed, attended by his three daughters; on right, the same man kneels at saint's feet (f. 193).

194–219v
Hours of the Virgin for Advent, with miniature for matins: Annunciation (f. 194); and six-line historiated initials for lauds: Visitation (f. 199v); prime: Nativity (f. 205); terce: Annunciation to the Shepherds (f. 207); sext (*midi*): Adoration of the Magi (f. 209); none: Presentation in the Temple (f. 211); vespers: Flight into Egypt (f. 213); compline: Coronation of the Virgin (f. 217).

220–46
Hours of the Virgin from the first day after the octave of Christmas to the Purification, with miniature for matins: Annunciation (f. 220); and six-line historiated initials for lauds: Visitation (f. 225); prime: Nativity (f. 230v); terce: Annunciation to the Shepherds (f. 233); sext (*midi*): Adoration of the Magi (f. 235v); none: Presentation in the Temple (f. 237v); vespers: Flight into Egypt (f. 240); compline: Coronation of the Virgin (f. 244).

247–55
Psalter of St Jerome with eight-line historiated initial: St Jerome kneeling before seated Virgin and Child (f. 247).

255–55v
Obsecro te

255v–256v
Prayer in honour of Our Lady, *Ave virgo gloriosa.*

257
Hymn, *Ihesu nostra redemptio.*

Late fourteenth-century additions

257v–261
Hours of the Holy Spirit, with pen flourished initials varying from five to seven lines in height for matins (f. 257v); prime (f. 258); terce (f. 258v); sext (f. 259); none (f. 260); vespers (f. 260v); and compline (f. 261).

261v–262v
Gospel of St Luke, *Missus est* and prayers in honour of the Annunciation.

262v–263v
Prayer in honour of body and blood of the Lord *In presencia corporis et sanguinis tui.*

Late fifteenth-century additions

264–70
Litany of the saints (Franciscan).

270v–271v
Litany of the saints for a sister of the Franciscan order.

Figure 1. Blanche of Savoy kneeling before the Trinity. *Savoy Hours*. New Haven, Yale University, Beinecke Rare Book and Manuscript Library, MS 390, f. 2. 201×147 mm.

Figure 2. Christ addresses Bonne of Luxembourg and Jean le Bon from the Cross. *Psalter of Bonne of Luxembourg*. New York, The Metropolitan Museum of Art. The Cloisters Collection (69.86), f. 329. 125×91mm.

Figure 3. Vision of Isaiah. *Hours of Jeanne of Navarre*. Paris, Bibliothèque Nationale, MS n.a. lat. 3145, f. 25. 180×135 mm.

Figure 4. St John the Baptist. *Petites Heures*. Paris, Bibliothèque Nationale, MS lat. 18014, f. 208. 215×145 mm.

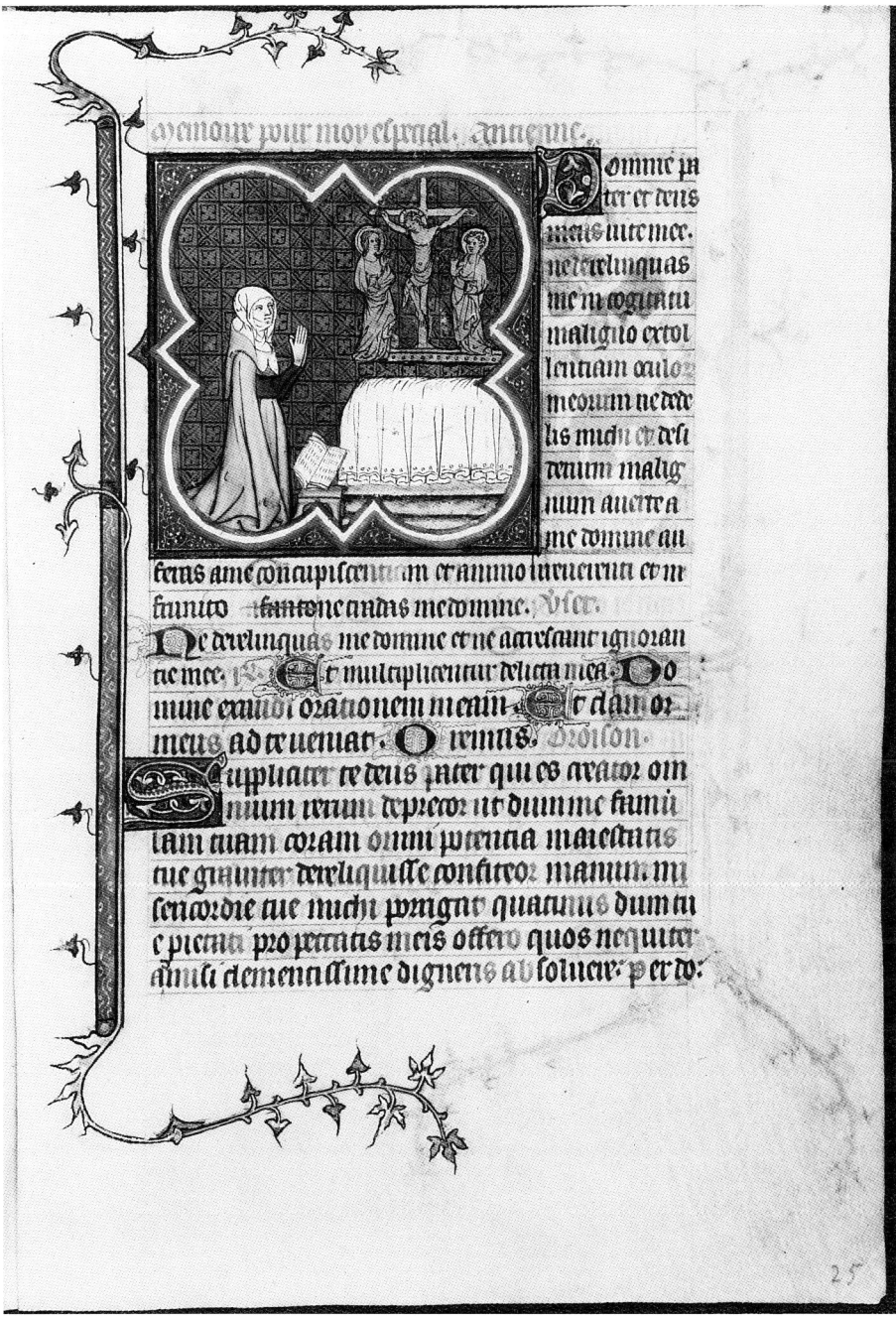

Figure 5. Blanche of Savoy at prayer. *Savoy Hours*. New Haven, Yale University, Beinecke Rare Book and Manuscript Library, MS 390, f. 25v. 201×147mm.

Figure 6. Annunciation. *Hours of Jeanne of Navarre*. Paris, Bibliothèque Nationale, MS n.a. lat. 3145, f. 39. 180×135 mm.

Figure 7. Entombment. *Hours of Jeanne of Navarre*. Paris, Bibliothèque Nationale, MS n.a. lat. 3145, f. 115. 180×135 mm.

Figure 8. Anointing of St Louis. *Hours of Jeanne of Navarre*. Paris, Bibliothèque Nationale, MS n.a. lat. 3145, f. 99. 180×135 mm.

Figure 9. The preaching of the Crusade. *Hours of Jeanne of Navarre*. Paris, Bibliothèque Nationale, MS n.a. lat. 3145, f. 106v. 180×135mm.

Figure 10. Jeanne de Navarre with her guardian angel gives alms to the poor. *Hours of Jeanne of Navarre*. Paris, Bibliothèque Nationale, MS n.a. lat. 3145, f. 123v. 180×135mm.

Figure 11. Jeanne de Navarre kneels before the Virgin and Child. *Hours of Jeanne of Navarre*. Paris, Bibliothèque Nationale, MS n.a. lat. 3145, f. 118v. 180×135 mm.

Figure 12. Jeanne de Navarre kneels before the Virgin and Child. *Hours of Jeanne of Navarre*. Paris, Bibliothèque Nationale, MS n.a. lat. 3145, f. 151v. 180×135 mm.

Figure 13. King Charles V kneels before St Anthony. *Savoy Hours*. New Haven, Yale University, Beinecke Rare Book and Manuscript Library, MS 390, f. 4 (upper). 201 × 147 mm.

64 THE ART OF THE BOOK: ITS PLACE IN MEDIEVAL WORSHIP

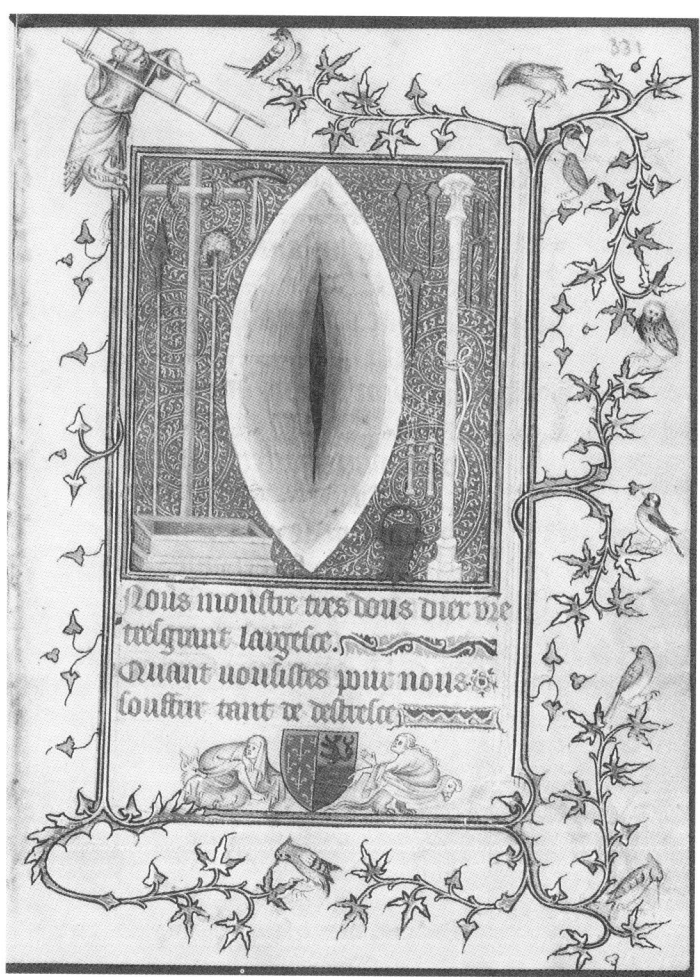

Figure 14. The wound of Christ and the instruments of the Passion. *Psalter of Bonne of Luxembourg*. New York, The Metropolitan Museum of Art. The Cloisters Collection (69.86), f. 331. 125×91mm.

Figure 15. The degrees of charity. *Psalter of Bonne of Luxembourg*. New York, The Metropolitan Museum of Art. The Cloisters Collection (69.86), f. 315. 125×91 mm.

Figure 16. Jean de Berry and his guardian angel. *Petites Heures*. Paris, Bibliothèque Nationale, MS lat. 18014, f. 199. 215×145 mm.

THREE

Books for a Dominican Nuns' Choir: Illustrated Liturgical Manuscripts at Saint-Louis de Poissy, c.1330–1350

Joan Naughton

PHILIPPE IV LE BEL, KING OF FRANCE began building the Dominican church and monastery at Poissy, on the Seine approximately thirty kilometres from Paris, in 1298. The nuns moved into the royal foundation in 1304, but not until almost thirty years later, and fifteen years after the king's death, was the large Gothic church consecrated—on 12 February 1331 (n.s.).[1] In a grand ceremony the Archbishop of Sens, in the presence of King Philippe VI de Valois and twenty-five archbishops and bishops, solemnly dedicated the church to the founder's grandfather,

---

[1] For a detailed study of the history of the building and the early appearance of the architecture and its sculptural embellishment see A. Erlande-Brandenburg, 'La priorale saint-Louis de Poissy', *Bulletin Monumental* 129 (1971), 85–112. The king's intention that the church be completed much earlier is evidenced by his petition for and the consequent granting of papal indulgences by Clement V in 1312 to those who would attend the dedication, its anniversary, and on other specified feast days during the year of dedication. The two Bulls were confirmed the day before the actual ceremony by his successor John XXII at Avignon: see T. Ripoll and A. Bremond, eds, *Bullarium Ordinis Fratrum Praedicatorum*, I (Rome, 1729), 122–23, 193.

St Louis (King Louis IX) who had reputedly been born at Poissy.[2] Two years later the saint's own grand-daughter Marie de Clermont, one of the founding nuns, was elected prioress.[3]

In 1346, however, the approach of the English army under Edward III caused the nuns to vacate their premises. They fled to Paris for an unknown period while the English king stayed in the monastery itself and the Black Prince took over the royal palace at Poissy. The army's sojourn was short, lasting only while the bridge at Poissy was repaired between 13 and 16 August. The English spared the monastery, but burnt surrounding towns and countryside. In this richly productive area the incendiary devastation of royal forest and of summer crops ripe for harvest was considerable, for it is recounted that the smoke was visible from Paris.[4] This no doubt diminished substantially the income of the extremely well-provided house since the nuns took revenues and daily sustenance from the area and had grazing, silvan and other rights there.[5]

---

[2] The future Pope Clement VI, then archbishop of Rouen, and the bishops of Paris and Chartres are among the ecclesiastics known to have taken part in the ceremony: M.-D. Chapotin, *A travers l'histoire dominicaine, ancienne et contemporaine* (Paris, 1903), 392. A lack of general conviction that Louis IX had been born in the royal palace at Poissy is implied by Philippe le Bel's protestation in the foundation charter of the monastery, dated 1304: 'où tout le monde sait qu'il avait pris naissance'; see Erlande-Brandenburg, 'La priorale', 89 n. 2. For a review of the disagreement between the chroniclers over this issue see E. Bories, *Histoire de la Ville de Poissy* (Paris, 1925), 33–34.

[3] Philippe le Bel persuaded the parents of Marie de Clermont to sever her betrothal of three years to Jean, Marquis de Montferrat. She took the Dominican habit, aged 14, in 1299 at Montargis, remaining there until the first nuns entered Poissy in 1304; she was elected to the prime office on the founding prioress' death in 1333; see Anselme de Sainte-Marie, *Histoire généalogique et chronologique de la maison royale de France*, I (Paris, 1726), 297; R. Labarraque, *Poissy à travers les âges* (Alençon, 1948), 30–31.

[4] For the events during August 1346 at Poissy and the surrounding area see H. Denifle, *La désolation des églises, monastères et hôpitaux en France pendant la guerre de cent ans* (Paris, 1899), I, 39–41; G. Fourquin, *Les campagnes de la région Parisienne à la fin du Moyen Age* (Paris, 1964), 225–26; S. Moreau-Rendu, *Le prieuré royal de saint-Louis de Poissy* (Colmar, 1968), 105–06; M. Mollat, *Histoire de l'Isle de France et de Paris* (Toulouse, 1971), 120, 150; and the chronicles which most fully deal with the events: J. Viard, ed., *Les Grandes Chroniques de France*, (Paris, 1920–53), IX, 275–79; S. Luce, ed., *Chroniques de Froissart*, (Paris, 1872), III, 148–50, with variant accounts 380, 383; fragment of a chronicle, Cambridge, Corpus Christi College MS 370, ff. 1–8, published in J. Moisant, *Le Prince Noir en Aquitaine 1355–1356–1362–1370* (Paris, 1894), 169–71.

[5] For the sources of the nuns' revenues see Philippe le Bel's foundation charter (Paris, Archives Nationales, JJ 2), published in Moreau-Rendu, *Prieuré royal*, 311–16; C.-V. Langlois, 'Registres perdus des archives de la chambre des comptes de Paris', *Notices et extraits des manuscrits de la Bibliothèque Nationale et autres bibliothèques* 40 (1916), 332–78; O. Dufourcq-Latron, Le monastère royal de saint-Louis de Poissy depuis la fondation (1304) jusqu'à l'institution de la Congrégation Gallicane (début du XVIe) in *Position des Thèses . . . École nationale des chartes* (Paris, 1929), 82–87. Surviving cartulary documents from Poissy

The Black Death, which was in the Paris region from mid-1348 to the end of 1349, probably had a similarly adverse effect on monastic income. Whether the plague directly affected the nuns themselves is not known since almost no documents survive from this period. However, the larger part of the nuns' royally endowed income came from the revenues of agricultural production on land owned in the regions of the Ile-de-France and Normandy and from varied riparian mercantile interests such as milling and the supply of goods to Paris via the Seine; very little came directly from the royal treasury. It is likely, therefore, that the material well-being of the house continued to be significantly reduced as a result of the particularly ravaging effects of the disease on the populations of Paris, Normandy and regions along associated water-routes.[6]

Six illustrated liturgical manuscripts made for use in the newly dedicated church have survived from the period outlined above. The closely knit group was produced in Paris and, except for the missal which was designed for the use of the priest-celebrant, the books pertain to the part played by the nuns in the celebration of the Divine Office and the Mass. The nuns' choir was located in the central nave of the church and here they daily chanted the Office and sang the appropriate sections of the ordinary and proper of the Mass.[7] In this paper I shall examine this group of manuscripts with special reference to the particular requirements of the Poissy nuns, in order to assess the extent to which these requirements influenced the form and appearance of the books and, more speculatively, to consider how the commission might have been carried out. To define more precisely the relationship between the appearance of the

---

dating from this period (and/or later copies) are catalogued in H. Lemoine, *Département de Seine-et-Oise, Inventaire-Sommaire des Archives Départementales antérieures à 1790, Archives Ecclèsiastiques*, Series H (Corbeil, 1944), 73H.

[6] On the effects of the Black Death in this area see, for example, F.A. Gasquet, *The Black Death of 1348 and 1349* (London, 1908), 56; E. Carpentier, 'Autour de la Peste Noire: famines et épidémies dans l'histoire du XIVe siècle', *Annales E.S.C.*, 17 (1962), 1062–92; R.S. Gottfried, *The Black Death: Natural and Human Disaster in Medieval Europe* (London, 1983), 54–55.

[7] The division of the church into architecturally and liturgically separate areas for choir nuns, lay sisters, friars, the royal family and the general public, based on Cistercian precedent, is analysed in A. Erlande-Brandenburg, 'Art et politique sous Philippe le Bel. La priorale Saint-Louis de Poissy', *Comptes rendus d'Académie des Inscriptions et Belles Lettres* (1987), 509–14. For a closer consideration of the layout of the nuns' choir at Poissy see J. Naughton, 'The Poissy Antiphonary in its royal monastic milieu (Melbourne, State Library of Victoria MS *096 1/R66A)', *La Trobe Library Journal* 13 (1993), 39–40, Diagram 1. The publication entitled 'Monastic architecture for women', *Gesta* 31.2 (1992) discusses a number of the architectural means used to preserve the enclosure of women within a building intended for wider liturgical use.

manuscripts and their specific function I shall compare them with selected liturgical books made contemporaneously in Paris.

The group consists of three unnoted breviaries and one antiphonal-hymnal for the Divine Office, and a missal and a gradual-prosar for the Mass (Table 2, p. 94).[8] The breviary now privately owned in London is perhaps the earliest of the group, liturgical dating placing it between 1332 and 1336.[9] It is a one-volume compilation. The other two breviaries (Paris, Bibl. de l'Arsenal MSS 107 and 602–603) are divided into separate summer and winter volumes. Together with the missal (London, BL Egerton MS 3037) they date liturgically to between 1336 and 1348.[10] Only the winter volume of Paris, Bibl. de l'Arsenal MS 107 is extant.[11] In the Dominican calendar which introduces each of these five volumes the Dedication of the Church of St Louis is inscribed on 12 February. In addition, express references to *sorores* in Masses for the Dead in the missal indicate that it was designated for use by the celebrant conducting services for the nuns.[12] In view of the disruptions to monastic life caused by the

---

[8] For catalogue descriptions of these manuscripts see the following: Melbourne antiphonal: K.V. Sinclair, *Descriptive Catalogue of Medieval and Renaissance Manuscripts in Australia* (Sydney, 1969), no. 218, 369–70; M.M. Manion and V.F. Vines, *Medieval and Renaissance Illuminated Manuscripts in Australian Collections* (London, 1984), no. 71, 176–79; Arsenal breviaries: V. Leroquais, *Les bréviaires manuscrits des bibliothèques publiques de France* (Paris, 1934), II, no. 393 (317–19; Bibl. de l'Arsenal MS 107) nos 410–11 (348–50; Paris, Bibl. de l'Arsenal MSS 602–603). London breviary: *Sotheby's Sale Catalogue*, 4 June 1974, no. 2919 (52–54); missal: *British Museum, Catalogue of Additions to the Manuscripts 1921–1925* (London, 1950), 311–13. The gradual has been only summarily catalogued: C.U. Faye and W.H. Bond, *Supplement to the Census of Medieval and Renaissance Manuscripts in the United States and Canada* (New York, 1962), 470. These manuscripts are also included in the catalogue which forms part of my PhD dissertation, 'Manuscripts from the Dominican Monastery of Saint-Louis de Poissy', University of Melbourne, 1995.

[9] The presence of St Servatus in the calendar and contents indicates that the manuscript could not have been written before 1332 when the addition of the saint's feast to the Dominican liturgy was confirmed, nor very long after 1336 since the feast of St Martial, confirmed in this year, has been added to the original text; see Leroquais, *Bréviaires*, I, ci.

[10] The feast of St Martial (confirmed 1336) is present and that of St Vincent, which was confirmed at the level of *totum duplex* in 1348 (ibid.), is still ranked at the previous level of *semi-duplex*.

[11] It appears that as early as the fifteenth century only the one volume was in existence since the inscribed ownership formula is in the singular, 'Ceste legende est a seurs ...', whereas the known two-volume breviaries at Poissy were inscribed during the same period in the plural, 'Ces legendes sont a seurs ...', once in each volume (Paris, Bibl. de l'Arsenal MSS 602–603) or 'Ces belles legendes appartiennent a seur ...' (*Belleville Breviary*, Paris, BN MS lat. 10483–4). It is conceivable that the winter volume only was completed.

[12] 'Sorores' and 'sororum' were added in the original corrector's hand in the margin of f. 227v for use instead of 'fratres' and 'fratrum'. In a number of respects a degree of confusion

wars and disease mentioned above, and the decimating effect which the plague had in Paris where the manuscripts were produced,[13] it may be reasonably inferred that all these books were made before the nuns' temporary departure from the monastery in 1346.

The chant books in the group are less readily dated and located since they contain only the sung Proper items and have no calendar. A Poissy provenance for the antiphonal (Melbourne, State Library of Victoria, MS *096 1/R66A) was first proposed by François Avril, and the late Pucellian-derived style of its illustrations dated to 1335–1345.[14] This provenance has now been confirmed by the identification of the antiphon to Sts Sebastian and Yves on folio 424 as a processional item pertaining uniquely to an altar at Poissy dedicated to these two saints.[15]

The liturgy in all these books is, of course, Dominican, as is that of the gradual (Philadelphia, Museum of Art, MS 45-65-7) which has been incorrectly catalogued for the Use of Paris even though it includes the Dominican feasts of Sts Dominic, Peter Martyr and Thomas Aquinas.[16] Like the other manuscripts, the gradual is illustrated and emphasises the feast of St Louis with a portrait. Here, though, such treatment of the feast is exceptional since Louis is the only post-biblical saint depicted in the book; not even Dominican saints are thus privileged. The Parisian style of the illustration reveals late-Pucellian influence (Fig. 17). The text is largely unabbreviated, stress marks are placed over even basic Latin words, and a *kyriale* with instructions in French was added later. These features point to a destination and later ownership at a female house, where neither

---

attended the first attempt to transcribe this missal. The original entries in the calendar omit the mandatory Dominican commemorations as well as the feast of St Louis, while the litany for Holy Saturday includes Olaf, Heinciui(?) and Ladislas in addition to the normal Poissy litany for the period. Though St Martial appears in the calendar, the Mass text for the feast is absent. Otherwise the contents are fully in accord with liturgical practice at Poissy as understood from other manuscripts made for the house. The inadequacies were rectified at the time of the manuscript's correction. Omitted feasts were added and intrusive litany items cancelled. These early additions and erasures were made during production, and before the book was illuminated, since the border on f. 175v is interrupted by the direction 'Officium sancti Servatii quare in fine libri .xx.' added in the corrector's hand. A *rituale* for Lent and Eastertide, inserted in the second half of the fourteenth century, specifically uses the feminine forms 'soror', 'cantrix', etc. (ff. 239v–241), thereby reinforcing the connection of the manuscript with the sisters in their choir.

[13] For passages concerning the drastic effects on the capital as described by Jean de Venette, the continuator of Guillaume de Nangis, and the chroniclers of St Denis and of the Carmelites in Reims see P. Zeigler, *The Black Death* (Harmondsworth, 1969), 78; G. Deaux, *The Black Death 1347* (London, 1969), 105; Gottfried, *Black Death*, 55.

[14] Manion and Vines, *Australian Collections*, 177–78.

[15] Naughton, 'Poissy Antiphonary', 39. The altar was added to those first established in the church.

[16] Faye and Bond, *Supplement to Census*, 470.

confidence in the pronunciation of Latin nor a literary comprehension of the language was likely to be universal.[17] There is, therefore, little doubt that the gradual was made for a wealthy establishment of Dominican nuns near (or in) Paris who especially venerated St Louis; this was almost certainly Poissy. The inclusion of a sequence for St Louis shows that his feast was celebrated at the highest grade, which was indeed the practice at the monastery.[18] Moreover, a gradual-prosar of a comparable personal size and with similar arrangement of texts was later made by one of the Poissy nuns, indicating that the particular format of this gradual was one

[17] The term 'phonetic literacy', the ability to sound aloud written words correctly, has been used to distinguish this skill from the more formidable and rarer 'comprehension literacy' among medieval readers, the capacity to read with understanding: P. Saenger, 'Books of Hours and Reading Habits in the Later Middle Ages', *Scrittura e Civiltà* 9 (1985), 240–41. The minimum literacy requirement for a Poissy choir sister was that she be able to read and sing the liturgy. Philippe le Bel requested the friars to find Dominican nuns for his foundation-to-be who 'sciant legere et cantare' so that they might transmit these skills to the postulants: letter from the king to the Dominican Provincial of France, dated 1299, transcribed by the fourteenth-century Dominican historian Bernard Gui, 'E notitia Provinciarum et Domorum Ordinis Praedicatorum' in *Recueil des historiens des Gaules et de la France* 23 (Paris, 1876), 191. The nuns' Constitutions likewise required that choir sisters achieve a phonetic and musical literacy in the range of liturgical texts; 'novicie et alie sorores que apte sunt in psalmodia et officio diuino studeant diligenter preter conuersas quibus sufficit ut sciant usque ad discant ea que debent pro horis dicere': Constitutions from Poissy dating c.1300, Munich, Bay. Staatsbibl., MS Clm. 10170, f. 138. Latin instructions are the norm in liturgical volumes made for Poissy; rubrics in French are confined to late additions. Marks placed over the stressed syllable of polysyllabic Latin words to aid in pronunciation are found in a number of manuscripts from the house; they have been mostly added to passages to be read aloud before a conventual gathering. I know of no other Poissy book in which sung texts are so treated, though here the stressmarks are confined to words chanted on a repeated or almost invariant note. Compare, though, the use of stress marks over all sung polysyllabic words in the modern plainchant compilation, the *Liber usualis*, suggesting a present-day phonetic illiteracy and rhythmic ignorance far more serious than that insured against at Poissy.

[18] All the sequences in the manuscript occur in two other compilations which were made and updated at Poissy in the fourteenth and fifteenth centuries: a c.1300 illustrated missal (Princeton University Library, MS Garrett 41) which was twice updated between c.1330–50 and a small, very modestly decorated prosar (Boston, Museum of Fine Arts, MS 80.504), probably made and first updated in the fifteenth century. Apart from certain commemorations of the Virgin, for which the liturgy was universal, sequences were chanted only during solemn Masses for the highest ranked (*totum duplex*) feasts; see W.R. Bonniwell, *A History of the Dominican Liturgy* (New York, 1944), 92. *Totum duplex* feasts were still relatively few at this period and, since the Dominican liturgy was by no means absolutely universal, an examination of the sequences can give some indication of the liturgical celebration and therefore identity of the house for which the book was made.

established in the house.[19] Stylistically its ornamentation dates between 1335 and 1345. It is thus contemporary with the other manuscripts in the group, all of which were probably made in the period 1332 to 1346.

If it is accepted that these six works—in seven volumes—were destined for Poissy from the outset, then can we discern whether any particular pattern was impressed on their production?[20] There are no large choir books: the size of the manuscripts ranges from 285x200 mm for the antiphonal—just inside the modern A4 sheet—to 169x121 mm for the gradual, about three-fifths this size (Table 2).[21] The thickness of the volumes increases with their dimensions (Table 2) so that each presents as a compact, rather chunky and slightly heavy book, portable but not without some effort. Similarities in their production are manifest. All are written on fine quality vellum, flawless and smooth, in a very clear Gothic liturgical hand using two sizes of script; there are few abbreviations even for liturgical instructions. Although transcription is by a single hand throughout each manuscript, most, if not all of the six books appear to involve a different scribe.[22] Two quire sizes are used: twelve folios for the breviaries and missal, which are written in two columns, and eight for the chant books, in which the music and text are written in long lines. The hierarchical decorative patterns are similar in all the manuscripts, and depend upon the differing size of initials rendered alternately in gold and blue, with pen-flourishing in blue or red.

---

[19] New York, Union Theological Seminary, The Bourke Library, MS DeR 52. The manuscript was made c.1580–90 by Marie de Fortia for her aunt Geneviève de Courtin, both nuns at Poissy. It measures 170x107 mm, the text block 137x86 mm. Compare the measurements 168x121 mm and 120x83 mm for the Philadelphia gradual.

[20] In order to compare more readily the imagery in the four types of liturgical compilation I have, in general, disregarded the psalter section of the breviaries, whose illustrative patterns conform to the eight-partite Parisian type: David harping for Sunday matins (Psalm 1), pointing to his eyes or anointed by Saul for Monday matins, (Psalm 26), etc.; the series is summarised in G. Haseloff, *Die Psalterillustration im 13. Jahrhundert* (Kiel, 1938), 21–33, Tables 4–6. Two very small, personal ferial psalter-processionals made in Paris for Poissy nuns at this period follow the same iconography; the design and execution of the manuscript sold at Sotheby's, 9 December 1974, lot 60 shares the modest but high-quality manufacture of the volumes considered in this article, while Waddesdon Manor MS 2 is an undertaking of the highest luxury; see L.M.J. Delaissé, J. Marrow and J. de Wit, *The James A. de Rothschild Collection at Waddesdon Manor. Illuminated Manuscripts* (Fribourg, 1977), 37–58; J. Hamburger, 'The Waddesdon Psalter and the Shop of Jean Pucelle', *Zeitschrift für Kunstgeschichte* 44 (1981), 243–57.

[21] The pages of the manuscripts have, however, been cropped during their later rebinding; none survives in its original covers.

[22] Dr Christopher de Hamel kindly examined photocopies from each manuscript, cautioning that, although there are differences between the hands of the six manuscripts, the scribes are very similar, and warning that some perceived differences could be due to the different scales involved.

The flourishing is modestly developed and extended into generous margins with the result that there is negligible competition with the text.[23] Calligraphic cadels provide another emphatic element in the chant books (Figs 17 and 22) and clarity is at all times paramount.[24] The calendars are unillustrated scribal productions, enlivened with a pen-flourished gold and blue 'KL' monogram for each month; gold, blue and red inks emphasize chosen feasts.

At a higher ornamental level are the pages on which selected feasts are illustrated, or highlighted by initials painted in a vine leaf pattern in gold, blues and pinks.[25] These are the only pages graced with a border, a narrow bar also painted in gold and colours, and extended to frame the text on at least three sides via unobtrusive vine leaf terminals (Figs 17–22, 24, Pl. 3). Sometimes the borders incorporate dragons, and very rarely a hybrid figure, while small birds perch in a few of the borders of the London breviary. Again, there is a minimum of interference with the words and notation, as is appropriate for books whose function was to prompt their users to particular verbal and musical responses at a precisely defined moment, usually in concert with others.

The number of illustrated pages ranges from seventeen in the gradual to thirty in the summer breviary (Paris, Bibl. de l'Arsenal MS 603). Most illustrations, though not all, are around six lines high and more or less square. They are very much a minor part of each manuscript; the majority of historiated initials and miniatures occupy little more than one-tenth of a page, while illustrated pages are limited to only 2–4% of the total number of pages in any one book (Table 2). But how is this decorative emphasis distributed in the manuscripts? The summary in Table 1 (pp. 93–4) points out two distribution patterns. Either the decorative elements are ranged singly and widely or, as in the London breviary and the missal, they are concentrated around selected feasts with the result that these two manuscripts present an air of heightened luxury when open at one of the chosen feasts. The celebrations given this treatment include the first Sunday of Advent and Easter Sunday in the missal (Pl. 3) and the feasts of the Dominican saints and St Louis in the breviary (Fig. 18).

Interestingly, the overall pattern of manuscript illustration, in which fewer feasts are emphasized in the *temporale* than in the *sanctorale*, is not shared by the gradual, where the decoration of the *sanctorale* is far less dominant, even to the extent of the complete omission of all Dominican

---

[23] In addition to the full-page reproductions from all manuscripts which accompany this article, see Manion and Vines, *Australian Collections*, Figs 175, 180.

[24] See also Manion and Vines, *Australian Collections*, Pl. 37, Fig. 179.

[25] One variant initial is filled with a red oakleaf design (missal, f. 209^v), a background motif which has been seen as characteristic of the 'Pucelle workshop': see K.B. Morand, 'Jean Pucelle and his workshop' (Diss., University of London, 1958), 215.

saints (Table 1). This has its origins in Dominican precedent, and can be traced back to the primary decorative emphases given to feasts in the 'prototype' manuscripts which were produced in the 1250s to disseminate liturgical reform in Paris, the Dominican liturgical centre of the period.[26] In all cases a relative concentration of decoration on the *temporale* gives the gradual a distinct Christological emphasis (Table 3, p. 95). The embellishment programme of the antiphonal also follows that of the earlier Dominican manuscripts.[27]

In general, though, the feasts selected for illustration are similar in all the manuscripts; the most common are documented in Table 4 (p. 96). To some extent, higher ranked feasts are more likely to receive pictorial definition, but there seems to be no absolute rule. Illustrative emphasis is placed on the major Christological events of the *temporale*, and Marian and Dominican festivities in the *sanctorale*, together with the feasts of Sts Louis and John the Baptist, both of whom were specially honoured at Poissy.[28] As was usual in France, the feast of the Trinity is represented by the 'Throne of Mercy' ('*Gnadenstuhl*')—the Father holding the crucified Christ while the dove-Holy Spirit descends between them (Fig. 17).[29] The preference accorded Pentecost (illustrated in all six books) over the Ascension (illustrated in four) may reflect the fact that in Dominican liturgy the celebration of Pentecost was extended into the next two days

---

[26] The completion of the revision and the readiness of exemplars for copying was announced at the Dominican Chapter General of 1256: Bonniwell, *Dominican Liturgy*, 84. The so-called 'prototype' manuscript of the complete liturgy and constitutions (now Rome, Santa Sabina, MS XIV. L. 1) was held at the Convent of Saint-Jacques in Paris; see Bonniwell, *Dominican Liturgy*, 85–94. A copy (now London, BL MS Add. 23935) was made in Paris shortly after, ostensibly for the Master General to settle any doubts concerning the contents of the manuscripts used in the houses he visited; see J. Wickham Legg, *Tracts on the Mass* (London, 1904), xxii–xxiii; G.R. Galbraith, *The Constitution of the Dominican Order 1216–1360* (Manchester, 1925), 193–98; Bonniwell, *Dominican Liturgy*, 94–96. The status of the Santa Sabina manuscript as the Dominican liturgical prototype has recently been challenged by Leonard Boyle and Simon Tugwell on codicological and other grounds at a colloquium on the manuscript held in Rome in March 1995; I am grateful to the Rev. Dr Simon Tugwell, O.P. for this information.

[27] For a more detailed comparison see Naughton, 'Poissy Antiphonary', 45, Table 1.

[28] St Louis was given a patron saint's eminence at Poissy. John the Baptist was to some extent regarded as an exemplar by the Dominicans, the Friars Preachers, who saw themselves as his successors, as preachers who should also operate from a basis of poverty; see J.J. Berthier, ed., Humbert of Romans, *Opera de Vita Regulari*, (Torino, 1956), I, 90. Processional Offices for the feasts of Sts Louis and John the Baptist (and the Nativity of the Virgin) were celebrated at Poissy in addition to the universal Dominican processional liturgy.

[29] The alternative representation of the Trinity—two identical seated figures towards whom the dove descends—was reserved for the more literal illustration of the opening words of Psalm 109: 'Dixit Dominus Domino meo, sede a dextris meis . . .'.

maintaining the highest rank (*totum duplex*) throughout, a privilege the feast shared with Easter Sunday. This may reflect the special meaning Pentecost had for a religious order such as the Dominicans; its members saw themselves as the successors of the Apostles whose divine empowerment for mission is commemorated in this feast.[30] The Ascension received a different sort of liturgical emphasis, being among the limited number of feasts whose celebration the Dominicans extended beyond the choir into a processional Office.[31]

Among the female saints, Mary Magdalen probably received an illustration because of the increased veneration accorded her by the Dominicans after 1295 when Pope Boniface VIII invested the friars with the official guardianship of the shrine at Saint-Maximin, believed to contain her body. Her feast was soon raised to the highest rank.[32] The Virgin was considered the special protectress of the Order,[33] and most of the

---

[30] W.A. Hinnebusch, 'Dominicans', *New Catholic Encyclopedia*, IV (New York, 1967), 974; M.-H. Vicaire, *L'imitation des apôtres: moines, chanoines, mendiants, IVe–XIIe siècles. Tradition et spiritualité*, II (Paris, 1963). All monastic incumbents considered themselves as such, the apostolic imitation of poverty and communal life being prescribed in the Benedictine rule: Cap. 48: 9; T. Fry, ed., *The Rule of St Benedict*, (Collegeville, Minn., 1981), 250–51. The Dominican precept, reflected in their motto 'Contemplare et contemplata aliis tradere', is aimed more towards apostolic evangelical ambitions. The teaching mission given the Apostles by Christ and the sacred power and authority imparted to them with the Holy Spirit was celebrated on the day of Pentecost, a model for the preaching activity of the Dominicans who likewise moved outwards from a central point. Part of the duty of the nuns, whose liturgical obligation was identical with that of the brothers, was vicariously to share this task by ensuring its success through devotion to liturgy and their prayers for the friars; see letters of the friars Raymond of Peñafort and Peter Martyr to the Dominican prioresses in Bologna and Milan, translated in S. Tugwell, *Early Dominicans* (London, 1982), 409–11; J.B. Walker, 'Dominicans—Sisters,' *New Catholic Encyclopedia*, IV (New York, 1967), 984.

[31] For some processionals used by the nuns at Poissy see M. Huglo, 'Les processionneaux de Poissy' in *Rituals: Mélanges offerts au Père Gy OP* (Paris, 1991), 339–46. For the feasts which merited a procession at the monastery during its first decades see the list from the Psalter-processional Waddesdon Manor MS 2, ff. 325–55v (not included by Huglo) in Delaissé *et al.*, *Rothschild Collection*, 39.

[32] Bonniwell, *Dominican Liturgy*, 204. The feast was elevated to *totum duplex* at the Chapters General of 1297–1300. It took some little time for the embarrassing reference to the saint's 'other' body, at Vézelay, to be removed from the Dominican martyrology.

[33] The last liturgical obligation of the day was the recitation of the *Salve Regina*, which was sung processionally after compline. The Dominicans were the first to institute this nightly hailing of the Virgin, who had recommended the Order to Christ, as their patron and protectress; see Bonniwell, *Dominican Liturgy*, 148–55; J.L. Cannon, 'Dominican Patronage of the Arts in Central Italy: The Provincia Romana ca. 1220–ca. 1320' (Diss., London, University of London 1980), 233. The nuns at Poissy may have been particularly well versed in the legends surrounding the special and intimate relationship between the Virgin and the Order. Two texts in a Dominican compilation housed there, containing

books illustrate the four Marian feasts observed in Dominican liturgy at the time—the Purification, Annunciation, Assumption and Nativity of the Virgin. But apart from these instances, and even though the books were made for use in a female house, there is no tendency to single out female saints for depiction. Indeed, in two of the breviaries (London, Private Collection, and Paris, Bibl. de l'Arsenal MS 603) a generalized group of female figures for the feast of the Eleven Thousand Virgins acts as a companion-piece to the next illustration, a similarly generic group of males for the feast of All Saints (cf. Figs 19 and 20). Apart from Mary Magdalen and the Virgin Mary, the only other female saint whose feast is highlighted is St Katherine, who attracts a small four-line votive illustration in Paris, Bibl. de l'Arsenal MS 603. (The same low illustrative emphasis is given to Sts Denis and Martin, specially revered in Paris; and these three feasts are illustrated only in this more expansively illuminated two-volume manuscript.) Since St Katherine was frequently depicted in Dominican works as a learned preacher who was martyred by unbelievers,[34] the illustration of the saint here probably also reflects Dominican preferences. One can thus conclude that in this group of manuscripts there is no overt emphasis of particular female saints because of any sense of identification, reverence or compassion on the part of the nuns. The same is not true of the patron saints of their church and their order, Sts Louis and Dominic.

Individual saints are most often shown in action, and only rarely in the alternative mode as standing figures with symbolic attributes. St Louis is an exception. He is always depicted as a sainted king, even to the extent of there being two almost identical portraits of him in the one book—the London breviary (e.g. Fig. 21). There is no attempt to render his miracles (nor, for that matter, those of other saints) despite their lengthy narration in the liturgy and the existence of Parisian models for their illustration both in books[35] and in stained glass.[36] Rather, St Louis stands nimbed, but

---

material for Marian devotion and worship (Paris, BN MS fr. 12483), treat the subjects 'Pour quel cause on dit .salve regina misericordie. apres complie en lordre des freres prescheurs' (f. 194v) and 'De nostre dame qui dessous son mantel gardoit especial les freres prescheurs' (f. 236v). The manuscript, now fragmentary, dates from the second quarter of the fourteenth century. The ownership inscription, dating from the seventeenth century, was written when the book already lacked its first twenty-two chapters. On this volume see also A. Långfors, 'Notice du MS fr. 12483 de la Bibliothèque Nationale,' *Notices et Extraits* 39.2 (1916), 503–62.

[34] Cannon, 'Dominican Patronage', 241, 256. A great number of Dominican houses, especially in the German and Italian Dominican Provinces, were dedicated to the saint.

[35] The lessons to be read during the feast of St Louis and its octave, which these manuscripts show to have been celebrated at the highest rank at Poissy, detail the saint's life and miracles. The same events which are described verbally in the liturgy were recreated pictorially to illustrate the Hours of St Louis and his life in books made for female members of the royal house and illustrated by Jean Pucelle and his close associates.

accoutred as the kings of France who had succeeded him. He, too, wears regalia, his clothing embroidered with a semé of fleurs-de-lys and his cloak lined with vair.[37] In his hands he holds variously a sceptre (antiphonal and gradual), a sceptre and book (London breviary), a model of the Sainte Chapelle and the *main-de-justice* (breviary, Paris, Bibl. de l'Arsenal MS 603) or the full royal coronation insignia of the sceptre and *main-de-justice* (missal and London breviary).[38] Like his successors he is usually clean-shaven; only in the missal is he shown with the beard which he wore in the later years of his life.[39] A similar representation of the saint had been added around 1317 to the *Registre des ordonnances de l'hôtel du roi* written between 1261 and 1317 (Paris, Archives Nationales, JJ 57, f. 20).[40] Crowned, nimbed and bearded, the king is dressed in coronation robes and holds the symbols of royal power: the sceptre and the

---

The following manuscripts are notable among those made in Paris: (1) *Hours of Jeanne d'Evreux* (New York, The Metropolitan Museum of Art, The Cloisters Collection (54.1.2) dated between 1325 and 1328; (2) a copy of Guillaume de Saint-Pathus' *Vie et Miracles de saint Louis* (Paris, BN MS fr. 5716) dated in the early 1330s; (3) *Hours of Jeanne of Navarre* (Paris, BN MS n.a. lat. 3145) dated c.1336–40. For dating and illustration of the St Louis series in each see: (1) F. Avril, *Manuscript Painting at the Court of France* (London, 1978), 53–59; ibid., 'Manuscrits' in *Les Fastes du Gothique: Le siècle de Charles V* (Paris, 1981), 292–93; (2) E.A.R. Brown, 'The Chapels and Cult of Saint Louis at Saint-Denis,' *Mediaevalia* 10 (1984), 293–95, 320, n. 55 citing François Avril; Avril, 'Manuscrits,' 299–300; (3) M. Thomas, 'L'iconographie de saint Louis dans les Heures de Jeanne de Navarre' in *Septième centenaire de la mort de saint Louis* (Paris, 1976), 209–31; Avril, 'Manuscrits', 312–14; and M.M. Manion (Chapter 2 above, 29-30, 33).

[36] Similar narrative models in stained glass had for some time been publicly visible at St Denis, completed by 1303 (since destroyed), and Fécamp, dated c.1310; see Brown, 'Chapels and Cult', 283–89.

[37] For reproduction of the initial in the Melbourne antiphonal see Manion and Vines, *Australian Collections*, Fig. 182.

[38] The sceptre and *main-de-justice*, in left and right hands respectively, entered the *ordo* of coronation drawn up in the 1260s, towards the end of Louis IX's reign: A. Erlande-Brandenburg, 'Le tombeau de saint Louis', *Bulletin Monumental* 126 (1968), 17; ibid., 'La priorale', 111; E.A.R. Brown, 'The ceremonial of double succession in Capetian France: The funeral of Philip V', *Speculum* 55 (1980), 279, n. 54.

[39] He probably wore a beard from the time of his first crusade in 1248 until his death during his second in 1270. On the consideration of thirteenth- and fourteenth-century bearded/non-bearded representations as portraiture/cultic imagery, with earlier bibliography, see C. Maumené and L. d'Harcourt, *Archives de l'art français* 15. Iconographie des rois de France, Part 1, De Louis IX à Louis XIII (Paris, 1928), 17–18; Erlande-Brandenburg, 'La priorale', 7–36; M.P. Lillich, 'An early image of Saint Louis,' *Gazette des Beaux-Arts* 75 (1970), 251–56, reviewed in A. Lefébure, 'Iconographie,' *Bulletin Monumental* 128 (1970), 156–57; P.-M. Auzas, 'Essai d'un répertoire iconographique de saint Louis' in *Septième centenaire de la mort de saint Louis* (Paris, 1976), 3–56.

[40] For reproduction see Erlande-Brandenburg, 'Tombeau de saint Louis', 19.

office of justiciar, the *main-de-justice*.⁴¹ This very imagery was soon to be used for sepulchral effigies of the French kings. The first, a *gisant* holding the sceptre and *main-de-justice*, and surmounting a shrine containing the heart of Philippe le Bel, was placed in the centre of the nuns' choir at Poissy in approximately 1327.⁴²

Several other comparable representations earlier than those in the Poissy manuscripts are known. A glass panel from Saint-Père de Chartres (1297–1305) shows the saint similarly clad, holding a book and sceptre.⁴³ A small sculptured figure of the standing king holding a sceptre and placed upon a tomb is depicted in the *Hours of Jeanne d'Evreux* (f. 102v)⁴⁴ and again, but this time set upon an altar and holding the *main-de-justice*, in a copy of Guillaume de Saint-Pathus' *Vie et miracles de Saint-Louis* (p. 370).⁴⁵ Arguably this object refers to an actual gilt-silver statue, now lost, which was paid for by the Abbey of St Denis in 1299, and which probably stood on the altar in the chapel dedicated to the saint.⁴⁶ Its pictorial representation points up the popularity of the devotional cult practised by royal and common people alike at the saint's tomb and altar.⁴⁷ The imagery used

---

⁴¹ M. François, 'Les plus beaux manuscrits à peintures conservés aux Archives nationales', *Les trésors des bibliothèques de France* 6 (1938), 170–72; Erlande-Brandenburg, 'Tombeau de saint Louis', 19. Exactly the same imagery was also used in the Franciscan breviary made for Queen Jeanne d'Evreux, contemporary with the Poissy group (Chantilly, Musée Condé MS 1887, f. 335v); for reproduction see S.C. Cockerell, *The Book of Hours of Yolande de Flanders* (London, 1905), Fig. 11.

⁴² Although the tomb was destroyed, probably at the French Revolution, it is known from drawings by Gaignières; for reproductions and discussion see Erlande-Brandenburg, 'La priorale', 111–12, Fig. 21; E.A.R. Brown, 'Persona and Gesta: The image and deeds of the thirteenth-century Capetians. 3. The case of Philip the Fair', *Viator* 19 (1988), 225–26, Fig. 9. The sculpture can be dated c.1327 when payment was made for the alabaster for the tomb; see B. Prost, 'L'histoire des arts en France', *Gazette des Beaux-Arts* 36 (1887), 237. It represented the king as laid out in coronation robes and regalia during the three days after death when he was still accounted 'alive'; see A. Erlande-Brandenburg, *Le roi est mort. Étude sur les funérailles, les sépultures et les tombeaux des rois de France jusqu'à la fin du XIIIe siècle* (Paris, 1975), 19–22; E.A.R. Brown, 'The ceremonial of double succession in Capetian France: The double funeral of Louis X', *Traditio* 34 (1978), 229; ibid., 'Funeral of Philip V', 276–86. Philippe le Bel was the first actually to hold the *main-de-justice* on his deathbed, as was later represented in the Poissy sculpture: Erlande-Brandenburg, *Le roi est mort*, 121.

⁴³ Lillich, 'Early image', 241–52, Figs 1 and 3.

⁴⁴ For reproduction see Avril, *Manuscript Painting*, Pl. 8.

⁴⁵ For reproduction see Brown, 'Chapels and cult', Pl. 11.

⁴⁶ G.S. Wright, 'The tomb of Saint Louis', *Journal of the Warburg and Courtauld Institutes* 34 (1971), 66–70; Brown, 'Chapels and cult', 292–95.

⁴⁷ The illustrations provide a logical sequence: in the Saint-Pathus *Vie*, 285, 370, crowds of cripples and others approach the unguarded shrine; in the *Hours of Jeanne*

for St Louis in our small group of manuscripts appears therefore to derive directly from a royally sanctioned artistic trend in Paris at the time, as exemplified by the representation added to the royal register described above; this was, in turn, strongly influenced by the sculptural image of the saint that was part of his cult at St Denis.

Martyrs are usually represented in these manuscripts undergoing the torments associated with their deaths rather than as standing votive figures holding the instruments of their martyrdom: Sts Paul and Peter Martyr are beheaded, Peter and Andrew tied to their crosses, Bartholomew flayed, Stephen stoned and Laurence roasted on the grill.[48] St Dominic, too, is invariably depicted at the point of his entry to eternal life, according to the vision of the prior of Brescia that occurred at the exact moment of the saint's death. The event is narrated in the final lessons for the octave of his feast:

> And he saw in his mind's eye a kind of opening made in the sky, and through the aperture were lowered two gleaming ladders. The one was held at the top by Christ the Lord, the other by his Mother. And angels of light were hurrying up and down the rungs. But look, between the two ladders was placed a seat with someone sitting upon it who appeared to be a friar, for his face was covered with his hood, in the way in which dead brothers of the Order are buried. Then gradually Jesus Christ and his Mother pulled the ladders upwards, the seated friar drawn with them until he was carried up to the psalm-singing angels in heaven. With his welcome there, and the return of the ladders and seat, the opening in the sky was closed and the vision disappeared.[49]

This theme, uncommon in France, is depicted with little variation in its five representations in the Poissy group (e.g. Figs 22 and 24).[50] All

---

d'Evreux, f. 102v, the queen prays before the image in the chapel, guarded by soldiers, which is now empty of other worshippers.

[48] For reproductions of martyrdom of St Paul (Melbourne antiphonal) and of Peter Martyr (London breviary) see Manion and Vines, *Australian Collections*, Figs 179 and 180.

[49] Paris, Bibl. de l'Arsenal MS 603, lessons 7-8 from Octave of feast of St Dominic, f. 287v. The Latin text is essentially identical with that printed in *Monumenta Historica Sancti Patris Nostri Dominici. II. Libellus de principiis ordinis praedicatorum, Acta canonizationis, Legendae Petri Ferrandi, Constantini Urbeveteri, Humberti de Romans*, ed. H.C. Scheeben, *Monumenta Ordinis Praedicatorum Historica* 16 (1935), 55.

[50] For reproductions of this initial in the London breviary and the breviary, Bibl. de l'Arsenal MS 603 see Manion and Vines, *Australian Collections*, Fig. 178 and Leroquais, *Bréviaires*, Pl. 41. Preliminary studies suggest that early use of this visual theme in Dominican books is found in the second half of the thirteenth to the early fourteenth century in female houses of the Dominican Province of Germania, its literary description already enlivening the numerous hagiographical accounts of the saint produced within the Order in the thirteenth century. A lectionary made for the nuns in Regensburg *c*.1267-76 contains an early representation (Oxford, Keble College MS 49, f. 130): M.B. Parkes, *The*

show one ladder instead of two and scant attention is paid to the details of the text: no seat is depicted, rarely do the holders of the ladder appear, and only in the London breviary is the saint shown with his cowl over his face, or as obviously dead. Nevertheless the illustrators seem to have had some knowledge of the particular iconography required since the heavenly opening, two or more angels, and the ladder with the saint on its lower rungs are consistently portrayed. Compare the deviation from the text in a contemporary Tuscan psalter-antiphonal where Dominic, alone, actively climbs a ladder held by a hand from heaven.[51] It is perhaps pertinent that this image had a built-in exemplary function, such a heavenly ascent being the goal held out to those who followed the Dominican way. In the Poissy manuscripts though, that message is only implied, unlike the quite explicit visual statement in a gradual of 1312 owned by the Dominican nuns at Sankt Katharinenthal in the Lake Constance region: in this version an angel grasps the raised hands of the saint to convey him up the ladder while a nun, identified by inscription as Katharina de Radegge, follows in identical pose three rungs below (Fig. 23).[52] Beneath the ladder is the exemplary means by which such grace is to be attained: Dominic sits in meditation resting his head upon his hand, his book closed on the desk before him.[53]

Medieval Manuscripts of Keble College Oxford (London, 1979), 227–42, Fig. 128. Another early example occurs in the c.1300 antiphonal made in Paris, almost certainly for use by Poissy nuns (London, BL Add. MS 30072, f. 213v). By the mid-fourteenth century the imagery is established in Italian books and altar panels (usually as a relatively small, subsidiary narrative image in the latter), and in Flemish manuscripts as well as the Paris-originating volumes described in this article. The ladder imagery, used widely in Byzantine and Western depictions of apotheosis and heavenly reward, stems directly from the biblical description of the link formed between earth and heaven by Jacob's Ladder (Gen. 28:12).

[51] *Sotheby's Sales Catalogue*, 7 December 1982, lot 70, f. 237v (illustrated).

[52] Zurich, Schweizerisches Landesmuseum MS LM 26117, f. 261v; E.J. Beer et al., *Das Graduale von Sankt Katharinenthal*, 2 vols (Lucerne, 1983); F.O. Büttner, *Imitatio Pietatis* (Berlin, 1983), *passim*.

[53] A well-known example of the visual use of saints as devotional examples for young Dominicans to follow during their contemplative periods is seen in the cells frescoed by Fra Angelico and his associates in the fifteenth century at San Marco in Florence, where a Dominican saint is depicted in an appropriate attitude before divine imagery. The verbal and pictorial descriptions of St Dominic's methods of prayer were produced to meet the same ends. See 'The Nine Ways of Prayer' in F.C. Lehner, ed., *Saint Dominic. Biographical Documents* (Washington, 1964), 148; S. Tugwell, 'The Nine Ways of Prayer of St Dominic' in *Early Dominicans*, 94–103, 475–76; J.-C. Schmitt, 'Entre le texte et l'image: les gestes de la prière de saint Dominique' in R.C. Trexler, ed., *Persons in Groups: Social Behaviour as Identity Formation in Medieval and Renaissance Europe* (New York, 1985), 195–214; W. Hood, 'Saint Dominic's Manners of Praying: Gestures in Fra Angelico's Cell Frescoes at S. Marco', *Art Bulletin* 58 (1986), 195–206; ibid., 'Fra Angelico at San Marco. Art and the liturgy of cloistered life' in T. Verdon and J. Henderson, eds, *Christianity and the Renaissance. Image and*

Except for the attention paid to the Dominican saints, the decorative and illustrative content of these manuscripts follows common Parisian patterns. Books of similar appearance, decorated in gold and illustrated to the same modest extent, were made around this time for Paris churches. The missal, Paris, Bibl. de l'Arsenal MS 608, is a case in point. Its eighteen small historiated initials illustrate a similar range of feasts and share with the Poissy manuscripts Parisian iconographical and compositional elements. Apart from a double-page rendering of the crucifixion and Christ in majesty at the canon of the Mass, it is so like our group of manuscripts that despite a liturgy which pertains to Notre-Dame in Paris it has often been incorrectly attributed to Poissy.[54] Our manuscripts also reveal a striking similarity in format, lay-out and decoration to a set of liturgical books dating to about 1300, and commissioned by Philippe le Bel from as early as 1298 for his new foundation at Poissy, though the nuns did not actually take up residence until 1304.[55] The distribution of decoration and illustration and the restrained use of gold are comparable in both sets of manuscripts. Modest pen-flourished or painted capitals and

---

Religious Imagination in the Quattrocento (Syracuse, 1990), 109–31; ibid., *Fra Angelico at San Marco* (New Haven and London, 1993), 195–207 and *passim*.

[54] The error has revolved around an obit for Philippe le Bel in the calendar: 'Obitus Philippi, regis Francie, fundatoris ecclesie Pissiaci.' Henry Martin, and others who have followed his provenance, have repeatedly placed the manuscript at the Dominican church of St Louis; see, for example, H. Martin, *Catalogue des manuscrits de la Bibliothèque de l'Arsenal*, I (1885), 457–58; ibid., *La miniature française du XIIIe au XVe siècle* (Paris, 1924), 93, despite Leroquais' subtle demur that the obit would, from the mention, only *seem* to imply a Poissy provenance—'la mention de l'église de Poissy paraît indiquer que le missel a été à l'usage de cette église'; V. Leroquais, *Les sacramentaires et les missels manuscrits des bibliothèques publiques de France* (Paris, 1924), II, 246. But there is no indication that the manuscript was ever with the nuns at Poissy, where it would have been of limited liturgical use, and, since it was later at the Church of St Lazare in Paris it seems unlikely that it ever left the city. The reference to the king's foundation at Poissy, which occurs in conjunction with related obits for his wife Jeanne (2 April) and his successors Louis X (4 June) and Charles de Valois (16 December), is merely a statement of his piety, as a similarly worded obit in a copy of an ancient obituary at the Premonstratensian Abbey of Joyenval makes clear—'Commemoratio domini Philippi, Francae regis, hujus nominis IV, cognomine Pulchri, sanctimonialium Pisciacensium fundatoris'; see A. Molinier, *Obituaires de la Province de Sens, II. Diocèse de Chartres* (Paris, 1906), 297.

[55] The commission was supervised by the Dominican friars in Paris. These manuscripts will be treated in a proposed article tentatively entitled 'Philippe le Bel and the Earliest Manuscripts at Poissy'. Comparable in type to the present set of manuscripts are a breviary (Chartres, Bibl. mun. MS 552, now destroyed), a missal (Princeton University Library, Garrett MS 41), an antiphonal (London, BL MS Add. 30072) and a diurnal (Rouen, Bibl. mun. MS 221). Slightly less directly comparable is a martyrology (Munich, Bayerische Staatsbibliothek, cod. Clm. 10170). For the king's register of payments see L. Delisle, *Notice de douze livres royaux du XIIIe et du XIVe siècle* (Paris, 1902), 58 (list incomplete) and J. Viard, *Les journaux du trésor de Philippe IV le Bel* (Paris, 1940), *passim*.

small-sized historiated initials for selected feasts establish similar hierarchies of decoration, and only the pages with historiated initials have decorated borders. Since the books from each period are written on like quality vellum and project an almost identical *mise-en-page*, their production is likely to have cost an equivalent amount of money.[56]

Table 4 indicates the degree of variation in the illustrative subject matter for the same feasts in our group of manuscripts, and so addresses the question as to whether there were strict rules laid down by the Dominicans in this regard. For instance, the first Sunday in Advent is illustrated in the Melbourne antiphonal by the Annunciation (f. 4v), even though this image is also used for the feast of the Annunciation itself (f. 249).[57] In the breviaries, however, the beginning of Advent is illustrated by the more usual depiction of Isaiah, the author of most of the readings for this season. He is shown either indicating his vision of the Lord in glory or standing beside the Virgin annunciate (Paris, Bibl. de l'Arsenal MS 107). (The Mass books, as customary, adhere to a literal rendering of the opening words of the introit (officium): *Ad te levavi animam meam* . . . by showing a priest standing before an altar who raises towards God his soul in the form of an *homunculus* or small child.) The feast of the Assumption of the Virgin is illustrated either by the Byzantine Dormition or by the more recent Western image of her Coronation, well-known since the twelfth century through its presence on the entry portals of Gothic cathedrals both in Paris and throughout the Ile-de-France.

The feast of the birth of John the Baptist prompts three different themes: an actual illustration of his birth; his baptism of Christ; or a representation of the saint with the *agnus dei* signifying Christ, the Saviour of the world, whose coming the Baptist had announced. To some extent the choice of theme depends on the particular text illustrated. In the London breviary, for example, the Baptism of Christ accompanies the opening words of the first lesson for matins: *Tu ille Iohannes qui deum baptizasti* . . ., while the responsory for the first lesson in the Melbourne antiphonal, *Fuit homo missus a deo* . . ., is heralded by a depiction of the saint's birth. However, a more-or-less literal visualization of the text is not routine, and a generalized image of the saint holding the *agnus dei* serves to introduce the Mass introit in both the missal and gradual, *De ventre matris mee vocavit me dominus nomine meo* . . . (Isaiah 49:1) as well as the gratuitous preliminary words of the first lesson for matins in the breviary,

---

[56] The two sets of liturgical books are not exactly equivalent, however. The feasts selected for illustration are less fixed in the earlier manuscripts, with the Apostles and St Katherine more prominent, and the representation chosen for St Dominic more variable.

[57] The two images are reproduced in Naughton, 'Poissy Antiphonary', 41, Pls 16 and 17.

Paris, Bibliothèque de l'Arsenal MS 603, *Sollempnitates nobis diversorum martirum* . . . .⁵⁸

Finally, the illustration of the newly introduced feast of Corpus Christi, which celebrates the doctrine of transubstantiation independent of the Mass service,⁵⁹ is still, however, visually dependent upon the ritual of the Mass. In all of the manuscripts the celebrant raises the host as he faces the altar. But whereas in the missal a human priest enacts this rite (Fig. 26), in the breviaries Christ himself is the priest (Fig. 27). Flanked by angel attendants instead of human ministers, his nimbed figure provides a visual interpretation of the vespers antiphon: *Sacerdos in eternum Christus . . . panem et vinum obtulit*. The development and spread of this image,

---

⁵⁸ It will be noticed that there are two sets of lessons for the feast in the Poissy breviaries. The sung items remain constant. I have found no record of any changes promulgated in the Dominican Chapter Acts. The 'Sollempnitates' set appear to be the earlier and are found in the Dominican 'prototype' (*c*.1256), the Poissy breviary Paris, Bibl. de l'Arsenal MS 603 (apparently dating after 1336), and the *Belleville Breviary* (*c*.1323–26). The series 'Dicte (Sancte) iohanes: tu ille iohannes' must be a replacement, perhaps peculiar to Poissy, since this Office follows with the newly confirmed Offices for Corpus Christi and Thomas Aquinas at the rear of the psalter-processional, Waddesdon MS 2, dated to the 1330s. Their presence in the London breviary (near-contemporary if not slightly earlier than Paris, Bibl. de l'Arsenal MS 603 in which the earlier Office persists) may indicate a greater knowledge by the scribe of the rite at the monastery, perhaps because better instructions were issued. But no updated version was transcribed in Oxford, Bodleian Library MS Rawl. liturg. e2, a late fifteenth-century compilation made by the Poissy nuns of Offices which had been added or had undergone change since the early fourteenth century. Possibly the use of these lessons was discontinued.

⁵⁹ Introduction of the feast was from the mid-thirteenth century supported by Dominicans associated with Liège, where the celebration had originated among the Beguines; see M. Rubin, *Corpus Christi: The Eucharist in Late Medieval Culture* (Cambridge, 1991), 164–85. Two different Offices were added around 1300 to an antiphonal at the Dominican monastery of Marienthal near Brussels (Brussels, Bibl. Royale MS 139, ff. 106–09); see L.M.J. Delaissé, 'A la recherche des origines de l'office du Corpus Christi dans les manuscrits liturgiques', *Scriptorium* 4 (1950), 221–23; T.J. Mathiesen, 'The Office of the New Feast of Corpus Christi in the Regimen Animarum at Brigham Young University', *Journal of Musicology* 2 (1983), 14–15. Yet the Dominican Order was in general slow to accept the feast, and only after 1324 does its celebration appear to have been enforced. Although first ratified by the Chapters General in 1304–06: Bonniwell, *Dominican Liturgy*, 224, and its adoption ordered by Pope Clement V in 1311, even in 1318 there seems still to have been no acceptable Office: 'De officio vero magister ordinis studeat providere'. The introduction was approved the following year. In 1321 an alteration in the instructions for the ordinary was introduced, including directions for the celebration of the feast of Corpus Christi as *totum duplex* with octave. This was confirmed in 1323, a year before the confirmation of the feast itself which would in future be obligatory throughout the order, and would use the Office *editum, ut asseritur* by Thomas Aquinas. For dates of decisions by Chapter General see B.M. Reichert, ed., *Acta capitulorum generalium ordinis Praedicatorum*, II (1304–78), *Monumenta Ordinis Praedicatorum Historica* 4 (1899), 109, 120, 128, 142, 149.

recently charted by François Avril, appears to have centred on work carried out for members of the French court and religious houses like Poissy, which were closely linked to it.[60] However, though the Mass theme consistently introduces Corpus Christi in the Poissy manuscripts, this was not obligatory in French Dominican books of the period; the Last Supper, for example, was chosen to illustrate the feast in a missal written in 1336 by a friar at the convent at Evreux (Chartres, Bibl. mun. MS 581, f. 163).[61]

It seems, therefore, that although each liturgical type of manuscript in the Poissy group generally follows Dominican precedent for the embellishment of a given feast, the specific subject-matter chosen to illustrate the feast, except perhaps in the case of Dominican saints, shows no evidence of a rigorous adherence to a fixed Dominican (or Poissy) visual canon.[62] Rather, it appears to depend on themes being explored by Parisian artists at large, with the result that in most cases the imagery is closely related—although not necessarily identical—from book to book.

A number of artists contributed to these manuscripts. The same historiator's hand does not appear in more than one book, while three or more illustrators worked on the London breviary and on Bibl. de l'Arsenal MSS 602-603. One artist worked right through the winter volume of the latter (Paris, Bibl. de l'Arsenal MS 602). His wide-eyed figures are earnestly intent; like the Virgin in the Nativity who hugs her child closely to her (Fig. 28), they recall Pucellian work.[63] Four historiators worked on the summer volume, each associated with a quite distinctive border construction and range of background patterns; most of the historiated initials are the work of two hands, the straight-backed, rather dour-looking figures of the artist of the psalter section and early *temporale* contrasting with the slightly stooping, and at times rather 'harum-scarum' figures later in the book whose robes are painted in rich, saturated colours

---

[60] F. Avril, 'Une curieuse illustration de la Fête-Dieu: l'iconographie du Christ prêtre élevant l'hostie, et sa diffusion' in *Rituals: Mélanges offerts au Père Gy OP* (Paris, 1991), 39–54.

[61] Leroquais, *Sacramentaires et missels*, II, 243; Avril, 'Illustration de la Fête-Dieu', 4.

[62] The absence of a fixed Dominican illustrative programme has also been observed for liturgical manuscripts made in the thirteenth century for use by the friars in the Roman province: see Cannon, 'Dominican patronage', 144.

[63] Compare, for instance, Pucelle's Flight into Egypt in the *Hours of Jeanne d'Evreux* (New York, The Metropolitan Museum of Art, The Cloisters Collection (54.1.2, f. 83): Avril, *Manuscript Painting*, Pl. 7. In the *Hours of Jeanne of Navarre* (Paris, BN MS n.a. lat. 3145), illustrated by Jean le Noir and other Pucelle-influenced artists, the Virgin in two depictions of the Nativity either suckles her child (f. 50—see K. Morand, *Jean Pucelle* (Oxford, 1962), 20, Pl. XVIIa), or holds him close to her (f. 143v) in scenes of similar immediacy and intimacy to that of Paris, Bibl. de l'Arsenal MS 602. The Christ child in the Nativity of the other manuscripts of the Poissy group lies in the usual crib-altar.

including a distinctive vivid green (Figs 19 and 20). Two other hands were responsible for two embellished pages each. One worked in an ungainly, strongly monumental style; the large, squat figures seem to burst out of the initial which itself escapes from its surrounds (Fig. 27). The other produced the two smallest initials, only four lines high, near the bottom of the page on widely-spaced gatherings.[64]

Most of the artists responsible for the illustration of the other manuscripts in this group worked in a late-Pucellian style. Their figures are relatively stocky and can be rather stiff (Fig. 17). Assailants are often pugnaciously energetic. In contrast to this trend is the work of the final painter in the London breviary whose tall, fine-featured, willowy females convey some of the refined elegance of Maître Honoré, the Parisian illuminator active in the later thirteenth century (Fig. 29).[65] The more painterly and softly rounded features of the missal miniaturist are at variance with the linearity characteristic of most of the other hands in these books, and instead of their strong colour contrasts (used to offset, for example, a cloak against its visible lining), attempts are made to render the effects of 'shot' silk and diaphanous materials (Fig. 26). Unfortunately, the paint work of the miniatures in this manuscript has worn extremely badly; it is muddied to an obfuscating dull grey-brown early in the book and is flaking elsewhere.

All of these finely crafted books, with their gold embellishments and small images framed by decorative borders, are unarguably luxury items. But their ornamentation is relatively restrained when compared with that of the breviary made at the same period for Blanche de France, a Franciscan nun at Longchamp and cousin to several choir sisters at Poissy.[66] The miniatures in her book are considerably larger and greater in number. At a height of twelve lines of text, they occupy a fifth of the page, while some eighty-nine pages of this breviary, including the

---

[64] The thoroughness of production of all these manuscripts should be remarked upon: letters lacking appropriate embellishment are almost non-existent. Such careful finishing may stem from the righting of any omissions which would be noticed when the text was corrected, as was mandatory, against a certified Dominican exemplar. It is tempting to imagine that the fourth artist in this volume, who is responsible for small initials, out of the way and easily missed, was involved in such a circumstance.

[65] In particular the depiction of the virgins who water the seven trees of the mystic garden in *La somme le roy* (London, BL MS Add. 54180, f. 69v): E.G. Millar, *The Parisian Miniaturist Honoré* (London, 1959), Pl. 4.

[66] Vatican, Bibl. Apostolica cod. Urb. lat. 603. The owner was the daughter of Philippe le Bel's third son King Philippe V and Jeanne d'Artois et Bourgogne. Although a nun she was sheltered by her protective mother and sisters who received papal dispensations to stay with her at the monastery before she took her vows, a privilege overused by the queen who then received a caution for too frequent visits: Brown, 'Funeral of Philip V', 271–72, nn. 16–17. Her devoted relatives may have commissioned the lavish book.

calendar, are illustrated; their illuminated borders are richly populated with hybrid figures. More lavish and costly ornamentation is also evident throughout the rest of book, for gilded and painted initials hierarchically order the text on every page and regularly project into the margins via decorated extensions inhabited by birds; this secondary ornamentation is also in great contrast to the discreet, and considerably less expensive flourishing in scribal inks which fulfils the same purpose in the Poissy manuscripts.[67]

A second contemporary breviary which provides a telling comparison with the Poissy group is the *Belleville Breviary*, produced under the direction of Jean Pucelle (Paris, BN MSS lat. 10483-4). This Dominican office-book was apparently made for a female lay patron, Jeanne de Belleville, and its design reveals a considerable didactic input by the friars.[68] The calendar and psalter are heavily illustrated with theological themes intended both to instruct and to stimulate contemplation, while a preliminary text in the vernacular explains the meaning of the pictures.[69] Throughout the manuscript no expense has been spared in preparation: multi-illustrated pages are numerous and an ivy-leaf border terminating in dragons or humorous hybrids surrounds the text on every page. The two volumes were also specially arranged to help cushion the difficulty of use during the Easter period. The apparent owner, a mature female wearing secular dress and wimple, is portrayed in three illustrations.[70] It seems clear that the book was produced for its lay female owner to follow—pictorially at least—while the Divine Office was chanted in a chapel or in church.

---

[67] A further distinction occurs in the rubrics: those in the Franciscan breviary are rendered in French while all the Dominican manuscripts retain the Latin of the primary exemplars, including the sometimes long introductory considerations of authorship before the lessons in the breviaries.

[68] Evidence from royal inventories indicates that this manuscript and a similarly finely made missal which has not survived were made for Jeanne de Belleville, and later confiscated by the Crown with other property from her husband Olivier de Clisson. For description and provenance of the manuscript see, for example, L. Delisle, *Recherches sur la librairie de Charles V*, I (Paris, 1907), 182–85; ibid., *Notice de douze livres royaux du XIIe et du XIVe siècle* (Paris, 1902), 81–88; Leroquais, *Bréviaires*, III, 204–205.

[69] The didactic theological content of calendar and psalter sections are analysed in F.G. Godwin, 'An illustration to the De Sacramentis of St Thomas Aquinas', *Speculum* 26 (1951), 609–14 and L.F. Sandler, 'Jean Pucelle and the Lost Miniatures of the *Belleville Breviary*', *Art Bulletin* 66 (1984), 73–96. For a recent, finely argued account of the programme's elaboration, with bibliography for the manuscript, see C. Sterling, *La peinture médiévale à Paris, 1300-1500*, I (Paris, 1987), 71–87.

[70] Winter volume, f. 203; summer volume, ff. 148 and 253. I draw attention to these aspects in my dissertation.

Nonetheless, some seventy years after its production the manuscript, its earlier leather binding now replaced with figured silk, was given by Jean de Berry to his niece, Marie de France, a nun at Poissy. In 1454 it was purchased from the Poissy community by the nun Marie Jouvenal des Ursins, who immediately replaced the closures displaying the royal arms with a new set bearing images that were made of fine gold.[71] It was probably also she who had all the page-edges painted with the Ursins arms amid foliage, at about which time the book must have received the red velvet covers still preserved with the manuscript today. From its treatment at Poissy it follows that the *Belleville Breviary* was not in normal use as a choir book. Since the liturgy lacks the nine-lesson octave for the feast of St Louis it was inadequate for the celebrations at the monastery; it was never updated with this or with newer feasts, not even in the calendar. The silk then velvet covers contrast markedly to the sturdy leather in which the breviaries of our group were rebound in about 1500, which presumably replaced earlier binding of similar robustness. Together with the golden clasps and painted page-edges, the rich but relatively poor-wearing fabric of the covers of the *Belleville Breviary* (and the very fact of their survival until today) attests to its use at Poissy, not daily in the choir like the breviaries of our group, but either on special occasions, perhaps as an item of display, or as a private devotional book, which its illustrative programme invites.

The considerable difference in the original purpose and function of the *Belleville Breviary* and the manuscripts of the Poissy group is highlighted by a comparison of their respective illustrations of the Office of St Dominic. In the Poissy books, as we have seen, this Office is accented by the one small depiction of Dominic on the heavenly ladder (Figs 22 and 24), an event which is narrated in the lessons for the octave of the feast. By contrast, the *Belleville Breviary* presents the user with an illustrated didactic account of Dominic as founder of the Dominican Order. Of the five scenes depicted from the saint's life only the first two refer to events recounted in the Office as transcribed in this manuscript: the early indication of his outstanding destiny through the star on his forehead (Paris, BN MS lat. 10484, f. 270v) and his role as preacher (f. 271). The events that follow (f. 272) do not belong to the liturgical texts they accompany.[72] At the top of

---

[71] For inventory descriptions and inscriptions in the two volumes of the *Belleville Breviary* that describe its history and former appearance see references cited in n. 68 above.

[72] These particular events are also absent from the breviaries in the group of manuscripts from Poissy. They did, though, form part of the far more extensive readings for the feast of St Dominic in Humbert's revised Dominican lectionary of the 1250s (London, BL Add. MS 23935, ff. 218v–223v) and are common to contemporary Dominican hagiographical accounts of the saint. See, for instance, Jacobus da Voragine, *Legenda Aurea*, ed. T. Graesse (Osnabrück, 1969; a facsimile of the 1890 edition), 468–69.

the page is the dream of Pope Innocent in which Dominic (representing the new Order) reinforces the toppling Lateran church. In the lower margin Innocent's successor, Honorius, hands Dominic the document of approval of the new Order. Dominic's vision, in which Sts Peter and Paul endorse the itinerant preaching vocation of the friars as a continuation of the apostolic tradition by presenting him with both book and staff, completes the sequence (Fig. 25).

The absence of this type of expansive pictorial content from the liturgical books expressly designed for Poissy reflects their intended function. The lay owner of the *Belleville Breviary* could either follow the text of the service or contemplate its didactic illustrations. A similar choice was not permitted the Poissy nuns. Two well-defined periods each day, one after matins-lauds, the other after compline, were prescribed by the Rule for meditation and contemplation.[73] The daily duties to be performed in choir were quite different, namely to sing (mainly in unison) correctly, loudly and clearly the Dominican liturgy as formulated in the Rule and charter.[74] Clarity of text and music were of paramount importance in the books intended to assist with this. Small illustrations which would help in finding the place after the necessary switching between various parts of the liturgy during services were thus appropriate, whereas visual narrative sequences which required a distracting meditative application were not. Based on Dominican-Parisian precedents, therefore, the illustrative and decorative schemes in the books of the Poissy group allowed a fine line to be drawn between functional tools and the *deluxe* possessions appropriate for liturgical use by nobly born women,[75] or, in the case of the missal, by the priest-celebrant in the imposing church of a royal monastic foundation.

Is it possible to glimpse any details of the commissioning of these books? Two of the breviaries in the group make visual reference to their

---

[73] Poissy Constitutions, Cap. 1 (Munich, Bay. Staatsbibl. MS Clm. 10170, 129v–130v); W.A. Hinnebusch, *The History of the Dominican Order*. I. Origins and Growth to 1500 (New York, 1965), 353.

[74] The Constitutions of the nuns at Poissy required that the liturgy be sung fluently and distinctly, *tractum et distincte*, which presupposes the ability to read (or reproduce from memory after the sung cues of the cantrix) words and music at sight from manuscripts in which the Office was necessarily correctly written and checked. It was not to be sung too fast, either, due care being given to observe the medial pauses—'in medio versus metrum cum pausa servetur'; Poissy Constitutions, 129v. The loud singing which Dominic had urged upon the choir was reiterated by the fifth Master General in his instructions to the Order; see Tugwell, *Early Dominicans*, 80; Humbert of Romans, *Opera*, II, 105.

[75] Philippe le Bel's Charter specified that the nuns were to be nobly born, otherwise his successors would need to approve their entry. During his lifetime he had the right to vet all postulants; see Paris, Archives Nationales, JJ 2, published in Moreau-Rendu, *Prieuré royal*, 315.

nun owners: in Paris, Bibl. de l'Arsenal MS 602 a nun-hybrid prays in the margin by an image of the Annunciation (f. 419); and in the London breviary three Dominican nuns sing before a lectern (Fig. 30), replacing the male cantors that usually illustrate the psalm *Cantate Domino* and, of course, summing up the book's purpose in a particularly identifiable way. Breviaries at Poissy, including these, were inscribed in the fifteenth century with the names of a pair of owners, who presumably had entered together and were destined to sit side by side daily in the choir stalls until one either succeeded to a special office or died.[76] Possibly, then, these breviaries were personally owned in this way from the outset, though the chantress and sacristan, who were officially responsible for the availability, correctness and good condition of the books to be used for the Divine Office and the Mass, probably advised on the purchase of new volumes.[77] The comparable decorative elements in each manuscript of our group, the matching quality of their materials and execution, and their consequent similar costs support this supposition. As discussed above both textual and stylistic elements point to a main production period after about 1335, so possibly the books were ordered as a consequence of the nuns' recent occupation of their new church in 1331. With the much larger church in use, more nuns could be accommodated in choir, so either more women entered Poissy at this time or those already there were now all able to attend choir together. The production of a new antiphonal, considering that one was already at the house, points to the need for a second chantress within the large choir space, a position which may have been dispensed with while the considerably smaller chapel of St Dominic was still serving the nuns.[78]

---

[76] Paris, Bibl. de l'Arsenal MS 107 was inscribed before 1473 by its co-owners: 'Ceste legende est a seurs K. la chandelliere. Et .K. Nicolas. Religieuses. en leglise monsr Saint loys de Poissy. Et demoura. Dutout a la survivant deulx deulx'. The breviary Paris, Bibl. de l'Arsenal MSS 602–603 was given to two sisters who flourished in 1469, and later belonged to two successive single owners who are known from the sixteenth century: 'Ces legendes sont a seurs Richarde et Jehanne Gouverne Religieuses en leglise monseigneur saint loys de poissy et a la sourvivant dicellez. Et leur donna seur marie helard, leur maistresse Religieuse ou cedit lieu'. 'Ces legendes cy sunt a seur guenegonde de monteigny Religieuse en leglise monseigneur saint louys de poissy.' 'Et appres le deces de soeur Claude de Belleville elles ont este donnees a Loffice de soubz prieure. Resquiescant in passe.'

[77] Humbert of Romans, *Opera*, II, 238–39, 249. I have so far found no evidence at Poissy of borrowing office-books from a common library as was practised by the friars at Barcelona. Between 1241 and 1491 forty-five breviaries and three diurnals were assigned to certain friars, apparently for the duration of the borrower's life; see C. Douais, *Les assignations des livres aux religieux du couvent des Frères Prêcheurs de Barcelone (XIIe–XVe siècles)* (Toulouse and Paris, 1893).

[78] An analogous situation occurred at Aix. In about 1330 a canon copied a two-part antiphonal then, some twenty years later, a second two-part antiphonal was transcribed by another canon. The four volumes were distributed so that the cantor on each side of the

While we have, of course, no idea how many more volumes, now lost, formed part of this comprehensive commission of books over a decade, the large number of people involved in production of the extant manuscripts—possibly six scribes and some twelve or more illuminators—might indicate that at least some were ordered at the same time. The distribution of the illustrative workload in Paris, Bibl. de l'Arsenal MSS 602-603 could even reflect some kind of deadline since the number of workers increases, and the proportion of gatherings each one illustrates decreases, as the book continues.

On the other hand, though, the manuscripts' similar format and appearance could be purely the result of patterns of production which had become established over a considerable period of time. Whether a specific circumstance elicited the books' production or not, however, the volumes were more than likely ordered during the term of the second prioress, Marie de Clermont, between 1333 and 1344; the wealthy grand-daughter of St Louis who had been brought up by his widow Marguerite de Provence,[79] she may well have been the driving force behind the *deluxe* purchases.

It is likely that, since the transcription of each manuscript required an appropriate Dominican exemplar, the scribal work for these books was carried out in the vicinity of the convent of St Jacques in Paris and if so, that their illumination took place in the same area. Recently Joan Diamond and Richard and Mary Rouse have demonstrated that in the late thirteenth century and well into the second decade of the fourteenth century Parisian manuscript production relied on a large number of small, closely situated establishments whose proprietors shared commissions.[80] One of these enclaves functioned near the rue Saint-Jacques.[81]

---

choir used one newer and one older transcription; see M. Huglo, *Les livres de chant liturgique* (Turnhout, 1988), 93.

[79] *Liste des prieures du monastere de S. Louis de Poissy . . . extraite des anciens comptes, et autres Monumens dudit Monastere . . .*, probably Paris, n. d. (reprinted from 1644 publication), 2. Marie de Clermont survived until 1372 so her influence on the house is unlikely to have ceased when she relinquished the office of prioress in 1344 after she became blind.

[80] J. Diamond, 'Manufacture and market in Parisian book illumination around 1300' in E. Liskar, ed., *Europäische Kunst um 1300* (Vienna, 1986), 101–10; R.H. and M.A. Rouse, 'The commercial production of manuscript books in late thirteenth-century and early fourteenth-century Paris' in L.L. Brownrigg, ed., *Medieval Book Production. Assessing the Evidence* (Oxford, 1990), 103–15.

[81] Rouse and Rouse, 'Commercial Production', 104. The same authors have demonstrated the strong and continued patronage, in the case of theological and university texts, that the Dominicans at St Jacques gave to the *libraire* situated nearest their convent between 1270 and 1342; see R.H. Rouse and M.A. Rouse, 'The book trade at the University of Paris, c.1250–1350' in L.J. Bataillon, B.G. Guyot and R.H. Rouse, eds, *La production du livre universitaire au Moyen Age. Exemplar et pecia* (Paris, 1988), 59–63, 73–75.

The continuation of such a situation into the 1330–1340s would explain both the large and disparate group of illustrators of our manuscripts who were nonetheless aware that the unusual, expressly Dominican imagery of St Dominic upon the heavenly ladder was currently the appropriate theme to associate with his feast. As well as being designed to meet the needs of the Poissy community, therefore, this group of manuscripts may also reflect an established tradition for liturgical book production and illustration as supervised by the Dominicans in Paris at this time.[82]

---

[82] This study formed part of my doctoral research and of a project *Art, Worship and the Book in Medieval Culture* funded by the Australian Research Committee (ARC). I also gratefully acknowledge the support which I received from an Australian Postgraduate Research Award, the Alma Hansen Travelling Scholarship and a Travel Grant-in-Aid from the University of Melbourne.

Appendix

TABLE 1. ILLUSTRATION/DECORATION PROGRAMMES

Includes only feasts emphasized with an illustration in at least one manuscript

H = Historiated initial with border   d = decorated initial   f = Pen-flourished initial   / = Outside range of book.

Feasts ranked *totum duplex* at time of production of the manuscripts are shown in capitals.

The triply decorated sections are London Breviary: first vespers; matins, first lesson; matins, responsory to first lesson; Missal: miniature(s) above or below rubric (Canon: *Te igitur* initial); *officium* (introit). Single historiations emphasize the first lesson of matins in the other breviaries, its responsory in the antiphonal and the introit in the gradual.

	Breviary Arsenal 107	Breviary Arsenal 602-3	Breviary Private Coll.	Missal BL Eg. 3037	Antiphonal Melb. SLV	Gradual Phil. Mus. Art
Temporale						
First Sunday of Advent	H	H	H d d	H H	H	H
NATIVITY OF THE LORD	H	H	d H	H d	H	H
Circumcision	H	H	d			
EPIPHANY	H	H	H f	H d	H	H
Palm Sunday		H				
Canon of Mass	/	/	/	H d	/	/
EASTER SUNDAY	H	H	d	H H d	H	H
ASCENSION	H			H d	H	H
PENTECOST	H	H	H d	H d	H	H
HOLY TRINITY	/	H	H d f	H	H	H
CORPUS CHRISTI	/	H	H	H d		
DEDICATION OF CHURCH		H	H	H		H
Sanctorale						
Andrew	H	H		H d	H	H
Nicholas		H				
STEPHEN		H	d		d	
JOHN THE EVANGELIST		H	d		d	
PURIFICATION OF THE VIRGIN	H	H	H d d	H d	H	
THOMAS AQUINAS	H	H	H d f			
ANNUNCIATION	H	H	H d f	H d	H	
PETER MARTYR	H	H	H d		H	
TRANSLATION OF DOMINIC	H	H	d H d	H	H	
BIRTH OF JOHN THE BAPTIST	/	H	H	H d	H	H
PETER AND PAUL	/	H		H	H	
Commemoration of Paul	/	H			H	
MARY MAGDALEN	/	H		H	H	
DOMINIC	/	H	H d f	H	H	
Laurence	/	H			H	
ASSUMPTION OF THE VIRGIN	/	H	H d f	H d	H	H
Bartholomew	/	H				
LOUIS	/	H	H H f	H	H	H

	Breviary Arsenal 107	Breviary Arsenal 602-3	Breviary Private Coll.	Missal BL Eg. 3037	Antiphonary Melb. SLV	Gradual Phil. Mus. Art
AUGUSTINE	/	H			d	
Beheading of Baptist	/	H				
BIRTH OF THE VIRGIN	/	H	H f f	H d	H	H
Michael Archangel	/	H		H d	H	H
Denis	/	H				
11000 Virgins	/	H	H d f			
ALL SAINTS	/	H	H d f	H d	H	H
Commemoration of the Dead	/	H			H	
Martin	/	H				
Katherine	/	H				
Office & Mass of the Virgin	d	H				

TABLE 2. MANUSCRIPTS: SIZE AND ILLUSTRATION

Manuscript	Museum	Size (mm)		Pages with illustration & border	
		Height x Width	Page thickness	Number	Percent of total
BREVIARY	London, Private Collection	215x144	65	28	2.8
BREVIARY (Winter)	Paris, Bibliothèque de l'Arsenal MS 107	240x163	70	21	2.6
BREVIARY	Paris, Bibliothèque de l'Arsenal MSS 602/3	237x161 235x165	70 69	25 30	2.6 3.3
MISSAL	London, British Library, Egerton MS 3037	211x138	38	23	4.2
ANTIPHONAL	Melbourne, State Library of Victoria MS *096 1/R66A	285x200	80	23	2.7
GRADUAL	Philadelphia, Museum of Fine Arts MS 45-65-7	168x121	32	17	2.4

TABLE 3. DISTRIBUTION OF MAJOR EMBELLISHMENT DEVICES IN DOMINICAN PROTOTYPAL AND POISSY GRADUALS

	'Prototype' Original	'Prototype' Copy	Poissy c.1340s
Temporale			
First Sunday in Advent	d	[d]	H
NATIVITY OF THE LORD	d	f	H
EPIPHANY		f	H
EASTER SUNDAY	d	f	H
ASCENSION		f	H
PENTECOST	d	f	H
HOLY TRINITY	d	f	H
DEDICATION OF CHURCH		f	H
Sanctorale			
Andrew			H
BIRTH OF JOHN THE BAPTIST			H
ASSUMPTION OF VIRGIN		f	H
LOUIS	/	/	H
BIRTH OF VIRGIN		f	H
Michael Archangel			H
ALL SAINTS		f	H
Commemoration of Dead		f	
Total feasts emphasised:			
GRADUAL Sanctorale	5	8	8
GRADUAL Temporale	0	4	7
ANTIPHONAL Sanctorale	4	7	6
ANTIPHONAL Temporale	7	15	17

H = Historiated initial with border
d = Decorated initial, usually vine-leaf pattern
f = Pen-flourished initial
[ ] = Space left for initial: incomplete
/ = Not applicable: book predates introduction of feast.
Feasts ranked *totum duplex* at time of manuscripts' production are in capitals.
Poissy Gradual = Philadelphia Museum of Art MS 45-65-7
Prototype original = Rome, Santa Sabina, MS in Dominican Archives
Prototype copy = London, British Library, Add. MS 23935

TABLE 4. ILLUSTRATION OF FEASTS.

Includes only feasts illustrated in three or more books

	Breviary Arsenal 107	Breviary Arsenal 602-3	Breviary Priv. Coll.	Antiphonal Melb. SLV	Missal BL Eg. 3037	Gradual Phil. Mus. Art
Temporale						
First Sunday of Advent	Isaiah and Virgin	Vision of Isaiah	Vision of Isaiah	Annunciation		Priest raises soul
NATIVITY OF THE LORD			Nativity of Christ			
EPIPHANY			Adoration of the Magi			
EASTER SUNDAY	Resurrection		—	Resurrection	Resurrection *Noli me tangere*	Resurrection
ASCENSION	Ascension	—	—		Ascension	
PENTECOST			Descent of Holy Spirit upon Apostles			
HOLY TRINITY	/	'Throne of Mercy' Trinity	'Throne of Mercy' Trinity	—	'Throne of Mercy' Trinity	
CORPUS CHRISTI	/	Christ-priest raises host	Christ-priest raises host		Priest raises host	—
DEDICATION OF CHURCH	—	Bishop dedicates church	Bishop dedicates church		Bishop dedicates church	
Sanctorale						
Andrew	Saint being tied to cross		—		Saint being tied to cross	
PURIFICATION OF BVM			Presentation of Christ			—
THOMAS AQUINAS		Saint teaching			—	—
ANNUNCIATION			Annunciation		—	—
PETER MARTYR	Standing saint		Martyrdom	Standing saint	—	—
TRANSL. OF DOMINIC	Dominic on ladder		Translation		Standing saint	—
BIRTH OF JOHN BAPTIST	/	Holds agnus Dei	Baptism of Christ	Birth scene	Holds agnus Dei	—
PETER AND PAUL	/	Peter's Crucifixion	—	Peter's Crucifixion	Standing saints	—
Commemoration of Paul	/	Martyrdom		Martyrdom	—	—
MARY MAGDALEN	/	Standing saint	—		*Noli me tangere*	
DOMINIC	/			Saint on ladder		
ASSUMPTION OF BVM	/	Coronation		Dormition		
LOUIS	/			King Louis		
BIRTH OF BVM	/			Birth scene		
Michael Archangel	/	Standing angels			Michael killing dragon	Coronation
ALL SAINTS	/		—	Group of saints		

/ = outside range of book — = feast unillustrated in manuscript See Table 2 for feasts illustrated in less than three books.

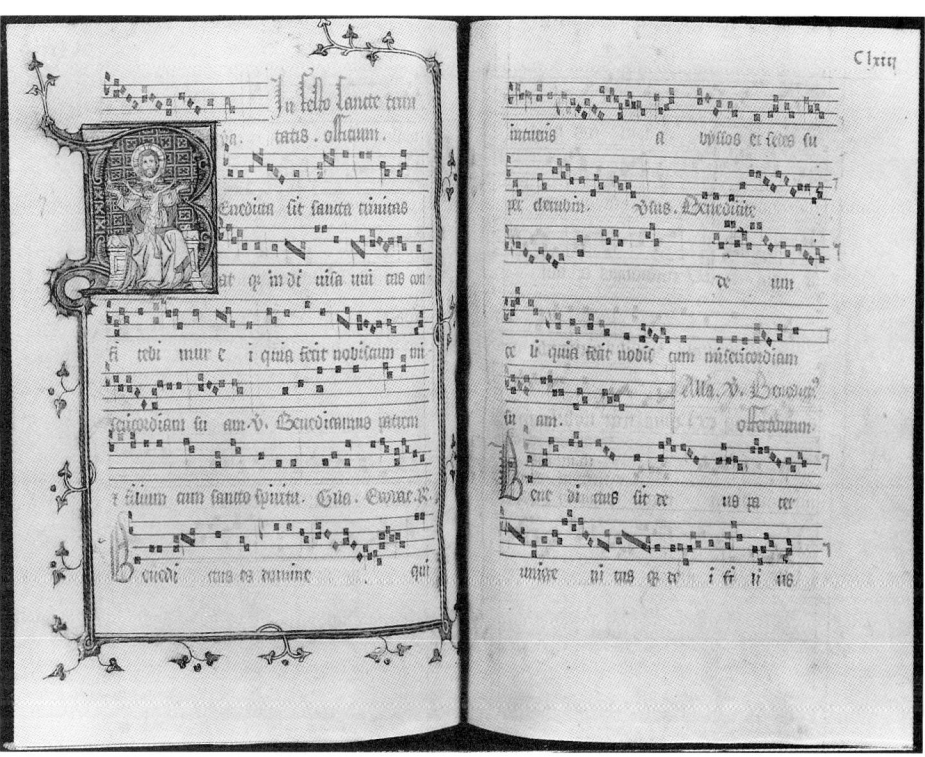

Figure 17. Trinity Sunday. Gradual. Philadelphia, Museum of Art, MS 45-65-7, ff. 162v–163. 168×121 mm (each page).

Figure 18. Feast of the Translation of St Dominic. Breviary. London, Private Collection, ff. 367v–368. 215×144 mm (each page).

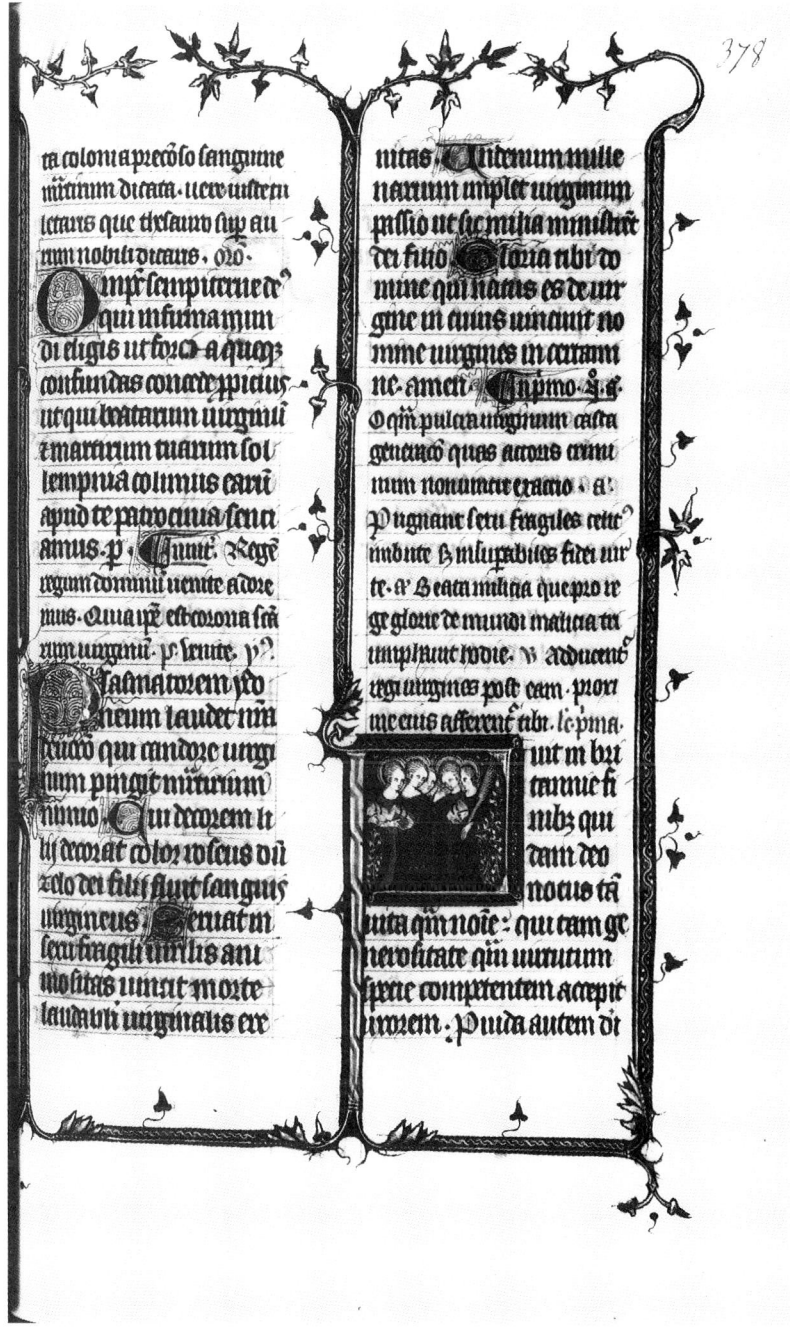

Figure 19. Feast of the Eleven Thousand Virgins. Breviary. Paris, Bibliothèque de l'Arsenal, MS 603, f. 378. 237×161 mm.

Figure 20. Feast of All Saints. Breviary. Paris, Bibliothèque de l'Arsenal, MS 603, f. 387. 237×161 mm.

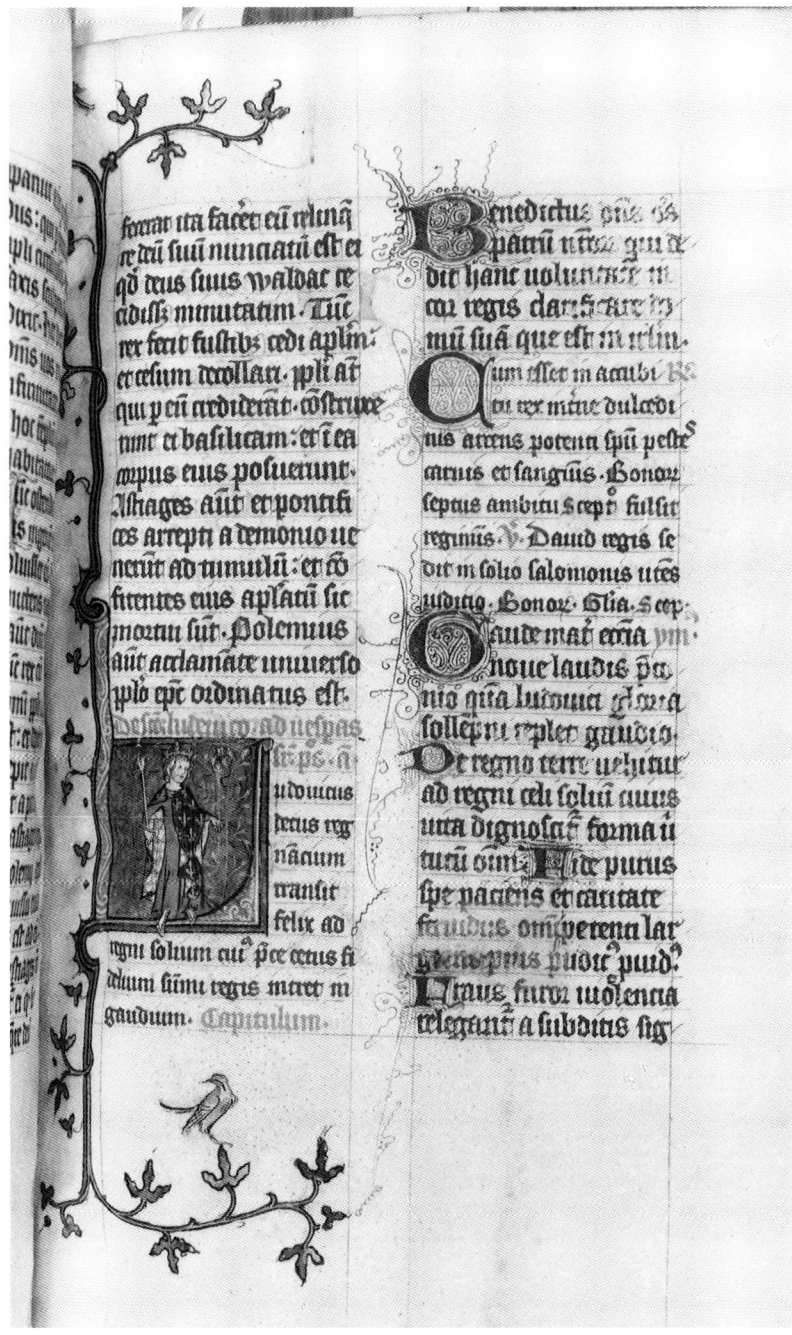

Figure 21. Feast of St Louis. Breviary. London, Private Collection, f. 422. 215×144mm.

Figure 22. Feast of St Dominic. Antiphonal. Melbourne, State Library of Victoria, MS *096 1/R66A, f. 294v. 285×200 mm.

Figure 23. Feast of St Dominic. Gradual. Zurich, Schweizerisches Landesmuseum, MS LM 26117, f. 261v. 550×375mm (detail).

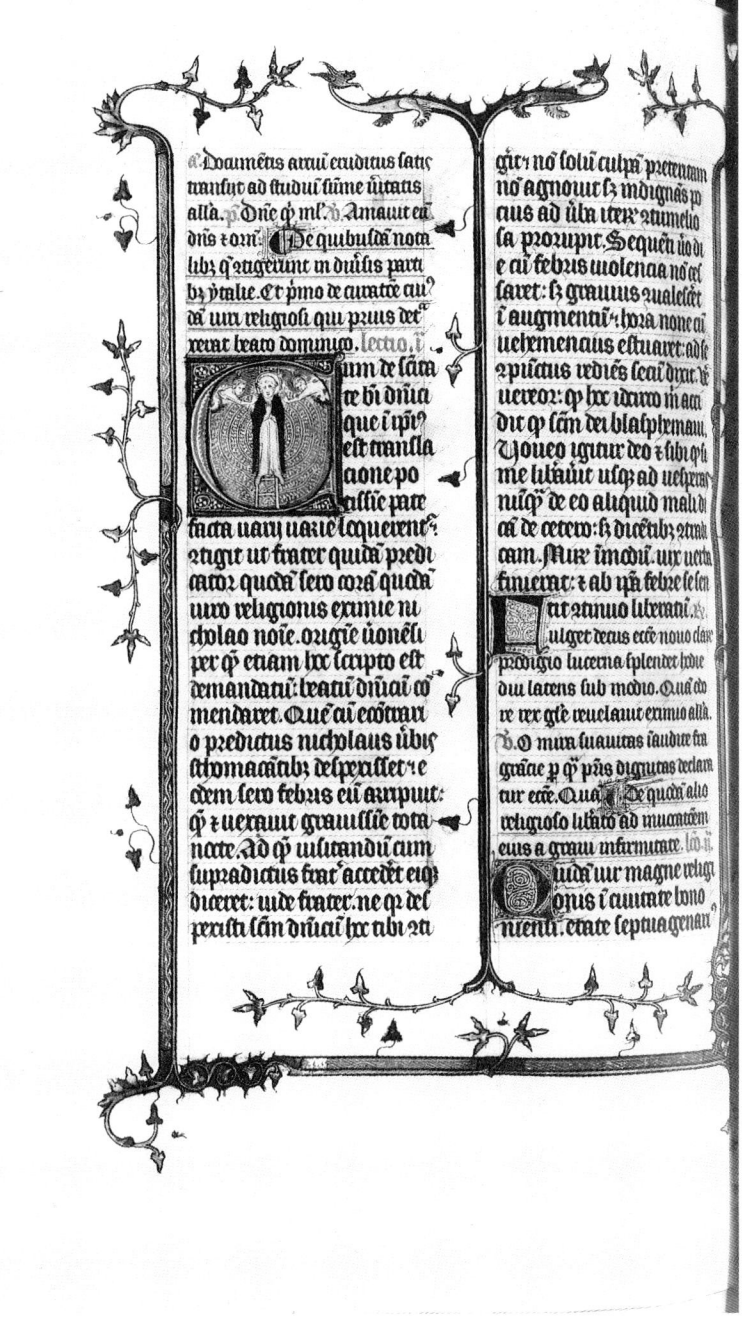

Figure 24. Feast of the Translation of St Dominic. Breviary. Paris, Bibliothèque de l'Arsenal, MS 107, f. 388v. 240×163mm.

Figure 25. Feast of St Dominic. *Belleville Breviary*. Paris, Bibliothèque Nationale, MS lat. 10484, f. 272. 240×170 mm.

Figure 26. Feast of Corpus Christi. Missal. London, British Library, Egerton MS 3037, f. 127. 211×138 mm.

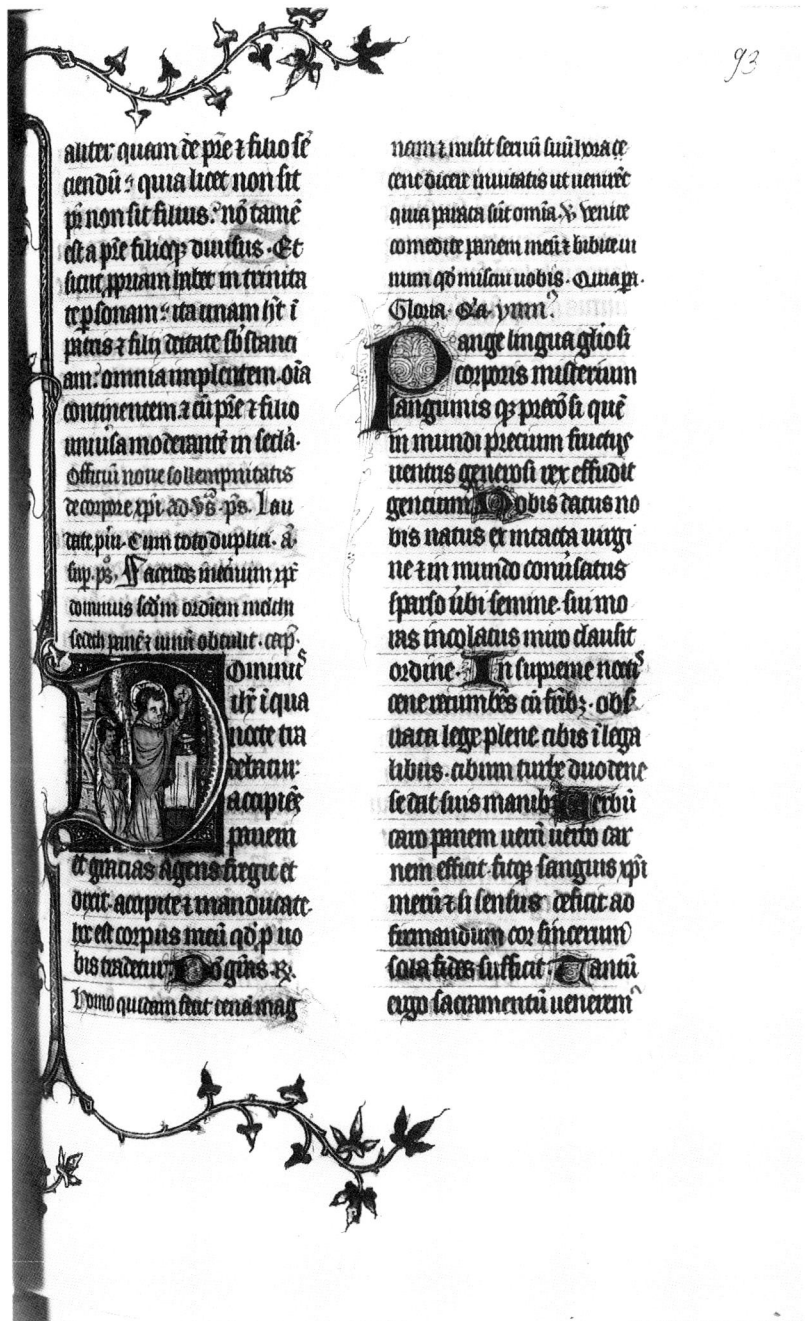

Figure 27. Feast of Corpus Christi. Breviary. Paris, Bibliothèque de l'Arsenal, MS 603, f. 93. 237×161mm.

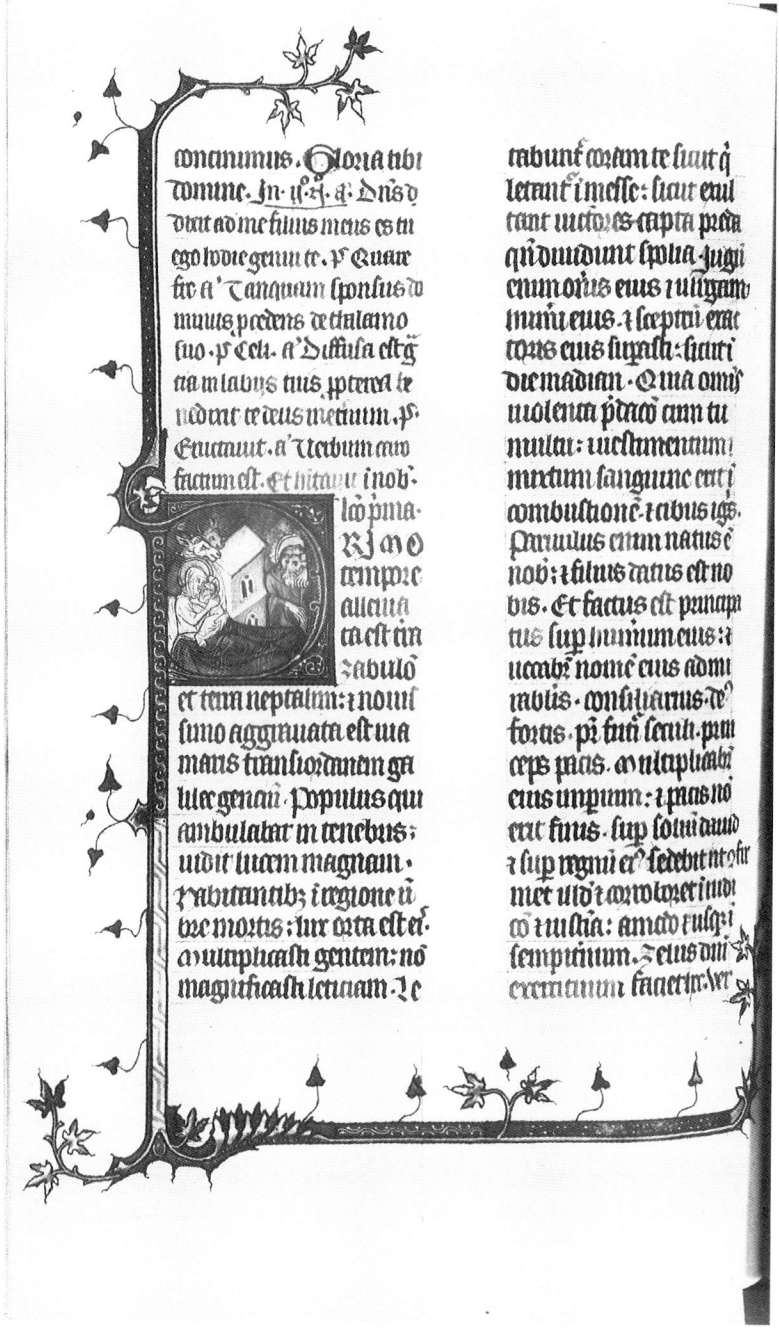

Figure 28. Feast of the Nativity. Breviary. Paris, Bibliothèque de l'Arsenal, MS 602, f. 122v. 237×161 mm.

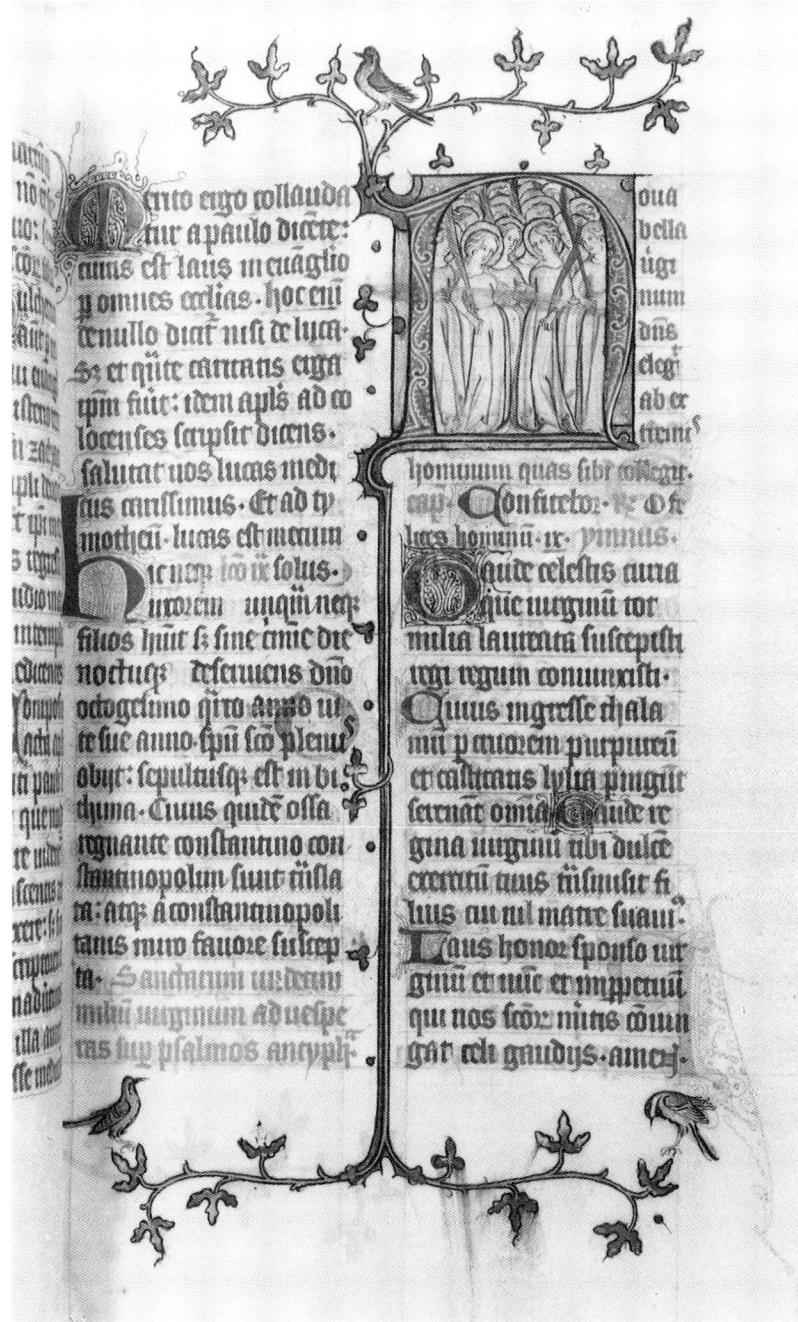

Figure 29. Feast of the Eleven Thousand Virgins. Breviary. London, Private Collection, f. 461. 215×144 mm.

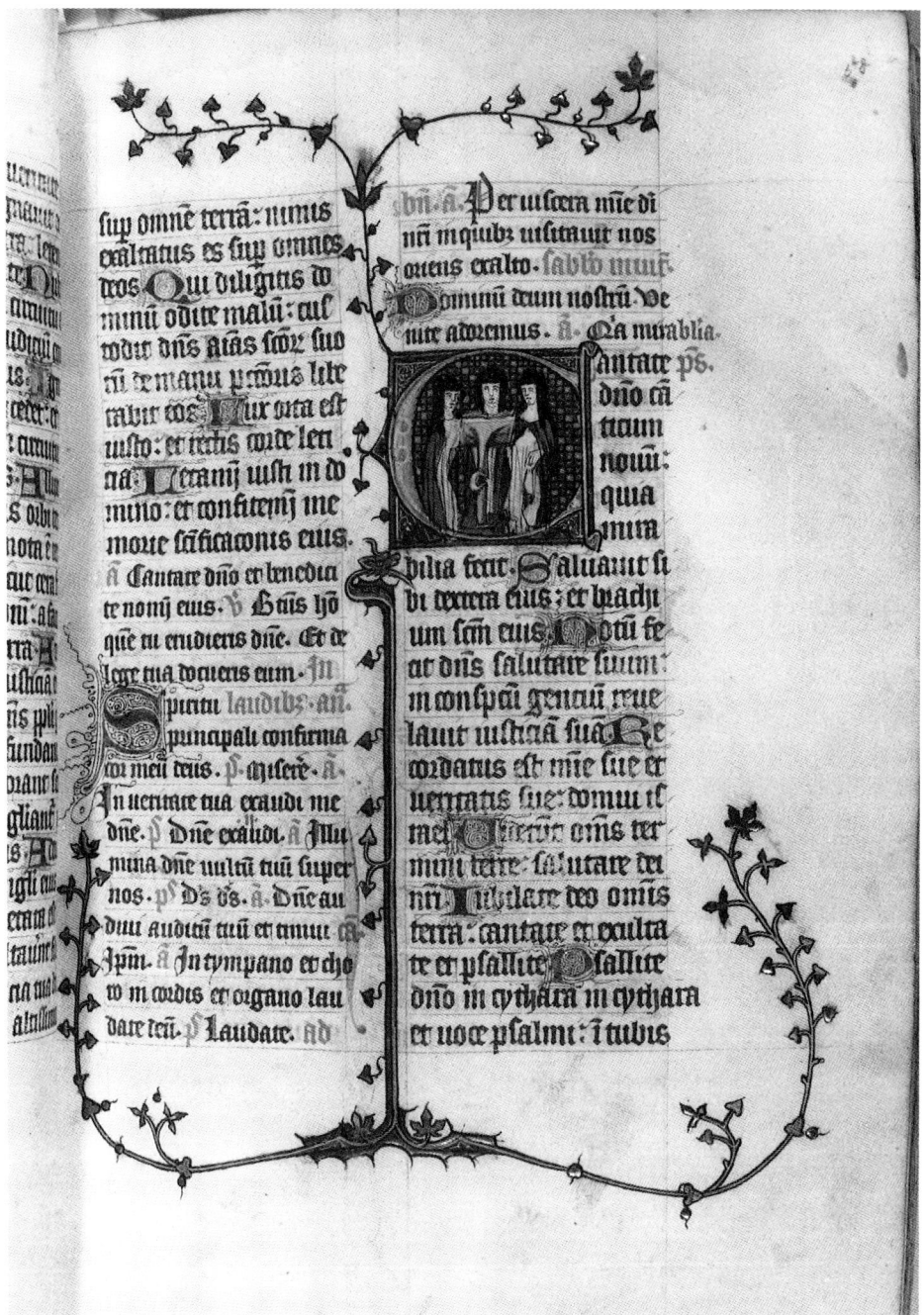

Figure 30. Psalm 97, *Cantate Domino*. Breviary. London, Private Collection, f. 58. 215×144 mm.

FOUR

The Illustrated Office of the Passion in Italian Books of Hours

Bronwyn C. Stocks

THE OFFICE OF THE PASSION OCCURS with reasonable frequency in books of hours from the late thirteenth century onwards; it is often illustrated. To date, however, the relationship between the text of this Office and its illustration has received little attention.[1] This study is based on a group of twenty-five Italian books of hours produced before 1425.[2]

The recitation of prayers at certain hours of the day in commemoration of the Passion has a long tradition. The *Apostolic Constitutions* of the second or third century state that the faithful should pray at the third, sixth, and ninth hours of the day because at the third hour Christ was condemned by Pilate, at the sixth he was crucified, and at the ninth

---

[1] See W. Lampen O.F.M., 'De Officio Divino in Ordine Minorum Iuxta S. Bonaventuram', *Antonianum* 2 (1927), 135–56; S. Sticca, 'Officium Passionis Domini: An unpublished manuscript of the fourteenth century', *Franciscan Studies* 34, annual XII (1974), 144–99, and A. Bennett, 'The Scheide Psalter-Hours', *Princeton University Library Chronicle* 55 (1994), 191, 205.

[2] These form part of a larger group of forty Italian books of hours dating from the late thirteenth to the first quarter of the fifteenth century that I have located in the course of my doctoral research on 'Text and Image in the Early Italian Book of Hours'.

'Christ was pierced in his side and shed forth blood and water and brought the rest of the time of that day in light to evening'.³ The persistence of this tradition ensured that, with the establishment of the canonical hours, the recitation of prayers at these periods became related to the observance of particular events of the Passion.⁴ This practice was further encouraged by medieval treatises such as the *De meditatione Passionis Christi per septem diei horas libellus*, attributed to Pseudo-Bede.⁵

Devotion to the Passion of Christ increased steadily during the Middle Ages, particularly from the twelfth century, and texts which treated the Passion narrative systematically and chronologically had widespread appeal.⁶ Devotional treatises such as Pseudo-Bernard's *Liber de Passione Christi et planctibus matris ejus* and Pseudo-Bonaventure's *Meditationes vitae Christi* (hereafter referred to as *The Meditations on the Life of Christ*) required their readers to contemplate the experiences, pain and sorrow of the Virgin and Christ, as though the events of the Passion were occurring before their very eyes.⁷ The doctrine of *compassio*, which was a feature of contemplative meditation, received wider circulation through these texts, which were written with a general audience in mind, and which many lay people found appealing.⁸ The author of *The Meditations*, for example, exhorts his reader to 'look', 'consider', 'regard' and 'marvel' at the events of the life of Christ.⁹ The Office of the Passion and the Hours of the Cross, which begin to appear in books of hours in the late thirteenth century and

---

³ G. Dix, *The Treatise on the Apostolic Tradition* (London, 1937), 62, verses 2–5; see also J.A. Jungmann, *The Early Liturgy to the Time of Gregory the Great* (London, 1960), 101–2.

⁴ See Jungmann, *The Early Liturgy*, 98–104; Sticca, *Officium*, 152–53. The Little Office of the Virgin or Hours of the Virgin was thus to be read in commemoration of the pain Mary suffered on behalf of her son. It was sometimes illustrated by a Passion cycle, as in the two Lombard missal-hours c.1380, Paris, BN MS lat. 757 and Paris, BN MS Smith-Lesouef 22; see V. Leroquais, *Les Livres d'heures manuscrits de la Bibliothèque Nationale* (Paris 1927), I, 1–7. This was by no means an exclusively Italian phenomenon. See J. Harthan, *Books of Hours* (London, 1977), 26–28; and R. Wieck, *Time Sanctified* (New York, 1988), 66.

⁵ See J.-P. Migne, ed., *Patrologia Latina*, 221 vols (Paris, 1844–64), 94.561–68.

⁶ See J. Leclercq, F. Vandenbroucke and L. Bouyer, *A History of Christian Spirituality*, vol. 2, *The Spirituality of the Middle Ages* (London, 1968), 243–50; J. Marrow, *Passion Iconography in Northern European Art of the Late Middle Ages and Early Renaissance* (Belgium, 1979); and *New Catholic Encyclopaedia*, 17 vols (Washington D.C., 1967-74), 10, 1059–61.

⁷ For *Liber de Passione Christi et planctibus matris ejus* see *Patrologia Latina*, 182.1133–42. For *Meditationes vitae Christi* see A.C. Peltier, ed., *Sancti Bonaventurae Opera Omnia* (Paris, 1868), 12, 509–630.

⁸ See Leclercq, *Christian Spirituality*, 314; Marrow, *Passion Iconography*, 10–12, and Sticca, *Officium*, 155.

⁹ I. Ragusa and R.B. Green, eds and trans., *Pseudo-Bonaventure: The Meditations on the Life of Christ* (Princeton, 1961); see especially 309–45.

early fourteenth century, respectively, further fostered compassionate identification with the sufferings of Christ, especially through their association of these events with particular hours of the day.[10]

There is sometimes confusion about the differences between the Office of the Passion and the Hours of the Cross in the literature dealing with books of hours, a confusion which often stems from the inconsistencies in the titles given to the two texts.[11] The Office of the Passion, however, is longer than the more popular Hours of the Cross—it contains eight hours by contrast to the seven of the Hours of the Cross. Whereas the Hours of the Cross are usually introduced by a rubric stating that they were composed by Pope John XXII,[12] the supposed author of the Office of the Passion, St Bonaventure, is only occasionally mentioned in the introductory rubrics; usually there is no reference to authorship at all.[13] More-

---

[10] Marrow, *Passion Iconography*, 11. The practice of reciting Offices in honour of the Passion at the canonical hours is very old. St Udalric, Bishop of Augsburg (died c.972), recited a Little Office of the Cross and some time later Aelsinus, a monk of the Newminster, composed a similar Office for his superior (Leroquais, *Livres d'heures*, I, xxvi).

[11] The Office of the Passion is variously introduced as, 'officium Passionis domini'; 'officium sacratissime Passionis domini nostri ihesu christi'; 'officium gloriose Passionis domini nostri ihesu christi'; 'officium Passionis et crucis domini nostri ihesu christi'; 'officium de cruce; officium sanctae crucis'; and 'magnum officium crucifixi'. In modern literature dealing with books of hours, the Office of the Passion is also described in a number of different ways; for example, Hours of the Passion; Little Office of the Passion; Hours of the Passion and Cross; or, Long Hours of the Cross.

[12] For example, 'Incipit officium crucifixi compositum per dominum Johannem papam xxii' (The *Adelaide Hours*, c.1375, State Library of South Australia; this manuscript is discussed in detail later in this essay). According to Leroquais, 'Plusieurs manuscrits du XIVe siècle attribuent soit les Heures, soit l'Office à Jean XXII (lat. 757, f. 2v; lat. 1026, f. 440v; lat. 1342, f. 35v); mais il convient d'observer que dès la fin du XIIIe siècle, on trouve l'Office de la Passion dans les Heures à l'usage de Thérouanne (lat. 14284, f. 1-41)' (*Livres d'heures*, xxvi). It seems, however, that he is confusing the two texts, since the attributions to John XXII in the manuscripts cited refer to the Little Hours of the Cross, while the hours for the use of Thérouanne contain the Office of the Passion. The Office of the Passion has never, to my knowledge, been attributed to John XXII.

[13] *S. Doctoris Seraphici S. Bonaventurae opera omnia*, edita studio et cura pp. Collegii a S. Bonaventura (Florence, 1882–1902), VIII, 152–58 lists thirty-eight codices containing this Office. Five contain an attribution to St Bonaventure. One such is Paris, BN MS lat. 16309, which states, 'Incipit Officium sanctae crucis completum a fratre Bonaventura ad preces domini Ludovici'. Tradition has it that the Office was commissioned from Bonaventure by Louis IX. The *Chronica XXIV Generalium* states, 'Hic Generalis ad instantiam domini et sancti Ludovici, regis Franciae, Officium devotissimum de cruce composuit'. *Analecta Francescana*, III (1897), 131. There has been some doubt, however, expressed over the attribution of this text to St Bonaventure; see I. Brady, 'The edition of the *Opera Omnia* of St Bonaventure (1882–1902),' *Archivium franciscum historicum* 70 (1977), 372–74.

over, the two texts often exist side by side in books of hours.[14] The quintessential element of the Office of the Passion is a series of eight hymns on the Passion—one for each canonical hour—of which *In Passione Domini* is the first.[15] The other components are the same as those for breviary Offices, namely psalms and antiphons, canticles, short lessons (at matins), *capitula*; versicles and responses, and concluding prayers for each hour (except matins) based on the collect form.

I have identified three distinct, recurring versions of the Office of the Passion in the twenty-five Italian books of hours that form the basis of this study. In twenty of these the text conforms to one of the three versions. The texts of the remaining five manuscripts are individual variations, most of which are based on the version I have designated as 'Type 3' (see Appendix, Table 1, p. 130). With the exception of the hymn *In Passione Domini*, all the textual elements—psalms, antiphons, lessons, *capitula*, prayers, etc.—vary from version to version and in their combinations.[16] The variations do not seem to indicate liturgical use, chronological period, geographical origin, or association with a particular religious order.

One of the earliest appearances of this Office in a personal prayer book occurs in the *Supplicationes Variae* (Florence, Bibl. Laurenziana MS Plut. XXV. 3) which was produced for use in Genoa in 1293.[17] It also appears in

---

[14] It should be noted that the Office of the Passion in these books of hours is not the first such Office known to us. St Francis also composed an Office of the Passion which he recited in addition to the daily Office. This Office, which was subsequently used by his order, bears little resemblance to the texts found in late medieval Italian books of hours. It is essentially a compilation of verses from selected psalms interspersed with the saint's own words. St Francis' Office has five separate variations, corresponding to changes in the liturgical calendar. See D. Gagnan, 'Office de la Passion, prière quotidienne de St François d'Assise,' *Antonianum* LV (1980), 3–86. For the text see *Legendae S. Francisci Assisiensis saeculis XIII et XIV conscriptae*, ed. Quaracchi (Florence, 1941). Anne Derbes has recently observed a number of interesting correspondences between this office of St Francis and late medieval Italian art; see *Picturing the Passion in Late Medieval Italy. Narrative Painting, Franciscan Ideologies, and the Levant* (Cambridge, 1996), 35, 65, 107–8.

[15] See G.M. Dreves and C. Blume, eds., *Analecta Hymnica Medii Aevi*, 55 vols (Leipzig, 1886–1912), L, no. 568; J. Julian, ed., *A Dictionary of Hymnology*, 2 vols (London, 1907), I, 232 and 566; II, 1187; F.J. Mone, *Lateinische Hymnen des Mittelalters*, 3 vols (Freiburg im Breisgau, 1964), I, 84–91, 112–16; and J. Szöverffy, '"Crux Fidelis . . ." Prolegomena to a history of the Holy Cross Hymns,' *Traditio* 22 (1966), 34–35. Most authors attribute only the hymn for matins, *In Passione Domini*, to St Bonaventure.

[16] See Appendix, Table 2 (138–41).

[17] See A. Neff, 'The *Supplicationes Variae* in Florence: A late Dugento manuscript', (Diss., Univ. of Pennsylvania, 1977) 4–5; A.M. Ciaranfi *Scelta per la Storia dell'Arte*

Boston, Public Library MS qMed. 131, an early fourteenth-century book from the Marches region, which, apart from this Office, contains only the Vigils of the Dead, and a calendar.[18] Strictly speaking, neither of these works is a book of hours; the *Supplicationes*, however, includes all the basic texts of this genre, as well as a large amount of other material; the Boston manuscript is a kind of excerpt of a book of hours. I have included them in this study since they provide early examples of the Office in association with illustrated cycles of the Passion. Both the Boston manuscript and the *Supplicationes Variae* contain the version of the Office ('Type 1') which has been ascribed to St Bonaventure in numerous editions of his works.[19] This version also appears in an early fourteenth-century Franciscan breviary (Vatican, B.V.A. MS lat. 10.000); it is therefore possible that it represents the original text.[20]

These two devotional manuals have extensive pictorial Passion cycles. In the *Supplicationes Variae* they form part of a larger group of forty-five tinted drawings which appear at the end of the manuscript, unaccompanied by text.[21] The Passion illustrations of the Boston manuscript are of particular interest because they are distributed throughout the text of the Office and thus provide an early example of the integration of text and image within the Office of the Passion. The distribution is as follows:

Invitatory	Agony in the garden
Matins	Betrayal
	Christ led away
Lauds	Christ before Annas
	Christ led away
Prime	Christ before Caiaphas
	Buffeting and Mocking of Christ
Terce	Christ before Pilate
	Flagellation

(Florence, 1988), 325–48, and B. Degenhart and A. Schmitt, *Corpus der italienischen Zeichnungen, 1300–1450*, 3 vols (Berlin, 1968), I, 7–16.

[18] See Sticca, *Officium*, 144–99.

[19] *S. Bonaventurae opera omnia*, VIII, 152–68; see above, n. 13. It should be noted that while the text of the Office of the Passion in the Boston manuscript conforms in general to 'Type 1', there are some slight deviations; for example, the psalm for compline is 'Beatus qui intelligit' (Psalm 40), instead of the usual Psalm 87, 'Domine Deus salutis meae'.

[20] See P. Salmon, *Les Manuscrits Liturgiques Latins de la Bibliothèque Vaticane. I: Psautiers, Antiphonaires, Hymnaires, Collectaires, Bréviaires* (Vatican, 1968), 191–92.

[21] The *Supplicationes* also contains an initial with the Flagellation and a rondel with the Crucifixion at matins. Subsequent hours are accompanied by images of single figures, some shown in prayer. See Neff, 'The *Supplicationes*, Fig. 22. For illustration of the *Supplicationes Variae* drawings see Degenhart and Schmitt, *Corpus*, 1, Pls 7–18 and Figs 12–14.

Sext	Christ before Herod
	Carrying the Cross
None	Christ stripped
	Crucifixion
Vespers	Longinus strikes Christ's side
	Deposition
Compline	Entombment [22]

In all but two of the twenty-five manuscripts in this group the Office of the Passion is accompanied by imagery of some kind. In eleven of the books it is associated with full Passion cycles and in one with an Old Testament cycle. In one matins is introduced by a depiction of the Man of Sorrows, in another by the Flagellation and the Crucifixion; in both of these manuscripts various religious figures preface subsequent hours. In seven of the manuscripts the beginning of the Office is marked by a representation of the Betrayal, the Crucifixion, or the Man of Sorrows, while one manuscript has a depiction of the cross at each hour. One book is embellished with decorative initials only and two of the group are not illuminated.[23]

Apart from the Boston manuscript, the Passion cycles in this group are normally made up of an introductory illustration for each hour of the Office. These scenes follow a chronological order which is present in the text of the Office itself; they often illustrate the particular episode from the Passion that is highlighted in the hymn and the concluding prayer for each hour. Text and image are thus closely paralleled. From time to time, however, this parallelism is modified and it would seem that textual and visual traditions developed with some independence of each other. Nevertheless, the underlying unity of sentiment throughout the Office and the intrinsic connection of all the Passion events means that even when the illustrations do not precisely match those singled out in the hymn or concluding prayer, they resonate with the general tenor of the text.[24]

In order to demonstrate more precisely the relationship between text and illustrative cycle in the Office of the Passion, I have selected one particular manuscript—referred to here as the *Adelaide Hours*—for detailed analysis. This approach also allows for comparisons to be made, as

---

[22] Photographs of the Boston manuscript were unavailable on account of the book's tight binding. See, however, Sticca, *Officium*, Pl. I –XVI.

[23] See Appendix, Table 1 (130–37).

[24] This synchronization is also often present in illustrated Hours of the Cross since the hymns and prayers of these shorter hours also progress systematically through the Passion narrative. It is not a feature, however, of the Little Office or Hours of the Virgin where the text is not structured chronologically.

appropriate, with other manuscripts in the group. The *Adelaide Hours*, now in the State Library of South Australia, was probably illuminated in central Italy (perhaps near Chiusi) c.1375.[25] Historiated initials illustrate its Office of the Passion as follows:

Matins	Betrayal
Lauds	Christ before Pilate
Prime	Flagellation
Terce	Carrying the Cross
Sext	Crucifixion
None	Crucifixion
Vespers	Deposition
Compline	Entombment[26]

MATINS AND LAUDS[27]

(i) Matins: Betrayal of Christ (Fig. 31)

The representation of the Betrayal of Christ in the opening initial of matins, though small in scale, exploits the dramatic potential of this theme. As in Giotto's depiction of the same subject in the Scrovegni Chapel, attention is focused on the emotional confrontation between Christ and Judas, expressed through the intensity and directness of their eye contact.[28] The crowding of the group of three-quarter length figures into the confines of the small space helps to convey the sense that Christ has been set upon and trapped, while with raised hand he seems to question what is taking place. By causing the figures to overlap parts of the initial, the illuminator takes the action into the viewer's space, a particularly effective device in an image designed to provide a contemplative focus during the recitation of the accompanying prayers.

The text for the hour of matins in the *Adelaide Hours* does not focus on any single event of the Passion narrative. Its invitatory versicle is a call to recite the Office in praise of 'Christ the King, the Lord, crucified',[29] and the hymn *In Passione Domini* which follows the invitatory psalm, encompasses the whole mystery of Christ's Passion and death, presenting the redemptive power of his sufferings as a source of compassion and hope

---

[25] See M. Manion and V. Vines, *Medieval and Renaissance Illuminated Manuscripts in Australian Collections* (London, 1984), No. 14 (70–71). This manuscript contains the version of the Office designated as 'Type 2' in Appendix, Table 1 (132–33).

[26] For details of the Passion cycles in other books in this sample and the way in which they compare with the *Adelaide Hours*, see Appendix, Table 1 (130–37).

[27] Biblical citations throughout are from the Douai Bible.

[28] See J.H. Stubblebine, *Giotto, The Arena Chapel Frescoes*, (London, 1969), Figs 41–42.

[29] 'Regem Christum crucifixum dominum.'

for the devout: 'In the Lord's Passion, by which salvation was given to man, let there be our rest and heart's desire.'[30] The reader is called upon to bear in mind all the details of the Passion—the punishments, the insults, the crown of thorns, the cross, the nails, the lance, the bitter drink of vinegar and gall—so that steeped in compassion for Christ's sufferings and worshipping him crucified, one may come to enjoy with him the fruits of salvation in heaven.[31] It is only in its concluding verse that the hymn refers specifically to the Betrayal, the opening scene in this grand scenario: 'Praise and honour, O Christ, sold and betrayed without cause, who suffered death for mankind, on the bitter gibbet.'[32]

Within this context, however, it is not difficult to interpret psalm 87, which follows on from the hymn, in terms of the betrayal and arrest of Christ. Both its antiphon, 'I was delivered up and came not forth: my eyes languished through poverty' (vs 9–10), and verses such as, 'Thy wrath hath come upon me and thy terrors have troubled me. They have come round about me like water all the day: they have compassed me about together. Friend and neighbour thou hast put far from me: and my acquaintance, because of misery' (vs 17–19), emphasize the theme of treachery and desertion; this is reinforced by the versicles and responses from Jeremiah (12:7) recited at the end of the psalm: 'I have forsaken my house, I have left my inheritance; I have given my dear soul into the hand of her enemies'.

By contrast, the lesson from Isaiah (53:2–5), which concludes matins, calls to mind the mystery of the Passion as such, rather than one particular episode. Along with an especially poignant image of 'a man of sorrows . . . familiar with suffering' the lesson emphasizes the redemptive nature of Christ's sufferings: 'he was wounded for our iniquities, he was bruised for our sins, on him lies a punishment which brings us peace, and through his wounds we are healed.' The accompanying versicle and response from the lamentations of Jeremiah (1:12) reiterate the theme of compassion, putting the words of the prophet into the mouth of the suffering Christ: 'O all ye that pass by the way, attend, and see if there be any sorrow like to my sorrow. Look all you nations and see my suffering.'

It is worth noting that while matins in the *Adelaide Hours* contains only this one lesson, most versions of the Office have three lessons which,

---

[30] 'In Passione domini/qua datur salus homini/sit nostrum refrigerium/et cordis desiderium.'

[31] 'Portemus in memoria/et penas et obprobria/Christi, coronem spinem/crucem, clavos et lanceam. Et plagas sacratissimas/omni laude dignissimas/acetum, fel, arundinem/ mortis amaritudinem. /Hec omnia nos satient/et dulciter inebrient/nos repleant virtutibus/et gloriosis fructibus.'

[32] 'Laus, honor Christe vendito/et sine causa prodito/passo mortem pro populo/in aspero patibulo.'

taken together, encompass the whole narrative of the Passion. In the Boston manuscript, for example, the first lesson combines John and Matthew's accounts of the scourging and mocking of Christ (John 19:1–3, Matthew 27:30); the second John and Luke's description of Christ carrying the cross to Calvary and his crucifixion (John 19:16–18, Luke 23:34); and the third gives John's account of Christ thirsting on the cross, the offer of vinegar, and his words, 'It is consummated '(John 19:28–30). The three lessons for the other versions of the Office are taken from the Gospel of Matthew (26:47–49, 50–65, and 27:27–46 respectively); they begin with the arrest of Christ and conclude with his death.

As the principal hour of the Office, matins thus directs the reader to contemplate the sufferings of Christ in a spirit of compassion and hope. The introductory historiated initial provides a visual cue to the narrative that unfolds in the course of the Office, as well as focusing more specifically on the theme of betrayal which is also present in the text.

(ii) Lauds: Christ before Pilate (Fig. 32)

The opening initial for lauds shows Christ interrogated by Pilate. Christ's head is bowed and he gathers his robe around him in a gesture of withdrawal, calling to mind his refusal to answer the charges of his accusers. The restricted space of the initial is again used to advantage, with the crowding together of the three nearly full-length figures adding to the sense of harassment.

It is customary for the recitation of lauds to follow directly on from matins and originally it was not thought of as a separate hour. Its text reflects this. The hymn, for example, like that of matins, is comprehensive in scope, and while referring to the 'blessed scars, spits, whips and insults' inflicted on the Saviour, celebrates his triumph over death and suffering, rather than dwelling on any particular episode of the Passion: 'Let the congregation praise Christ the leader who through his cross, redeemed us from the enemy. Let our happy company exalt the heavens with praises.'[33] The concluding prayer that rounds off both matins and lauds sums up the whole series of events associated with 'the early morning hour' (*matinali*):

> Lord Jesus Christ, who at the early morning hour allowed yourself to be betrayed, seized, bound, struck on the face and spat upon for the salvation of mankind, grant that we may seek reproaches and insults for the glory of your name and that we may continually recall this your most sacred Passion

---

[33] Christum ducem/qui per crucem/redemit nos ab hostibus/laudet cetus/noster letus/ exultet celum laudibus.

so that through it we may deserve happily to arrive at the comfort of your resurrection.[34]

Partly, it would seem, because of the more indeterminate nature of lauds in the framework of the canonical hours, it is illustrated in this group of manuscripts by a variety of different subjects drawn from the early part of the Passion. A late fourteenth-century book of hours, probably for Treviso use (London, BL Add. MS 15265; Fig. 33) for example, depicts the Mocking and Buffeting of Christ. As well as being referred to in both the hymn and the concluding prayer, these torments are also conjured up by the words of Jeremiah used for the versicle and response after the hymn: 'He shall give his cheek to him that striketh him: he shall be filled with reproaches ' (Lamentations, 3:30). Devotional treatises of the period often focussed on this aspect of Christ's sufferings and may well have influenced the illustrative programmes of books of hours. The author of *The Meditations*, for example, dramatically recreates the scene:

> Now they examine him and procure false witnesses . . . who condemn him and spit on his most sacred face, blindfold him, smite him, strike him, saying, 'Prophesy, who is it that struck you'.[35]

While the various interrogations and trials of Christ—before Annas and Caiaphas, Pilate and Herod—were also important in both literary and visual tradition, it is more usual for the appearance of Christ before Pilate to illustrate prime in this group of manuscripts, for reasons which I will discuss shortly. The position of this scene at lauds, however, in the *Adelaide Hours* is logical chronologically, and it resonates with Psalm 58 which is recited at this hour. According to tradition this psalm was composed by David when he was being persecuted by Saul, and its antiphon (vs. 4) throws into relief the theme of persecution by the powerful: 'For behold, they have caught my soul: the mighty have rushed in upon me.'

THE LITTLE HOURS: PRIME, TERCE, SEXT AND NONE

As with the breviary model on which they are based, these shorter hours all follow the same format: a hymn of only two stanzas; antiphon and psalm; *capitulum*; versicles and responses; and concluding prayer. Texts here focus more sharply on the particular events of the Passion that had come to be associated with each hour.

---

[34] 'Domine Ihesu Christi qui hora matinali pro salute humana tradi capi et ligari alapis cedi et conspui voluisti. Fac nos quesumus contumelias et obprobria pro tui nominis gloria letanter suscipere et sic huius tue sacratissime Passionis memoria continue recordari ut ad tue resurrectionis confortium mereamur feliciter pervenire.'

[35] Ragusa and Green, eds, *Meditations*, 326–27.

(i) Prime: Flagellation (Pl. 4)

The dramatic close-up type of composition, often favoured by the illuminator of the *Adelaide Hours*, is at its most compelling in the depiction of the Flagellation. Not only is the tension between Christ and his assailant feelingly communicated, but the vulnerable, semi-naked body of the Saviour almost startlingly confronts the viewer, inviting emotional participation in the scene.

While the hymn for prime refers to the blindfolding and mocking of Christ: 'You, O sun of justice, whose face was veiled and who was ridiculed by fickle people on bended knee',[36] the concluding prayer is based on the tradition that at the first light or watch of the day Christ was brought before Pilate:

> Lord Jesus Christ, the judge of judges, you who at the first hour of the day were brought before the presidium of Pilate and underwent the harshest of judgements, we humbly beseech you that you may come to us wretched ones as judge so that we may not be damned to eternal suffering but deserve to be in the company of your faithful in heaven.[37]

Understandably, in five manuscripts of this survey Christ appears before Pilate at prime.[38] The Flagellation is also appropriate, however, since it resulted from Pilate's order and the intense confrontational image of this subject in the *Adelaide Hours* movingly encapsulates the theme of physical assault and indignity present in both the mocking and buffeting of Christ and his scourging.

(ii) Terce: Carrying of the Cross (Fig. 34)

At terce the image of Christ carrying the Cross is precisely paralleled in the hymn:

> Christ, who at the third hour were led to execution, bearing the cross on your shoulders for us wretched ones, make us so to love you and to live such holy lives that we may enjoy heavenly rest at home with you.[39]

The illustration also reflects the concluding prayer:

---

[36] 'Tu qui velatis facie/fuisti sol iustitie/flexus illusus genibus/cesus quoque verberibus.'

[37] 'Domine Ihesu Christe qui hora diei prima pilato presidi presentatus fuisti iudex iudicum [sic] iudicium durissimum pertulisti tibi humiliter supplicamus ut nobis miseris subvenias iudicando ne in extremo iudicio eterno dampnemur supplicio. Sed [cum] tuis in celestibus mereamur fidelibus sociari.'

[38] See Appendix, Table 1 (130-37).

[39] 'Hora qui ductus tertia/fuisti ad supplicia/Christe, ferendo humeris/crucem pro nobis miseris./Fac nos sic te diligere/sanctamque vitam ducere/ut valeamus requie/frui celestis patrie.'

Lord Jesus Christ, you who at the third hour of the day were led to the punishment of death for the salvation of the world, we beseech you to destroy all our sins by virtue of your most holy Passion and lead us mercifully to your eternal glory.[40]

A sense of movement in Christ's body as he advances on his painful journey is expressed by the way in which his body overlaps part of the letter 'D', so that he appears to move towards the viewer's space.

Often illustrations of this scene include men armed with hammers, ladders and nails as in the illustration which accompanies terce in London, BL Add. MS 15265. This is in keeping with Psalm 108, used here and its antiphon (vs. 3):

They have spoken against me with deceitful tongues. They have compassed me about with words of hatred: they have fought me without cause.

The illuminator of the *Adelaide Hours*, however, has chosen to stress the theme of compassion, and depicts Christ surrounded not by his persecutors but by his sorrowing friends—the Virgin on the left and a nimbed male figure on the right.

The *capitulum* exhorts the faithful to follow the suffering Christ:

Christ also suffered for us, leaving you an example that you should follow his steps; who did no sin, neither was guile found in his mouth ' (1 Pet. 2:21–23).

The versicle and response hold up to the devout the ideal of Christ's inner freedom and quiet courage: 'He offered because it was his own will, and he opened not his mouth' (Isaiah 53:7). While terce is most often illustrated by the Carrying of the Cross, variations occur in some manuscripts to allow for more emphasis on earlier events or because of different approaches to the illustration of matins and lauds that have a flow-on effect.[41]

(iii) Sext: Christ Crucified, Offered Vinegar to Drink (Fig. 35)

The frequent inclusion of two illustrations devoted to the Crucifixion is one of the most distinctive characteristics of Passion cycles in Italian books of hours. This is in contrast to French or Flemish programmes where it is more usual for the illustration of the Crucifixion at sext to be followed by

---

[40] 'Domine Ihesu Christi qui hora diei tertia ad mortis poenam pro mundi salute ductus es te suppliciter obsecramus ut per virtutem tue sancti sanctissime Passionis omnia peccata nostra deleas et [misericorditer nos per ducas] ad tue beatudinis gloriam [sempiternam].' The scribe of the *Adelaide Hours* omits the text in brackets.

[41] See Appendix, Table 1 (130–37).

the Deposition at none.⁴² In the *Adelaide Hours* the dying Christ is offered vinegar to drink at sext; at none he is shown dead on the cross (Fig. 36).

This concentration on the details of the crucifixion narrative reflects the fact that traditionally the sixth hour marked the raising of Christ on the cross and the ninth the hour of his death. In Italian books of hours both text and images adhere closely to this tradition, which is also kept alive in contemporary devotional literature such as the *Meditations on the Life of Christ*.⁴³ The introductory historiated initial in the *Adelaide Hours* provides a simple and effective cue to the sentiments expressed in the concluding prayer:

> Lord Jesus Christ, at the sixth hour of the day, you mounted the gibbet of the cross and thirsting on it for our salvation, you permitted yourself to be given vinegar and gall. Grant us to thirst for the chalice of your Passion with ardent hearts set on fire and to delight perpetually in you the one God and crucified Lord.⁴⁴

There were of course rich visual as well as literary renderings of the Crucifixion for the illuminators of these books to draw on, and the compositions in some of the other manuscripts are far more detailed. The illustration for sext in the Bolognese book of hours, London, BL Add. MS 34247, for example, provides a literal interpretation of the words of the hymn: 'His sacred hands and feet were pierced by nails' (Fig. 37).⁴⁵ In an image of great immediacy Christ is nailed to the cross; the whole composition is tilted towards the viewer, who is spared none of the horrifying details.⁴⁶ The dramatic quality of this scene suggests the possible influence of contemporary Passion plays or of passages such as the following from *The Meditations*:

---

⁴² This assessment is based on examples of narrative Passion illustrations in French and Flemish manuscripts in Leroquais, *Livres d'heures* and *Supplement* (Macon, 1943), and Wieck et al., *The Book of Hours*. There are, of course, well known examples of French and Flemish manuscripts which do not fit this generalisation, but instead follow the pattern of Italian illustrative programmes; for example, the *Très Riches Heures,* Chantilly, Musée Condé MS 65, and the *Petites Heures,* Paris, BN MS lat. 18014.

⁴³ Ragusa and Green, eds, *Meditations*, 333–38. I am grateful to Margaret Manion for suggesting to me the significance of *The Meditations*.

⁴⁴ 'Domine Ihesu Christe qui hora diei sexta crucis patibulum ascendisti in qua salutem nostram siciens felle et aceto potari te permisti. Te suppliciter deprecamur ut accenso et inflammato corde nostro sicire nos facias tue calicem Passionis et in te solo deo ac domino crucifixo iugiter delectari.'

⁴⁵ 'Crucem pro nobis subiit/et stans in illa sitiit./Ihesus sacratis manibus/clavis fossique pedibus.'

⁴⁶ Other images of the Passion in this manuscript are similarly evocative. This is partly because of the masterful use of perspectival space by the artist. The quatrefoils appear as windows through which the viewer glimpses the dramatic events.

With your mind's eye see some thrusting the cross into the earth, others equipped with nails and hammers, others with the ladder and other instruments, giving orders about what should be done, and others stripping him.[47]

Psalm 21, parts of which were quoted by Christ on the cross, is recited in the *Adelaide Hours* at sext. It, too, prompts the reader to contemplate diverse aspects of the crucifixion drama. The cruelty of the mocking crowd of onlookers, for example, is conjured up in the antiphon (vs. 8), 'All they that saw me have laughed me to scorn: they have spoken with the lips, and wagged the head'; and the evangelists themselves interpreted the verses, 'They have dug my hands and feet . . . They have parted my garments amongst them; and upon my vestments they cast lots' (vs. 18–19), as referring to the nailing of Christ to the cross and to the division of His garments among the soldiers.[48]

Whereas the illustrations in the *Adelaide Hours* operate as effective cues to the theme of a particular hour by virtue of their very selectivity, the illumination of the Office of the Passion in the Bolognese book of hours, Kremsmünster, Stiftsbibliothek MS Cim. 4, is characterized by a wealth of detail.[49] Although much of this resonates with the relevant psalms and with contemporary devotional literature, there is not the same degree of synchronization with the schedule of events laid down in the hymn and prayer for each hour. Only one crucifixion scene, for example, appears in this cycle and this is at none (Fig. 38). It incorporates several phases and aspects of the event into the one composition after the manner of contemporary Trecento fresco and panel painting, including such dramatic and emotional motifs as the crowd of onlookers that stare and point at Christ, the soldier offering him vinegar to drink, Longinus about to pierce his side with a lance, the sorrowing Magdalen and the swooning Virgin.

(iv) None: Christ Dead on the Cross (Fig. 36)

In the historiated initial for none the death of Christ is subtly and effectively differentiated from the torments of the crucifixion commemorated at the preceding hour. While the general configuration of the two illustrations is remarkably similar, the head of Christ is now bowed, and drooping arms and sagging torso replace the taut physique of the figure on the cross in the illustration for sext; blood pours forth from the wounds in his hands, feet and side. The viewer is exhorted to ponder these mysteries

---

[47] Ragusa and Green, eds, *Meditations,* 333.
[48] See Matt. 27:35.
[49] At least two episodes of the Passion are depicted in most of the historiated initials.

with compassion and steadfastness through identification with the Virgin, standing resolutely by the cross from the sixth to the ninth hour. She is joined at none by the sorrowing St John, who replaces the soldier and his offer of the bitter drink that increased rather than assuaged the torments of Christ's dying moments.

The illustration for none is very much in tune with the hymn for this hour which focuses on the heroic and redemptive nature of Christ's death rather than its indignities:

> May the blessed Passion of Christ be our liberation, and through it may the joys of heaven be prepared for us. Glory to Christ the Lord who, hanging on the cross, surrendered his spirit and, with a cry, saved a lost world.[50]

Similar sentiments are expressed in the concluding prayer:

> Lord Jesus Christ at the ninth hour of the day, with hands spread out on the cross and head bowed, you surrendered your spirit to God your Father opening paradise with your noble death. Grant in your mercy, to us unworthy ones, what we beg of you, that at the hour of our death our souls may come to you who is true paradise.[51]

Whereas the illuminator of the *Adelaide Hours* shows only the blood pouring from the wounds of Christ, sometimes the illustration for none includes the image of Longinus thrusting a lance into Christ's side.[52] This episode, based on the Gospel of St John, has a long history in the representation of the Crucifixion; but its popularity in late medieval art seems to have been heightened by the development of an intense devotion to the wounds of Christ.[53] Another reflection of this devotion is an introductory rubric in some manuscripts (for example, in the Bolognese hours at Kremsmünster) recommending that five verses of each psalm in the Office of the Passion be recited in honour of the five wounds of Christ.[54]

---

[50] 'Beata Christi passio/sit nostra liberatio/ut per hanc nobis gaudia/parata sint celestia./Gloria Christo domino/qui pendens in patibulo/clamans emisit spiritum/mundumque salvans perditum.'

[51] 'Domine Ihesu Christe qui hora diei nona expansis in cruce manibus et inclinato capite deo patri spiritum tradidisti et clave tue dignatissime mortis paradisum reserasti. Concede nobis indignis supplicationibus nostris ut in hora mortis nostre animas nostras ad te qui vere paradisus es facias misericorditer pervenire.'

[52] See Appendix, Table 1 (130–37).

[53] See M. Rubin, *Corpus Christi, The Eucharist in Late Medieval Culture* (Cambridge, 1991), 157 and 302–6; J. Leclercq, *Spirituality*, 185; and *New Catholic Encyclopaedia*, 14, 1035–37; see also M.M. Manion (Chapter 2 above, 37–38).

[54] 'Incipit officium sacratissime Passionis domini nostri Ihesu christi in quod quolibet psalmo [sic] dicuntur quinque versus tantum in memoria quinque vulnerum Ihesu christi . . .' This reflects the recommendation of St Joscia of St Bertin that psalms be sung in honour of the five wounds; see Leclercq, *Spirituality*, 185.

An unusual illustration for the hour of none in another Bolognese book of hours, London, BL Add. MS 34247 (Fig. 39), dwells in detail on St John's account of the piercing of the side of Christ:

> but when they (the soldiers) came to Jesus, and saw that he was already dead, they did not break his legs: but one of the soldiers opened his side with a spear; and immediately there came out blood and water (John 19:33–34).

The Fathers of the Church interpreted this passage as denoting the birth of the Church, which springs, like another Eve from the side of Christ the second Adam; and they associated the water and the blood with the life-giving sacraments of baptism and the Eucharist.[55] The illustration follows this interpretation quite literally with the Crucifixion being flanked by the celebration of the eucharist on one side and a baptism on the other. The blood from the wound in Christ's side flows into the chalice and the water into the font. Here the Crucifixion itself is rendered as a kind of vision, with the neophyte looking up towards Christ whose body seems to hover mid-way between the two sacramental representations.

VESPERS AND COMPLINE

The spirit of the final two hours of the Office of the Passion is that of quiet mourning over the body of Christ in the company of the Virgin and a few of Christ's trusted friends and disciples.

The structure of vespers is distinguished from that of the 'little hours' of prime, terce, etc., by a longer hymn, comparable to those of matins and lauds, and the inclusion of the canticle of the *Magnificat*, a regular component of vespers in Offices of the breviary. Like all the other hours, the remaining texts of vespers comprise a psalm, antiphon, versicles, responses, *capitulum* and concluding prayer in the collect form. Compline has the shorter two-stanza type of hymn and the canticle *Nunc dimittis*, traditionally part of the last hour of the day. Otherwise its textual elements are the same as for vespers and the 'little hours'.

(i) Vespers: Deposition (Fig. 40)

In the introductory historiated initial for vespers of the *Adelaide Hours* the taking down of the body of Christ from the cross is combined with a pietà-type image of Mary mourning her dead son. While the cross and ladder in the background allude to the Deposition, Christ is already being embraced by his mother at its foot in the respectful and sympathetic presence of Joseph of Arimathea, St John and one of the holy women. Psalm 56, which begins this hour, is a song of vigil whose antiphon aptly evokes an

---

[55] See *Jerusalem Bible*, English edition (London, 1966), New Testament, 189, n. 19r.

image of the Lord finally delivered from his tormentors: 'God hath sent his mercy and his truth and he hath delivered my soul from the midst of the young lions. I slept troubled' (vs. 5); and the psalmist's plea for the mercy and shelter of God while he waits until the 'iniquity pass away', so that he may 'arise early' may be interpreted as an expression of hope in the Resurrection.

The hymn for vespers, like those of matins and lauds, while referring to a number of Christ's sufferings celebrates the mystery of salvation rather than singling out any particular episode for contemplation. The concluding prayer, however, makes explicit reference both to the Deposition and Mary's reception of Christ's body:

> Lord Jesus Christ, having been put to death for the sake of humanity, at the hour of vespers you were taken down from the cross already dead and, according to pious belief, willingly gave yourself into your mother's arms, graciously grant that having laid down the burden of our sins, we may be worthy to be presented before your divine majesty.[56]

The illustration of the *Adelaide Hours* is in complete accord with this prayer.

(ii) Compline: Entombment (Fig. 41)

As with the illustrations of the Crucifixion at sext and none, those for vespers and compline reflect different phases of a common theme and are visually closely related. The composition for compline repeats the close-up presentation of the dead Christ in the vespers initial; and a similar, though not identical, group of figures grieves with the Virgin; but Christ is now shrouded in burial clothes, and leafy trees replace ladder and cross in the background, indicating that the setting has changed from Golgotha to the burial site. The emphasis here, too, is on the compassion of Mary and a small band of faithful followers.

The hymn for compline calls on the reader to turn to Christ, identifying with the mysterious experience of his body awaiting the resurrection: 'You, O innocent king, who lay dead in the stone tomb, you grant that we may always rest in you and give you praise.'[57] The last part of the text for this hour is missing, but it can be reconstructed by reference to other manuscripts containing the same version of the Office. It is

---

[56] 'Domine Ihesu Christe qui hora vespertina pro humana salute iam morte peremptus de cruce deponi et in tue matris manibus, ut pie creditur, recipi voluisti, concede propitius, ut depositis peccatorum nostrorum sarcinis, ante conspectum divine maiestatis tue presentari valeamus.'

[57] 'Qui iacuisti mortuus/in petra, rex innocuus/fac nos in te quiescere/semperque laudes reddere.'

highly probable, therefore, that the concluding prayer was also a call to remember with compassion the death of Christ:

> Lord Jesus Christ, who at the last hour of the day lay quietly at rest in the sepulchre, wept and lamented over by your most worthy mother and the other women, grant, we beseech you, that your Passion may make our passionate tears run freely and that with all the devotion of our hearts we may always lament that same Passion and with ardent desire keep its memory ever fresh.[58]

The inclusion of the Deposition and the Entombment at vespers and compline, respectively, in illustrative Passion cycles seems to be a characteristic of Italian books of hours and most of the cycles in this survey follow this pattern.[59] The concentration on the time between the death of Christ and his Resurrection is, as we have seen, present in the text itself and flows from the association of the evening hours with a time of waiting or vigil in anticipation of the Resurrection that begins the new day. As with the inclusion of two Crucifixion scenes, this emphasis seems further to distinguish the Italian programmes from their French and Flemish counterparts, since the latter often conclude the Passion cycle with an image of the Resurrection.[60]

This analysis demonstrates how the subject-matter of both the text and the illustration of the Office of the Passion is systematically related to specific times of the day. In particular the hymns and concluding prayers for each hour make explicit this connection. The psalms and other scriptural passages from which the versicles, responses, *capitula* and lessons are taken lend themselves to interpretation in the light of the declared focus of the hour, but there is also another dynamic at work. Along with the phased presentation, the Passion is also presented as a single entity: all of Christ's sufferings are part of the mystery of redemption and salvation, and the reader is urged throughout to identify compassionately with these sufferings precisely because they are the witness of Christ's love for the human race and a source of hope.

As the text and the images move through the Passion narrative they constantly remind the reader of earlier stages and anticipate others; building up a rich network of associations in the course of the day. It is not difficult to understand, therefore, the popularity and the effectiveness

---

[58] 'Domine Ihesu Christi qui hora diei ultima in sepulchro quievisti et a matre tua meritissima et aliis mulieribus planctus et lamentatus fuisti. Fac nos quesumus Passionis tue cum Passionis lacrimis abundare et tota cordis devotione ipsam Passionem tuam semper plangere et eam quasi recentem cum ardenti desiderio retinere.'

[59] See Appendix, Table 1 (130–37).

[60] See the many examples of narrative Passion illustrations in French and Flemish manuscripts in Leroquais, *Livres d'heures* and *Supplement*, and Wieck, *Time Sanctified*.

of this devotion in honour of the Passion, in which text and image mutually reinforce one another particularly, it would seem, in Italian books of hours.

Appendix

TABLE 1. Illustration of the Office of the Passion according to textual 'types'

TYPE 1

Manuscript	Illustration			
	invitatory	matins	lauds	prime
[1] Florence Biblioteca Laurenziana MS Plut. XXV.3 Genoa 1293	—	Flagellation Crucifixion	—	Man holding a torch
[2] Boston, Public Library MS qMed.131 Marches c.1325	Christ Agony in the garden	Betrayal Christ led away Beardless male saint Beardless male saint Bearded male saint	Christ before Annas Christ taken to Caiphas Christ	Christ before Caiaphas Mocking of Christ Christ blindfolded Christ
[3] London, British Library MS Add. 34247 Bologna late 14th century	—	Crucifixion Christ blessing	Flagellation Christ blessing	Christ before Pilate
[4] Oxford Bodleian Library MS Canon.Liturg. 146 Bologna late 14th century	—	Man of Sorrows	—	—
[5] Rovigo Biblioteca dell'Accademia dei Concordi MS Silv. 53 Florence? late 14th century	—	Crucifixion Resurrection	—	—

TYPE 1

Illustration

terce	sext	none	vespers	compline
[1] Poor Clare, reading	Franciscan, reading	Dominican, pointing to a book	Young man (added later)	Young woman
[2] Christ before Pilate	Christ before Herod	Christ stripped	Crucifixion	Entombment/ Lamentation
Flagellation	Carrying the Cross	Crucifixion	Deposition	
[3] Mocking of Christ	Christ nailed to Cross	Crucifixion	Deposition/ Pietà	Entombment
[4] —	—	—	—	—
[5] —	—	—	—	—

TYPE 2

Manuscript	Illustration			
	invitatory	matins	lauds	prime
[6] Vatican Biblioteca Apostolica MS Reggiana 165 L'Aquila c.1400	Man of Sorrows	Betrayal	Christ before Caiaphas	Christ before Pilate
[7] Adelaide State Library of South Australia n.n. Central Italy c.1375	—	Betrayal	Christ before Pilate	Flagellation
[8] Munich Bayerische Staatsbibliothek MS Lat. 23215 Milan c.1378	—	Betrayal	—	Christ before Caiaphas
[9] London British Library MS Add. 15265 Treviso late 14th century	Betrayal	Christ before Caiaphas Man of Sorrows	Mocking of Christ St John the Baptist	Christ before Pilate St Peter(?)
[10] Oxford Bodleian Library MS Canon. Liturg. 268 Fiesole late 14th century	—	Crucifixion	—	—
[11] Oxford Bodleian Library MS Canon. Liturg. 274 Milan early 15th century		[decorated initials at each hour]		

TYPE 2

Illustration

terce	sext	none	vespers	compline
[6] Carrying the Cross	Christ nailed to Cross	Crucifixion	Deposition	Entombment
[7] Carrying the Cross	Crucifixion	Crucifixion	Deposition/ Pietà	Entombment
[8] Christ before Pilate	Christ nailed to Cross	Crucifixion	Deposition	Entombment/ Pietà
[9] Carrying the Cross	Crucifixion	Deposition Resurrection	Entombment	'Noli me Tangere'
Male saint	Christ	Christ	Male saint	Male saint
[10] —	—	—	—	—
[11] —	—	—	—	—

TYPE 3

Manuscript	Illustration			
	invitatory	matins	lauds	prime
[12] Rimini Biblioteca Civica Gambalunga Sc. MS 23 Florence c.1450		[not illustrated]		
[13] Novara Biblioteca Seminario MS 1 Siena c.1375	—	Crucifixion	—	—
[14] Paris Bibliothèque Nationale MS Lat. 1342 Venice? c.1380	—	Man of Sorrows	—	—
[15] Paris Bibliothèque Nationale MS Lat. 1352 (missal-hours) Padua late 14th century	—	Last Supper	Trans- figuration	Agony in the garden
[16] Vatican Biblioteca Apostolica MS Chigi. D IV 52 Bologna late 14th century	—	[missing]	Cross	Cross
[17] Florence Biblioteca Nazionale MS Landau-Finaly 22 Milan c.1394–95, c.1428–30	—	Punishment of Achan Joshua stops the sun	Ehud presents a gift to Eglon	Ehud slays Eglon
[18] The Hague Koninklijke Bibliotheek MS 76 F 6 Milan c.1400	—	Betrayal	[decorated initials at sub- sequent hours; completed c.1500 in Spain]	
[19] Modena Biblioteca Estense MS Lat. 831 Siena? early 15th century	—	Man of Sorrows	Angel in prayer	Dominican in prayer

TYPE 3

Illustration

terce	sext	none	vespers	compline
[12] —	—	—	—	—
[13] —	—	—	—	—
[14] —	—	—	—	—
[15] Betrayal	Flagellation	Crucifixion	Entombment	Resurrection
[16] Cross	Cross	Cross	Cross	Cross
[17] Jael slays Sisera	Jephtha sacrifices his daughter	Samson slays a lion	Samson slays the Philistines	Foxes with firebrands
[18]				
[19] Figure in prayer	Religious figure in prayer	Saint with book	Dominican saint with book and arrow	Hermit saint

TYPE 3

Manuscript	Illustration			
	invitatory	matins	lauds	prime
[20] Oxford Bodleian Library MS Canon.Liturg. 246 Venice early 15th century	—	Crucifixion	—	—

TYPE 3 variation A[61]

Manuscript	invitatory	matins	lauds	prime
[21] Kremsmünster Stiftsbibliothek MS Cim. 4 Bologna 1349	Raising of Lazarus / Entry into Jerusalem	Last Supper / Washing of Feet / Agony in the Garden	Betrayal / Peter cuts off Malchus' ear	Flagellation / Pilate enthroned
[22] Oxford Keble College MS 59 (psalter-hours) Padua early 15th century	—	David in prayer	Agony in the Garden	Mocking of Christ

TYPE 3 variation B

Manuscript	invitatory	matins	lauds	prime
[23] Modena Biblioteca Estense MS Lat. 842 Milan c.1390	—	Betrayal Saints Ambrose and Augustine	Flagellation	Christ before Pilate
[24] London British Library MS Add. 17466 Pavia? 1412	Last Supper	Figure kneeling in prayer	—	Betrayal

---

[61] The following four manuscripts represent two variations based on 'Type 3'. For the most part, they share the same lessons, *capitula*, prayers, versicles, responses and many of the antiphons of Type 3. They differ in their psalms; and while many of these are also held in common they occur in different sequences.

TYPE 3

Illustration

terce	sext	none	vespers	compline
[20] —	—	—	—	—

TYPE 3 variation A

| [21] Man of Sorrows | Pilate frees Barabbas/ Carrying the Cross | Crucifixion | Deposition | Entombment/ Pietà |
| [22] Carrying the Cross | Christ nailed to Cross | Crucifixion | Deposition | Entombment |

TYPE 3 variation B[62]

| [23] Carrying the Cross | Christ nailed to Cross | Crucifixion | Deposition | Entombment |
| [24] [removed] | Flagellation | Carrying the Cross | Crucifixion | Entombment |

---

[62] The Office of the Passion, missal-hours, Paris, BN MS lat. 757, c.1380, the twenty-fifth manuscript in this sample, appears to be a unique version. Every textual element is different from those found in other manuscripts. It is not illustrated, but preceded by a Last Judgement miniature.

TABLE 2. Three recurring 'types' of the Office of the Passion:

Abbreviations

Ant.	antiphon	Or.	*oratio*
Cant.	canticle	Ps.	psalm (number indicated in brackets)
Cap.	*capitulum*	R.	response
Inv.	invitatory	V.	versicle
Les.	lesson		

	Type 1	**Type 2**	**Type 3**
matins			
V. (all) Domine labia mea aperies			
R. (all) Et os meum annuntiabit laudem tuam			
V. (all) Deus inadiutorium meum intende			
R. (all) Domine ad adiuvandem me festina			
Inv.	Christum captum	Regem christum	Regem christum
Ant. (all) Venite adoremus			
Ps. (all) Venite exultemus			
Hymn (all) In Passione Domine			
Ant.	Insurrexerunt	Traditus sum	Novit dominus
Ps.	Quare fremuerunt [2]	Domine, Deus [87]	Beatus vir [1]
Ant.	—	—	Astiterunt
Ps.	—	—	Quare fremuerunt [2]
Ant.	—	—	Non timebo
Ps.	—	—	Domine quid [3]
Les. 1	Apprehendit pilatus	Non est ei species	In illo tempore orante
R.	Seniores populi	O vos omnes qui	Seniores populi
V.	Collegerunt	Attendite universi	Collegerunt
Les. 2	Susceperunt autem	—	Tunc accesserunt
R.	Tanquam ad	—	Tristis est anima
V.	Cumque iniecissent	—	Ecce ad propinquabit

Les. 3	Postea sciens Ihesu	—	Mare autem facto
R.	Sicut ovis ad	—	Tenebre facte
V.	Tradunt in mortem	—	Cum ergo accepisset

Cant. (all) Te Deum

lauds

V. (all) Deus in adiutorium etc.

Ant.	Contumelias	Quia ecce ceperunt	Attendite universi populi
Ps.	Usquequo [12]	Eripe me [58]	Laudate dominum [150]
Cap.	Spiritus oris	Recogitate	Comunicantes

Hymn (all) Christum ducem, qui per crucem

V.	Dabit percutienti	Dabit percutienti	Ego sui flagellatus
R.	Saturabitur opprobriis	Saturabitur opprobriis	Et castigatio mea
Ant.	Proprio filio	Proprio filio	Tradar ego

Cant. (all) Benedictus dominus deus israel

Or. [all] Domine Ihesu Christe qui hora matinali[63]

prime

V. (all) Deus in adiutorium etc.

Hymn (all) Tu qui velatis facie

Ant.	Faciem meam	Astiterunt reges	Cum ducerunt
Psalm	Iudica me [42]	Quare fremuerunt [2]	Iubilate deo [99]
Cap.	Recogitate	Communicantes	Christus passus
R.	Deo gratias	Spiritus oris	Deo gratias
V.	Cum male diceretur	Captus est	Colaphicabant
V.	—	Proposite sibi	—
R.	Cum pateretur	Omni confusione	Et spoliabant

Or. [all] Domine Ihesu Christe qui hora diei prima

terce

V. (all) Deus in adiutorium etc.

Hymn (all) Hora qui ductus

Ant.	Dominus tanquam	Locuti sunt	Vide Domine

---

[63] The prayers in each of the textual variations of the Office of the Passion begin in the same way, however, the phrasing and, sometimes, the meaning differs from version to version. While I have supplied the incipits which apply to each of the versions, it is not practical to give details of the entire prayers here.

Ps.	Exaudi deus [63]	Deus, laudem [108]	Ad te levavi [122]
Cap.	Christus passus	Christus passus	Christus formam
R.	Deo gratias	—	—
R.	Proposite sibi	Proposite sibi	
V.	Omni confusione	Omni confusione	Ad duxerunt
V.	Oblatus qui	Oblatus qui	—
R.	Et non aperuit	Et non aperuit	Et condemnaverunt

Oro. [all] Domine Ihesu Christe qui hora diei tertia

sext

V. (all) Deus in adiutorium etc.

Hymn (all) Crucem pro nobis

Ant.	Posuerunt supra	Omnes videntes	O vos omnes
Ps.	Credidi propter [115]	Deus, deus meus [21]	Circumdederunt [21:17-21]
Cap.	Tradebant autem	Humiliavit semetipsum	Aspiciamus
R.	Oblatus est quia	Oblatus est quia	Iesu Christi crucifixe
V.	Et non aperuit	Et non aperuit	Et perpetua vulnera
V.	Tradidit in mortem	Tradidit in mortem	—
R.	Et cum sceleratis	Et cum sceleratis	—

Or. [all] Domine Ihesu Christe qui hora diei sexta

none

V. (all) Deus in adiutorium etc.

Hymn (all) Beata Christi passio

Ant.	Cum accepisset	Laboravi clamans	Iesu autem cum gustasset
Ps.	Voce mea [141]	Salvum me fac [68]	Hec est generatio [23:6-8]
Cap.	Decebat enim	Christus semel	Frates gaudete
V.	Tradidit in mortem	Tradidit in mortem	Ad propinquabant
R.	Et cum sceleratis	Et cum sceleratis	Quem cuncte
V.	Vere languores	Vere languores	—
R.	Et dolores nostros	Et dolores nostros	—

Or. [all] Domine Ihesu Christe qui hora diei nona

vespers

V. (all) Deus in adiutorium etc.

Ant.	Dignus es	Misit Deus	Ad vesperum demorabitur

Ps.	Exaltabo te [29]	Miserere [56]	Domine non est [130]
Cap.	Videmus Ihesum	Videmus Ihesum	Fratres michi autem
Hymn (all) Qui pressura			
V.	Disciplina pacis	Disciplina pacis	Lanceaverunt
R.	Cuius livore	Livore cuius	Et sparserunt
Ant.	Recessit	Cum accepisset	Deponentes

Cant. (all) Magnificat

Oro [all] Domine Ihesu Christe qui hora vespertina

compline

V. (all) Converte nos etc.

Ant.	Plangent eum	Homo pacis	Tullit Ioseph
Ps.	Domine Deus [87]	Beatus qui [40]	Laudate dominum [150]
Hymn (all) Qui iacuisti			
Cap.	Christo igitur	Christo igitur	Christo igitur
R.	Oportuit in	Oportuit in	Facebat in sepulcro
R.	Et ita intrare	Et ita intrare	Et spoliabat
V.	Oportuit pati	Oportuit pati	—
R.	Resurrexit propter	Resurrexit propter	—
Ant.	Salvator mundi	Salve nos	Ecce crucem

Cant. (all) Nunc dimittis

Oro. [all] Domine Ihesu Christe qui hora diei ultima

Figure 31. Betrayal of Christ. Book of Hours. Adelaide, State Library of South Australia, f. 15. 102×79mm.

Figure 32. Christ before Pilate. Book of Hours. Adelaide, State Library of South Australia, f. 21v. 102×79 mm.

Figure 33. Mocking and Buffeting of Christ. Book of Hours. London, British Library, Add. MS 15265, f. 102. 140×94mm.

Figure 34. Carrying of the Cross. Book of Hours. Adelaide, State Library of South Australia, f. 29. 102×79 mm.

Figure 35. Christ crucified, offered vinegar to drink. Book of Hours. Adelaide, State Library of South Australia, f. 34. 102×79mm.

Figure 36. Christ dead on the Cross. Book of Hours. Adelaide, State Library of South Australia, f. 39v. 102×79 mm.

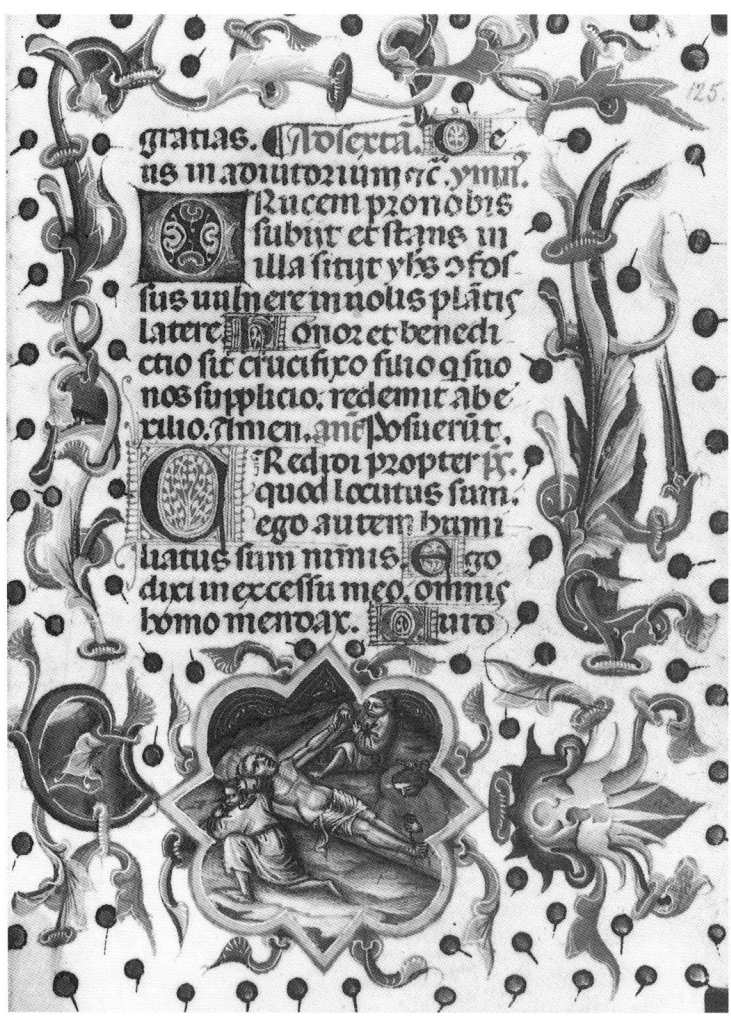

Figure 37. Christ is nailed to the Cross. Book of Hours. London, British Library, Add. MS 34247, f. 125. 134×100 mm.

Figure 38. Crucifixion. Book of Hours. Kremsmünster, Stiftsbibliothek, MS Cim.4, f. 150. 152×110 mm.

Figure 39. Crucifixion, with Mass and Baptism. Bolognese Book of Hours. London, British Library, Add. MS 34247, f. 127. 134×100 mm.

Figure 40. Deposition. Book of Hours. Adelaide, State Library of South Australia, f. 45v. 102×79mm.

Figure 41. Entombment. Book of Hours. Adelaide, State Library of South Australia, f. 49. 102×79 mm.

FIVE

An Unusual Image of the Assumption in a Fourteenth-Century Dominican Choir-Book

Margaret M. Manion

THE CHOIR-BOOKS NOW IN THE BIBLIOTECA COMUNALE AUGUSTA, in Perugia, which were made for the convent of S. Domenico in that city, probably between the years 1305 and 1315 are significant for a number of reasons.[1] Not least of these is their impeccable provenance, all but one of the fourteen volumes of the original commission having remained in their city of origin.[2] They are also the source of valuable information about the practice of medieval liturgical music, a fact which John Stinson demonstrates with his

---

[1] This article will also be published in slightly different form in a festschrift for George Tibbits (Department of Architecture and Building, The University of Melbourne). It arises out of a study made of the Perugian choir-books with John Stinson, supported by a grant from the Australian Research Council. For the place of these *corali* in the history of Umbrian painting, see F. Todini, 'Gli antifonari de San Domenico e la miniatura a Perugia nel primo Trecento' in *Francesco d'Assisi. Documenti e Archivi. Codici e Biblioteche. Miniature* (Milan, 1982), 218–36; and E. Lunghi, 'per la fortuna della Basilica di S. Francesco ad Assisi: i corali domenicani della Biblioteca "Augusta" di Perugia', *Bolletino della deputazione storia Patria per l'Umbria* 88 (1991), 43–68.

[2] The missing volume was apparently dismembered and the decorated pages sold individually. Three of these pages are now in the Cini Foundation, Venice; see Todini, 'Antifonari', 230–36.

edition of the text and music for the Office of the feast of the Assumption;[3] and, since they were written and embellished at a time of major innovation in Umbrian painting, they are important for the history of Italian book illumination. The artists responsible for their twenty-eight large historiated and figurative initials were in touch with the latest developments in fresco and panel, as well as being expert in the manuscript medium. Indeed, both in scale and conception, several of these compositions suggest independent paintings; at the same time, however, they are firmly anchored in the liturgical book, being inscribed within the contours of particular letters and accompanied by one or more lines of music and text for the chants of the feast which they introduce. These initials have been attributed to three main artists: 'Il Primo Miniatore Perugino', 'Il Secondo Miniatore Perugino' and Marino da Perugia, whose signature on a painting of the *Maestà* now in the Galleria Nazionale dell' Umbria indicates that he was also a painter of large scale panels.[4] The work of all three artists reflects the interaction of the Umbro-Roman classical revival with emotive northern Gothic elements, and the influence not only of earlier traditions of manuscript illumination, but also of the great series of late thirteenth- and early fourteenth-century frescoes in the Church of S. Francesco at Assisi.[5]

The historiated initial for the Office of the feast of the Assumption (Perugia, Biblioteca Comunale Augusta, MS 2785, f.91v) which is the subject of this essay, is the work of Marino da Perugia, in many ways the most progressive artist of the group.[6] This unusual composition, which to date has received little scholarly attention, is a particularly striking example of the interaction between monumental painting and manuscript illumination; it also demonstrates how literary and visual imagery, combined in fresh and unexpected ways, may reflect both the rich resources of the Christian cultural tradition and individual artistic creativity. Within the context of the medieval choir-book, and more particularly the words and music for the feast of the Assumption, this image bears testimony both to the distinctiveness and vigour of Umbrian art in the early Trecento and to the spiritual vitality of the Dominican and Franciscan orders responsible for the commissioning of such works.

---

[3] See Chapter 6 below. The Office for the Feast of the Assumption is in the antiphonal volume, Perugia, *Biblioteca Comunale Augusta*, MS 2785, ff. 84v–108; it measures 620x430 mm and contains 190 folios.

[4] See Todini 'Antiphonari', 218–19, 234–36; M. Boskovits, *Pittura Umbra e Marchigiana tra Medioevo e Rinascimento* (Florence, 1973), 12–13; and L. Bellosi, 'La Sala dei Notai, Marino de Perugia e un "antequem" per il "problema di Assisi"' in *Per Maria Dionini Visani. Scritti di amici* (Torino, 1977), 22–25.

[5] Todini, 'Antifonari', 234–36.

[6] See Todini, 'Antifonari', 218–19, 234–36.

The historiated initial 'V' (Pl. 2), which introduces the responsory for the first lesson of matins for the feast of the Assumption, shows Mary and Christ enthroned in the clouds above an empty tomb. Worshipful angels surround them and Mary's jewel-studded robe proclaims her royal status; as is the case with Christ and the attendant angels, her head is encircled by a gold nimbus. What is particularly striking about this image is the way in which the public and regal celebration of Mary's triumph over death is combined with the depiction of an unusually intimate relationship between herself and Christ. As though overcome with weariness or emotion she leans her head and the weight of the upper part of her body against his shoulder. Christ's arm protectively enfolds her, and the couple clasp hands in front. This unusual configuration appeared in a small group of Umbrian, or Umbrian-related, fresco and panel paintings in the early Trecento and just this once, it seems, in an illuminated manuscript, again in the heart of Umbria.[7]

Certain aspects of the composition reveal the influence of older traditions, such as the enthronement of Mary at the side of Christ and his arm around her shoulder, which go back to the twelfth century mosaic in the Church of S. Maria in Trastevere, Rome,[8] while the close physical relationship between Mary and Christ reflects images of the Virgin and Child, and of the Deposition or Lamentation where, however, it is Mary who cradles the head of her dead son. The representation of St John leaning on the bosom of Christ at the Last Supper provides perhaps the closest visual and emotional comparison, with the inclination of the Apostle's head against Christ's body being a similar expression of intimate affection and trust. This image, however, was long sanctioned by the Gospel text and rendered familiar through widespread use, whereas the depiction of the *madonna assunta* in the embrace of her son had a much more transitory existence. As the theme of the Assumption grew increasingly popular in fourteenth century Italy, it was the majestic figure of a frontally enthroned Virgin, ascending without her son to heaven, that was preferred.[9] Why this was so will be discussed later;

---

[7] See M. Meiss, 'Reflections of Assisi: A tabernacle and the Cesi Master', in *Scritti di Storia dell' Arte in Onore di Mario Salmi* (Rome,1962), II, 75-111; and D. Gordon, 'Art in Umbria (1250–1350)' (Diss., Courtauld, London, 1979), 209-210. The group comprises, in addition to the cycle at Assisi, fresco cycles in S. Giuliana, Perugia; Sacro Speco, Subiaco, by Meo da Siena; the Palazzo Trinci, Foligno, by Ottaviano Nelli; and an altarpiece, now in the *Musée Ile de France*, St Jean Cap Ferrat, attributed to the Cesi Master. There are some striking similarities between the image in the Cap Ferrat altarpiece and that in the choir-book, and Dillian Gordon says that the illuminator must have seen the altarpiece (*Art of Umbria*, 209). I concentrate here, however, on the archetypal composition of Cimabue, especially because other compositions in the Perugian choir-books make it clear that the illuminators were familiar with the fresco cycles there.

[8] Meiss, 'Reflections of Assisi', 90-91.

[9] Meiss, 'Reflections of Assisi', 96.

here it is timely to observe that this rare and evocative image seems to have been the creation of the great Tuscan painter, Cimabue, appearing first in the now much damaged fresco cycle dedicated to the Virgin in the apsidal tribune of the upper Church of S. Francesco, *c*.1270–80.[10]

Two things are significant about the Assisi fresco in the present context. In the first place the Assumption scene occurs there as part of a narrative series concerned with the last days on earth of the Virgin, her death and subsequent glorification. Secondly, this cycle is based on a literary source, *The Golden Legend*, a book on the principal feasts of the Church's year written by the north Italian Dominican Jacopo da Voragine between 1255 and 1266.[11] This work was probably designed as a guide for clerics in the preparation of homilies and sermons, although it was later translated from Latin into the vernacular of many European countries and became popular reading among the lay aristocracy as well as in clerical and religious circles. In his presentation of the lives of the saints and of important feasts in honour of Christ and the Virgin, Jacopo combines commentaries on the relevant liturgical readings with material based on apocryphal writings and earlier hagiography.[12] This he does with serious theological intent, often using fanciful anecdote to emphasize orthodox doctrine.[13] Thus in his treatment of the Assumption he combines a reference to the words from the Song of Songs, traditionally used in the Office for the feast, with an apocryphal legend attributed to St John. Part of Jacopo's account reads as follows:

> When the Blessed Mary saw all the Apostles gathered together, she blessed the Lord and sat down among them in the midst of lighted lamps and candles. At about the third hour of the night, Jesus came with the ranks of the angels, the troop of the patriarchs the host of the martyrs, the army of the confessors, and the choir of the virgins; and all took their places before the throne of the Virgin, and their voices mounted in sweet and solemn song. And the aforesaid book, ascribed to John, tells us what obsequies were then celebrated. Jesus Himself began and said: 'Come, my chosen one, and I shall place thee upon my throne, for I have desired thy beauty!' And she answered: 'My heart is ready, O Lord, my heart is ready!' Then all who had come with Jesus sweetly intoned: 'This is she whose bed was free of sin, and who shall have fruit in the refection of holy souls!' And she herself sang: 'All generations shall call me blessed, because he that is mighty hath done great things to me, and holy is his name!' Then Christ, singing more fairly than all, intoned: 'Come from Libanus, my spouse, come from Libanus, come: thou

---

[10] For a descripton of the frescoes and their reproduction, see E. Lunghi, *The Basilica of St. Francis at Assisi* (London, 1996), 28-33.

[11] See *The Golden Legend of Jacobus de Voragine*, translated and adapted from Latin by G. Ryan and H. Ripperger (New York, 1969).

[12] See H. Maddocks, 'Pictures for aristocrats: The manuscripts of the *Légende dorée*,' in M.M. Manion and B.J. Muir, eds, *Medieval Texts and Images* (Sydney, 1991), 1–24.

[13] See Maddocks, *Légende dorée*, 2.

shalt be crowned!' and she responded: 'Behold I come, for in the head of the book it is written of me that I should do thy will, O my God; for my spirit hath rejoiced in God my saviour!' And in this manner Mary's soul went forth out of her body, and flew upward in the arms of her Son; and she was spared all pain of the body, as she had been free from corruption without. And Our Lord said to the Apostles: 'Carry the body of the Virgin my Mother to the valley of Jossaphat, and lay it in the new tomb which ye will find there; and await me for three days until I come to you!' At once the Virgin was surrounded with red roses, signifying the troops of the martyrs, and with white lilies, signifying the hosts of the angels, confessors, and virgins. And the Apostles called after, saying: 'O Virgin most prudent, whither goest thou? Be mindful of us, O Lady!' Then the assemblage of those who had stayed behind in heaven, in admiration of the choiring of those who ascended, went swiftly forth to meet them; and seeing their King bearing in his own arms the soul of a woman, *and her leaning upon him*, they began to exclaim, saying: '*Who is this that cometh up from the desert, flowing with delights, leaning upon her beloved?*' And those who accompanied her answered: 'Fair is she among the daughters of Jerusalem, as ye have seen her filled with charity and love.' And in this wise she was taken up into Heaven rejoicing, and placed upon a throne of glory at the right hand of her son. And the Apostles saw that her soul was of such whiteness as no tongue of mortal man could express.[14]

The scenes that line the lower part of the walls of the choir of S. Francesco, incorporate several features of this account.[15] Their sequence is:

(i) *The Virgin takes leave of the Apostles.* Mary is shown seated on a bed surrounded by nimbed Apostles; Christ stands at its foot, elevated above the group, and gestures towards her;

(ii) *The Death or Dormition of the Virgin*: Mary's prostrate body is surrounded by throngs of nimbed Apostles and patriarchs; in the centre, Christ holds her soul in the shape of a small child;

(iii) *The Assumption*: Christ is seated beside Mary in a mandorla held by angels; Mary leans on his shoulder; his left arm enfolds her and his right hand crosses her left; below, patriarchs and prophets are ranged in tiers behind an empty tomb;

(iv) *Christ and the Virgin enthroned in heaven*: Around the enthroned couple are serried ranks of angels, prophets and saints; they are joined by nimbed Franciscan friars at the foot of the throne for whom Mary appears to intercede.

As well as the obvious similarities between these literary and visual accounts, there are also significant differences. In keeping with a tradition

---

[14] *The Golden Legend*, 451–52.
[15] For reproductions, see Lunghi, *The Basilica of St. Francis*, 30–33.

that the spiritual and corporeal Assumption of Mary took place in distinct stages, Jacopo narrates not only the ascent of the Virgin's soul to heaven, but also the carrying of her body in ritual procession to the tomb, where it remains for three days until summoned forth by Christ. Then reunited, her body and soul are triumphantly assumed into heaven. In Cimabue's cycle, however, there is no distinction between the spiritual and bodily Assumption of Mary, the empty tomb in the scene of the ascent signifying the simultaneous escape of both body and soul from the corruption of death. This reflects the growing emphasis on the integration of the spiritual and corporeal aspects of the mystery of the Assumption. Nor indeed does Jacopo's overall attitude differ in essentials from that of Cimabue, for after relating various, and sometimes contradictory, legends associated with Mary's death, he reflects on the nature of the Church's belief in this mystery, and appealing to the testimony of the Fathers of the Church and the saints he concludes that while much of what he has reported may be apocryphal, the underlying truth is that, 'the glorious Virgin Mary was assumed and exalted wholly, honourably, joyously, and in an excelling manner. She was assumed wholly, in body and soul, as the Church piously believes: and this many of the saints not only assert, but set themselves to prove with many reasons'.[16] Acknowledging that this is an event shrouded in mystery he rests his case by citing the authority of St Augustine:

> If the death of all the saints is precious, the death of Mary is beyond price. Therefore I deem that it must be confessed that Mary, by the bounty of Christ, was assumed into the joy of eternity, and was received more honourably than others, since she was honoured above all others by grace; and that she was not dragged down to the common lot of humanity, which is corruption, the worm and the dust, since she had borne her Saviour and the Saviour of all . . . We well know that all these things could not be preserved in the order of nature, but we doubt not that on behalf of Mary's integrity, grace was more powerful than nature. Christ therefore made Mary to rejoice in her own son, in soul and body, nor allowed any blemish of corruption to come upon her who had suffered no impairment of her integrity in bringing forth so great a son, that she whom such excelling grace had bathed might be ever without stain, and she who had begotten the flawless life of all might have life in its fullest. If therefore, O Christ, I have spoken as I ought, do thou and thine, approve; if not, do thou and thine, I pray, forgive me![17]

The allusions to the Song of Songs in Jacopo's account link it with the liturgy for the feast of the Assumption, where the antiphonal verses and responsories for the Office of the feast in the Dominican rite are based largely on this great love poem of the Old Testament, traditionally attributed to King

---

[16] *The Golden Legend*, 455–56.

[17] *The Golden Legend*, 465.

Solomon.[18] The particular verses (italicized in the passage from Jacopo above) that give rise to Cimabue's distinctive depiction of Christ and the Virgin come at the conclusion of the Song of Songs when the chorus welcomes the approaching bride and groom: 'Who is this coming up from the desert leaning on her beloved' (8:5).[19] They echo the words applied earlier to the triumphant appearance of the king's retinue: 'Who is this coming up from the desert like a column of smoke breathing of myrrh and frankincense and every perfume the merchant knows? See, it is the litter of Solomon. Around it are sixty champions, the flower of the warriors of Israel' (3:6–7). The description of the bride emerging from the desert on the arm of her betrothed, moreover, is immediately preceeded and followed by images of sleep: 'I charge you daughters of Jerusalem, not to stir my love, nor rouse it, until it please to awake' (8:4), and, 'I awakened you under the apple tree, there where your mother conceived you' (8:7). This has prompted commentators to see the bride's entrance into a land where the flowers of spring have replaced the barrenness of the desert as a sign of her awakening to a new life in which, 'love is strong as death' (8:6).[20] In both Cimabue's painting and the illustration in the Perugian choir-book, the Virgin's form is suffused with langour, her head resting heavily on Christ's shoulder. This is in keeping with her being lovingly aroused from sleep, and it is pertinent here to recall that Mary's death was traditionally interpreted, especially in the East, as 'a falling asleep' or 'dormition'. Furthermore, while the biblical verse (8:5) suggests, in the first instance a bridal procession, in both the fresco and the antiphonal the rendering of the pair as seated and locked in a tender embrace evokes also those passages in the Song of Songs which celebrate a more intimate exchange of love, several of which feature in the Office of the Assumption.[21]

From early Christian times this biblical celebration of love was interpreted as symbolizing the betrothal of God—and by extension the glorified Christ—to his spouse the Church.[22] This interpretation was also in keeping with Judaic tradition which often represented Israel or the chosen people as the betrothed of God.[23] The Fathers of the Church extended this allegorical approach to the Virgin Mary, whom they presented for veneration not only as *Theotokos* or Mother of God, but also as *Mater Ecclesiae* or

---

[18] Other texts come from Ecclesiasticus and Gospel passages that refer to Mary; see Stinson (Chapter 6 below), 168.

[19] Biblical citations are from *The Jerusalem Bible* (London, 1966).

[20] See, for example, the Commentary to *The Jerusalem Bible*, nn. e and f, 1003.

[21] See the text edited by Stinson (Chapter 6 below).

[22] See the Introduction and Commentary to the Song of Songs, *The Jerusalem Bible* (991–1003).

[23] See Hosea, *passim*, and Isaiah 54:5–10.

the Church; hence the use of excerpts from the Song of Songs in liturgies in her honour.[24]

The setting for this depiction of Christ and the Virgin at Assisi is a pictorial cycle based largely on legendary material; the Perugian antiphonal, however, provides a different contextual emphasis both visual and literary. In keeping with the illustrative pattern followed throughout the choir-books a single historiated initial functions as the visual cue to the feast, so that this one scene now sums up the mystery of the Assumption. Furthermore, the image is aligned with scriptural and liturgical sources that are free of legendary embellishments, so that text and illustration mutually reinforce one another. As is customary, the initial introduces the responsory for the first lesson of matins, which in this case is a paraphrase of various verses of the Song of Songs: 'I saw my beautiful one ascending like a dove above the banks of the waters; the fragrance of her vesture was exceeding wondrous. And like the days of spring roses and lilies of the valley surrounded her'. The accompanying versicle is taken from Chapter 3, verse 6 of the same text: 'Who is this coming up from the desert like a column of smoke, breathing of myrrh and frankincense and every perfume that the merchant knows?' These words apply in the first instance to Solomon or the royal bridegroom; but here they are adapted to refer to Mary. The only specific reference to Chapter 8, verse 5 is in the versicle for the fifth responsory and the citation is abbreviated: 'This is she who comes up from the desert, flowing with delights'. Thus, nowhere in the Office do the actual words, 'leaning on her beloved', occur. Nevertheless, to those familiar with the Song of Songs, the association must have been obvious.

This leads one to consider the particular audience to whom this image was addressed. Whereas the Assisi cycle decorated a place of public worship, the Perugian choir-books were made for the specific use of the community at S. Domenico. Matins of the Divine Office was regularly sung in religious houses either at midnight or between midnight and dawn, and it is unlikely that members of the public would have attended this service. Although, therefore, the choir-books may have been proudly shown to visitors from time to time, their primary purpose was to meet the needs of a small group of male religious, who were well versed in the scriptural and theological traditions of the Church and, no doubt, equally well acquainted with the writings of their fellow Dominican, Jacopo, for it was precisely to assist such clerics in their teaching and preaching that *The Golden Legend* had been compiled. For them the Song of Songs and this composition, which so movingly encapsulated its meaning, expressed the love of God for his people whom, as in the case of the Virgin Mary, he was pledged to rescue from death and corruption.

---

[24] See H. Rahner, *Mary and the Church*, trans. S. Bullough (London, 1961), especially 1–12.

On a more personal level, the Song of Songs was seen to symbolize the mystical betrothal of the Lord with the soul of the devout Christian, and the spiritual life of religious, whether male or female, had long been presented in these terms.[25] Therefore, particularly for a conventual audience, the representation of Mary leaning trustfully on the shoulder of a supportive and tender Christ in her ascent heavenwards could also be construed as a visual commentary on the relationship between Christ and the soul of the individual religious.

Why was it, asks Millard Meiss, that this arresting rendering of the Assumption did not persist in Italian art beyond the early years of the fourteenth century, especially, one might add, since it originated in such an important place of public worship and was associated with a greatly respected artist?[26] He suggests that one reason may have been that the intimacy of the composition was less in tune with the spirit of the later Trecento which, he argues, favoured a more detached monumentality. Meiss also says that, 'perhaps Cimabue's composition was too condensed, combining and therefore also perhaps blurring the successive moments of the Assumption, the arrival on the throne, and the Coronation'.[27] This is an interesting comment in relation to the context of the image in the choir-book of S. Domenico. It is true that both medieval writers and artists tend to represent eternal verities in an episodic way, as if they were subject to the spatial and temporal limitations of this life. Indeed, this approach often helps to bring the forces of the imagination to bear on particular aspects of a mystery, and it by no means necessarily implies a simplistic or naive interpretation of the subject. Cimabue himself presented the Assumption within the context of a fresco series based on a literary narrative, and it seems that whenever the composition was repeated it was within a sequential framework, except for this particular example. Condensation is effective here because of the intrinsic relationship of the image to the liturgy, so that it becomes a visual gloss on the biblical love song and related texts. Both text and gloss, moreover, must have communicated their meaning transparently to one group in particular, namely those celebrating the feast in sacred music and song, and thereby contributing to the expounding of its central theme of trustful, enduring love.

---

[25] See G. Schiller, *Ikonographie der christlichen Kunst* (Gütersloh, 1980) 4.2, 83–140.

[26] Meiss, 'Reflections of Assisi', 96.

[27] Meiss, 'Reflections of Assisi', 96.

SIX

The Dominican Liturgy of the Assumption: Texts and Music for the Divine Office

John Stinson

THE LITURGICAL CHANT OF THE WESTERN CHURCH has attained an illusory familiarity: most educated listeners recognize it at first hearing, but fewer and fewer have chant melodies on the turntable of their inner gramophones. Indeed, the known repertoire is coeval with the gramophone: both had their origins in the 1890s, respectively through the editions of Solesmes and the invention of Thomas Edison; and both have largely disappeared, through widespread misinterpretations of the liturgical reforms of the Second Vatican Council and the advent of digital technology.[1] It might also be noted that while the revival of medieval church music in the first half of this century made available a substantial body of chants in editions more reliable than any previously published, this by no means adequately represented the corpus of liturgical chant in

---

[1] Article 166 of the Constitution on the Sacred Liturgy 'acknowledges Gregorian chant as distinctive of the Roman liturgy', and goes on to say 'other things being equal, it should be given pride of place in liturgical services'; see the edition by M.E. Simcoe, *The Liturgy Documents* (Chicago, rev. 1985), 1–36. According to R. Schuler, the revised (Latin) liturgical books published after the Council 'remained almost totally unknown, and in some dioceses, their use was prohibited by local legislation that forbade the use of Latin'; see 'A chronicle of reform Part V: The place of music in eucharistic celebrations', *Sacred Music* 110 (1983), 5–11.

use in the Middle Ages. Recent research indicates that although some 10,400 different chants have been published since the revival began, this accounts for less than a quarter of the medieval repertoire currently indexed.[2] Furthermore, of the works published, only the chants for the Mass became widely known, as this was the main service attended by lay congregations. The chants of the Divine Office, especially the responsorial chants for matins, have remained largely unedited and unsung, except by monastic communities of regular observance.

This essay seeks to contribute to the knowledge and understanding of medieval chant, by a study of the Office for the feast of the Assumption of the Virgin Mary as it appears in a set of early fourteenth-century Dominican choir-books, made for the Church of San Domenico in Perugia, together with other related Dominican sources.[3] It presents an edition of the text and music of the Office, much of which has not been published in modern times. For reasons which will become clear in the course of the article, this edition differs from the accepted meaning of the term 'critical', although the melodies and related texts are placed within the context of the transmission of the liturgy especially from the ninth to the fourteenth centuries.

The chanting of the Divine Office was one of the key activities of the monastic life instituted by St Benedict in the sixth century and as various

---

[2] The printed chant books were indexed by J.R. Bryden and D.G. Hughes in *An Index of Gregorian Chant* (Cambridge, Mass., 1969). Their index covers all publications by the monks of Solesmes and the *Editio Vaticana* and some of the manuscripts published in facsimile in the series *Paléographie Musicale*—the *St Yrieux Gradual* (F–Pbn 903), the *Beneventan Gradual* (I–Bc 34), the *Lucca Antiphonal* (I-Lc 601), the *Worcester Antiphonal* (GB–Wc 160) and W.H. Frere's *Graduale Sarisburiense* (London, 1894). More recent indices by L. Dobszay and G. Prószeky, *Corpus Antiphonalium Officii Ecclesiarum Centralis Europae* (Budapest, 1988); the *Cantus* project of the Catholic University of America, under the direction of R. Steiner, and A. Hughes' *Late Medieval Liturgical Offices* (Toronto, 1994) have vastly extended the horizons of the repertoire of chant. A total of 170,000 chants, representing some 46,035 different works, have been indexed to September 1996, excluding those from Central Europe in the Dobszay-Prószeky project. The Solesmes publications, including facsimiles and printed editions indexed by Bruden and Hughes, represent 22.56% of the indexed chants.

[3] This set of choir-books from the first decades of the fourteenth century was the focus of research by M.M. Manion and J. Stinson in the project 'Decoration, Text and Music in Italian Medieval Choirbooks', supported by the Australian Research Council. The complete contents of the *corali*, which constitute an annual cycle of chants for both the Office and the Mass, were the basis of *The SCRIBE Database*, in which text, music, decoration and liturgical function can be searched electronically. The present edition is produced from this database using the *SCRIBE* program, written by B. Parish and J. Stinson—see *Directory of Computer Assisted Research in Musicology*, ed. W.B. Hewlitt and E. Selfridge-Field (Menlo Park, Ca., 1988), 100–101. The Perugian choir-books have been described in detail in G. Ciliberti, *Musica e Liturgia nelle Chiese e Conventi dell'Umbria. Secoli X–XV* (Perugia, 1994), 51–70.

expressions of his Rule flourished and proliferated in the later Middle Ages, the performance of the Office remained central to the Benedictine tradition, the daily singing of the psalms, the chanting of the interspersed readings from the Old and New Testaments and the lives of the saints, constituting a large part of the devotional life of both monks and nuns.[4] Before the rise of the mendicant orders in the thirteenth century, there were two fundamental patterns of the Office: the 'monastic' *cursus* which had been directly shaped by the prescriptions in the Rule of St Benedict and the 'secular' or 'Roman' *cursus* used in cathedrals and collegiate churches.[5] The essential differences between the two lay in the number of psalms at vespers and the disposition of psalms, responsories and readings at matins. In the monastic *cursus* four psalms were sung at vespers, while the number was five in the secular. The festive secular *cursus* for matins usually had three nocturns, each of three psalms with antiphons, followed by three readings, preceded by their own responsories and verses. The monastic *cursus* for festive matins had six psalms with antiphons and four lessons with responsories in the first two nocturns, then three canticles with a further four lessons and responsories in the third nocturn.

The text for the Office of the Assumption appears in the earliest surviving sources, the *Compiègne Antiphonal* (c.870) and the *Codex Hartker* (early eleventh century).[6] While there is remarkable consistency over the centuries in the biblical sources on which the words of the Office are based, perhaps even more remarkable is the inconsistency with which such texts are assigned to particular hours. The order in which they occur in each hour also varies greatly. Of the thirty-three manuscripts, for example, surveyed for the preparation of this edition, no two have the same texts in the same order for any of the hours, except for lauds (see Table 1).[7] Even allowing for the differences between the secular and

---

[4] For an overview of the role of the liturgy in the Benedictine order, see J. Leclerq, *The Love of Learning and the Desire for God*, trans. C. Mansfield (New York, 2nd ed., 1974).

[5] The monastic and secular *cursus* are discussed in J. Harper, *The Forms and Orders of Western Liturgy from the Tenth to the Eighteenth Century* (Oxford, 1991), 73–108; and also by A. Hughes, *Medieval Manuscripts for Mass and Office* (Toronto, 1982).

[6] The standard critical edition of the texts used in the Divine Office is R. Hésbert, *Corpus Antiphonalium Officii* (Rome, 1968–1970). In this monumental six-volume work Hésbert examines twelve manuscripts, six from the secular or Roman cursus and six from the monastic cursus which he considers to be broadly representative of the two traditions. Volume 3 contains 4,516 *invitatoria* and antiphons and Volume 4 contains 2,455 responsories with their verses, versicles and hymns, making a total of 6,971 texts. In the *Cantus* index and the Dominican chants in the Perugian manuscripts there are many texts not edited by Hésbert.

[7] The most consistent settings were for lauds, in which most manuscripts had the same

monastic *cursus* this surprising variety, especially for matins and vespers, suggests that while the compilers of liturgical Offices drew on a common pool of antiphons and responsories, they exercised considerable flexibility in their arrangement. It is certainly clear that the variations cannot be explained simply by regional distinctions or the traditions of individual orders, since Offices of similar provenance, and of houses of the same order, sometimes differ. Rather, they reflect the lack of uniformity in liturgical observance before the reforms of the Cistercians, Dominicans and Franciscans in the later Middle Ages and the subsequent normative reforms of the Councils of Trent and the Second Vatican Council.

The biblical sources that feature consistently in the Office of the Assumption are New Testament passages that contain explicit references to Mary such as: Luke 1:46, 48 (*Magnificat anima mea Dominum . . . Beatam me dicent omnes generationes*) and Old Testament passages from the Song of Songs, and less frequently from *Ecclesiaticus*, which are applied figuratively to Mary, such as Song of Songs 8:5 (*Quae est ista);* and Ecclesiasticus 24:13, 15 (*Sicut cedrus exaltata sum in libano, et sicut cypressus in monte Sion . . . quasi myrra electa dedi suavitatem odoris*). The use of these sources varies from direct citation to paraphrase. There are also a number of texts which praise the Virgin or ask for her intercession in terms that mingle allusions to Scripture with more direct reference to the feast itself or to the traditional titles of the Virgin and her intercessory relationship with Christ.[8] The text, *Vidi speciosam quasi columbam,* a paraphrase of several elements of the Song of Songs, is one of the most stable in its position as the first responsory for matins. It is found in the *Codex Hartker*, the earliest antiphonal containing musical notation, and in all the other manuscripts surveyed for this edition. The first responsory for matins is the text frequently selected for illustration or decoration, and in the Perugian choir-books the unusual depiction of the Assumption discussed by Margaret Manion introduces *Vidi speciosam.*[9]

While the texts of the Office suggest a loosely-regulated selection and adaptation from a common pool, its music reflects more complex patterns of transmission. The association of the melodic repertoire of western liturgical chant with Pope Gregory (died 604) has been called into question in recent scholarship.[10] Certainly no known manuscripts with music

---

five anthiphons: *Assumpta est Maria in caelum; Maria virgo assumpta est; In odore unguentorum tuorum; Benedicta filia tu a domino;* and *Pulchra es et decora filia.*

[8] See, for example, the antiphons *Paradisi Portae* and *Ascendit Christus.*

[9] See Chapter 5 above.

[10] H. Hucke, 'Toward a new historical view of Gregorian chant', *Journal of the American Musicological Society* 33 (1980), 437–67; D. Hiley, 'Recent research on the origins of Western

notation go back to this period. On the other hand, the similarity of melodies in manuscripts from many parts of Europe in the tenth and eleventh centuries indicates that they depend either on a common heritage of earlier lost written sources or else on a strong oral tradition. The extant manuscripts show that melodies which are substantially the same differ in many details—sometimes the distinctions are no more than those of musical spelling, sometimes there are minor variants in the notes themselves; at others whole phrases are transposed or significantly different. These variants have been interpreted either as deviants from lost written originals or as accurate representations of inevitable differences in orally transmitted repertoires.[11] If operating on the principle that these distinctions result from a lost original, editorial practice has attempted to restore the original melodies by the application of techniques based on the editing of texts. This has involved the normalization of melodies according to an hypothetically reconstructed lost 'original'.[12] If, however, one proceeds on the assumption that the extant melodies derive from different oral traditions rather than from one original written source, then the differences need to be noted but not normalized, as each oral tradition may lay claim to being 'authentic'.

A further complication is that at certain critical stages in the history of liturgical chants, melodies were deliberately altered to conform to what was at the time understood as 'correct' musical theory. Thus the transmission of Dominican melodies may have combined both written and oral unaltered ancient melodies with those altered in earlier monastic reforms as well as those altered by the Dominicans themselves. The complexities of this transmission emerge more clearly, when one considers the history of the development of musical notation.

Before the development of a system of representing relative pitch, European music notation represented the melodic contour of individual syllables with signs called neumes, often derived from punctuation marks. The *punctum*, the regular sign for the end of a sentence, indicated a falling of pitch; the *quilisma*, related to many signs for the question mark,

---

chant', *Early Music* 16 (1988), 202–13; D.G. Hughes, 'Evidence for the traditional view of the transmission of Gregorian chant', *Journal of the American Musicological Society* 40 (1987), 377; K.C. Levy, 'Charlemagne's archetype of Gregorian chant', *Journal of the American Musicological Society* 41 (1988), 566–78; H. van der Werf, *The emergence of Gregorian chant: a comparative study of Ambrosian, Roman, and Gregorian chant* (Rochester, N.Y., 1993).

11 For a critical view of the relevance of the oral and written paradigms to the transmission of medieval music, see L. Treitier, 'Orality and literacy in the music of the Middle Ages,' *Parergon*, New Series 2 (1984), 143–74.

12 The most important study based on the paradigm of the 'lost' original is *Le Gradual Roman: edition critique par les moines de Solesmes* (Solesmes, 1957–62). For an account of the Solesmes edition, see D. Hiley, *Western Plainchant: A Handbook* (Oxford, 1992), 624–29.

indicated a rising inflection.[13] To sing the music from such manuscripts required the singer to know the melody beforehand, since the notation served only as a reminder of its details. To complement this notation some manuscripts identified the 'mode' in which the melody was to be sung, whereby common formulas establish the framework of the melody. Contemporary with the earliest musical manuscripts is a highly developed theory of eight modes derived from Greek models. These modal formulas were gradually made more explicit by the application of mathematical acoustics which provided precise techniques of tuning individual intervals. In the eleventh century, the use of the monochord to tune each of the intervals of the scale was related to the visual identification of intervals by the employment of horizontal lines labelled with the letter-names of notes. This technique, attributed to Guido d'Arezzo, enabled singers to read music in the modern sense, that is, to sing accurately melodies not previously known by providing visual guides to intervals which could be accurately pitched on the monochord. Throughout the Middle Ages musical education included an increasingly more refined conjunction of modal theory, mathematical acoustics and empirical experimentation on the monochord. By the beginning of the thirteenth century there was a large body of literature that gave very precise instructions in the practice of singing in the modal system. In these, Pythagorean mathematical acoustics, in which the pitch of every note was calculated by proportions of the length of a vibrating string, were applied to the theory of the eight modes and exemplified from the repertoire of liturgical chant.

The earliest noted antiphonals and graduals contain developed settings of both the Office and the Mass of the Assumption. These melodies can be read with accuracy only by collating the neume notation with later staff notation that used the labelled horizontal lines developed by Guido. Staff notation began to replace neume notation from the eleventh century. The introduction of a staff of from one to six lines greatly facilitated the accurate reading of musical pitch; through its use it became possible to *read* music not previously known, whereas the neume notation depended on an orally transmitted knowledge of the melody.

This change from an annotated aural/oral tradition to a written one was not universally welcomed. The twelfth-century theorist John of Afflighem frequently corrected what he considered to be inaccurate transcriptions into the new notation, either because the new transcription

---

[13] The derivation of neumes from punctuation marks is discussed by L. Treitler, 'Reading and singing: on the genesis of occidental music-writing', *Early Music History* 4 (1984), 135–208, K.C. Levy, 'On the origin of the neumes', *Early Music History* 7 (1987), 59–90; S. Corbin, *Die Neumen* (Cologne, 1977); and E. Cardine, *Sémiologie Grégorienne* (Solesmes, 1970; trans. by R. Fowels, 1982).

differed from his aural experience or because the new orthography did not conform to the current musical theory of mode.[14] Thus by the end of the twelfth century there was a perceived need to 'correct' some of the liturgical melodies, either because the new notational style differed from local practice or because the melodies were found not to conform to the developing theoretical system. The theory of mode, which had begun as a descriptive aid to singing known melodies, was now formulated in terms of the relative size of intervals which could be measured on the monochord. Modal theory was thus used to justify the alteration of even the most ancient melodies—descriptive aids had become prescriptive norms.

Existing liturgical repertoires were 'reformed' according to modal theory first by the Cistercians,[15] then by the Dominicans.[16] The first widespread reform of liturgical chant was initiated by St Bernard of Clairvaux in an attempt to restore liturgical chant to its authentic Gregorian models. The letter of St Bernard prefacing a treatise on chant reform begins:

> Among the various endeavours in which our fathers, the founders of the Cistercian Order, strove to excel was one to which they paid the most scrupulous and zealous attention: that in the divine praises they should use the chant which was found to be the most authentic. To this end they sent several men to transcribe and bring back the Antiphonary of the Cathedral of Metz, for it was said to be 'Gregorian'. But they found matters to be different from what they had heard. For upon examining it, they were disappointed because in respect to both music and text it was discovered to be corrupt, very poorly structured, and despicable from almost every point of view. Nevertheless, because they had begun, they continued to use it, and they retained it until our time. At last, however, since our brother Abbots of the Order could no longer endure it, and since they decided it should be revised and corrected, they committed the task to my supervision.[17]

---

[14] The following passage from John of Afflighem's *De Musica* exemplifies this concern for correcting even melodies well-established in the tradition: 'The antiphon *Gaudendum est nobis*, although it is in the [first mode], cannot be sung in its natural location because in certain places it demands, according to some, a whole tone below [low C (i.e. a low Bb)], which is not there. Yet if begun on A, it proceeds to the same end without going astray. Thus too the antiphon *Magnum hereditatis mysterium*.' See W. Babb, *Hucbald, Guido and John on Music* (New Haven, 1978), 127–28.

[15] The Cistercian reforms were based on the *Epistola Sancti Bernardi de revisione cantus Cisterciensis*; see J.-P. Migne, ed., *Patrologia Latina*, 221 vols (Paris, 1844–64), 182.1121–1132; a more reliable edition with English translation by F.J. Guenther, S.J., has been published by the American Institute of Musicology—*Corpus Scriptorum de Musica* 24 (1974).

[16] The Dominican reforms are discussed by R. Haller, O.P., in his doctoral dissertation, 'Early Dominican Mass chants: a witness to thirteenth-century chant style' (Diss., Catholic University of America, Washington D.C., 1986).

[17] 'Inter cetera quae optime aemulati sunt patres nostri, Cisterciensis videlicet ordinis inchoatores, hoc quoque studiosissime et religiosissime curaverunt ut in divinis laudibus id

As there were no extant Gregorian manuscripts even in the twelfth century, the reform was carried out along what could be called characteristically fundamentalist lines. For example, because there is no B flat in the lowest octave, B flat was to be avoided in all other octaves; because there were only ten commandments and ten strings on the biblical psaltery, no melody was to exceed the range of a tenth; melodies in authentic modes were to be clearly authentic and plagal clearly plagal; melodies were not to mix authentic and plagal modes. Just as the Cistercians preferred their architecture to be plain and unadorned, their liturgical chant was to be purged of all excess ornament and repetition. Manuscripts which transmitted melodies older than square notation were marked so that offending passages could be recognized and new copies made with these passages omitted. In their attempt to find the most 'authentic' melodies for liturgical chant, the Cistercians systematically altered those melodies which did not conform to their norms. Some modern Cistercian scholars regard this reform as 'a terrible mistake'.[18]

Soon after the foundation of the Dominican order, Humbert of Romans, the Master General during the time of the liturgical reform, reflected on the need for liturgical uniformity:

> . . . at the beginning of the Order there was a great deal of variety in the Office, and therefore a single Office was compiled in order to achieve uniformity everywhere. In the process of time four of the brethren from four provinces were commissioned to bring [the Office] into better order, which they did, and their arrangement was confirmed. But because there were still some things to be corrected, a commission was again approved at three chapters by the Master-General Humbert.[19]

---

canerent quod magis authenticum inveniretur. Missus denique qui Metensis ecclesiae antiphonarium—nam id Gregorianum esse dicebatur—transcriberent et afferent, longe aliter rem esse quam audierant invenerunt. Itaque examinatum displicuit, eo quod et cantu et littera inventum sit vitiosum et incompositum nimis, ac paene per omnia contemptibile. Quia tamen semel coeperunt, usi sunt eo, et usque ad nostra tempora retinuerunt. Tandem aliquando non sustinentibus iam fratribus nostris abbatibus ordinis, cum mutari et corrigi placuisset, curae nostrae id operis iniunxerunt.' Guentner (ed.), *Epistola S. Bernardi* (1974), 21 (text) and 42 (trans.).

[18] C. Waddell, O. Cist., 'The origin and evolution of the Cistercian antiphonary: reflections on two Cistercian chant reforms,' in M.B. Pennington, ed., *The Cistercian Spirit: A Symposium*, Cistercian Studies 3 (Spencer, Mass., 1970), 207: 'the whole chant reform associated with St Bernard's name had been a terrible mistake.'

[19] 'Postea sciendum quod ab initio Ordinis fuit multa varietas in officio, et ideo compilatum fuit unum officium propter uniformitatem habendam ubique. Processu vero temporis commissum fuit quatuor fratribus de quatuor provinciis, ut melius ordinarent; quod et fecerunt, et eorum ordinatio confirmata est. Sed quia adhuc erant ibi alique corrigenda, facta fuit iterum commission per tria capitula approbata Magister Humberto.' Humbert of

The new uniform Dominican liturgy, which retained some of the Cistercian reforms and made further alterations in order to make the melodies conform to contemporary music theory and aesthetic taste, also generated some resistance. The General Chapter in London in 1250, for example, registered complaints. Later chapters, however, at Metz (1251) and Buda (1254) enjoined the observance of the edited chants on the whole order. In 1256, a tax of twenty pounds per province was imposed for the production of the prototype manuscript under the direction of Humbert of Romans.[20] This carefully prepared volume in large format (480x320 mm; 500 folios) is now in the Dominican archives in Rome (MS XIV L 1). Chapters in 1258 and 1265 insisted on all liturgical books being copied from this prototype,[21] and in 1267 Clement IV gave papal approval to the reforms approved by the Chapter of Buda in 1256. A smaller (175x265 mm), more portable prototype was made for the use of the Master General some time after 1262;[22] it is now in the British Library (Additional MS 23,935). The set of choir-books now in Perugia and the *Poissy Antiphonal*, discussed in this volume by Joan Naughton,[23] may have been copied from one of these exemplars or from one of the other copies made about the same time.[24]

The melodies as they appear in the Perugian manuscripts have sometimes been through two reforms, and may differ substantially from those in the earliest sources. An example is the antiphon to the *Magnificat* for first vespers of the Assumption, *Ascendit Christus super coelos*.

The text of this antiphon is not listed in Hésbert's *Corpus Antiphonalium Officii*, which indicates that it did not occur in the twelve manuscripts, six

---

Romans, *Opera de Vita Regulari* (Rome, 1889; reprinted Turin, 1956), II, 152–53; cited in R. Haller, *Early Dominican Chants*, 349.

[20] 'Ad facienda communia ordini pro divino officio et ad providendum procuratori ordinis in curia de quibusdam expensis quilibet prior provincialis solvat .xx. libras Turonenses quas mittant priori Parisiensi et volumus quod accipiant pecuniam istam de primis libris vacantibus nisi per definitores capitulorum provincialium ordinetur quomodo dicta pecunia solvatur.' Paris, 1256. *Acta capitulorem generalium Ordinis Praedicatorum in Monumenta Ordinis Fratrum Predicatorum Historica* (Rome, 1898), III, 81–82; cited in Haller, 347.

[21] These rules are found in the *Poissy Antiphonal*, State Library of Victoria, MS*096.1 R66A, f. 4. For a discussion of these and other contemporary rules for copying chant manuscripts, see M. Huglo, 'Règlement du XIIIe siècle pour la transcription des livres notés', *Festschrift Bruno Stäblein zum 70. Geburtstag*, ed. M. Ruhnke (Kassel, 1967), 121–33.

[22] The Office of St Peter Martyr, canonized in 1262, was copied into the smaller exemplar in its original hand.

[23] See Chapter 3 above.

[24] W.R. Bonniwell, *A History of the Dominican Liturgy* (New York, 1945), 97, notes the existence of two other copie, one in Salamanca and the other in Oxford.

monastic and six secular, on which his critical edition is based. However, it does appear in Cistercian sources—for example, in Arouca at the monastery of Sts Peter and Paul.[25] Since the early Dominican Office books were modelled on Cistercian sources,[26] the presence of this antiphon may well be evidence of Cistercian origin. It is also found in the Barnwell[27] and Worcester[28] antiphonals, both thirteenth-century English sources of secular and monastic cursus respectively, which have a related, but substantially different, melody. Part of the Cistercian and Dominican reforms of liturgical chant involved the avoidance, wherever possible, of the *b rotundum*, or B flat. When melodies were written in the fifth mode, of which F is the *finalis*, it was customary to flatten the B above F in order to avoid the interval F–B, as this tritone was considered melodically discordant. In *Ascendit Christus super coelos* the melody as it appears in the English manuscripts begins with the same opening gesture as the Dominican version, except that the latter is transposed up a perfect fifth. This results in the complete avoidance of a flattened B; but in the process the melody is very substantially changed. These two forms of the melody may represent different oral traditions. Alternatively, the Cistercian and Dominican version may represent a deliberate attempt to make the melody conform to the rule of avoiding the B flat. The opening two lines (see Example 1 below) illustrate the differences and the similarities.

Since it was common practice to use a good melody more than once, many antiphons in medieval choir-books share the same melody. Thus the antiphon *Exaltata es, sancta Dei genetrix* shares a melody with more than a dozen different antiphons (see Example 2 below). Furthermore, the antiquity of the texts and the ambiguity of pitch in the earliest chant manuscripts make it impossible to assign with certainty a particular melody to a specific text, as the neumes in the oldest sources can be interpreted in more than one way.

---

[25] See W.D. Jordan, *The Liturgical Manuscripts of the Cistercian Monastery of Saint Peter & Saint Paul, Arouca, Portugal* (Brisbane, 1990).

[26] See Bonniwell, *A History of the Dominican Liturgy 1215–1945* (New York, 1945) and Haller, *Early Dominican Mass Chants*.

[27] Cambridge, University Library, MS Mm.ii.9, a rubricated Sarum antiphonal (probably from St Giles Abbey, an Augustinian house at Barnwell, England), second quarter of the thirteenth century; secular cursus; 567 pages; 340x240 mm; square notation on four-line staff (this description is from *Cantus*).

[28] Worcester, Cathedral Chapter Library, MS F. 160, a compendium of liturgical material, including an antiphonal, from Worcester Cathedral; dated *c.*1230, with fourteenth-century additions; 354 folios; quadratic notation on four red line staves; monastic cursus; facsimile in *Paléographie Musicale*, Series 1, xii (this description is from *Cantus*).

EXAMPLE 1: TWO VERSIONS OF *Ascendit Christus*

The first responsory for matins on the feast of the Assumption, *Vidi speciosam sicut columbam*, belongs to a family of responsories which all use the same melodic formula (see Example 3). Whereas *Exaltata es* illustrates the use of the same melody for different texts, *Vidi speciosam* may exemplify the practice of formulaic elaboration of psalm-tones. By this means, formulas which could be adapted to virtually any text were elaborated in the responsories to large-scale musical items, such elaborations being made, for the most part, in the period prior to the first surviving manuscripts. Thus while the text of *Vidi speciosam* is one of the most constant in the manuscripts surveyed, the improvised nature of responsories makes an exhaustive, critical comparison of its melodies inappropriate.

The variety of melodic versions was constrained by the reforms of the Premonstratentians and Cistercians in the twelfth century and by the Dominicans and Franciscans in the thirteenth. These orders required their liturgical books to be copied according to strict rules from approved exemplars: no syllable of text, ligature or pitch could be changed. Franciscans and Dominicans were obliged to use the new square notation, in which the pitch of each note was unambiguously indicated, but which lacked the expressive subtlety of the neumes. Cistercians, however, continued to use neumes in conjunction with the four-lined staff well into the fifteenth and sixteenth centuries, although their variety became more restricted as the expressive meaning of the older neumes grew less and less meaningful.[29]

The Office for the Assumption of the Virgin as transmitted by Dominican manuscripts dating from the time of Humbert's reform includes antiphons from the earliest manuscripts. The only two not included in Hésbert's *Corpus Antiphonalium Officii* are the *Magnificat* antiphon *Ascendit Christus super coelos* and the responsory verse *Regina mundi hodie de seculo*. *Ascendit Christus* occurs in English secular and monastic sources. It appears also in the *Processionale Monasticum* (1887–93, reprinted 1983) set to the same melody as in the Dominican exemplars, the Perugian choir-books, and the *Poissy Antiphonal*. *Regina mundi hodie de seculo* is paired with the responsory *Hodie Maria Virgo coelos ascendit*. Of the twelve sources indexed by Hésbert this association occurs only in Ivrea, Biblioteca Capitolare, MS CVI, an eleventh-century manuscript from that city. In the sources indexed in the *Cantus* project it appears in one monastic source (Arras, MS 465, from the monastery of Saint-Vaast) and one secular source (Cambrai, Bib. Municipal, MS C 38, from Cambrai Cathedral); in neither of these locations, however, is it paired with *Regina mundi hodie de seculo*. These two exceptions may help to establish part of the lineage of this Office. While the similarity between Dominican to Cistercian sources has been noted, the nature of the transmission of the music for individual Offices from one order to the other has not been studied in detail.[30]

The review of the text and music for the feast of the Office of the Assumption indicates the abundant opportunities that exist for further research into the transmission of liturgical texts and their musical settings. This field of investigation, moreover, has wide ramifications. There is the challenge, for example, of accessing and making available music that has remained largely unknown to date beyond the confines of the monastic community. Again, the association of Gregorian chant with such richly evocative texts as the Song of Songs is relevant both for the history of Christian spirituality and for medieval art, as Margaret Manion demonstrates.[31] The set of fourteenth-century Dominican choir-books in Perugia has proved a valuable resource in the investigation of these interlocking strands and offers considerable scope for further study.

---

[29] See M. Huglo, 'Règlement du XIIIe siècle pour la transcription des livres notés,' in Ruhnke, *Festschrift Bruno*, 121–33.

[30] The most comprehensive study is by Haller, *Early Dominican Chants*. His thesis deals with the chants for the gradual, as does the other substantial study of Dominican liturgy by D. Delaland, *Le graduel des Prêcheurs* (Paris, 1949).

[31] See Chapter 5 above.

TEXTS AND MUSIC FOR THE DIVINE OFFICE

EXAMPLE 2: MELODIES RELATED TO *Exaltata es*

EXAMPLE 3: MELODIES RELATED TO *Vidi speciosam*

177

Appendix

THE ASSUMPTION OF THE BLESSED VIRGIN MARY

Perugia, Biblioteca Comunale 'Augusta', MS 2785

First Vespers

Compline

Matins

Invitatorium, folio 89v

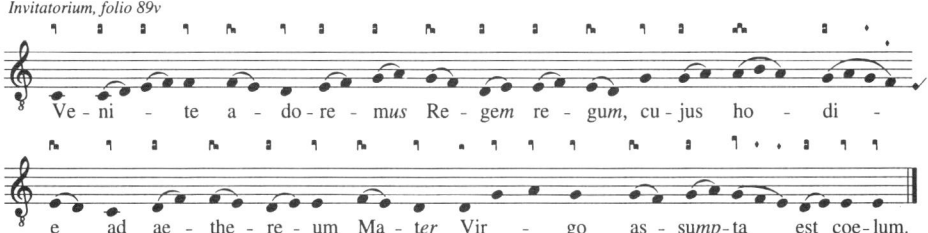

First Nocturn

Antiphona 1, folio 90r

Antiphona 2, folio 90v

Antiphona 3, folio 91r

Second Nocturn

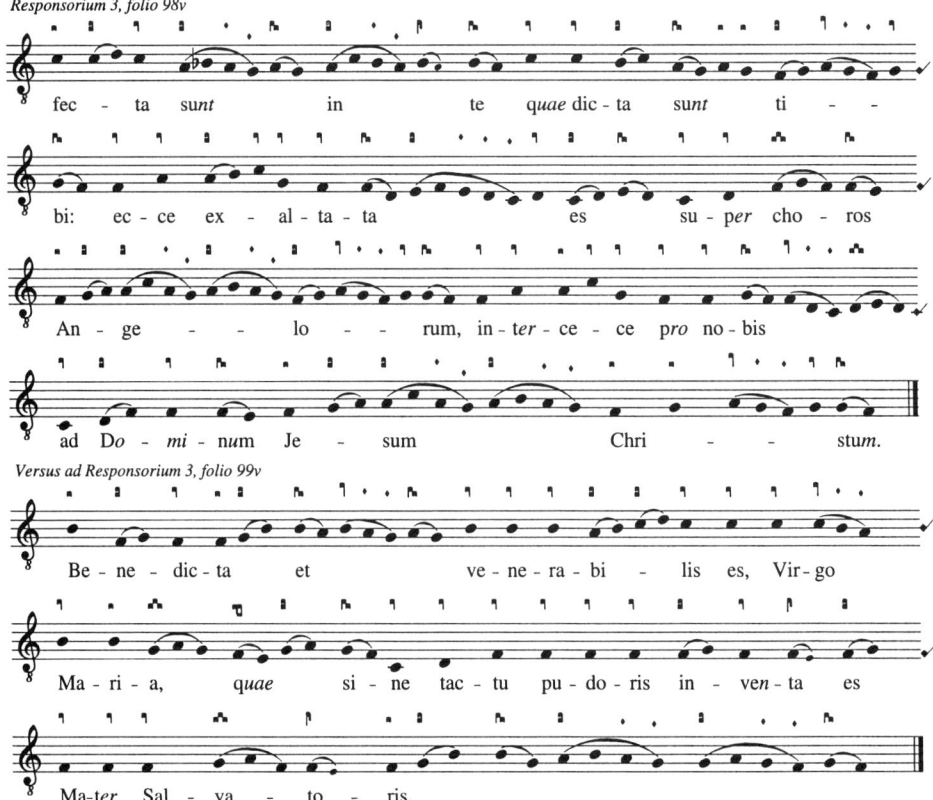

Third Nocturn

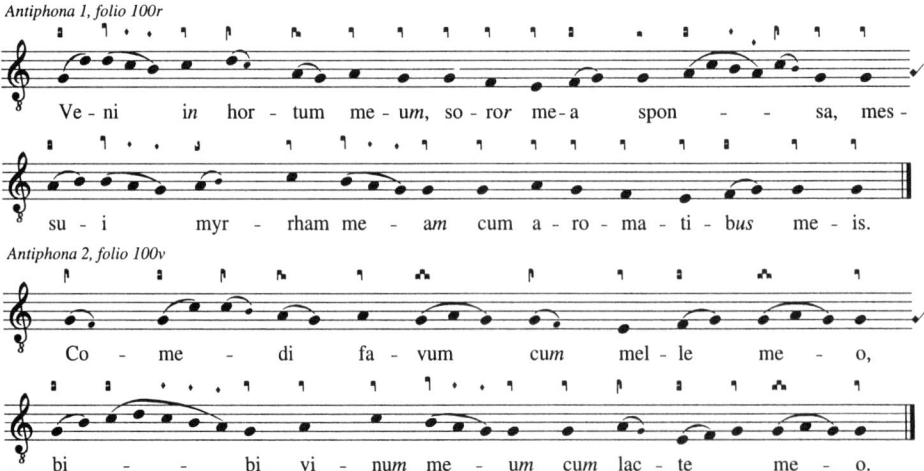

Lauds

Second Vespers

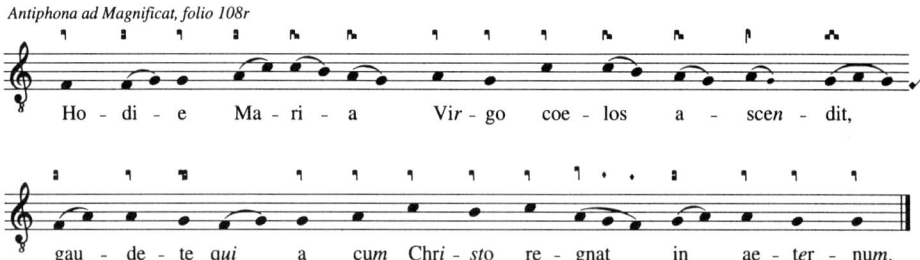

The Dominican Office for the Assumption

Hour	Item	Incipit	CAO	Concords	Modern Editions	Facsimiles
Vespers	Antiphon	Tota pulchra es, amica mea	5162	BRkglnsabpqzjh3dv	PM 274; VD 644	WA 360
	Magnificat Ant	Ascendit Christus super coelos	Not listed	2efv	VD 646	WA 358
Compline	Antiphon	Virgo Maria, non est tibi similis	5453	EMVw	PM 186	
	Nunc Dimit. Ant	Sub tuum praesidium confugimus	5041	CEMFSLApojh	AR 134;LU 1861; PM 287; VP37	
Matins	Invitatory	Venite adoremus Regem regum	1177	DFswanproqzjhv	LR 373	LA 442; WA 354
Nocturn 1	Antiphon	Exaltata es, sancta Dei Genitrix	2762	CGBEMVHRDFSLklmswagbcnproqzjh3d		LA 442
	Antiphon	Paradisi portae per te nobis	4215	CBEMVHRDFSLklmswagbcnproqzjh3dv	LR 374; VP 201	H 296;LA 442
	Antiphon	Hortus conclusus es, Dei Genitrix	3137	BEHRDFSklnagbnpxqh3d		H 299
	Responsory	Vidi speciosam sicut columbam	7878	CBEMVHRSLklmswagbcproqzjh3v	PM 178	H 296; LA 60
	Responsory Verse	Quae est ista, quae ascendit	7878a	CBEMVHRSswagbcqz3v	PM 178	H 296
	Responsory	Sicut cedrus exaltata sum	7657	CBEMVHRFSLklmswagbcproqzjh3v		H 296; LA 443
	Responsory Verse	Sicut cinnamomum et balsamum	7657	CBEMVHRFSLklmswagbcproqzjh3v		H 296; LA 443
	Responsory	Quae est ista, quae processit	7455	CBEMVHRDFSLklmswagbcproqzjh3v		H 297; LA 443
	Responsory Verse	Et sicut dies verni circumdabat	7455b	SLklmswagbcproqzjh3v		LA 443
Nocturn 2	Antiphon	Emissiones tuae paradisus malo	2641	BVRklmsapqzhdv		WA 354
	Antiphon	Fons hortorum, puteus aquarum	2887	BVRSklsapqzhdv	LR 250;PM 275	WA 354
	Antiphon	Veniat dilectus meus in hortum	5329	BVRSklnsapq,cv		LA 456,WA 354
	Responsory	Super salutem et omnem	7726	CBRFklnsagbcproqjh3dv	PM 263; LR 377	WA 357
	Responsory Verse	Exaltata es, sancta Dei Genitrix	5063	BHRfagc		H 385
	Responsory	Ista est speciosa inter filias	6994	CBEHRDFSLklmsagbcproqjh3dv	LR 378;PM 312	H 385; WA 366
	Responsory Verse	Ista est quae ascendit de deserto	6994	CBEHRDFSLklmsagbcproqjh3dv	LR 378;PM 312	WA 366
	Responsory	Beata es, Virgo Maria Dei Genitrix	6165	CGBEMVHRDFSLklmswagbcnproqzjh3dv	AM 1081; AR 126*; LR 249; LU 1686, VP 200	H 299; LA 447
	Responsory Verse	Benedicta et venerabilis es	6165b	SLklmswagbcproqzjh3v	AR 126*; LR 249; LR 258, VP 200	
Nocturn 3	Antiphon	Veni in hortum meum, soror mea	5325	BVRSklsapqdv	PM 275	LA 458; WA 355
	Antiphon	Comedi favum cum melle meo	1856	Vklmsapqzhv		LA 458; WA 355;
	Antiphon	Talis est dilectus meus	5098	Vklsaqz		LA 458
	Responsory	Hodie Maria Virgo coelos ascendit	6851	Enj		
	Responsory Verse	Regina mundi hodie	Not listed	2ef		
	Responsory	Beatum me dicent omnes	6172	CBEMVHRDFSLlmswagbcnproqjh3v		H 297
	Responsory Verse	Magnificat anima mea Dominum: lmswagbcproqjh3v				
	Responsory	Felix namque es, sacra Virgo Maria	6725	BEMVHRFSLlmswapruqz3v		H 307; LA447
	Responsory Verse	Ora pro populo, interveni pro clero	6725	BEMVHRFSLlmswapruqz3v		H 307; LA 447
Lauds	Antiphon	Assumpta est Maria in coelum	1503	CBEMVHRDFSLklmswagbcnproqzjh3dv	AR 127*; PM 242 AR 127*; PM 242	H 298; LA 448; WA 358
	Antiphon	Maria Virgo assumpta est	3707	CBEMVHRDFSLklmswagbcproqzjh3dv	AR 820; AR 875; AM 101; LU 1605;	H 298; LA 448; WA 358
	Antiphon	In odore unguentorum tuorum	3261	CBEMVHRDFSLklmswagbcproqzh3dv	LU 1605	H 299;LA 448; WA 358
	Antiphon	Benedicta filia tu a Domino	1705	CBEMVHRDFSLklmswagbcnproqzjh3dv	AR 821; LU 1233, 1606	H 299;LA 448; WA 358
	Antiphon	Pulchra es et decora, filia	4418	CBEMVHRDFSLklmswagbcnproqzjh3dv	AR 821; LU 1606; AM 1015	H 299; LA 448; WA 358
	Benedictus Ant.	Quae est ista quae ascendit	4425	CBEMVHRDFSLklmswagbcproqzjh3dv	AR 821; LU 1600;	H 299; LA 449; WA 358
The small hours have no proper chants						
Vespers 2	Magnificat Ant.	Hodie Maria Virgo coelos ascendit	3105	CBEMVHRDFSLabcdeglhijklnopqr	LU 1607	H 300; LA 449; WA 360

Abbreviations for Manuscript Sources

B	Bamberg, Staatsbibliothek, lit. MS 23
C	Paris, B.N. MS lat. 17436
D	Paris, B.N. MS lat. 17296
E	Ivrea, Chapter Library MS 106.
F	Paris, B.N. MS lat. 12584
G	Durham, Cathedral Chapter Library, MS B.III.11
H	St Gallen, Stiftsbibliothek MSS 390-391
L	Benevento, Chapter Library MS V. 21
M	Monza. Basilica S. Giovanni C. 12/75
R	Zürich, Zentralbibliothek, MS 28
S	London, British Library, Add. MS30850
V	Verona, Chapter Library MS XCVIII
a	Graz, Universitätsbibliothek, MS30
b	Klosterneuburg, Augustiner-Chorherrenstift, MS 1017.
c	Linz, Bundesstaatliche Studienbibliothek, MS 290 (183)
d	Vorau, Stiftsbibliothek, MS 287 (29)
e	Melbourne, State Library of Victoria, MS *096.1 R66A
f	Arouca, Monastery of Sts Peter and Paul, MS 1
g	Bamberg, Staatsbibliothek, lit. MS.25 (Ed.IV.2).
h	Karlsruhe, Badische Landesbibliothek, MS Aug. LX.
i	Toledo, Biblioteca capitular, 44.2.
j	Paris, BN, MS n.a. lat. 1535.
k	Arras, Bib. Municipale, 465 (893)
l	Cambrai, Bib. Municipale, MS C 38 (40).
m	Cambrai, Bib. Municipale, MS Impr. XVI C 4.
n	Paris, BN, MS lat. 1090
o	Paris, BN, MS lat. 12044
p	Paris, BN, MS lat. 12601
q	Paris, BN, MS lat. 15181 and lat. 15182
r	Paris, BN, MS n.a. lat. 1535
s	Cambridge, University Library, MS Mm.ii.9
t	London, British Library, Add. MS 23935
v	Worcester, Cathedral Chapter Library, MS F. 160
w	Florence, Arcivescovado s. c.
x	Lucca Biblioteca Comunale, MS 601 (*Paléographie Musicale*, series 1, ix)
z	Piacenza, Biblioteca Capitolare 65.
1	Rome, Archivium Generale Ordinis Predicatorum, MS XIV 11
2	Perugia, Biblioteca Comunale 'Augusta', MS 2785
3	Utrecht, Bibliotheek der Rijksuniversiteit, MS 406 (3.J.7)

NOTE: upper case silgla are from R. Hésbert, *Corpus Antiphonalium Officii*, 6 volumes, Rome, 1968-1970.

Abbreviations for Modern Editions

AM	*Antiphonale monasticum pro diurnis horis...* Paris, Tournai, Rome: Descleé. c. 1934.
AR	*Antiphonale sacrosanctae Romanae ecclesiae...* Paris, Tournai, Rome: Descleé, 1949.
CAO	R. Hésbert, *Corpus Antiphonalium Officii*, 6 volumes, Rome, 1968-1970.
LA	Lucca, Biblioteca Capitolare MS 601 (*Paléographie Musicale* IX, Tournai, 1906).
LR	*Liber responsorialis pro festis I classis* ... Solesmes, 1895.
LU	*The Liber Usualis with introduction and rubrics in English*, Tournai, New York, 1961.
PM	*Processionale Monasticum*, Solesmes, 1887-93, R 1983.
VD	*Vesperarum Liber iuxta pitum Sacri Ordinis Praedicatorum*, ed. Andreae Frühwirth, Rome, 1900.
VP	*Variae preces ex liturgia tum hodierna tum antiqua collectae aut usu receptae*, Solesmes, 5th edition, 1901.
WA	Worchester, Cathedral library MS F. 160 (*Paléographie Musicale* XII, Tournai, 1922).

Matins for the feast of the Assumption
A synoptic view of selected sources

Genre / Context	Cortona 7 Franciscan, 13thC	Florence Secular, 12thC	Arouca Cistercian, 14thC	Perugia Dominican, 13-14thC	Cambrai Secular, 14thC	Cambrai XIV Printed 1508-1518
First Nocturn						
Invitatory	Venite adoremus	Venite adoremus	Ave Maria gratia plena	Venite adoremus	Virgineae castitatis	Virgineae castitatis
Antiphon	Exaltata est sancta dei	Exaltata est sancta dei	Ecce tu pulchra es amica	Exaltata est sancta dei	Ecce tu pulchra es amica	Exaltata est sancta dei
Antiphon	Paradisi portae per te	Paradisi portae per te	Sicut lilium inter spinas sic	Paradisi portae per te	Sicut lilium inter spinas sic	Paradisi portae per te
Antiphon	Benedicta tu in mulieribus	Benedicta tu in mulieribus	Favus distillans labia tua	Hortus conclusus es	Favus distillans labia tua	Sicut myrrha electa odorem
Antiphon		Specialis virgo inter agmina			Exaltata es sancta dei	
Antiphon		Caeli regina Maria te juro			Paradisi portae per te	
Versicle		Virgo creatoris caelorum			Sicut myrrha electa odorem	
Responsory	Exaltata es*	Specie tua et pulchritudine tua	Ave Maria gratia plena		Exaltata es sancta dei	Exaltata es*
Responsory verse	Vidi speciosam	Vidi speciosam	Vidi speciosam	Vidi speciosam	Vidi speciosam	Vidi speciosam
Responsory	Quae est ista quae ascendit	Quae est ista quae ascendit	Quae est ista quae ascendit	Quae est ista quae ascendit	Viderunt eam filiae Sion	Viderunt eam filiae Sion
Responsory verse	Sicut cedrus exaltata sum	Sicut cedrus exaltata sum	Sicut cedrus exaltata sum	Sicut cedrus exaltata sum	Sicut cedrus exaltata sum	Sicut cedrus exaltata sum
Responsory	Et sicut cinnamomum	Et sicut cinnamomum	Et sicut cinnamomum	Sicut cinnamomum	Sicut cinnamomum	Sicut cinnamomum
Responsory verse	Quae est ista quae processit	Quae est enim quae processit	Quae est enim quae processit	Quae est ista,quae processit	Quae est ista quae ascendit	Quae est ista quae ascendit
Responsory verse	Et sicut dies verni	Et sicut dies verni	Osculetur me osculo oris	Et sicut dies verni	Sicut dies verni	Sicut dies verni
Second Nocturn						
Antiphon	Specie tua et pulchritudine	Specie tua et pulchritudine	Veni in ortum meum	Emissiones tuae paradisus	Emissiones tuae paradisus	
Antiphon	Adjuvabit eam deus vultu	Adjuvabit*	Comedi favum cum melle	Fons hortorum puteus	Fons hortorum puteus	
Antiphon	Sicut laetantium omnium	Sicut laetantium*	Anima mea liquefacta est	Veniat dilectus meus	Veniat dilectus meus	
Antiphon		Gratia caelestis reparatrix	Talis est dilectus meus		Specie tua et pulchritudine	
Antiphon		Sanctificans dominus templum	Descendi in ortum meum		Adjuvabit eam deus	
Versicle		Aula Maria dei casti	Hortus conclusus est		Sicut laetantium omnium	
Responsory	Assumpta est Maria	Diffusa est*	Benedicta tu in mulieribus	Super salutem et omnem	Assumpta est Maria	Assumpta est Maria
Responsory verse	Ornatam in monilibus filiam	Beatam me dicent omnes	Beatam me dicent omnes	Exaltata es sancta	Beatam me dicent omnes	Beatam me dicent
Responsory	Astitit regina a dextris tuis	Et misericordia ejus	Et misericordia ejus	Ista est speciosa inter filias	Et misericordia ejus	Et misericordia ejus
Responsory verse	Ornatam in monilibus filiam	Ornatam in monilibus filiam	Ornatam in monilibus filiam	Ista est quae ascendit	Ornatam in monilibus filiam	Ornatam in monilibus filiam
Responsory	Astitit regina a dextris tuis	Astitit regina a dextris tuis	Astitit regina a dextris tuis	Beata es Virgo Maria	Astitit regina a dextris tuis	Astitit regina a dextris tuis
Responsory verse	Beatam me dicent omnes	Veni electa mea et ponam in	Beata es virgo Maria dei	Benedicta et venerabilis es	Super salutem et...dilecta es	Super salutem et...electa es
Responsory	Et misericordia ejus	Specie tua et pulchritudine tua	Ave Maria gratia plena		Valde eam nobis oportet	Valde te nobis oportet
Responsory verse	Beata es Maria		Felix namque es sacra virgo			
Responsory verse	Ave Maria gratia plena		Ora pro populo interveni pro			

* denotes that the manuscript contains the incipit only

Third Nocturn

	MS 1	MS 2	MS 3	MS 4	MS 5	MS 6
Antiphon	Gaude Maria virgo	Beatam me dicent omnes	Veni in hortum meum		Veni in hortum meum	Gaude Maria*
Antiphon	Dignare me laudare te virgo	Et misericordia ejus	Comedi favum		Comedi favum	Maria virgo assumpta est
Antiphon	Post partum virgo inviolata	Ornatam in monilibus filiam	Talis est dilectus meus		Descendi in hortum meum u	Ista est speciosa inter
Antiphon		Astitit regina a dextris tuis			Gaude Maria virgo...	Ista est quae ascendit de
Antiphon		Veni electa mea et ponam in			Dignare me laudare te virgo	Beata es virgo Maria dei
Versicle		Specie tua et pulchritudine tua			Post partum virgo inviolata	Beata es et venerabilis virgo
Responsory	Maria virgo assumpta est	Surge virgo regia et aeterno	Post partum Virgo	Ilodie Maria Virgo	Maria virgo assumpta est	Felix namque es
Responsory verse	Diffusa est gratia in labiis	Beata es virgo Maria dei	Ista est speciosa inter	Regina mundi hodie	Ista est speciosa inter	Ora pro populo
Responsory	Mirra et guttura	Ave Maria gratia plena	Ista est quae ascendit	Beatam me dicent	Ista est quae ascendit de	
Responsory verse	Beata es virgo Maria dei	Diffusa est gratia in labiis	Cum esset Rex in accubitu	Magnificat anima mea	Beata es virgo Maria dei	
Responsory	Ave Maria gratia plena	Dilexisti justitiam et odist	Pulchra sum et decora	Felix namque es	Beata es et venerabilis virgo	
Responsory verse	O gloriosa femina excelso	Beata es Maria quae omnium	Super salutem et omnem	Ora pro populo,	Felix namque es	
	Sola fuit mulier patuit	Ave Maria gratia plena	Exaltata es Sancta Dei Genetrix		Ora pro populo	

Manuscript Sources

1. Cortona, Biblioteca Comunale, MS 6 *Thirteenth-century Franciscan antiphonal*.
2. Florence, Arcivescovado s. c. *Twelfth-century antiphonal from Florence Cathedral*.
3. Arouca, Monastery of Sts Peter and Paul, Ms 1 *Thirteenth-century Cistercian antiphonal*.
4. Dominican sources. Four concordant sources are represented in this column: Rome, Santa Sabina, Dominican Archives MS XIV L 1; London, British Library MS Additional 23935, Perugia, Biblioteca Comunale 'Augusta' MS 2785 and Melbourne, State Library of Victoria, MS *096 1/R66A.
5. Cambrai, Bibliothèque Municipale, MS C 38 (40). *Antiphonal from Cambrai Cathedral, c. 1230-1250 (with later additions)*.
6. Cambrai, Bibliothèque Municipale, MS Impr. XVI C 4. *Antiphonal for Cambrai printed in Paris by Simon Vostre between 1508 and 1518. Secular cursus.*

SEVEN

A Centre for Devotional and Liturgical Manuscript Illumination in Fifteenth-Century Besançon

Vera F. Vines

THE IDENTIFICATION OF REGIONAL CENTRES of manuscript illumination and the plotting of their activities have attracted increasing attention over recent years. The extensive exhibition of French manuscripts dated between 1440 and 1520 which opened at the Bibliothèque Nationale, Paris, in November 1993 introduced much new research on Parisian ateliers and other well known centres of late medieval illumination such as Rouen and Tours. Its 240 exhibits and the accompanying catalogue by François Avril and Nicole Reynaud also addressed many less well-documented—and in some cases hypothetical—regional centres of French manuscript production.[1] This paper focuses on one such centre, metropolitan Besançon, with which a number of fifteenth-century manuscripts in quite disparate styles have been associated.[2]

---

[1] Paris, Bibliothèque Nationale. F. Avril and N. Reynaud, *Les Manuscrits à Peintures en France 1440–1520* (Paris, 1993).

[2] See Avril and Reynaud, *Manuscrits*, 193–210.

From the second quarter of the fifteenth century onwards, to judge from the numerous extant examples, illuminated liturgical and devotional books for use in the archdiocese of Besançon were in steady demand. Manuscripts destined for Besançon have been identified through their texts, which include particular antiphons, responses and *capitula* in the Hours of the Virgin and the Office of the Dead, and regional and local saints in the litanies and calendars.[3] Two feasts accorded the highest gradings in the calendar are the most precise indicators that a book was intended to be used within the archdiocese of Besançon—the dedication of the cathedral of St John the Evangelist (May 5) and the dedication of the altar of the co-cathedral of St Stephen (October 3). However, the archdiocese embraced a wide region, with some of its dependent dioceses extending beyond the Franche-Comté; and while it is relatively easy to identify liturgical books designed for use in the metropolitan churches of Besançon itself, there is much greater variation in the calendars and litanies of books made for other parts of the archdiocese, especially in calendars of books of hours.

Nor can it be assumed that all fifteenth-century liturgical and devotional manuals broadly described as of Besançon Use were made in that city, still less that they reflect an entrenched local tradition of illumination. When manuscript production in Paris was disrupted by English occupation from 1420 to 1436, artists seem to have scattered to find work in outlying areas and in so doing helped to mould distinctive regional styles.[4] Scholars, however, disagree about the precise origins of the varied influences discernible in fifteenth-century books made for Besançon. For example, in a fine book of hours for the Use of Besançon (New York, Morgan MS M.293, dated c.1430) John Plummer and Millard Meiss recognized the hand of a miniaturist trained in the Egerton Master's early fifteenth-century Parisian workshop. They based their judgements on the artist's compositional style, on his evangelists' facial types, and on his technique of applying glazed metal to create glistening ornamental patterns.[5] Plummer saw no reason to doubt that this Parisian-trained illuminator later worked within or near Besançon, in an established workshop which employed artists capable of producing fine quality books and who were involved in the training of others. Hence, he maintained

---

[3] See J. Plummer, 'Use and Beyond Use' in R.S. Wieck, ed., *Time Sanctified: The Book of Hours in Medieval Art and Life* (New York, 1988), 149–56.

[4] See J. Plummer, *The Last Flowering: French Painting in Manuscripts 1420–1530* (New York, 1982).

[5] Plummer, *Last Flowering*, no. 36 (26); and M. Meiss, *French Painting in the Time of Jean de Berry: The Limbourgs and their Contemporaries*, 2 vols (New York, 1974), I, 384–88.

that the Master of Morgan MS. M.293 exercised a persistent influence on locally produced manuscripts.[6]

François Avril's reading of the situation differs from Plummer's in that he believes that the artist of Morgan MS M.293 came from Burgundy rather than Paris, exercising his considerable influence on Besançon illumination chiefly through the work of one particular—and possibly native—illuminator who was active for more than twenty years, from 1450 or earlier. Avril argues that this follower's different phases of development over a considerable period could account for the marked stylistic differences evident amongst his manuscripts.[7]

Disparate styles also appear in books for Besançon Use, with illuminators trained in traditions as diverse as those of the Northern Netherlands and Savoy apparently working together on the same commission. For example, in a book of hours for Besançon Use (New York, Morgan MS M.28, c.1470) we find the hand of an illuminator whose work shows certain Northern Netherlandish influences. This artist's style occurs in other manuscripts for Besançon Use, and in Morgan, MS M.28 he collaborated with a more accomplished colleague whose style Plummer identified as originating in Savoy.[8] Plummer suggested that the latter was in charge of the project, though his only supporting evidence is the fact that the 'Savoyard' illuminator executed the first six miniatures and their borders while his collaborator was responsible for the manuscript's last eleven miniatures together with many of the borders and the twenty-four calendar roundels. Since calendars were often produced last, the 'Savoyard' illuminator could have worked first on the book; this does not necessarily mean, however, as we shall see later, that he dictated its decorative programme.

Another book of hours for Besançon Use (New York, Pierpont Morgan MS M.196, considered by Plummer to have been produced about 1470, and thus roughly contemporary with Morgan MS M.28) was entirely illustrated by another Savoyard illuminator.[9] This artist has been identified by Avril as the Saluces Master, a superlative craftsman whose major manuscript achievement was the magnificent *Saluces Hours* (London, BL Add. MS 27697, c.1440–65).[10] According to Avril, Morgan MS M.196 was produced in Besançon soon after 1450—that is to say, considerably earlier

---

[6] Plummer, *Last Flowering*, no. 36 (26).

[7] Avril, *Les Manuscrits*, no. 109 (197).

[8] Plummer, *Last Flowering*, no. 75 (57–58). Plummer notes that this book has a calendar feast for the dedication of a church at Dôle, a subsidiary diocese of Besançon; its patron may have been resident there.

[9] Plummer, *Last Flowering*, no. 73 (56).

[10] F. Avril, 'Le Maître des Heures de Saluces: Antoine de Lonhy', *Revue de l'Art* 85 (1989), 9–34.

than Plummer's date for this manuscript—during an early stage in the career of the Saluces Master, whose travels ranged from Burgundy to Savoy. Plummer, on the other hand, attributes the miniatures of Morgan MS M.196 to a follower of the Saluces Master and suggests that the book may have been illuminated in either north-western Savoy or a neighbouring region, proposing such centres as 'Geneva, Lyons, Mâcon, or Chalons-sur-Saône' as a possible place of origin.[11]

These divergent views indicate the need for further historical research to complement stylistic observations, if we are to identify more precisely the location and nature of the production of manuscripts for Besançon Use in the fifteenth century. I have previously drawn attention to two miniatures in a missal made for Charles de Neufchâtel after his installation as archbishop of Besançon in 1464 (Auckland Central City Library, Special Collections, Med. MSS G138-39) which through their use of medieval legend and liturgical pageant reveal an intimate knowledge of local traditions and customs of that city.[12] I present here additional evidence from this important and elaborate commission which indicates that, at least from the 1470s to the close of the century, Besançon supported an active centre of manuscript production to which certain works may be confidently attributed. This centre, encompassing both text-copying and illuminating activities, was directly associated with the patronage of the archbishop and his entourage; it produced liturgical books and books of hours for patrons connected with the archdiocese of Besançon. Some of its products, moreover, reveal a blend of distinctive local stylistic characteristics with diverse foreign elements, a mix that suggests that itinerant artists of high quality were attracted to work there.

Before turning to the Auckland missal it will be helpful to recall the geographical and political implications of the location of Besançon as capital city of the Franche-Comté. Fifteenth-century Besançon was situated on one of the major trading routes winding from Italy through the Savoy alps to Northern Europe; it thus played an important linking economic role in the region and a considerable number of merchants and financiers resided there. Protected geographically by the U-bend of the River Doubs, the city was relatively free from turmoil and was home to several important local industries, including leather tanning and parchment making. Its countryside, moreover, was much richer than neighbouring mountainous Savoy. As a result, there was a continuous movement of Savoyard artisans into the Franche-Comté throughout the later

---

[11] Plummer, *Last Flowering*, 56.

[12] V.F. Vines, 'Reading medieval images: Two miniatures in a fifteenth-century Missal' in M.M. Manion and B.J. Muir, eds, *Medieval Texts and Images: Studies of Manuscripts from the Middle Ages* (Sydney, 1991), 127–47.

Middle Ages. Manuscript craftsmen could well have been amongst them.[13]

From the twelfth century onwards Besançon had also an been an important imperial city governed by a prince-archbishop who owed allegiance to the Holy Roman Emperor as well as to the Pope. During the fifteenth century, however, Besançon's chief loyalties were to the Duchy of Burgundy although at times the city governors could exercise independent judgement, as when in 1463 they ignored the recommendation of Philip the Good and supported the claim of the young candidate, Charles de Neufchâtel for the archbishopric of Besançon.[14] Then, in 1480, when Louis XI sought to take the region for the French monarchy, the archbishop and his family attempted to persuade the city to surrender to the royal invaders. For this Charles was branded as a traitor by both the townspeople and the nobility still loyal to the Burgundian cause, and he was forced into exile. Although given the bishopric of Bayeux, he remained archbishop of Besançon until his death in 1498.[15]

The splendid Auckland missal, which bears the coat-of arms of Charles de Neufchâtel, was probably produced some time in the early 1470s (Pl. 5).[16] It is divided into a summer and a winter volume and has an unusually rich illustrative programme. The text of the canon, which is written in full in each volume, is introduced by two full-page miniatures of the Crucifixion and Christ in Majesty; the individual Masses of the temporal and sanctoral are illustrated by small single column paintings, making a total of seventy-two miniatures. This illustrative programme was carried out by two stylistically unrelated collaborators. One of these is the illuminator who was responsible for the greater part of Morgan MS M.28. His style ultimately derives from the northern Netherlands.

---

[13] See C. Fohlen, ed., *Histoire de Besançon. Des origins à la fin du xvie siècle* (Paris, 1964); R. Fiétier, *La Cité de Besançon de la Fin du xiième au Milieu du xivème siècle. Etude d'une Société Urbaine*, 3 vols (Lille, 1978); M. le Commandant Revel, 'Savoie et Franche Comté' in *Aca-démie des Sciences Belles-Lettres et Arts de Besançon* (Besançon, 1927); F.M. Fournier, 'L'Immigration Savoyarde en Franche-Comté avant 1789' in *Mémoires de la Société d'Emulation du Doubs*, N.S. (1959), 3–41. For Besançon and merchant activities along north Italian and Burgundian trade routes see L. Gauthier, *Les Lombards dans Les Deux-Bourgogne* (Paris, 1909).

[14] See M. Rey and R. Fiétier, 'Les Grandes Epreuves' in Fohlen, 507–53.

[15] See M. Piquard, 'Charles de Neufchâtel Archévêque de Besançon et la Conquête de la Franche-Comté par Louis XI', *Les Annales de Bourgogne*, 5 (1933), 260–63.

[16] For a full description of the missal, see M.M. Manion, V.F. Vines and C. de Hamel, *Medieval and Renaissance Manuscripts in New Zealand Collections* (London, 1989), no. 18 (55–58). The date of the production of the missal is now set at c.1471 instead of 1464, since Romain Jurot has informed me that the feast of the Visitation (vol. 2, f. 170) was not adopted in Besançon until 1471. M. Jurot has completed a doctoral dissertation on the medieval liturgy of the archdiocese of Besançon.

Since his work appears in a number of manuscripts for Besançon, he must have been in the region for some time and he will be referred to here as 'the Besançon illuminator'. The other illuminator's artistic vocabulary seems to have been acquired in Provence.[17]

While most of the illustrations in the Auckland missal conform to widespread iconographical patterns, a small number refer to events of specific interest to Besançon and its archbishop; these do not rely on established visual precedents. Such innovations should not be under-rated; in light of the predominance of traditional programmes of illustration—especially for liturgical texts—it was surely no accident when artists altered established images or replaced them with new ones.[18]

This point has already been made in an earlier study with reference to two particular miniatures from the missal[19]; however, in order to present the case as fully as possible for the local production of this manuscript, I refer to them again briefly here. Each illustrates a legend which enjoyed considerable popularity in medieval Besançon: St Antidius' ride to Rome on a devil to berate an errant pope; and the Meeting of the Three Kings on their way to Bethlehem (Figs 42 and 43). Instead of using traditional visual schema such as an iconic full-length figure of St Antidius to mark his feast, or a portrayal of the Adoration of the Magi for the Epiphany, the illuminators of the Auckland missal produced two iconographically novel compositions. The depiction of the local saint winging his way across the sky on the back of the tamed forces of evil highlights the role of romance and metaphor in medieval thought, while the Meeting of the Three Kings is given an added historical dimension by the inclusion of a black youth who wears an exotic shawl, and stands as if declaiming a dramatic speech. He is part of the legendary narrative since his presence identifies the nearby horseman as the king of Nubia. But he also em-bodies a real-life character of late medieval Besançon, who was to be dressed in 'Persian' costume and blackened to look like a 'Moor' prior to participating in the Epiphany procession of the Three Kings—an annual adjunct to the Besançon liturgy.[20]

---

[17] For an analysis of the two artists' styles, see Manion, Vines and de Hamel, *Manuscripts in New Zealand*, 57–58. The Provençal hand, which I believe to be related to that of the painter and illuminator Enguerrand Quarton, has not to date been associated with any other manuscripts for Besançon. The Besançon illuminator was responsible for the miniatures in the missal reproduced in Figs 1, 4–6, and 8 in the Manion *et al.* catalogue; the Provençal illuminator executed the miniatures reproduced in Figs 2–3.

[18] See J.J.G. Alexander, *Medieval Illuminators and their Methods of Work* (London, 1992), 52.

[19] See Vines, 'Reading Medieval Images', 127–47.

[20] See K. Young, 'La Procession des Trois Rois à Besançon', *The Romanic Review* 4 (1913), 76–83. I am grateful to M. Jurot for this reference. Young discusses a French translation, dated 1629, of an earlier Latin text (now lost) which gives stage directions for the choir-

Two other miniatures refer to specific episodes in the history of Besançon. Their innovative character can best be appreciated if considered alongside some of the missal's more traditional imagery. For example, three different, but well-established compositions, introduce feasts associated with St John the Evangelist, patron saint of the metropolitan church of Besançon: he holds the poisoned cup (December 27), he is shown unscathed in a pot of boiling oil (May 6), and, for the feast of the dedication of the metropolitan church in his honour (May 5), a bishop accompanied by two acolytes raises his hand in blessing outside a church. The depiction of the Stoning of St Stephen for the feast of his martyrdom (December 26) is also sanctioned by scriptural and visual tradition (Fig. 44).[21]

On the other hand, the two images from the *sanctorale* that mark the Invention of St Stephen's relics (August 3) and the Dedication of his altar in the co-cathedral (October 3) can only be understood with reference to historical events of special importance to Besançon. The scene that illustrates the Invention of St Stephen's relics has a sparse interior setting (Plate 5); it shows a room with a vaulted ceiling and, in the background, a tapestried couch and cushion beneath four windows. In the middle ground a youth with tonsure and halo is asleep on a stool, his head held in one hand, while an older man stands in the foreground, pointing to a bier on the floor. This scene explicitly refers to the discovery of the saint's relics.[22]

According to legend, the early Christian priest, Lucien, recorded in a letter that an imperious old man claiming to be Gameliel had visited him three times in a dream.[23] On each occasion he exhorted Lucien to rescue his relics from their hiding place alongside the body of St Stephen protomartyr and to restore them to a place of honour. Lucien alerted the Patriarch, John of Jerusalem, who thereupon recovered both Gameliel's

---

boys taking part in the procession: 'on habille trois petits garçons à la mode de pages de Perses avec habillement à ce propres, l'un desquels on doibt noircir par le visage et les mains qui représent le Roy more . . .' (81). Young found that other earlier Latin Ordinals did not contain details regarding stage make-up (81, n. 4). It is possible, therefore, that the black youth in the missal's miniature (c.1471) is the earliest pictorial reference to Besançon's dramatic ceremonial for the Epiphany. Fifteenth-century depictions of the three kings advancing towards Bethlehem occur in some Besançon Books of Hours (where they replace the 'Adoration of the Magi'); see, for example, New York, Pierpont Morgan MS M.41, f. 55; Paris, Hôtel Drouot sale, 7 December 1960, Lot 6, miniature 9; none of them, however, contains the figure of a youthful 'Moor'.

[21] See Manion, Vines and de Hamel, *Manuscripts in New Zealand*, Pl. 14 .

[22] For the legend of the translation of St Stephen's arm-bone, see B. de Vregille S.J., *Hugues de Salins, Archevêque de Besançon (1033–1066)* (Besançon, 1983), 381–82.

[23] Lucien's letter is published in J.-P. Migne, ed., *Patrologia Latina*, 221 vols (Paris, 1844–64), 41.807–18. I am grateful to Bernard de Vregille for this reference.

relics and Stephen's body. Tradition also has it that St Stephen's body was subsequently divided into many parts, the most valuable of these being the main bone of one arm which showed the actual marks of the martyr's stoning. After many vicissitudes the arm-bone found its way to Besançon. The city proudly claimed that the relic had been in place beneath the main altar of the Carolingian church of St Stephen since before the year 1000, and it had long been the object of civic as well as religious cele-bration.[24]

At the instigation of the great medieval churchman Hugues de Salins, liturgist, reformer, statesman, and benefactor, who was archbishop of Besançon from 1031 to 1066, the Carolingian church of St Stephen was restored and enlarged; its ecclesiastical status was also officially designated as 'co-cathedral', second only in rank to the metropolitan basilica and cathedral of St John.[25] At the same time, the liturgy of Besançon was reformed and rewritten, almost certainly by Hugues, who also provided St Stephen's relic with a new and sumptuously ornamented gold reli-quary in the shape of an arm, with the archbishop's name engraved thereon. During a dedication ceremony on 3 October, 1050, Pope Leo IX placed the reliquary beneath the altar of the rebuilt church.[26]

The miniature in the Auckland missal which introduces the Mass for the dedication of the altar of St Stephen alludes to this event (Fig. 45). The pope, identified by his triple tiara, kneels with his hand raised in benediction; he is accompanied by two tonsured clerics who stand on either side of the altar. No attempt has been made to reproduce the cathedral's sanctuary realistically, the altar and the rounded windows behind it being conventional motifs used to express the general idea of a church interior. The image is, nevertheless, of considerable historical interest, since it is a unique pictorial record of a significant event in Besançon's medieval past. For the patron, Charles de Neufchâtel, it must have had personal overtones as well, reminding him of the venerable traditions of his ancient see and of his pastoral responsibilities as Hugues de Salins' successor.

Other relics venerated in Besançon also receive visual emphasis in the Auckland missal although in more traditional formulations. The feasts of the translation of the relic of the crown of thorns, and of the relics of St Nicholas, for example, are both illustrated by the customary theme of the

---

[24] The early medieval reliquary containing the city's most precious relic was a major visual focus for processions and other ceremonial occasions; see n. 29.

[25] De Vregille, *Hugues de Salins*, 78–82. The Bull of Union of the two chapters was promulgated in the thirteenth century; see Fiétier 'L'administration Diocésaine', *La Cité de Besançon*, II, 921–24.

[26] The Pope also placed the skull of St Agapité beneath the main altar beside the arm-bone of St Stephen; see de Vregille, 'Hugues de Salins' in C. Fohlen, ed., *Histoire de Besançon*, 267.

procession. In each scene two clerics are shown carrying a reliquary mounted on a pair of poles which they support on their shoulders. The setting for the procession of the relic of the crown of thorns (vol. 2, f. 204) is a churchyard; that for the translation of St Nicholas' relics (vol. 2, f. 146) a hilly landscape (Fig. 46). Such processions were popular in the medieval church; and an eleventh-century pontifical reflects their long history in Besançon:

> On the day before the new church is consecrated, the relics are placed in the bier that has been built in the other church or in a tent, and there let vigils be held on that very night in honour of the saints whose relics are to be stored… and on the following day, after the rites of consecration of the church itself, they go to that place where the relics have been during the vigils on the previous night, and let them be carried with very great honour right to the entrance-door of the church and, after the homily to the people, then let the bishop receive the bier with the deacon, and during the approach let the priest say the antiphon: 'We approach, blessed Lord'.[27]

Such occasions would have been familiar to Charles de Neufchâtel from his early years and his rebuilding of the chapel dedicated to St Nicholas in the basilica of St John, for his own private use, some time after 1465, no doubt involved him personally in such a ceremonial.[28]

The portrayal of clerics processing through a hilly terrain in the Auckland missal may also reflect the actual role of processions in the liturgy of Besançon, which resulted from the custom of sharing religious observances between the co-cathedral of St Stephen, situated on the citadel above the city and the metropolitan church of St John below. Christmas, the Epiphany, Easter, and Pentecost were celebrated in St John's basilica while the Ascension, the feasts of St Stephen and some other important saints were celebrated in St Stephen's. For each major festival the canons of the chapters of the two cathedrals came together, one group processing to meet the other at the appointed place. Solemn processions through the city streets and into the nearby countryside must certainly have been a familiar sight.[29]

Textual evidence from the Auckland missal further reinforces the specific nature of this manuscript commission. The most distinctive feature of the missal, and of particular interest to musicologists and students of liturgy, is its Pentecost *Exultet*. Recently described as a 'liturgical

---

[27] Pontifical, Use of Besançon, Montpellier, Bibl. de la Fac. de Médicine, MS 303, ff. 113–14. I am indebted to B. de Vregille for this reference.

[28] See Fiétier, *Cité de Besançon*, II, 941, for comments on the archbishop's private chapel of St Nicholas.

[29] See B. de Vregille, 'Les célébrations liturgiques' in Fohlen, 351–70; and Abbé Guibard, 'Cérémonies qui se pratiquaient au Moyen Age . . .' in *Annales franc-comtoises. Revue, Religieuse historique et littéraire* 6e Année 12 (1869), 3–15.

curiosity of no little interest',[30] this chant was sung during the Vigil of Pentecost in the basilica of St John over many centuries. Elegantly transcribed, with full musical notation, it occupies nine pages in the Auckland missal and is introduced by a large illuminated capital (Fig. 49). The text is an amplification of the Holy Saturday *Exultet* (Fig. 48), carefully modified to suit the theme of praise of the Holy Spirit. The benediction and lighting of the candle, features of the Easter Vigil, were also incorporated into the Pentecost observance at Besançon to symbolize the gift of the Holy Spirit to the faithful.[31]

In his definitive study of this subject, Bernard de Vregille concludes that the author of the Pentecost *Exultet* was almost certainly the eleventh-century prelate Hugues de Salins who, in addition to his reputation as a statesman, was also known for his special devotion to the Paraclete. The earliest extant record of this liturgical innovation occurs in an eleventh-century missal (Besançon, Bibl. mun. MS 72) associated with the collegiate church of the Madeleine in Besançon; it was probably made for Hugues' own use.[32]

By the fifteenth century the Pentecost chant had become an established part of the liturgy of the basilica of St John. It appears, but without any accompanying melody, in two other contemporary Besançon missals, Besançon, Bibl. mun. MSS 76 and 77. A third missal (Besançon, Bibl. mun. MS 75) contains an abbreviated reference to the chant in the form of

---

[30] 'Pentecost Exultet'. *New Catholic Encyclopedia* (New York, 1967), 5, 766. The chant occurs in vol. 2 of Charles de Neufchâtel's missal (ff. 25–29v); the Easter *Exultet* is in vol. 1 (ff. 125–29). I am indebted to John Stinson for helpful discussions of the two variant chants.

[31] See A. Strittmater O.S.B., 'The Pentecost Exultet of Reims and Besançon' in D. Miner, ed., *Studies in Art and Literature for Bella Costa Greene*, (Princeton, 1954), 384–400. Strittmater's pioneering research brought to light a hitherto neglected manuscript in the Walters Library, Baltimore. He was unable to explain, however, the short-lived existence of the chant in the medieval liturgy of Reims Cathedral. De Vregille, 'Les célébrations litur-giques,' having identified Hugues de Salins as the author of Besançon's *Exultet*, observed that as pontifical legate he attended the consecration and crowning of Philippe I at Reims on 23 May 1059. Indeed, Hugues was the main celebrant at the royal ceremony, which took place on the feast of Pentecost. De Vregille suggests (in private communication) that the Archbishop of Besançon may have included the Pentecost *Exultet* in this special liturgical celebration, which could account for its use at Reims for a brief period. It is incorrectly stated in Manion, Vines and de Hamel, *Manuscripts in New Zealand*, 57, that the Pentecost *Exultet* was short-lived at both Reims and Besançon, instead of at Reims only.

[32] De Vregille, 'Les célébrations liturgiques', 332–33 and 447–48. See V. Leroquais, *Les Sacramentaires et Missels: manuscrits des bibliothèques publiques de France,* 3 vols (Paris, 1924), I, 173. Leroquais, however, does not refer to the Pentecost *Exultet* (See Strittmater, 'Pentecost Exultet', 399).

a rubric which directs the celebrant back to the Holy Saturday *Exultet*.[33] Presumably, the archdeacon who intoned the *Exultet* would have had access to a choir-book containing the fully-noted version.

In contrast to these three manuscripts, Charles' missal contains complete, fully noted versions of both the Easter and Pentecost *Exultet*. Comparison shows that the Pentecost melody is an amplified variant of the Easter music, modified to accommodate the altered wording. The fact that the feast of Pentecost occurs in a separate volume from the Holy Saturday liturgy is the most likely reason why the Pentecost *Exultet* was written out in full in the Auckland missal. However, the attention accorded it through full transcription highlights again the spiritual affinity between Charles de Neufchâtel and his venerable predecessor Hugues de Salins, originator of this liturgical embellishment. Years later, despite his status of exile, Charles was to associate himself explicitly with Hugues in an act of public patronage. In 1486, he joined with the Besançon chapter to repair the reliquary of St Stephen.[34] An inscription added to the stand of the new 'Bras' acknowledges three donors.[35] The first is archbishop Hugues, *Unus Praesul Hugo Dudum Qui Sedet In Astris* ('the first bishop Hugh, now in heaven for a long time'). The other two donors are the cathedral chapter and Charles de Neufchâtel.[36]

In the miniature for the feast of All Saints in the Auckland missal two figures occupy a pre-eminent position in the group of male saints (Fig. 49). One of them is St John the Evangelist; he is clearly identifiable by his attribute, a poisoned chalice from which issue several vipers. Mitre, crook and ceremonial chasuble identify the figure who turns towards him as a bishop. His identity, however, is uncertain. Standing slightly behind him to the left is St Lawrence, recognisable from the gridiron that he holds and clad in a deacon's dalmatic. Conceivably the bishop stands for St Nicholas, whose relics, it has already been noted, were venerated in Besançon, and whose chapel in St John's cathedral Charles had refurbished for his own private use. Certainly, liturgical dress sets this figure and St Lawrence apart from the rest of the group, and super-imposes on the basic theme of All Saints the image of a bishop being assisted by a deacon in his

---

[33] See Leroquais, *Sacramentaires et Missels*, III, no. 740 (172–73), (Besançon, Bibl. mun. MS 75); no. 741 (173) (Besançon, Bibl. mun. MS 76); and no. 844 (256–57) (Besançon, Bibl. mun. MS 77). Leroquais makes no mention of the Pentecost *Exultet*.

[34] See B. de Vregille, 'Les Diocèses de Besançon et de S. Claude' in M. Rey, ed., *Histoire des Diocèses de France* (Paris, 1977), VI, 79–80.

[35] The reliquary, shaped like an arm, was known as the 'Bras,' the name also given to the episcopal coinage; see J. Gauthier and P. Brune, 'Etude sur l'orfèvrerie en Franche-Comté du VII-XVIIIe', *Bulletin d'Archéologie* 30 (1900), 282–372, 302–3.

[36] De Vregille, *Hugues de Salins*, 437–38.

ceremonial responsibilities. Moreover, the pair appear in the company of St John, patron saint of the cathedral in which Charles de Neufchâtel was to use the missal for precisely such ritual occasions. Thus this miniature, too, seems to make reference to the epis-copal owner of the book.[37]

It is possible, however, that the bishop in the miniature is meant to represent Hugues de Salins. Charles would have been aware of the earlier move to canonize his revered predecessor, and as has already been observed, he was explicitly associated with Hughes in the inscription on the new reliquary of St Stephen, while the miniature in the missal for the dedication of the altar of St Stephen (Fig. 45) was a reminder of Hugues' labours on behalf of the see of Besançon. The fully noted version of the Pentecost *Exultet* would also have prompted the young prelate to emulate his saintly forbear's devotion to the Holy Spirit.

The detailed knowledge of Besançon's ecclesiastical history reflected in this splendid manuscript indicates that it was produced under the close supervision of clerics familiar with that history, while the complexity of the undertaking and the careful layout of the two-volume work required an integrated group of artists and crafts-people experienced in the production of illuminated manuscripts. Moreover, the meticulous transcription of the musical notation of the Pentecost *Exultet* shows that the scribe was well versed in copying liturgical music, probably from exemplars in the store of cathedral choir-books. Besançon had a widespread reputation for its performance of church music in the fifteenth century, the maintenance of which must have demanded constant recourse to musical texts for the training of choristers. This in turn points to the local production of choir-books.[38] The combined evidence indicates that the Auckland missal was produced in a manuscript workshop that operated in close association with the Besançon ecclesiastical authorities. The likeliest location for such a workplace would have been within or near the precincts of either the basilica of St John or the co-cathedral of St Stephen.

Further evidence, external to the missal, supports this conclusion. A pontifical also produced for Charles de Neufchâtel and bearing his arms has remained in Besançon (Bibl. mun. MSS 115–17; Fig. 50).[39] Its dimen-

---

[37] Hugues was only once referred to as 'saint' during the fourteenth and fifteenth centuries; in the *Vitae* of the Franche-Comté saints he is described as 'bienheureux'; see de Vregille, *Hugues de Salins*, 272.

[38] Dufay, arguably the greatest musician of the fifteenth century, visited the co-cathedral of St Stephen in Besançon in 1458, where he was consulted on the mode of an antiphon and was greeted by a former colleague from the papal choir, Pierre Grosseteste, who had retired to a canonry there; see D. Fellows, *Dufay* (London, 1982), 72, 242 and 247.

[39] V. Leroquais, *Les Pontificaux manuscrits des bibliothèques publiques de France*, 4 vols (Paris, 1937), I, no. 86 (75–78).

sions, ornamentation and illustration suggest that it was designed as a companion piece to the Auckland missal; the style of the miniatures, however, reveals more specific Flemish influences, although it is also related to that of the 'Besançon' illuminator. A smaller pontifical (Besançon, Bibl. mun. MS 157; Fig. 51) made for Charles's cousin Antoine, bishop of Toul from 1461, also belongs to this group.[40] Once again, another hand is responsible for the miniatures, but the compositions, interiors, landscapes, figure proportions, etc., are closely related to those of the missal. The half-page miniature of the Crucifixion in one of the three missals mentioned earlier (Besançon Bibl. mun. MS 77; Fig. 55) is also an example of this style. Moreover, the coat-of-arms in the initial beneath the illustration reveals that this missal was later adapted for Charles's successor, François de Busleyden, archbishop of Besançon (1498–1502).[41]

Perhaps even more interesting is the fact that at least two books of hours are also linked to the Auckland missal, indicating that the workshop did not confine itself to the production of liturgical books. As noted earlier, eleven miniatures and the calendar roundels of Morgan MS M.28 are by the Besançon illuminator; some of these compositions are virtually identical with those of the missal (Figs 52 and 53). The book of hours, Besançon, Bibl. mun. MS 125, also bears the stamp of the Besançon illuminator, although it may be the work of an assistant (Fig. 54).

Plummer, it will be recalled, in attributing the first six miniatures in Morgan MS M.28 to an illuminator trained in Savoy, suggested that this artist was in charge of the project. He saw his influence in three later books of hours for Besançon Use,[42] which implies that the Savoyard artist may have worked in the city for some time. It is the Besançon illuminator, however, whose style is consistently present in the group of manuscripts discussed here. He and his assistants or successors seem to have carried out several commissions for the archdiocese of Besançon from the 1470s. During this period the cathedral workplace also attracted talented artists from other regions such as Savoy and the south of France, who made substantial contributions to particular projects.

Jonathan Alexander has recently demonstrated the great variety of practices that operated in medieval manuscript production and has

---

[40] Leroquais, *Pontificaux,* I, no. 28 (86–88), Pl. 98. The bishopric of Toul was part of the archdiocese of Besançon.

[41] Leroquais, *Sacramentaires et Missels,* III, no. 844 (256–57). The missal, Besançon, Bibl. mun. MS 76, also has a half-page miniature of the Crucifixion; this is more Savoyard in style, with overtones of the Saluces Master.

[42] New York, Public Library, MS 41 (*c*.1475); sale, Paris, Hôtel Drouot, 7 Dec. 1960; and New York, Charles Scribner's Sons, cat. 170, no. 6; and Ossing, William Salloch, cat. 300, no. 47 (present whereabouts unknown).

shown that it is dangerous to assume that the terms 'workshop' or 'atelier' mean the same as in later Renaissance art, where artists were more likely to train in the manner of a particular master.[43] Still less should these terms be interpreted as standing for an organizational structure unvarying from place to place throughout the Middle Ages. For example, in the workshop or 'workplace' where the Auckland missal was produced, clerics may have been largely responsible for the task of writing the manuscripts, especially given the likely association with the cathedral and the number of liturgical books commissioned. Clerics—in orders, but not necessarily ordained—continue to feature among the ranks of scribes in the later Middle Ages and, in fact, two scribes and an illuminator are explicitly mentioned in a record of the clerks employed by a fourteenth-century archbishop of Besançon.[44] On the other hand, the fine quality of the border decoration and ornamentation of initials in these manuscripts, together with their detailed illustrative programmes, suggests that a group of professional illuminators found steady employment in this workplace over a considerable period of time. It is also clear that the local ranks were often swelled with talented itinerant artists. That the illuminators worked closely to the instructions of clerical advisers, possibly the scribes, has already been demonstrated.

Etaix and de Vregille have established a list of over forty manuscripts—mostly dating from the eighth to the twelfth centuries—that were once located in the ecclesiastical libraries of Besançon; about a dozen of these are associated with the cathedral of St John.[45] They have also shown that, although by no means all of these manuscripts were written in Besançon, a scriptorium existed there at least from the eleventh century.[46] Two fourteenth-century works relating to the archbishopric of Besançon have also been identified,[47] as well as the archival reference to two scribes and an illuminator, cited above.[48] There is, however, no known documentary evidence associating the making of fourteenth- and early fifteenth-century liturgical and devotional books with specific

---

[43] Alexander, *Medieval Illuminators*, 127.

[44] 'Deux écrivains, donc scribes, un clericus illuminator' (Fiétier, *Cité de Besançon*, II, 1011). Fiétier comments that this is an 'indice rare et combien précieux d'une activité artistique'.

[45] See R. Etaix and B. de Vregille, 'Les manuscrits de Besançon, Pièrre-François Chifflet et la Bibliothèque Bohier', *Scriptorium* 24 (1970), 27–39. The great majority of these early medieval manuscripts belonged to the library of the abbey and church of St Paul, Besançon. A community of canons regular who followed the rule of St Augustine occupied this site.

[46] Etaix and De Vregille, 'Les manuscrits', 39.

[47] Troyes MS 602 and Troyes MS 695; Etaix and De Vregille, 'Les manuscrits'.

[48] See n. 44.

centres in Besançon, and more detailed historical and liturgical research is needed to help resolve the often conflicting theories concerning regional attribution at this time.[49] Nevertheless, the cumulative evidence presented here indicates that in the latter part of the fifteenth century metropolitan Besançon had at least one established centre for the production of liturgical and devotional illuminated books, where under the patronage of the archbishop both local and itinerant artists found employment. In all probability this workplace was within or near one of the city's two cathedral precincts.

---

[49] This uncertainty is again exemplified by two further books of hours, kindly brought to my attention by Christopher de Hamel: Sotheby's, London, 20 June 1995, no. 90, Use of Besançon; and, of much finer quality, Sotheby's, London, 22 June 1993, no. 99, Use of Rome. See also Sotheby's Preview, July 1993, for a miniature of St George and the Dragon reproduced as a coloured cover-plate. Despite the different Usages, the calendars and memorials together suggest a likely connection with either Dijon or Besançon. In addition, the compositional forms, figurative style, and the palette of both manuscripts show undoubted affinities with the decoration and illustration of the Besançon missal.

Figure 42. St Antidius rides to Rome on the back of a devil. Missal. Auckland, Central City Library, Special Collections, Med. MS G. 139, f. 157. 318×238mm (detail).

Figure 43. Meeting of the Magi. Missal. Auckland, Central City Library, Special Collections, Med. MS G. 138, f. 22. 305×225mm (detail).

Figure 44. Stoning of St Stephen. Missal. Auckland, Central City Library, Special Collections, Med. MS G. 138, f. 15v. 305×225 mm (detail).

Figure 45. Dedication of the altar of St Stephen. Missal. Auckland, Central City Library, Special Collections, Med. MS G. 139, f. 242. 318×238mm (detail).

Figure 46. Translation of the relics of St Nicholas. Missal. Auckland, Central City Library, Special Collections, Med. MS G. 139, f. 146. 318×238mm (detail).

Figure 47. Feast of All Saints. Missal. Auckland, Central City Library, Special Collections, Med. MS G. 139, f. 253. 318×238mm (detail).

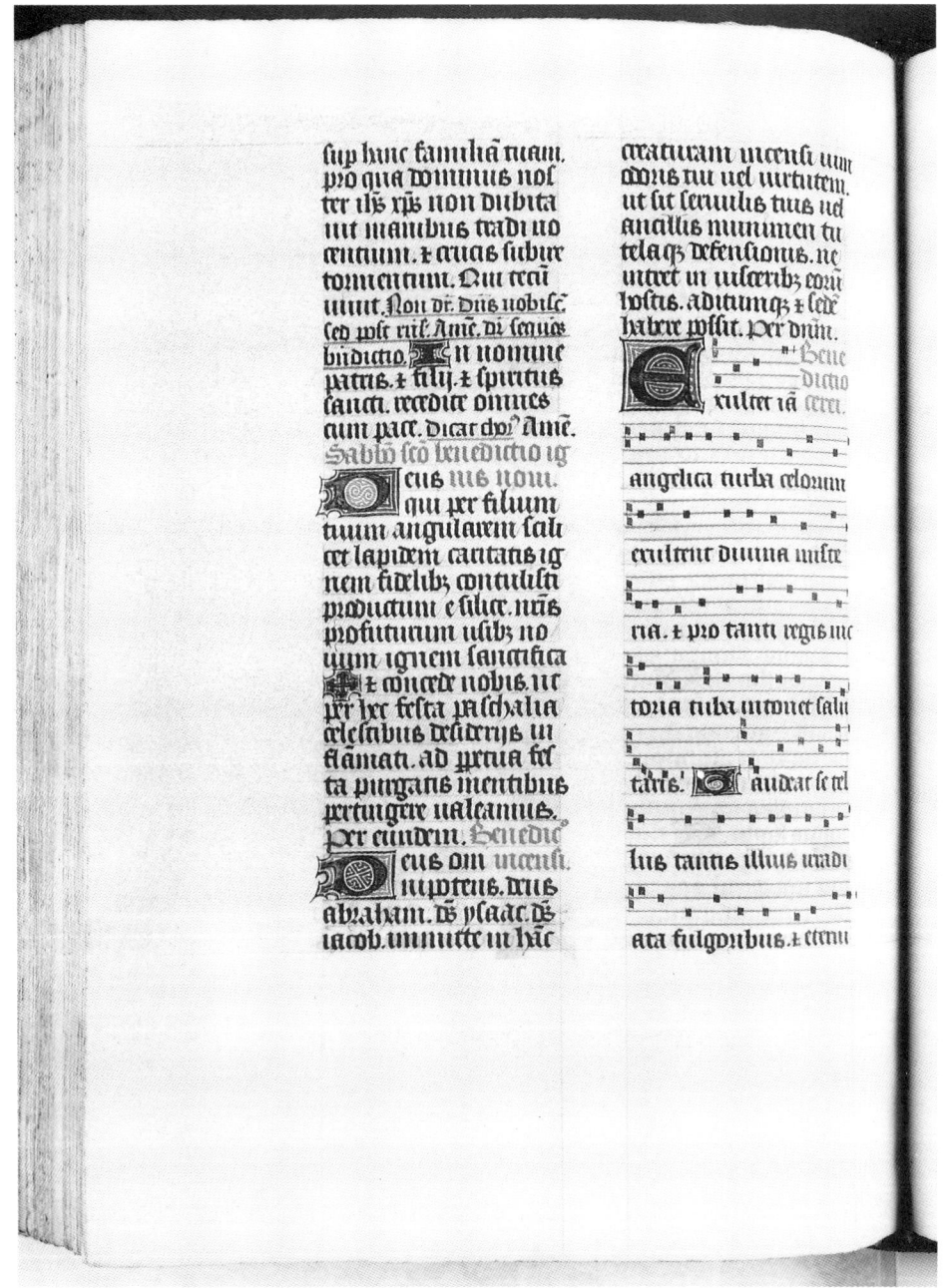

Figure 48. Holy Saturday *Exultet*. Missal. Auckland, Central City Library, Special Collections, Med. MS G. 138, f. 125v. 305×225 mm.

Figure 49. Pentecost *Exultet*. Missal. Auckland, Central City Library, Special Collections, Med. MS G. 139, f. 25. 318×238mm.

Figure 50. Ordination to the subdiaconate. Pontifical. Besançon, Bibliothèque municipale, MS 115, f. 14. 302×218mm.

Figure 51. Ordination to the diaconate. Pontifical. Besançon, Bibliothèque municipale, MS 157, f. 34. 180×135 mm.

Figure 52. Visitation. Book of Hours. New York, Pierpont Morgan Library, MS M.28, f. 40. 201×155mm.

Figure 53. Visitation. Missal. Auckland, City Central Library, Special Collections, Med. MS G. 139, f. 170. 318×238 mm (detail).

Figure 54. Presentation in the Temple. Book of Hours. Besançon, Bibliothèque municipale, MS 125, f. 40. 195×110mm.

Figure 55. Crucifixion. Missal. Besançon, Bibliothèque municipale, MS 77, f. 233v. 360×250 mm.

EIGHT

The Master of Jacques de Besançon and a Fifteenth-Century Parisian Missal

Hilary Maddocks

THE MISSAL NOW KNOWN AS PARIS, BIBLIOTHÈQUE MAZARINE MS 412, is one of the most elaborately illuminated liturgical books produced in the French capital during the last decade of the fifteenth century. The artist responsible illustrated numerous secular and religious books for a clientele ranging from provincial bourgeois merchants to French and English royalty. It is only recently, however, that the Master of Jacques de Besançon, as he is now called, has been reinstated as a significant figure in the history of fifteenth-century French illumination.

In 1892 Paul Durrieu identified a group of forty-seven illuminated manuscripts and twenty-eight printed books containing hand-painted miniatures or coloured engravings as the products of the same flourishing Parisian workshop whose activities spanned half a century (c.1449–98).[1] A colophon in one of these manuscripts—a noted Office of St John the Evangelist (Paris, Bibl. Mazarine MS 461)—states that it was made in 1485 and given to the Confraternity of St John the Evangelist by the 'bâtonnier' Jacques de Besançon, who also refers to himself as

---

[1] P. Durrieu, *Un grand enlumineur parisien au XVe siècle: Jacques de Besançon et son oeuvre* (Paris, 1892).

'enlumineur'.² Having identified the style of the larger and more accomplished of the two miniatures decorating this small book as typical of the work of his reconstituted Parisian workshop Durrieu named its *chef d'atelier* 'Jacques de Besançon'. Subsequent research however, has resulted in certain modifications of Durrieu's original thesis. It is now agreed that there were three distinct chronological phases in the activity of this workshop, each of which may be associated with a particular artistic identity: the Master of Jean Rolin, c.1445–65; the Maître François, c.1460–85; and the Master of Jacques de Besançon, c.1480–98. For some time the artist who headed the workshop in its last phase was known as 'the Chief Associate of Maître François', since it was argued that Jacques de Besançon specialized in the illumination of initials and borders etc., rather than in figurative painting and that the colophon in the Office of St John referred to his commissioning of this manuscript as 'bâtonnier' of a confraternity dedicated to the craft of the book. Nicole Reynaud has recently drawn attention to the importance of the works produced in the last phase of the workshop and has grouped them again under the name of Jacques de Besançon, adding, however, the qualification 'Master of' to allow for the possibility that Jacques de Besançon commissioned, rather than executed, the miniature in the Office of St John, which is the touchstone for the style of the last phase of this workshop.³

Now that this period has been identified with an artist in his own right, individual manuscripts are beginning to attract the detailed attention that they deserve.⁴ One such manuscript is the missal, Mazarine MS 412. The large dimensions and the elaborate decoration of this liturgical manuscript indicate that it was destined for use in an important church or chapel.⁵ Unlike, however, the series of missals executed in the

---

² 'L'an mil IIIIc–IIIIXX. cinq. fut fait ce livre en l'onneur de Dieu. et da la glorieuse vierge Marie. et de Monseigneur saint Jehan l'Euvangeliste. par Jacques de Besançon enlumineur lui estant bastonnier de la confrarie. Monseigneur Saint-Jehan fondee en l'eglise de Saint Andry-des-Ars a Paris pour servir a la dicte confrarie. Et prye aux freres et suers qu'il pryent Dieu. et monseigneur saint Jehan l'Euvangeliste pour lui. et qui plaise au benoit saint accepter le petit don' (Paris, Bib. Maz. MS 461, f. 33v).

³ For the most recent discussion of this workshop and the artists associated with it see F. Avril and N. Reynaud, *Les Manuscrits à Peintures en France 1420–1520* (Paris, 1993), 255–56. See also C. Sterling, *La Peinture médiévale à Paris*, 2 vols (Paris, 1987, 1990), 2, 177–228.

⁴ In her unpublished dissertation, *The Maître François and His Atelier* (Harvard, Cambridge, Mass., 1931), Eleanor Spencer presented a list of manuscripts attributable to this artist. Spencer and other scholars such as Plummer, Avril and Reynaud have since attributed more manuscripts to him; however, a definitive catalogue has not yet been published. Patrons of the Master of Jacques de Besançon include Charles VIII, Henry VII of England, Louis XII, Pierre II, duc de Bourbon, Antoine de Chourses and Katherine de Coëtivy.

⁵ Vellum, 452 folios, 455x320 mm. (justification 290x192 mm.), 28 lines of liturgical

1460s by this workshop for the archbishop of Autun which display the coat-of-arms of Cardinal Jean Rolin quite prominently in several places, the Mazarine missal lacks any reference to a particular clerical patron.[6] It is true that a priest appears in the large initial introducing the Proper of the first Sunday of Advent on folio 1 (Pl. 6); but the figure is not identified by any heraldic insignia, and the image of a kneeling cleric holding a small naked child as the personification of his soul had long served as a literal illustration of the opening words of the Introit for this feast: *Ad te levavi animam meam.* A possible allusion to a royal patron, however, appears in the miniature for the feast of the Nativity of the Virgin on folio 333v (Fig. 56). The scene shows a reclining St Anne holding the infant Virgin;

---

script, rubrics in red and blue; special feasts in the calendar are emphasized in gold. The miniatures are as follows: f. 1, First Sunday in Advent: the 'Procès de Paradis', Annunciation, seven 'O antiphons'; f. 14, Introit of midnight Mass of Nativity: Adoration of the Shepherds; f. 17, Introit of daytime Mass of Nativity: Flowering of Aaron's rod, the Nativity, twelve sibyls; f. 22, Introit of Epiphany: the Adoration of the Magi; f. 103v, Introit of Mass for Palm Sunday: Christ's entry into Jerusalem (intial); f. 4v, Prefaces of the Canon: the Church, Noah's Ark, Moses and the Synagogue; f. 6v, Crucifixion framed by scenes from the Passion (full page); f. 7, *Maiestas* with angels and prophets (full page); f. 8, Canon (*Te igitur*): Calvary and the Last Supper; f. 151, Introit for Easter Sunday: the Resurrection with border of virtues, patriarchs, prophets, etc.; f. 175, Introit for the Ascension: the Ascension; f. 183, Introit of Pentecost: Descent of Holy Ghost; f. 194v, Introit for Trinity Sunday: Trinity above the Apostles with orb of the world, the crippled and possessed; f. 195v, Introit of Corpus Christi: Abraham and Melchisedech, the Last Supper; f. 257, Introit of theVigil of St Andrew: the crucifixion of St Andrew; f. 277, Introit for the Purification: Purification at the temple; f. 282v, Introit for the Annunciation: The Annunciation with Old Testament kings and prophets; f. 298, Introit for the Nativity of St John the Baptist: Nativity of St John the Baptist; f. 300v, Introit for the Visitation: the Visitation; f. 310v, Introit for St Mary Magdalene: 'Noli me tangere'; f. 315, Introit for St Germanus of Auxerre: St Germanus and St Lupus with St Genevieve; f. 322v, Introit for Assumption of the Virgin: Assumption of the Virgin; f. 333v, Introit for the Nativity of the Virgin: Nativity of the Virgin; f. 352, Introit for All Saints: saints arranged in four descending tiers of apostles, confessors, martyrs and virgins; f. 357, Introit for the Presentation of the Virgin: Presentation; f. 362, Mass for the Vigil of an Apostle: the Apostles; f. 364, Common of a Martyr: torture of St Eustace; f. 369v, Mass for Many Martyrs: martyrs arranged in four tiers; f. 378, Introit for the Mass for a Confessor Bishop: confessor bishops arranged in three tiers; f. 382v, Introit for the Mass for many Virgin Martyrs: virgin martyrs; f. 410, Mass for the Dead: burial scene; f. 424, Ash Wednesday: benediction of the ashes; f. 432, Maundy Thursday: washing of the disciples' feet. The last two miniatures are by the Master of Anne of Burgundy who, like the Master of Jacques de Besançon, was the head of a large Parisian atelier. He was responsible for the decoration in another Parisian missal, BN MS lat. 859. For Mazarine MS 412, see V. Leroquais *Les Sacramentaires et Les Missels Manuscrits des Bibliothèques Publiques de France*, 4 vols (Paris, 1924), no. 712, 3, 149–50; Sterling, *Peinture Médiévale*, 2, 227–28; and Reynaud, *Manuscrits à Peintures*, no. 139 (259–61).

[6] For the Autun missals, see Avril and Reynaud, *Manuscrits à Peintures*, nos 8–9, (40–41).

she is attended by her husband Joachim and two midwives. In the framed archway above the canopied bed appear the royal arms of France: three *fleurs de lys* on an azure ground surmounted by a crown. Above the crown are three lilies and a tiny bust of the Virgin and Child with a banderole bearing the words *Ego flos campi et lilium convallium* ('I am the flower of the field and the lily of the valley'). From medieval times the lily referred both to the Virgin and to the French monarchy; here, the artist has made the connection quite explicit.[7] Durrieu and others have suggested that the use of the royal arms in the context of a miniature honouring St Anne may allude to the marriage of Anne of Brittany to Charles VIII in 1491.[8] This date, moreover, is in keeping with the style of both miniature and border decoration. The inclusion in the missal of a rare votive Mass for the king as head 'of church and state' is also suggestive of royal patronage. Neither text nor illumination, however, contains any of the specific references to Charles VIII, which are characterisic of books known to have been commissioned for the king's own use from this workshop. His portrait, for example, occurs quite frequently in such manuscripts as well as the insignia of the Order of St Michael—a cockle-shell pendant on which hangs a gold image of the archangel spearing a dragon.[9]

Textual evidence, moreover, points to the probability that the missal was designed for use in the Cathedral of Notre Dame in Paris or in a church dependent on it and not, as was originally proposed, for the Saint-Chapelle, the celebrated chapel attached to the royal palace. While the definition of the *incipit usum ecclesie parisiensis* is confirmed by the number of Parisian feasts in the calendar and Masses of the missal, three particular feasts and their octaves, which Robert Branner has shown to be characteristic of books made for use in the Sainte-Chapelle are not accentuated. These are the commemoration of the relics of the chapel (September 30); the reception of the crown of thorns (August 11); and the dedication of the chapel (April 26).[10] Mazarine MS 412 lists the feasts of the dedication and reception in its calendar, but includes only the latter among its Masses. This feast was observed throughout the diocese of Paris

---

[7] For the religious and nationalistic symbolism of the lilies, see C. Beaune, *The Birth of an Ideology: Myths and Symbols of Nation in Late-Medieval France* (Berkeley, 1991), 201–25.

[8] Durrieu, *Jacques de Besançon*, 60.

[9] The Master of Jacques de Besançon and his shop illuminated several books for Charles VIII including two psalters (New York, Morgan MS M.934 and Paris, BN MS lat. 774), a book of hours (Madrid, Bibl. Nac. MS vit. 24-1), an abridged life of St Denis (Paris, BN MS fr. 5868) and a printed book, Josephus' *De la bataille Judaique* (BN MS Vélins 696).

[10] R. Branner, 'The Sainte-Chapelle and the Capella Regis in the thirteenth century', *Gesta* 10 (1971), 19–22; and 'Le Premier Evangéliaire de la Sainte-Chapelle', *Revue de l'art* 3 (1969), 37–48.

and appears in all missals 'usum Parisiensis'. The feast of the Commemoration of the relics of the Sainte-Chapelle on September 30 is not mentioned at all in the missal.

On the other hand, the feast of the *susceptio reliquiarium*, the reception of relics at the Cathedral of Notre Dame, is registered in the calendar on December 4 in the missal and has its own Mass. This feast was observed only at the Cathedral of Notre Dame and its collegiate churches.[11] The missal also includes saints honoured in the cathedral liturgy, though not exclusive to it, such as Denis, Germanus of Paris, Germanus of Auxerre, Geneviève, Eligius, Stephen and Marcel. These saints are commemorated in both the calendar and sanctoral. St Geneviève, the patron saint of Paris, has three feasts, and the sanctoral contains an illustration of her meeting with St Germanus of Auxerre (Fig. 57). Furthermore, one of the rubrics of the missal includes a rare reference to a Mass in honour of the milk of the Virgin, which featured among the relics at Notre Dame.[12] It is probable, therefore, that this book was designed for use at Notre Dame or at a church associated with the cathedral. Indeed, it may well have been donated to the cathedral or its incumbent by a royal patron, since the royal family had close ties with Notre Dame. Anne and Charles were married there and a year later, on 9 July 1492, Anne was formally welcomed at a Mass in the cathedral, following her coronation at St Denis.[13]

Complex illustrative programmes are not usually compatible with the primary function of a liturgical book which is to ensure the efficient celebration of church ritual; and while images in non-liturgical manuscripts might be perused by an individual at will, a book such as the missal normally had very limited application outside the Mass and related ceremonies. Although missals, therefore, might receive rich embellishment, their illustration was often confined to a pair of full-page miniatures of the *Maiestas* and the Crucifixion at the canon, and small

---

[11] C. Wright, 'The feast of the reception of the relics at Notre Dame of Paris', in A.D. Shapiro, ed., *Music and Context: Essays for John M. Ward* (Harvard, 1985), 1–13; R.A. Baltzer, 'Another look at a composite Office and its history: The feast of the *Susceptio Reliquiarum* in medieval Paris', *Journal of the Royal Music Association* 113 (1988), 1–27.

[12] The rubric, written in alternate lines of red and blue between the introit and collect of Septuagesima Sunday reads, 'Non dicitur Gloria in Excelsis usque ad Pascha praeterquam in die Purificationis et Annunciationis et in ecclesia Parisiensi sabbato post Letare quando fit missa de lacte beate Marie' (f. 32). Leroquais discusses this Mass, which he found in only two missals (not including this one) in *Le Missel Manuscrit de l'Eglise Saint-Gervais à Paris* (Paris, 1930), 5–6.

[13] That the missal was made for a member of the royal family for use in the 'capella regis' or one of the royal chapels is also unlikely since by the fifteenth century these books followed the use of Rome, not of Paris. See Branner, 'The Sainte-Chapelle and the Capella Regis', 20.

one-column sized miniatures or historiated initials to introduce important feasts. In Mazarine MS 412 the Master of Jacques de Besançon has enlivened and diversified the tradition of missal illustration by drawing on a variety of motifs and compositional arrangements, which were, for the most part, developed by his predecessors to illustrate books of personal devotion or large-scale narrative and allegorical works. He has, nevertheless, ensured that the basic liturgical function of the missal remains paramount.

The text of Mazarine MS 412 is clearly set out in traditional two-column format with the canon of the Mass written in a larger hand. Two-line decorated initials denote the beginning of each section of the Propers, while rubrics and headings in red and blue act as a clear guide to the celebrant throughout. Also in keeping with tradition are the series of small one-column miniatures that highlight particular feasts in the temporal, sanctoral and common of the saints. Two more such miniatures mark the beginning of the prefaces and the introductory words of the canon; at the end of the book, a further two—in the hand of another master—head the rituals for the blessing of the ashes on Ash Wednesday and the washing of the feet on Maundy Thursday (ff. 424 and 434). Large scale compositions are reserved for the canon and the first Sunday of Advent which is also the beginning of the book. In addition to their small introductory miniatures, Christmas and Easter are highlighted by an elaborate architectural border that frames the whole page and contains a series of figures or allegorical depictions relevant to the theme of the feast. Within this relatively restrained and traditional format, the Master of Jacques de Besançon has enriched the illumination in a variety of ways.

The depiction of narrative scenes in a lively dramatic mode seems to have been one of the features of this workshop that continued to be popular with patrons throughout the course of its long life, and many of the small column miniatures of the missal exploit this element. Thus in contrast to the quasi-iconic scenes of standing saints with their attributes that so often characterize illustrations of the sanctoral, the focus here is frequently on a specific event. The picture that prefaces the introit for the common of a martyr, for example, depicts in graphic detail the sufferings of one particular martyr, St Eustace (Fig. 58); that for the feast of St Germanus shows the bishop and his clerical colleagues in the act of meeting St Geneviève and her companions (Fig. 57); and fresh energy is engendered into the long-established composition of the Nativity of the Virgin (Fig. 56) by the stately canopied bed being presented frontally instead of in profile, thus centering attention on the spritely midwives who prepare the baby's bath, rather than on the static group of St Anne and her new born child and attendant husband.

It would appear, too, that patrons had no objection to the repetition of compositions that had already been developed by the workshop and used quite extensively in a variety of contexts. The miniature introducing the Requiem Mass on folio 410 (Fig. 59), for example, is a readily recognizable variation on the depiction of a burial service that appears in numerous *horae* and a psalter by the Maître François (Fig. 60). On the other hand, the miniature for the feast of the Trinity combines a number of elements to form a rather unusual illustration of this subject (Fig. 61). Associated with each of the three men that represent the Trinity in the clouds of heaven are images which identify them through the doctrine of appropriation, with a particuar divine operation. Thus, beneath the representation of a bearded God the Father on the left is a large orb of the land, sea and sky that refers to the act of creation; on the right a group of people, including one lame and one possessed by a demon, look towards God the Son for deliverance in his name; while in the centre of the composition the Apostles are gathered around the Virgin in a Pentecost scene directly under God the Holy Spirit.

Equally context-specific is the small two-tiered miniature that introduces the text of the *Te igitur* of the canon (Fig. 62). Here the representation of Christ on the cross is used to stress the sacrificial character of the Mass. Devoid of narrative elements except for that of the centurion who pierces Christ's side with a spear, the miniature shows the blood of the crucified being poured into two chalices held by hovering, adoring angels. The figure of Christ on the cross is also part of a rendition of the mercy-seat theme of the Trinity, with God the Father shown in the half circle of glory above him and the dove of the Holy Spirit appearing between Father and Son. In the register below the unusual depiction of the Last Supper has a marked liturgical emphasis. Only Christ and St John, who leans on the Saviour's breast, are seated; the rest of the Apostles stand in two formal groups around the altar-table, the rods in their hands identifying them as successors to the priesthood of the Old Testament. Miniatures introducing the chants for the prefaces (f. 4v) and the feast of Corpus Christi (f. 195v) also use a two-tier format and typological subject-matter. The Church is likened to the ark as the vessel of salvation in the illustration to the prefaces, while Abraham's meeting with Melchisedech is presented in association with the Last Supper as a type of the Eucharist.[14]

The elaborate framing devices used on certain pages of the missal not only structure the compositions in striking ways, but also enhance their significance. For example, the full-page miniatures at the canon are presented in the format of a richly gilded altarpiece (Figs 63 and 64). This

---

[14] See Leroquais, *Sacramentaires*, Pl. LXXXVI for a reproduction of f. 4v.

helps to position the crowded narrative scene of the Crucifixion on the left-hand page within the context of a detailed Passion sequence, which extends, in the smaller side panels, from the agony in the garden to the carrying of the cross, and concludes, in the frieze below, with the carrying of Christ's body to the place of entombment. On the facing page, simulated niches in the golden frame that encloses the *Maiestas* composition contain alternating images of angels and prophets, while the base of the frame features, in sculptured relief, an Old Testament sequence from the creation and fall to the death of Abel. The four evangelists and their symbols in the corner spandrels of the *Maiestas* offer a counterbalancing New Testament point of reference. Thus, in addition to a rich pictorial setting for the traditional themes of the Crucifixion and the *Maiestas*, these pages also provide a succinct summary of the drama of salvation history, and their allusion to the altarpiece format locates individual figures and scenes within the context of Christ's redemptive sacrifice, made ritually present on the altar at each Mass.

Numerous explanatory banderoles feature in three other pages highlighted by architectural frames containing subsidiary figures and scenes. This characteristic, which was common in the large-scale narrative and allegorical books illuminated in the workshop, is further evidence of the designer's concern to present the various pictorial elements as an integrated and lucid commentary on a central theme. The pages for Easter and Christmas are virtually identical in format (Figs 66 and 65). A small one-column miniature, arched at the top, prefaces the introit, and a simulated stone architectural border encloses the text. The horizontal top of the frame contains a series of sculptured relief panels of foliate design, while the vertical inner margin and the space between the two columns of text are patterned with a double lancet-type motif. The considerably wider outer and lower sections of the border-frame are divided into twelve Gothic niches containing clearly labelled figures or symbols with lengthy inscribed banderoles.

The scenes that accompany the image of the Resurrection for Easter day (Fig. 66) emphasize the universal character and import of this mystery; they comprise testimonies from the virtues—justice, faith, hope, and charity—the patriarchs, prophets, and Fathers of the Church, the dead risen from their graves, the pagan world, represented by the oracle of the sibyl, the cosmic elements of sun and moon, the myrtle, symbol of immortality, and the Lord's disciples, together with all peoples—Jews and gentiles—to whom his Resurrection has brought eternal life. The inscriptions on the banderoles are carefully related to each image and are all of biblical derivation except for that accompanying the figure of the sibyl, which is taken from the *Divinarum Institutionum* of Lactantius.[15]

This detailed programme may have been explicitly designed for Mazarine MS 412 or else it is an appropriate and skilful adaptation from a larger work. We know more about the sources for the illustration of the page introducing the second Mass for Christmas Day (Fig. 65). The column miniature on this page depicts the flowering of Aaron's rod in its upper register and the Nativity below. Aaron was an Old Testament type of Christ and the flowering of his dry rod in the tabernacle was interpreted as a prefiguration of the Saviour's birth from the Virgin. The association of this scene with the Nativity is thus readily understandable in terms of biblical typology although its use in missal illustration is distinctive. The series of figures that occupy the twelve Gothic niches set into the simulated architectural frame are clearly labelled as the ancient sibyls and the inscriptions on the banderoles which they bear are extracts from oracles attributed to them.[16]

Many years ago Emile Mâle argued that the representation of the sibyls in this missal, together with the accompanying texts—all of which may be interpreted as referring to the coming of Christ—was based on the *Discordantiae nonnullae inter sanctum Hieronymum et Augustinum* by the Italian

---

[15] Lactantius' full text reads, 'et mortis fatum finiet et morte morietur tribus diebus somno suscepto et tunc ab inferis regressus ad lucem veniet primum resurrectionis initium ostendens'; (VII, xviii), cited in E. Mâle, *L'Art Religieux de la fin du moyen âge en France* (Paris, 1922), 257, n. 2.

[16] The texts of the oracles in Mazarine MS 412 read as follows (top to bottom): *Persica*: 'Ecce bestia condulcaberis et gignetur dominus in orbem terrarum et gremium virginis erit salus gentium', *Libyca*: 'Ecce veniet dies et solventur nexus synagoge et desinent labia hominum et videbunt regem viventium tenebit illum in gremio virgo matris eius erit statua cunctorum'; *Delphic*: 'Nascetur propheta absque matris coitu ex virginis eius; *Chimica*: In prima facie virginis ascendet puella sedens super sedem stratam puerum nutries dans ei ad comedendum lac de coelo missum'; *Erythraean*: 'In ultima aetate humiliabutur Deus et humanabitur proles divina jungetur humanitati divinitas Jacebit in feno agnus; *Samian*: Ecce veniet dies et nascetur de paupercula et bestiae terrarum adorabunt eum clamabatur et dicent laudate eum in atriis coelorum'; *Cumana*: 'Magnus ab integro seculorum nascitur ordo iam redit et virgo redeunt saturnia regna iam nova progenies celo dimittitur alto'; *Hellespontica*: 'De excelsis coelorum habitaculo prospexit Deus humiles suos et nascetur in diebus novissimis de virgine hebraea in cunnabulis terrae'; *Phrygia*: 'Et olimpi excelsus veniet et firmabitur consilium in coelo et annunciabitur virgo in vallibus desertorum'; *Tiburtina*: 'Nascetur Xristus in Bethleem et annunciabitur en Nazareth regente Tauro pacifico fundatore quietis O felix illa mater'; *Europa*: 'Veniet ille et regnabit in paupertate et dominabitur in silentio et egredietur de utero virginis'; *Agrippina*: 'Invisibile verbum palpabitur et circumdabitur alvus materna et nascetur ex matre ut deus et conversabitur ut peccator'.

Dominican Filippo Barbieri, published in 1481.[17] Mâle also claimed that this illustration was the first example in France where twelve sibyls rather than the ten referred to in the *Divinarum Institutionum* of Lactantius were represented.

Esther Gordon Dotson has since shown that Barbieri actually published two editions of his treatise in 1481 and that both of these reflect a fresco programme commissioned by Cardinal Orsini some time before his death in 1438. While these frescoes are no longer extant they are known to have been described in two fifteenth-century manuscripts as well as in the treatise of Barbieri; they also included woodcut illustrations.[18]

The sibyls in Mazarine MS 412 are based on Barbieri's second edition of 1481 which, while following the Orsini programme for the most part, associates different texts with the Erythraean and Hellespontic sibyls. Pictorial versions of the sibyls based on both Lactantius and the Orsini-Barbieri programmes were current in Italy in the late fifteenth and sixteenth centuries, although the Orsini version (Barbieri's first edition) is the most popular. There are fewer examples of the theme extant in the North; nonetheless it is is evident that the three versions of the oracles were also known there.[19] The earliest known French reference to Barbieri's second edition remains, however, Mazarine MS 412.

Barbieri describes the appearance of each of the sibyls, down to the colour of their clothing and hairstyle.[20] The iconography of the Mazarine sibyls reflects these descriptions quite closely. The Delphic sibyl, for example, has 'dark clothing and hair wound around her head'. This suggests that the composition in the missal may have been based directly on Barbieri, an hypothesis which is strengthened by the fact that it seems to be quite independent of the French pictorial tradition that developed in the second half of the fifteenth century.[21] These sibyls, as instanced in the *Hours of Louis de Laval* (Paris, BN MS lat. 920) have completely different attributes from those of Mazarine MS 412.[22]

The connection of the sibyls in this missal with an Italian text, together with their very inclusion in a liturgical work, is evidence of the influence of Italian humanism on French intellectual life, an influence which was to grow significantly under the patronage of François I. Moreover, they do

---

[17] Mâle, *L'Art Religieux*, 265.

[18] E. Gordon Dotson, 'An Augustinian interpretation of Michelangelo's Sistine Ceiling, Part II', *Art Bulletin* 61 (1979), 405–29.

[19] Mâle, *L'Art Religieux*, 256–66; and Gordon Dotson, 'An Augustinian interpretation', 406–407 and nn. 166–67.

[20] See Mâle, *L'Art Religieux*, 258–60. These are for Barbieri's second edition.

[21] Mâle, *L'Art Religieux*, 266–74.

[22] Three of these sibyls are reproduced in Mâle, *L'Art Religieux*; Figs 134–36.

not seem to have been part of the workshop repertoire before this time, by contrast to so many of the other motifs which enliven the illustrative programme of the missal. This suggests that the Master of Jacques de Besançon may have been responding to the directives of a patron or a learned adviser, eager to include a pictorial reference to recent humanist writings.

The fact that the page which introduces Advent in the missal also functions as a frontispiece to the manuscript probably accounts for the elaborate nature of its decoration (Pl. 6). Again, the illumination is organized around a simulated architectural frame; but here the illusion is somewhat different, for the two lateral borders are crowned by circular turrets and the whole edifice is set against a starry blue sky, so that it resembles, especially in the upper part, a triumphal gateway rather than an altarpiece.

In the large central panel, the beginning and end of the saga of redemption are combined: Gabriel is summoned by God to announce the Incarnation and a tiny figure of the infant Christ bearing his cross and the scourge to be used in the Passion descends towards earth, accompanied by the Holy Spirit in the form of a dove. At the same time angelic musicians rejoice at the fulfilment of the Messianic prophecy expressed in the words of Psalm 84:11, 'Mercy and truth have met; justice and peace have kissed', and the four virtues are shown being reconciled. Below, Gabriel's Annunciation to Mary is witnessed by four virgin daughters of Jerusalem, while in the side panels various categories of the unredeemed human race plead for the coming of the Saviour. Two columns of text, ten lines in length, are incorporated into the overall design of the page in the guise of a placard or billboard suspended in front of a dramatic presentation.

The representation of the reconciliation of the virtues was probably influenced by contemporary theatre, in particular the Passion play by Arnoul Gréban first performed in Paris around 1452.[23] The play is prefaced by a debate before the Trinity in heaven between justice and truth, who argue that the sin of mankind deserves punishment, and mercy and peace, who advocate a reprieve. The case is settled when God decrees the incarnation, sending the archangel Gabriel to announce the news to the Virgin. Gréban's play ends with Christ ascending to heaven and the reconciliation of the virtues.

The pictorial composition of the *Procès de Paradis* in the Mazarine missal originated with Maître François, who used it to illustrate matins of the hours of the Virgin in several books of hours produced in the 1470s and early 1480s [24] The Master of Jacques de Besançon also drew on this

---

[23] See M.M. Manion, *The Wharncliffe Hours* (London, 1981), 14–15.

[24] See, for example, Pierpont Morgan MS M.73, f. 7 (c.1470, possibly Le Mans); London,

theme for the feast of Advent in the *Légende dorée* which he illuminated with the Maître François (Paris, BN MS fr. 244, f. 107; Fig. 67).[25] The *Procès de Paradis* in the missal is distinguished, however, from other renditions by its positioning within the enlarged context of the seven scenes of the framing border. Here, groups of imploring, kneeling figures are labelled with banderoles bearing the words of the 'O antiphons' sung in the Office at the *Magnificat* on the seven days before the vigil of Christmas. The antiphons take the form of cries to the Saviour to come and redeem sinful humanity, and the messiah is invoked under a series of titles derived from the Old Testament: *Sapientia, Adonai, Radix Jesse, Clavis David, Oriens, Rex Gentium* and *Emmanuel*.[26]

Several other antiphons augmented these basic seven, the most venerable of which is incorporated into the scene of the annunciation in the Advent page of the Mazarine missal. Banderoles record the dialogue between the virgin daughters of Jerusalem, who stand behind Gabriel to the right of the composition, and the Virgin Mary: 'O Virgin of virgins, how does this come about? For one like you has never been seen before, nor will there be another.' 'O daughters of Jerusalem, why do you marvel at me? The mystery which you perceive is divine in nature.'[27] It is interesting to note that one of the churches where this antiphon was in use during the Middle Ages was Notre Dame de Paris.[28]

The immediate visual source for the depiction of the seven principal 'O antiphons' in the border of the missal is a French translation of Voragine's *Legenda aurea* illuminated by the Maître François and the Master of Jacques de Besançon, sometime between 1477 and 1485, for Antoine de Chourses, chamberlain to Louis XI, and his wife Katherine de Coëtivy (Paris, BN MS fr. 244–45). Advent in this *Légende dorée* opens with a full page illumination (Fig. 68) in which eight scenes are divided by the slender, veined columns characteristic of the workshop at this time and which continue to be used as a framing device for smaller miniatures in

---

BL Egerton MS 2045, f. 25 (before 1475, Paris); Melbourne, National Gallery of Victoria MS Felton 1, f. 15 (*c*.1475; calendar for Angers); Lisbon, Gulbenkian Collection, f. 13 (soon after 1481; calendar for Angers).

[25] The composition also appears, in a slightly truncated form, for matins of the Hours of the Virgin in a book of hours by the Master of Jacques de Besançon (Oxford, Bodleian Library liturg. Canon MS 43, f. 24).

[26] For the complete texts of the 'O antiphons' and their English translations see B.J. Muir, *The Exeter Anthology of Old English Poetry* (Exeter, 1994), 46–65.

[27] 'O Virgo virginum, quomodo fiet istud, quia nec primam similem visa es nec habere sequentem?' 'Filiae Jerusalem, quid me admiramini? Divinum est mysterium hoc quod cernitis.' (Muir, *Exeter Anthology*, Lyric no. 4, 49–50).

[28] C. Wright, *Music and Ceremony at Notre Dame of Paris* (Cambridge, 1989), 106–7.

the Mazarine missal (see Figs 56–59, 62). The introductory text is confined to two columns of four lines each in a panel suspended before the illumination. In the central scene of the top register, the infant Christ descends from heaven, with cross and scourge, towards the kneeling Virgin in the landscape below. The other seven panels illustrate the 'O antiphons'. The text of the *Légende dorée* discusses in detail these antiphons and their significance for the season of Advent, and the corresponding illustrations devised for Paris, BN MS fr. 244 incorporate details of both the antiphon texts and of Voragine's commentary on them. Thus the ignorant are depicted as shepherds, the unredeemed as jailed men; those 'in chains' are in a prison house, those 'held captive' in a pit, those who 'sit in darkness' in a shadowy room; and 'those in exile' in a boat on stormy seas. The Old Testament figures, to whom God gave the Law, emerge from the hell mouth of limbo.[29]

These compositions are adapted for use in the Mazarine MS 412 with only minimal change: the order in which the antiphons appear is slightly different to accommodate the different page lay-out of the missal, the prison bars in the illustrations of the second and fourth antiphons are dispensed with, and the room is not so emphatically darkened in the illustration of the fifth. The missal page also gives greater visual priority to the text in keeping with the book's liturgical function.

Another work by the Master of Jacques de Besançon, which has been dated slightly earlier on stylistic grounds, shows that his enrichment of missal illustration was not confined to this one manuscript, though it seems to have reached its peak here. The missal, Paris, Mazarine MS 410, is somewhat smaller in size than Mazarine MS 412 and its illustrative programme is less extensive.[30] It has recently been established, however, that a detached leaf of the Crucifixion surrounded by six Passion scenes, now Prague, Narodni Gallery, K.36879, originally formed part of this manuscript.[31] This full-page composition foreshadows that of the canon page of Mazarine MS 412, though the elaborate architectural frame is lacking. The first folio of Mazarine MS 410 has been removed, so it is not possible to establish whether or to what extent the complex Advent composition of the later missal was also anticipated. Certainly none of the eighteen miniatures that introduce selected Masses in the temporal, sanctoral and common of the saints of Mazarine MS 410 are linked with figurative border decoration in the way that occurs in Mazarine MS 412 and there are no typological parallels drawn even in the miniature that introduces the *Te igitur*, which depicts instead the celebration of the Mass.

---

[29] Jacobus de Voragine, *The Golden Legend: Readings on the Saints* (Princeton, 1993), 5–6.

[30] See Leroquais, *Sacramentaires*, no. 707, 3, 147. The manuscript measures 381x275 mm.

[31] See Avril and Reynaud, *Manuscrits à Peintures*, no. 139 (261).

The missal, Mazarine MS 412, is an unusual and distinguished example of late fifteenth-century missal illustration wherein diverse iconographical and compositional elements are skilfully integrated in a way that respects the primary liturgical function of the book. At the same time, the combination of erudition and ingenuity displayed in its decorative programme, and the explicit citation of motifs devised by the workshop for other manuscript genres, make it reasonable to suggest that this missal may have been displayed and discussed outside the context of the liturgy as an object reflecting the humanist and artistic interests of the patron or owner. The sumptuous nature of its decoration indicates a high ranking patron who, there is reason to believe, may have been associated with the court of Charles VIII, and the book amply demonstrates why the Master of Jacques de Besançon was ranked among the foremost illuminators of his day.[32]

---

[32] Research for this paper was assisted by an Australian Research Council Grant for the project *Art, Worship and the Book in Medieval Culture*, and also by a travelling fellowship from the Australian Academy of the Humanities.

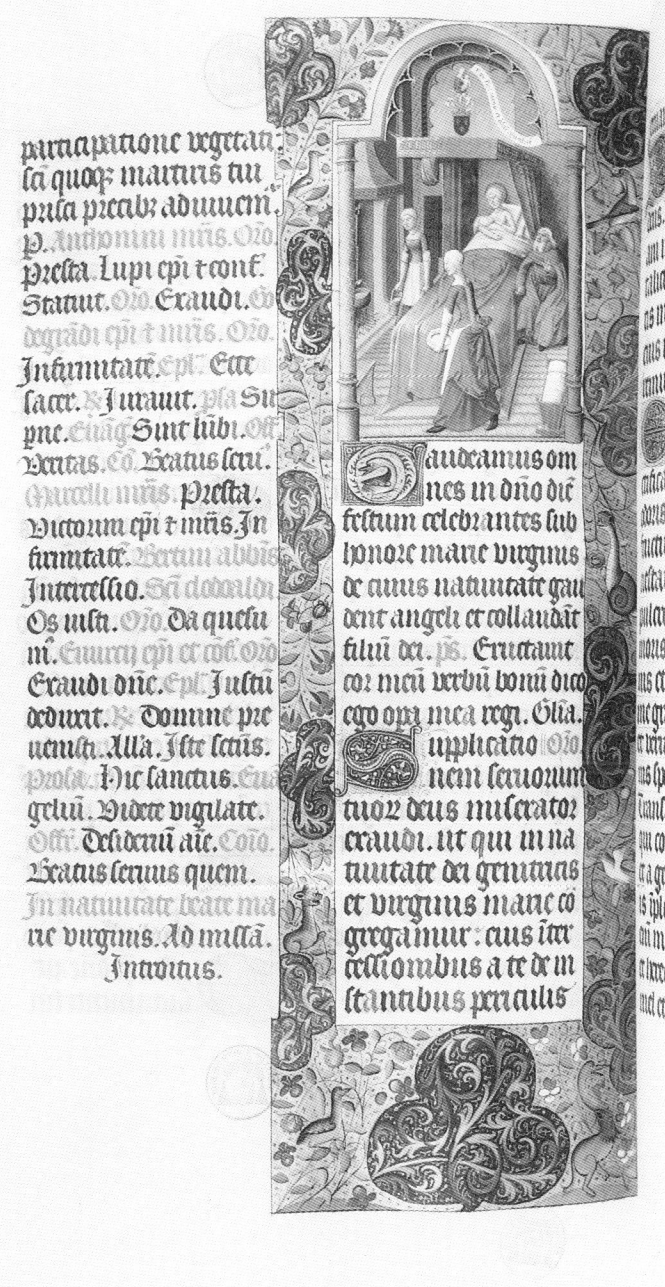

Figure 56. Nativity of the Virgin. Missal. Paris, Bibliothèque Mazarine, MS 412, f. 333v. 455×320mm.

Figure 57. St Genevieve meets St Germanus. Missal. Paris, Bibliothèque Mazarine, MS 412, f. 315. 455×320 mm.

Figure 58. Martyrdom of St Eustace. Missal. Paris, Bibliothèque Mazarine, MS 412, f. 364. 455×320 mm.

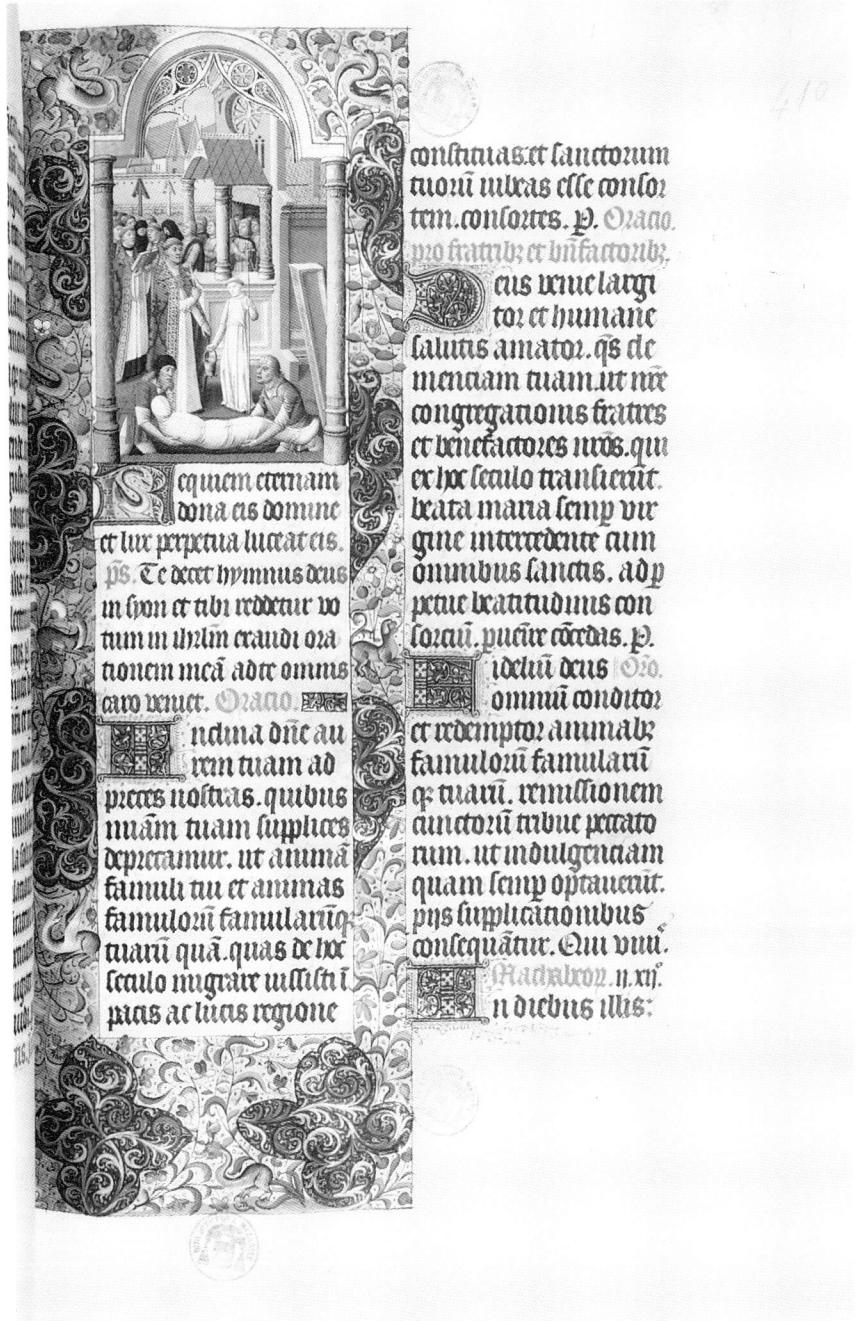

Figure 59. Burial service. Missal. Paris, Bibliothèque Mazarine, MS 412, f. 410. 455×320 mm.

Figure 60. Burial service. Psalter and Vigils of the Dead. Paris, Bibliothèque Nationale, MS Smith-Lesouëf 9, p. 349. 252×182mm.

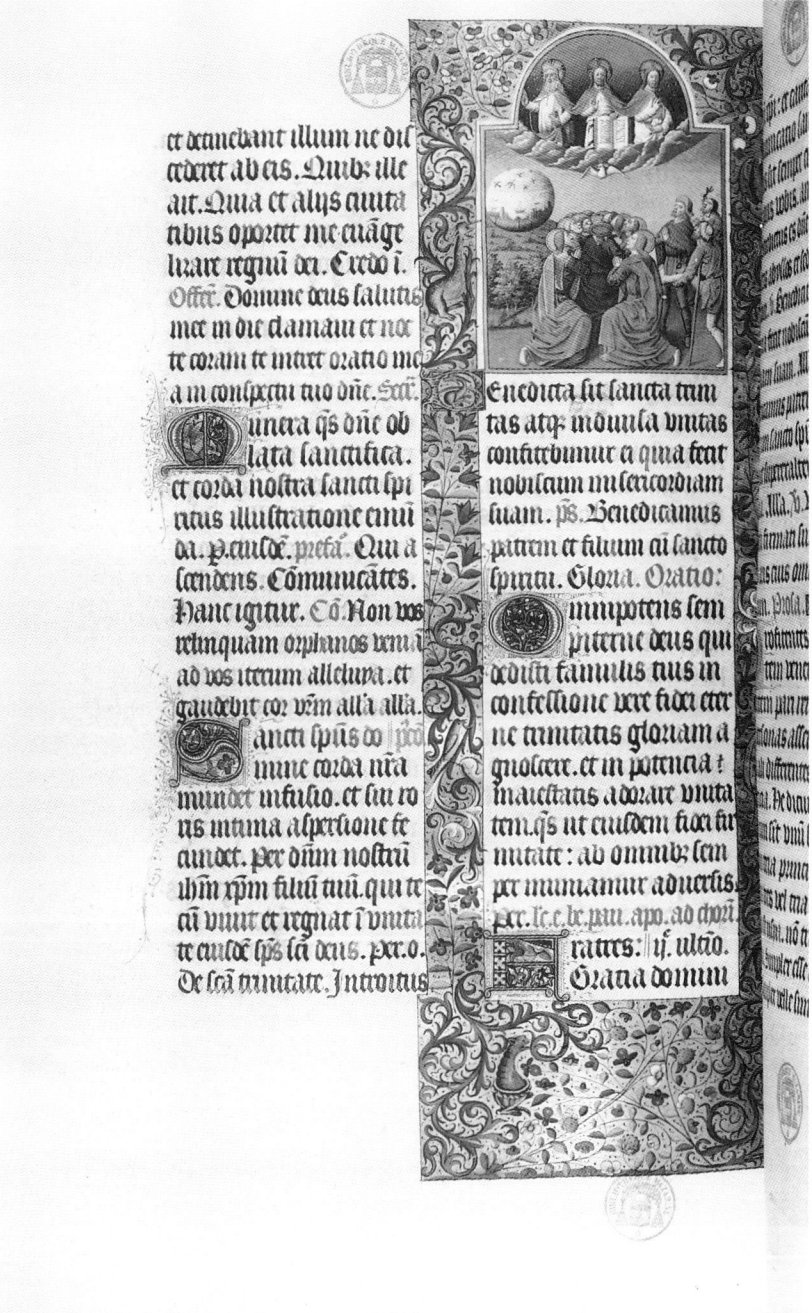

Figure 61. Feast of the Trinity. Missal. Paris, Bibliothèque Mazarine, MS 412, f. 194v. 455×320mm.

Figure 62. Last Supper and Crucifixion. Missal. Paris, Bibliothèque Mazarine, MS 412, f. 8. 455×320 mm.

Figure 63. Crucifixion and Passion scenes. Missal. Paris, Bibliothèque Mazarine, MS 412, f. 6v. 455×320 mm.

Figure 64. *Maiestas*. Missal. Paris, Bibliothèque Mazarine, MS 412, f. 7. 455×320 mm.

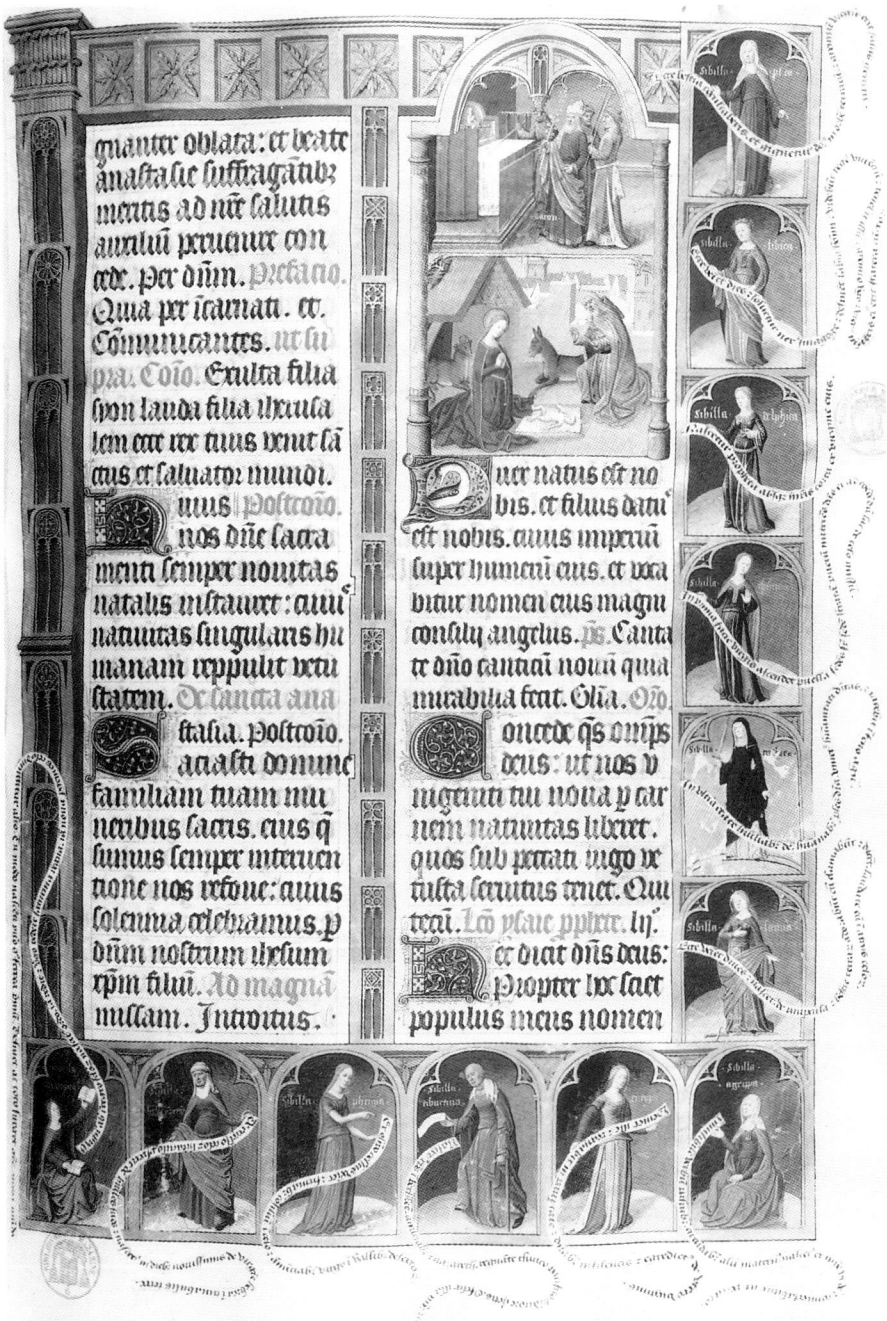

Figure 65. Feast of Christmas. Missal. Paris, Bibliothèque Mazarine, MS 412, f. 17. 455×320 mm.

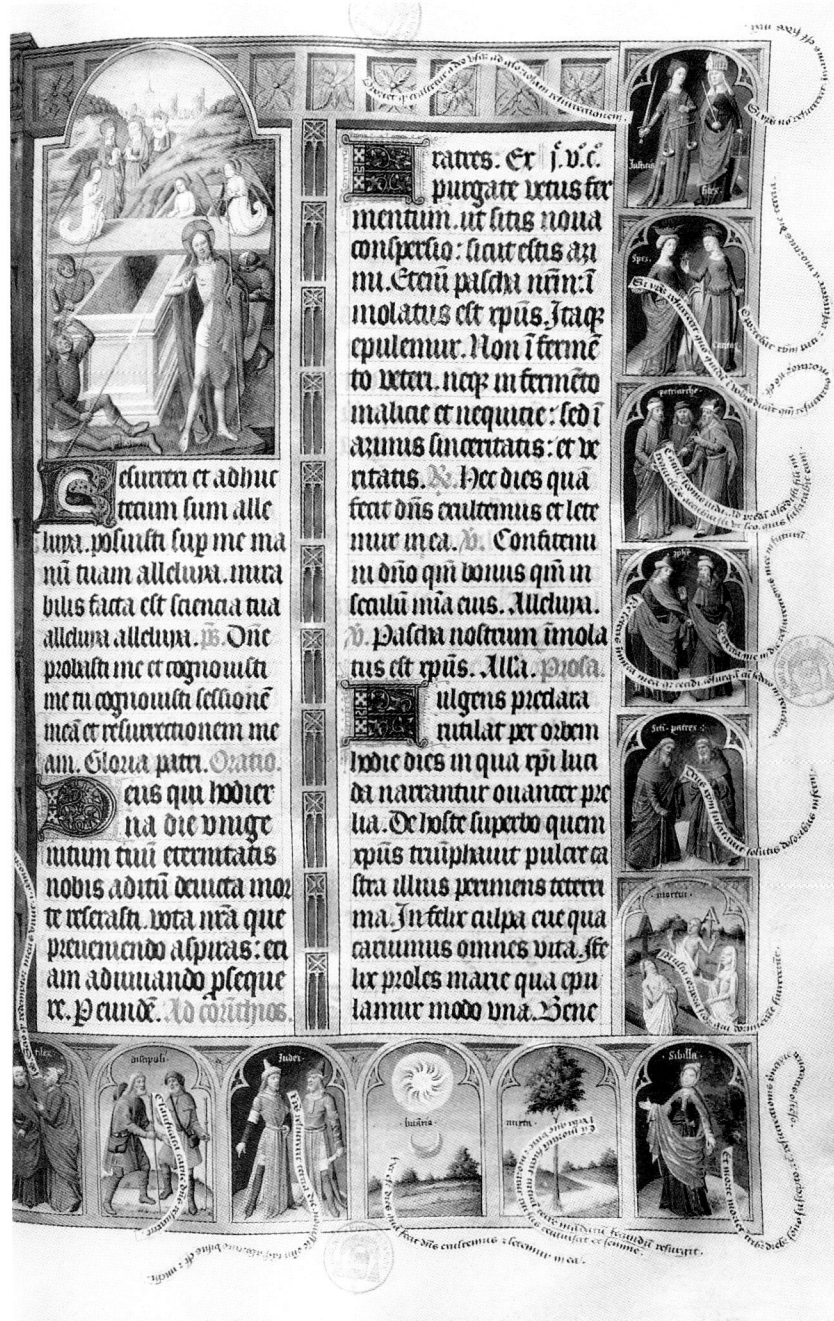

Figure 66. Easter Sunday. Missal. Paris, Bibliothèque Mazarine, MS 412, f. 151. 455×320 mm.

Figure 67. Feast of the Annunciation. *Légende dorée*. Paris, Bibliothèque Nationale, MS fr. 244, f. 107. 390×290 mm.

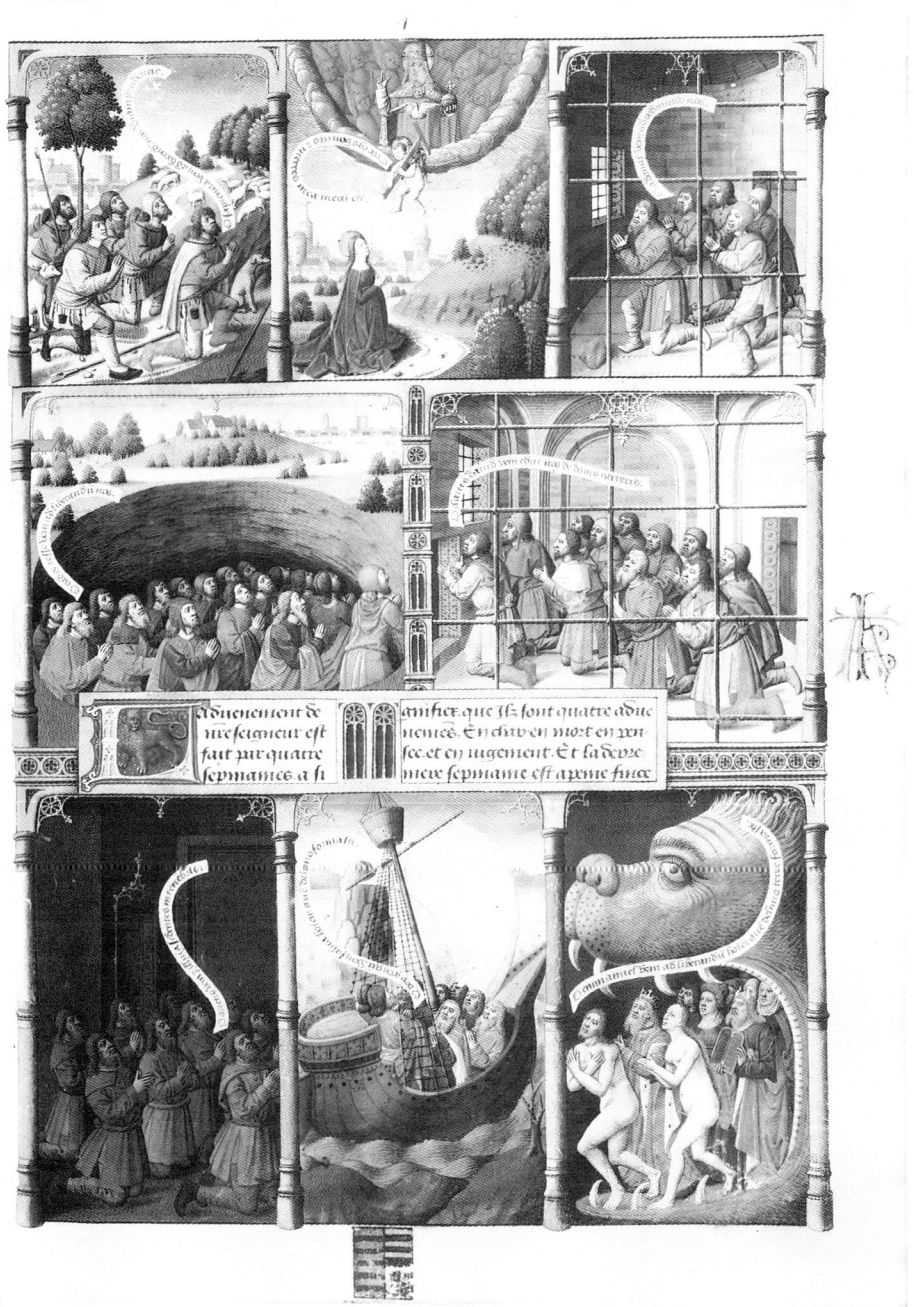

Figure 68. Advent Season. *Légende dorée*. Paris, Bibliothèque Nationale, MS fr. 244, f. 4. 390×290 mm.

NINE

Marginalized Jewels: the Depiction of Jewellery in the Borders of Flemish Devotional Manuscripts

Kate Challis

SINCE 1948, WHEN OTTO PÄCHT WROTE on the illusionistic borders of late medieval Flemish manuscripts, objects such as skulls, pilgrim badges, peacock feathers, shells and the even more frequently depicted flowers, insects and fruit have been associated with this kind of decoration.[1] Studies on Flemish manuscripts, however, have rarely acknowledged the presence of the jewelled border; when they do, it is only in passing.[2] In this essay I wish to draw attention to the wealth of material

---

[1] O. Pächt, *The Master of Mary of Burgundy* (London, 1948). See also G. Hulin de Loo, 'La vignette chez les enlumineurs gantois entre 1470–1500', *Académie Royale de Belgique. Bulletin de la Classe des Beaux-Arts* 21 (1939), 158–80.

[2] See G. Dogaer, *Flemish Miniature Painting in the Fourteenth and Fifteenth Centuries* (Amsterdam, 1987), 16; M. Smeyers and J. van der Stock, eds., *Flemish Illuminated Manuscripts 1475–1550*. St Petersburg State Hermitage Museum (Leuven and Antwerp, 1996), 14; D. Thoss, *Flämische Buchmalerei Handschriftenschätze aus dem Burgunderreich* (Graz, 1987), 18; E. Trenkler, *Das Rothschild-Gebetbuch. ms Ser. N. 2844 der Österreichischen Nationalbibliothek*. Codices Selecti LXVII (Graz, 1979), 89; F. Wormald and P.M. Giles, *A Descriptive Catalogue of the Additional Manuscripts in the Fitzwilliam Museum acquired between*

in this area and to some of the ways in which its analysis can contribute to our knowledge of late medieval Flemish illumination, and to an understanding of the beliefs and interests of the owners of these books.

The term 'the Ghent-Bruges School' was coined by Durrieu in 1891 to describe the followers of the Master of Mary of Burgundy.[3] Whilst acknowledging the importance of these two centres in the development of late medieval Flemish illumination, both Alfons Biermann[4] and Georges Dogaer[5] later questioned the expanded use of this term to denote a stylistic category that referred to a whole period rather than to a particular region. All the manuscripts, however, that are the subject of this study appear to have been executed in either Ghent or Bruges; thus the use of the term is appropriate here.

The particular style of manuscript illumination which flourished in these two centres between 1475 and 1520, whose origins have been associated with the Master of Mary of Burgundy, was preoccupied with illusionism.[6] Through a fundamental reorganization of the folio, the visual conflict that had previously existed between the flat two-dimensional surface of the page and the three-dimensional space construction of the miniature was resolved.[7] This spatial unity was achieved by dividing the folio into two zones: behind and in front of the surface of the page. The religious scene of the miniature appears to take place behind the surface of the folio. We witness the event at a distance, as through a window that creates an illusion of vast space (Fig. 69). On the other hand, the flowers, fruit, birds, pilgrim badges, jewellery etc. that are painted upon a coloured area or border extending around the main miniature seem to exist in front of the folio, creating the illusion of an intimate and accessible reality. Clever devices were used by other practitioners of this style to create *trompe-l'œil* effects, such as the casting of

---

1895 and 1979 (Cambridge, 1982), 145; F. Unterkircher, *Das Gebetbuch Jakobs IV von Schottland und seiner Gemählin Margaret Tudor*. Codices Selecti LXXV (Graz, 1987), 53–54; K. Köster, 'Religiöse Medaillen und Wallfahrts-Devotionalien in der flämischen Buchmalerei des 15. und 16. Jahrhunderts', *Buch und Welt. Festschrift für G. Hofmann* (Wiesbaden, 1965), 459–504. These writers refer only briefly to the presence of jewels in Flemish borders. Unterkircher questions their meaning and Köster suggests that they warrant research.

[3] P. Durrieu, 'Alexandre Bening et les peintres du Bréviaire Grimani', *Gazette des Beaux Arts* 5 (1891), 353–67; 6 (1891), 55–69 (especially 67–68).

[4] A. Biermann, 'Die Miniaturenhandschriften des Kardinals Albrecht von Brandenburg (1514–1545)', *Aachener Kunstblätter*, 46 (1975), 15–310 (especially 43).

[5] Dogaer, *Flemish Miniature Painting*, 16.

[6] See Pächt, *The Master of Mary of Burgundy*; and J.J.G. Alexander, *The Master of Mary of Burgundy—A Book of Hours for Engelbert of Nassau* (London, 1970).

[7] See Pächt, *The Master of Mary of Burgundy*, 24.

shadows by these objects or even the impression that pendants and brooches are actually pinned or sewn onto the page (Pl. 7).

Various factors, acting relatively independently, seem to have contributed to the use of jewels in the illusionistic borders of Flemish manuscripts. In the first place the depiction of jewellery suited the *trompe-l'œil* dimension of this type of decoration, with its emphasis on the close-up detailing of secular objects. Furthermore, the meticulous representation of surface texture characteristic of fifteenth-century Flemish panel painting exercised a considerable influence on book illumination of the period and jewels feature prominently in such paintings. One of the remarkable features of Jan van Eyck's famous *Ghent Altarpiece, c.*1432, for example, is the way in which it captures the luminosity and textural quality of gems and gold. It is also relevant that from the mid-fourteenth century Bruges was a major centre for the purchase and making of jewellery.[8]

The flourishing of book illumination in Bruges at this time coincided with a period of great prosperity for that city. It had in fact become one of the wealthiest towns in Europe, attracting affluent professionals from all over the continent as well as the court of Burgundy.[9] The patronage of these people stimulated the Flemish book industry from 1450 onwards, with members of the local aristocracy and patrician classes attempting to imitate the Burgundian dukes and thereby creating demands for luxury objects including richly illuminated manuscripts.[10]

Artists also benefited from the opportunities that Bruges provided as an international trading centre with its strong local and export market,[11] and restrictions by the powerful librarians' guild, such as the 1426 ban on the sale of imported miniatures especially from Utrecht, resulted in many illuminators settling in Bruges.[12] The list includes David Aubert, Philippe

---

[8] Merchants brought raw materials to Bruges and commissioned goldsmiths to make a specified number of items. These were then sold by the merchants throughout Europe. Bruges was one of the first cities to have expert diamond cutters ('diamantslypers'); and the technique using a diamond for the cutting process was invented there. See R.W. Lightbown, *Medieval European Jewellery* (London, 1992), 16 and 41; and V. Vermeersch, *Bruges and Europe* (Antwerp, 1992), 311–13.

[9] For Bruges as an international trading centre see, W. Prevenier and W. Blockmans, *The Burgundian Netherlands* (Antwerp, 1985), 111; and W. Blockmans 'Bruges, a European Trading Centre', *Bruges and Europe*, 41–55. For Bruges as a residence for the Dukes of Burgundy see, Vermeersch, *Bruges and Europe*, 215.

[10] Vermeersch, *Bruges and Europe*, 244.

[11] Vermeersch, *Bruges and Europe*, 299.

[12] The librarians' guild was founded in 1403; its members consisted of all trades and crafts relating to the production and sale of books. It was independent of the artists' guild; see Vermeersch, *Bruges and Europe*, 77–78.

de Mazerolles, Loyset Liédet, Lieven van Laethen and Willem Vrelant.[13] Such immigration intensified the artistic climate of the town and had a stimulating effect upon book illumination.

The information presented here on the use of jewellery on Flemish illumination is based on the study of thirty-seven devotional manuscripts, mostly books of hours, produced either in Bruges or in the neighbouring city of Ghent between 1475 and 1520 (see the Appendix).[14] The only exception is the *Hours of Catherine of Cleves* which was produced in Utrecht c.1440, some thirty-five years before the others. Some 227 folios of these thirty-seven manuscripts feature jewels in their borders. I have systematized this material into three categories according to the way in which the jewellery is presented. The first category comprises the depiction of single jewels on blank vellum; in the second category the pieces form part of a vertical strip border; and in the third they appear in full borders which enclose all four sides of the page.[15] Jewels in vertical strip borders occur the least frequently, accounting for only 13% of this sample. In 52% of the folios the jewels appear in full borders; 35% of the folios contain single jewels on blank vellum.

CATEGORY ONE: SINGULAR JEWELS ON BLANK VELLUM

Jewelled rosaries, pendants, brooches and rings lie upon the blank vellum of these folios (Fig. 70). In most cases they ornament pages of text, although they also occur on folios with half-page miniatures and a few lines of text. This type of marginal decoration does not serve to indicate the beginning of a particular prayer or Office and it is subsidiary to the text itself. The prayer books in which it appears tend to be lavishly illuminated, with marginal decoration featuring throughout the entire book and thus on pages which in less richly embellished books are often left bare.

The number of jewels and their positioning on a folio vary from manuscript to manuscript. A singular pendant placed underneath or beside a text is the most restrained representation. In a book of hours,

---

[13] Vermeersch, *Bruges and Europe*, 244 and 280.

[14] 'Marginalised Jewels. The depiction of jewellery in the borders of late fifteenth and early sixteenth century Flemish manuscripts' (B.A. Hons. thesis, University of Melbourne, 1994).

[15] I have distinguished between margins, borders and frames as follows: margins are the blank spaces around the text or image on which the jewels are depicted, borders are ruled spaces beside or surrounding an image and/or text; frames mark the inner and outer boundaries of the borders. Of the two borders running vertically alongside the text or miniature, the term 'outer margin' refers to the one closer to the edge of the folio, whereas the 'inner margin' indicates the margin closer to the binding.

Vienna, ON MS 1984, eight folios display just one jewel each.¹⁶ The margins of six folios of the book of hours, Rome, B.A.V. MS Ross. 94, depict a series of rosaries or brooches. One piece is placed underneath the text and the other on the outer margin of each folio.¹⁷ On folio 177 of ON MS 1984 three pieces of jewellery are positioned around the text: on the upper, lower and outer margins respectively. Similarly, folio 88 of another book of hours in Vienna, ON MS 1979, depicts three items, in this case rosaries, in its margins (Fig. 71). A rare example of the positioning of a piece of jewellery on each of the four sides of the text can be seen on folio 130 of the *Blumen-Stundenbuch* (Munich, Bay. Staatsbibl. MS Clm. 23637): on the inner, bottom and top margins there are three gold pendants, round, diamond and cross-shaped, respectively. Five threaded beads and a tassel hang from each; on the outer margin appear four rings threaded onto a scroll of vellum.¹⁸

This type of free-floating marginal decoration is not confined to the representation of jewellery. In fact, insects, flowers and animals were more frequently depicted. On occasions, flora, small creatures and jewellery share the same folio as seen in the *Hours of Joanna of Castile* (London, BL Add. MS 18852), where on folio 239 a bird sits on the top of the text, a rooster pecks at the ground below, and a diamond-shaped brooch occupies the outer margin. Folio 243 of the same hours displays a violet, a pendant and a ring topped with a sprig of four daisy buds (Fig. 70), while an animal, a jewel and a flower share folio 362.

Page 300 of the *Hours of Catherine of Cleves* (New York, Morgan MS M. 917; Fig. 72) and folio 13 of ON MS 1979 feature characteristics of both Categories One and Three. The jewels are depicted upon blank vellum, yet do not resemble any of the previously mentioned examples, since although not technically contained by full borders, they are nevertheless structured into particular patterns or objects which fulfil a similar framing function. Thus the dense arrangement of the beads on page 300 of the *Hours of Catherine of Cleves* resembles the framing border on folio 156 of volume 1 of the Hours of Albrecht of Brandenburg (formerly Amsterdam, Bibl. Philosophica Hermetica, MS 40).¹⁹

In these two cases instead of the jewellery being subsidiary to the script it is the marginal decoration that visually prevails. These embellish-

---

¹⁶ Folios 22, 23, 30v, 114, 144, 172 and 172v.

¹⁷ M. Thomas, *Livre d'Heures*. Ross. 94. Codices Selecti 56 (Fribourg, 1983), ff. 109v, 110, 119v, 120, 166v and 167.

¹⁸ B. Brinkmann and E. König, *Das Blumen-Stundenbuch* (Lucerne, 1991), f. 130.

¹⁹ Mainz Landesmuseum, H. Reber, *Albrecht von Brandenburg. Kurfürst. Erzkanzler. Kardinal. 1490–1545* (Mainz, 1990), 190. This collection has recently been sold and the present whereabouts of this manuscript is unknown.

ments, moreover, signify the beginning of a new section of the manuscript. In ON MS 1979 the beautifully decorated folio 13 marks the beginning of the Hours of the Virgin, and the marginal jewels combine with the half-page miniature to fulfil the function of a signifier.

CATEGORY TWO: JEWELS IN A VERTICAL STRIP BORDER

Vertical strip borders containing jewels occur always on the outer margins of a folio (Figs 73–75). On the verso they thus appear to the left of the text or miniature, and on the recto they are positioned to the right.

When vertical strip borders appear on pages of text it is not to denote the beginning of a new section (Fig. 75). Like the jewels depicted against the blank vellum in Category One, they adorn continuous pages of text in more lavishly illuminated manuscripts. Almost every one of the 490 folios of the *Hours of James of Scotland* (Vienna, ON MS 1897) has an illuminated border. Three hundred and forty-nine are of the vertical strip variety, seventeen of these feature jewels; and they seem to appear randomly throughout the Offices.[20]

When the vertical strip occurs beside a half-page miniature, both image and decorative border combine to mark the beginning of a particular section of the book. For example, on folio 15 of the book of hours (Oxford, Bodl. Douce MS 256), the border together with the miniature representing St Luke painting the Virgin introduces the Gospel reading for the feast of the Annunciation (Fig. 74).

The border itself is normally framed. Frames are usually gold and vary in style. The simplest consists of a gold line drawn around the edge of the strip as illustrated on folio 183v of Douce MS 256. This type of frame is also employed extensively in the *Hours of James of Scotland*. Thirteen of its jewelled vertical strip borders are enclosed by gold lines; the remaining four folios have simulated moulded, gilt picture frames (Fig. 75). Not all illusionistic picture frames are in crafted wood: the frame of the border on folio 15 of Douce MS 256, for example is made of gilt branches with knots, twigs and a sprouting acanthus leaf (Fig. 74).

In addition to the frames, coloured backgrounds delineate the perimeters of these vertical strips. Ranging from sombre greys to vibrant reds and pale blues, they accentuate the beauty of the jewellery and intensify the overall splendour of the folio. This setting-off of treasures on display, as it were, may be compared to the Kunstkammer of Archduke Ferdinand II at Schloß Ambras, the earliest known example of an

---

[20] For reproductions, see Unterkircher, *Das Gebetbuch Jakobs IV*. Refer to Appendix for folio numbers.

explicitly aesthetic presentation of a collection.[21] The cabinets of this Kunstkammer were lined in coloured felt to enhance the natural beauty of the objects on display, and particular attention was also paid to the arrangement of the treasures within the cabinets. Similarly, illuminators seem to have carefully organized the placement of jewelled objects within the border. Their efforts, however, were constrained by the relatively small size and elongated shape of the vertical strip. Often the jewellery was simply and quite sparsely arranged. On folio 70v of the *Hours of James of Scotland* a rosary hangs down the entire length of the border.[22] Frequently one piece was positioned directly above another as on folio 101v of Douce MS 256 (Fig. 73). In between the larger jewels on such folios loose pearls are placed at regular intervals. In the majority of cases, however, the border is divided into small subsections by basic geometric patterns and it is into these that the jewels are placed. Thus on folio 178 of Douce MS 256 three painted rectangular frames, one surmounting the other, form niches for the jewels.

Gilt and enamelled branch-work fashioned into many different shapes also created a framework for jewellery. What at first sight may appear to be flora or fauna are in fact representations of enamelled brooches shaped as flowers and branches.[23] On folio 441v in the book of hours, Oxford, Bodl. Douce MS 8, for example, three branches run across the border from left to right, while brooches and unmounted pearls lie above and below them. On folio 348, of the same hours, three brooches are separated by two horizontal branches; their ends are curved, as if they had just been torn from a tree. Even more rustic is folio 15 of Douce MS 256 (Fig. 74). Twigs with dangling acorns sprout from either side of the frame; their ends interlock, thereby creating three ornate arches, one on top of the other, from which three enamelled flowers are suspended. Two pairs of branches are laid across each other and form X-shapes on folio 50 of the *Hours of James of Scotland*.[24] Separating these branches, which are positioned one on top of the other, is a large crucifix pendant made of five red stones set in a gold clasp. Folios 86v and 183v of Douce MS 256 both feature two branches that swerve down the length of the border, overlapping at three points to create smaller units of space inside which lie enamelled flowers or pearls and acorns with golden caps and gems for the nuts. In some

---

[21] See E. Scheicher, 'The Collection of Archduke Ferdinand II at Schloß Ambras: Its purpose, composition and evolution' in O. Impey and A. MacGregor, eds., *The Origins of Museums: The Cabinet of Curiosities in Sixteenth and Seventeenth Century Europe* (New York, 1985), 29–38.

[22] Unterkircher, *Das Gebetbuch Jakobs IV*, f. 70v.

[23] Lightbown, *Medieval European Jewellery*, 174–76. For reproductions of existing enamelled pieces see 440 and 452.

[24] Unterkircher, *Das Gebetbuch Jakobs IV*, f. 50.

cases gilt branches are cut to form letters and phrases which are divided by pieces of jewellery (Fig. 75). The more functional role of such border ornamentation is discussed below in relation to Category Three where the appearance of gilt branch phrases is more frequent.

A highly sophisticated articulation of the border space is achieved by the use of a more geometric structure. Here, a lattice made of gilt wood encrusted with a row of pearls is laid on the border. Within its diamond-shaped niches nestle enamelled flowers, pendants, jewelled acorns and gold initials, as on folios 149v–150 and 199v–200 of the *Hours of James of Scotland*.[25] At the junction points of the lattice appear small enamelled flowers or large pearls. Thorns could also be represented protruding from this framework. Gilt branches and pearl lattices are not exclusive to the vertical strip border, they also feature in Category Three and are discussed below.

CATEGORY THREE: JEWELS IN A FOUR-SIDED BORDER

These borders extend around all four sides of a central panel which contains either a miniature, text or both. They are certainly the most magnificent expression of the jewelled borders (Figs 69, 76-82 and Pl. 7).

Although all four-sided borders, regardless of whether they frame a miniature or a page of text, share the same general characteristics, there are, nevertheless certain subtle differences. Let us first consider the border around a full miniature. The holy scene is witnessed through an arched window, with the surrounding border creating a plane between the reader and the religious world of the miniature (Figs 69, 77, 81). These images usually appear on the verso and generally mark the start of a new Office or prayer to a saint which follows on the opposite folio and which may also feature jewels in its border (Figs 78, 80). The borders of these facing folios, however, do not necessarily match each other. In the *Hours of Joanna of Ghistelles* (London, BL Egerton MS 2125; Fig. 76) for example, the border on folio 143 develops the theme of communion in the main miniature, introduced on folio 142v with the illustration of the Last Supper; it thus reverses the relationship between central and border space on the opposite folio. Some pairs do match exactly, for example, folios 52v–53 of the *Hours of Ferdinand of Austria* (Vienna, ON MS Ser. n. 2624) and folios 84v–85 of the *Rothschild Hours* (Vienna, ON MS Ser. n. 2884; Figs 77, 78) where the borders share the same coloured backgrounds, subject matter and design. Others may feature jewellery in both borders, yet vary in overall appearance. Not only are the backgrounds different on folios

---

[25] Unterkircher, *Das Gebetbuch Jakobs IV*, ff. 149v-150, 199v-200.

221v–222[26] of the *Rothschild Hours*, but the arrangement of the jewels within each border is too. Jewelled borders extending right around a text may also appear opposite full-page miniatures which lack a border altogether as on folios 300v–301 of the *Seelengärtlein* (Vienna, ON MS 2706)[27] or represent another subject such as flowers, as on folios 176v–177 of the Vienna book of hours, ON MS Ser. n. 13238.

Four-sided borders are usually reserved for openings with miniatures and/or pages of text that mark a new prayer or section, the opening lines of which will sometimes begin under the miniature or the facing verso (Figs. 69, 80). Folio 231v of a book of hours, London, BL Add. MS 35313, is an example of one of the relatively rare occasions where the work of the scribe and the illuminators are in some conflict (Pl. 7). The splendid miniature of Mary Magdalen and the elaborate jewelled border clearly are designed to introduce the suffrage in honour of this saint. The three lines of text above the miniature, which are highlighted both by their position and framing, are, however, the conclusion of a prayer in honour of St Anne from the preceding folio.

In the full-page miniatures of the folios I have investigated, the window through which one sees the religious world is invariably arched at the top, while the panels in which the texts are displayed are rectangular in shape (Figs 69, 76–82). In both cases, however, the central panels are always placed off-centre, closer to the top, and nearer to the spine of the book. Most of the decoration, therefore, tends to be concentrated in the lower and outer vertical sections of the border frame. Three rosaries with gold tassels narrowly fit into the inner border of folio 40 of the *Hours of Engelbert of Nassau* (Oxford, Bodleian Library, Douce MSS 219 and 220).[28] A brooch, enamelled flowers and pearls lie along the inner section folio 67 of the *Huth Hours* (London, BL Add. MS 38126). On the other hand, on folio 244v of the Vienna *Seelengärtlein* there is only room for a row of six small pearls and a small enamelled flower by the arched corner of the window.[29] The illuminator left these spaces empty on folio 183v of the *Hours of James of Scotland*, except for a jewelled acorn squeezed into the top right corner (Fig. 81).

The surface on which the jewellery is represented is usually one solid colour. There are, however, exceptions, such as the multi-coloured folio

---

[26] Unterkircher, *Das Gebetbuch Jakobs IV*, 120 and Trenkler, *Das Rothschild-Gebetbuch*, f. 221v.

[27] F. Dörnhöffer, *Hortulus Animae. ms Bibl. Pal. Vindob. 2706. The Garden of the Soul* (London, 1907–1910), Pl. 662.

[28] Alexander, *Hours of Engelbert of Nassau*, Fig. 35 and G.I. Lieftinck, *Boekverluchters uit de Omgeving von Maria van Bourgondie c.1475–1485* (Brussels, 1969), vol. 2, Fig. 77.

[29] Dörnhöffer, *Hortulus Animae*, Pl. 488.

635v of the *Grimani Breviary* (Venice, Bibl. Marciana, MS lat. 1, 99) where each niche created by the twisting branches has either an apricot, lime or *lapis* background.[30] A netting-like fabric appears to be stretched over the surface of folio 579v of the same manuscript.[31] Other folios display a light scattering of gold spangle, for example folio 244v of the Vienna *Seelengärtlein*.[32] Such embellishments and colours intensify the magnificence of the entire folio.

Border Frames and Jewel Arrangements

Two frames mark the perimeters of the four-sided border. The inner one either acts as the window for the miniature scenes, or encloses the textual passage, whilst the outer one extends around the entire illuminated surface. On folios 33v–34 in the modestly illustrated book of hours, Vatican, B.A.V. MS Ross. 94,[33] these frames give an illusion of being constructed of wood, whilst branches with springs sprout from their rustic counterparts on folio 223v in the *Seelengärtlein*[34] and folio 105v of the book of hours, Darmstadt, Landesbibliothek, MS 69.[35] On folio 40 of the *Hours of Engelbert of Nassau*, the frames are simple gold lines.[36] Such restraint, however, is relatively rare. Simulated moulded gilt picture frames are most common (Fig. 69). Some particularly flamboyant examples are pieces of jewellery in their own right, like the gilt frames on folio 319v of the Vienna *Seelengärtlein* which are embedded with pearls,[37] and the gilt wooden frame on folio 10v of London, BL Add. MS 35313, which is embossed with ornamental patterns.

The arrangement of the jewellery in these borders is quite diverse; indeed no two borders are identical. Certain general principles of organization, however, are discernible and allow the manuscripts to be categorized into a number of general groups.

Least complicated is the placement of the jewels at regular intervals. The pieces arranged side-by-side around the central panel are mainly enamelled flowers, brooches and pendants. Gaps created between these are occupied by smaller jewels such as loose pearls, enamelled flowers, jewelled acorns, pendants or a combination of these (Fig. 76 and Pl. 7).

---

[30] M. Salmi, *The Grimani Breviary* (London, 1972), Pl. 80.

[31] Salmi, *The Grimani Breviary*, Pl. 69.

[32] Dörnhöffer, *Hortulus Animae*, Pl. 488.

[33] Thomas, *Livre d'Heures*, ff. 33v–34.

[34] Dörnhöffer, *Hortulus Animae*, Pl. 446.

[35] Biermann, *Aachener Kunstblätter*, Fig. 36.

[36] Alexander, *Hours of Engelbert of Nassau*, Fig. 35 and Lieftinck, *Boekverluchters*, vol. 2, Fig. 77.

[37] Dörnhöffer, *Hortulus Animae*, Pl. 638.

Spatial patterns are also created by chains of beads or rosaries. On folio 3v of the *Legend of St Adrian* (Vienna, ON MS Ser. n. 2619) six rosaries are twisted into loops around the miniature.[38] Within and between them lie enamelled flowers and black pearls. In the *Marley Cutting* (Cambridge, Fitzwilliam Museum, Sp. 5) a girdle encircles an image of four virgin martyrs.[39] Inside its loops the jewels are placed. On folio 156 of vol. 1 of the *Hours of Albrecht of Brandenburg* (in Amsterdam), three strings of beads, consisting of a row of white, followed by a row of gold and another of white beads, run the vertical and horizontal length of the border.[40] Four enamelled flowers, positioned at uniform distances apart, divide the long strings into smaller sections. Less formal in their placement are the four rosaries that encircle a miniature of the Assumption of the Virgin in a book of hours, Cambridge, Fitzwilliam Museum, MS 294e.[41]

Wooden tracery connects the frames of folio 319 in the *Hours of Joanna of Castile* (Fig. 79), creating niches in which rosaries are displayed. Reminiscent of a Gothic chancel screen are the borders of folio 282 in the Vienna *Seelengärtlein*[42] and folio 706 of the *Grimani Breviary*.[43] The jewels are placed in niches within these ornate dividers. Some wooden frames are much less exotic: on folio 32v of the *Hours of Philip II Convault* (Oxford, Bodl. Douce MS 223), five dividers, fastened to a backing panel with bolts, run horizontally across the folio.[44] Picture-like frames, lined up next to each other, create compartments for the representation of jewellery on folio 224v of the *Rothschild Hours*.[45]

Rows of pearls encased in gold were woven into many formations. Around the Adoration of the Shepherds on folio 96v of BL Add. MS 35313 one such chain twists itself serpent-like along the bottom horizontal and up the vertical borders. At regular intervals fronds sprout, their ends blossoming into white enamelled flowers. On folio 224 of the same hours, similar flowers and cluster pendants lie inside the pearl-embossed roundels (Fig. 80). These circles are tightly packed beside one another. At the points where they touch smaller enamelled flowers are displayed. Rows of pearls form cognate loops around the Flight into Egypt folio 103v

---

[38] Thoss, *Flämische Buchmalerei*, Pl. 13 and Lieftinck, *Boekverluchters*, vol. 2, Fig. 263; and Smeyers and van der Stock, *Flemish Illuminated Manuscripts*, Fig. 46.

[39] Cambridge, The Fitzwilliam Museum, A. Arnould and J. Massing, *Splendours of Flanders. Late Medieval Art in Cambridge Collections*, (Cambridge, 1993), 87.

[40] Reber, *Albrecht von Brandenburg*, 190.

[41] Arnould and Massing, *Splendours of Flanders*, 96.

[42] Dörnhöffer, *Hortulus Animae*, Pl. 563.

[43] Salmi, *Grimani Breviary*, Pl. 89.

[44] Lieftinck, *Boekverluchters*, Fig. 282.

[45] Trenkler, *Das Rothschild-Gebetbuch*, f. 224v.

of the *Blumen-Stundenbuch*. Four pendants and an enamelled flower occupy the loops, which extend to the frames. Small spaces are created between the frames and the points where the pearl bands overlap. Here, the illuminator has depicted loose pearls, filling areas where the larger pieces could not fit.[46] Diamond-shaped spaces feature on folio 235v of BL Add. MS 35313. Flourishes embellished with pearls protrude from the sides of the framework, while the centres of the niches are reserved for the 'hanging' of a piece of jewellery.

An elaborate design of pearls embedded in gold is replicated in three manuscripts: folio 236 of BL Add. MS 35313, folio 183v of the *Hours of James of Scotland* (Fig. 81) and folio 210 of the *Rothschild Hours*.[47] Chains of small pearls run along either side of the border, meeting at intervals to form small trefoil-like enclosures which house pendants, enamelled flowers or large jewelled initials. Lining the frames of folio 11 of BL Add. MS 35313 are small pretzel-like shapes formed by tiny pearls set in gold, with centres of three larger pearls.

A more geometric space-divider is the frequently depicted lattice made of gold encrusted with pearls (Fig. 69). Within the diamond shapes created by the lattice on folio 148 of the *Hours of Albrecht of Brandenburg* (Los Angeles, J. Paul Getty Museum, MS Ludwig IX. 91) appear jewelled acorns, enamelled flowers and pendants. At the points where the diagonal running strips overlap, either brooches, enamelled flowers, shells or pearls are attached.[48] Cast shadows give the impression that the lattice on folio 514v of the *Grimani Breviary*, is elevated above the vellum surface.[49] More rustic lattices are made of branches with knots and sprigs as on folio 42v of the book of hours, Vienna, ON MS Ser. n. 2600.

Gilt and silver branches appear in large numbers of the folios considered in this study. On folio 221v of the *Rothschild Hours* they lie at diagonals forming X-shapes.[50] More malleable branches on folio 234v are twisted into crescents, around which the jewellery is arranged.[51] X-shaped branches appear on folios 99 and 241v of the *Hours of James of Scotland* (Fig. 82), while on folio 48v of the same manuscript the jewellery is suspended

---

[46] Brinkmann and König, *Das Blumen-Stundenbuch*, f. 103v.

[47] Trenkler, *Das Rothschild-Gebetbuch*, f. 210.

[48] Von Euw and J. Plotzek, *Die Handschriften der Sammlung Ludwig II* (Cologne, 1982), vol. 2, Fig. 516.

[49] Salmi, *Grimani Breviary*, Pl. 65.

[50] Unterkircher, *Das Rothschild-Gebetbuch*, 120 and Trenkler, *Das Rothschild-Gebetbuch*, f. 221v.

[51] Unterkircher, *Das Rothschild-Gebetbuch*, 130 and Trenkler, *Das Rothschild-Gebetbuch*, f. 234v.

from a crescent form.⁵² Jewelled pieces hang from branches which run horizontally across the border on folio 177 of the book of hours, Vienna, ON MS Ser. n. 13238. Gilt branches are also sometimes twisted into long plait-like configurations (Figs 77, 78 and Pl. 7) which run along the length of the two frames. Letters composed of branches often appear in conjunction with these.

On some folios branches cut into letters formulate entire words and phrases. These are often specifically related to the miniature or text and may act as a mnemonic device, indicating the theme of a particular text or hour. Thus, the angel Gabriel's greeting: *Ave maria, gratia plena, Dominus tecum*, appears around the Annunciation on folio 14v of the *Hours of Johann Albrecht of Mecklenberg* (Cassel, Murhandsehe Bibliothek, MS 4⁰ math. et art. 50);⁵³ and the Virgin's response: *Ecce ancilla Domini fiat mihi* around the same scene on folio 84v of the *Rothschild Hours* (Fig. 77). Occasionally the letters comprise initials, like the monogram 'IHS' for the name of Jesus, that accompanies the text of the *Stabat Mater* and an image of the Crucifixion, on folio 241v of the *Hours of James of Scotland* (Fig. 82). On folio 183v of the same hours, the initials of the owner, James, and his wife Margaret Tudor, appear in gold and pearls (Fig. 81), demonstrating that the letters do not always have a religious significance.

Phrases always run anti-clockwise, starting at the top left corner of the verso of a folio or on the lower border of the recto. They may extend around the entire perimeter of a double folio as in the *Rothschild Hours* where Mary's words *Ecce ancilla domini fiat mihi*, begin on folio 84v and part of the angel's message *Spiritus sanctus superveniet in te et virtus* continues on folio 85 (Figs 77, 78).⁵⁴

These decorative letters are not always made of gilded jewelled branches. On folio 95v of BL Add. MS 35313, the words *Gloria in excelsis* are in the same crimson red as the background, only the gold highlighting rendering them legible. Pearls, on occasion, are employed to form words, as seen on folio 7 of volume 2 of the *Hours of Albrecht of Brandenburg*

---

⁵² Unterkircher, *Das Gebetbuch Jakobs IV*, ff. 48v, 99.

⁵³ For a reproduction, see P. de Winter, 'A Book of Hours of Queen Isabel la Catolica' in *The Bulletin of The Cleveland Museum of Art* 66 (December, 1981), 379.

⁵⁴ 'Behold the hand maid of the Lord: be it unto me (according to your word)' (Luke, 1:38). 'The Holy Ghost shall come upon you; and the power (of the Most High shall overshadow you)' (Luke, 1: 35).

(formerly Amsterdam), folio 301 of the *Seelengärtlein* and folio 189v of the *Hours of James of Scotland*.[55]

Garlands such as those held by the cupids in Gerard David's 'The Justice of Cambyses: the Arrest of the Judge Sisamnes', Groeninge Museum, Bruges, also feature in this type of border illumination.[56] Composed of berries, foliage, flowers and gilt acanthus leaves, they occasionally incorporate brooches and cameos, which are linked into the garlands through their hooks. This was a feature of badges at the time, enabling the owners not only to sew jewellery onto their clothing, but also into their prayer books, as seen on folios 47v, 58v–59 and 74 of Douce MS 51; lead pilgrim badges are sewn onto all these folios. Rosaries and pendants lie scattered between the daisy chains and lily heads of folios 5 and 9v of the *Hours of Johann Albrecht of Mecklenberg*,[57] while rosaries and badges appear among the gilt acanthus leaves, columns, and classical looking structures on four folios of volume 2 of the *Hours of Albrecht of Brandenburg* (formerly Amsterdam).[58]

All the frames that enclose either image or text in folios that were examined for this study are based on the same illusionistic approach, with the exception of folio 53v of the book of hours, Vienna, ON MS 1887.[59] This belongs to a separate tradition of border illumination. The central panel of the Annunciation to the Shepherds is not arch-shaped at the top, nor does it give the impression of a view through a window. Instead of being enclosed by a contrasting illusionistic surface, it has a solid narrow gold frame to which a series of alternating enamelled flowers and loose pearls are fastened in a manner which is strikingly similar to the frame of the *Norfolk triptych* (*c*.1415) by the Mosan Master in the Museum Boymans van Beuningen, Rotterdam.[60] The miniature thus suggests an altarpiece rather than a vista that opens directly onto a heavenly world.

The Role of the Jewelled Border

Patrick de Winter has noted that the illuminators of the Ghent–Bruges School 'sought to reach a wider clientele at the court and were aware that

---

[55] For a reproduction of the *Seelengärtlein*, see Dörnhöffer, *Hortulus Animae*, Pl. 563. For a reproduction from the Hours of James of Scotland, see Unterkircher, *Das Gebetbuch Jakobs IV*, f. 189v.

[56] J. Snyder, *Northern Renaissance Art* (New York, 1985), Fig. 184.

[57] Biermann, *Aachener Kunstblätter*, 108 and 111.

[58] The four folios are 65, 71, 78 and 97. For a reproduction of f. 97 see, Sotheby's, London, *Twenty Illuminated Manuscripts from the celebrated collection of William Astor, first Viscount Astor*, sales cat., 21 June 1988 (London, 1988), 91.

[59] De Winter, *The Bulletin of the Cleveland Museum*, 386.

[60] Snyder, *Northern Renaissance Art*, Fig. 73.

in their commissions such patrons called also for pleasing effects of colour and shape';[61] but was the role of the jewelled border merely to embellish and beautify, or did it also act within the book in a symbolic way? And if so, how are the concepts of ornamentation and symbolism related?

To answer these questions it is important to note that jewelled borders seem only to occur in books designed for worship; no examples have so far been located in secular texts. Moreover, the significance of precious materials such as gems and jewellery in late medieval life needs to be considered. Certainly, jewels, privately owned and worn as body adornments, were objects of desire. For the medieval person, however, jewellery was not only a form of conspicuous consumption. According to the book of the Apocalypse such magnificent materials reflected the divine glory and splendour of the Heavenly Jerusalem:

> And the building of the wall thereof was of jasper-stone; but the city itself pure gold, like unto clear glass. And the foundations of the wall of the city were adorned with all manner of precious stones ... (21:18–21)

Lapidaries and treatises on medieval aesthetics stressed that God was manifest in gems, and the writings of Bonaventura and Thomas Aquinas explain that even though *lux* (light) was physical, it was fundamentally considered a metaphysical reality. As gems had an ability to receive and transmit this *lux*, these transparent bodies acquired a metaphysical disposition.[62]

Because of their spiritual connotations these precious materials could be invoked as an aid for contemplation of the Divine, as the famous passage in the writings of the twelfth century Abbot Suger indicates:

> When my whole soul is steeped in the enchantment of the beauty of the house of God, when the charms of many-coloured gems lead me to reflect, transmuting things that are material into the immaterial, on the diversity of the holy virtues, I have a feeling that I am really dwelling in some strange region of the universe which neither exists entirely in the slime of earth, nor entirely in the purity of Heaven; and that by God's grace I can be transported from this inferior to that higher world in an anagogical manner.[63]

---

[61] De Winter, *The Bulletin of the Cleveland Museum*, 362.

[62] See U. Eco, *Art and Beauty in the Middle Ages* (London, 1986), especially 49–50 for Bonaventura and Aquinas's view on *lux* and its relationship to metaphysical reality. For the popularity of lapidaries and treatises on the magical properties of stones in the Middle Ages, see K. Vollmöller, *Ein Spanisches Steinbuch von Marbodus dem Bischof von Rennes* (Heilbronn, 1880), and Lightbown, *Medieval European Jewellery*, 96.

[63] E. Panosky, *Abbot Suger on the Abbey Church of Saint Denis and its Art Treasures* (Princeton, 1946), 65.

Abbot Suger, however, was referring to the splendid liturgical items of his majestic abbey church, as opposed to the individual pieces of jewellery—rings, rosaries, brooches and the like—which embellish the borders of manuscripts of the Ghent-Bruges School. So, can one confidently conclude that the representation of secular jewellery in prayer books, had a similar impact on the worshipper and performed the same meditative function as the spectacular objects which adorned the house of God?

Certainly it would be incorrect to interpret the significance of personal pieces within a secular context only. Cult images, such as that of Our Lady of Impruneta near Florence, were regularly adorned with offerings of jewels given in the quest for aid and protection.[64] The image of a saint or holy person surrounded by pieces of jewellery was, therefore, a familiar one; and it is interesting to note that the majority of jewelled borders in manuscripts appear in association with the representation of holy personages as opposed to religious narrative scenes. Such illumination could well have evoked the ritualistic experience of worshipping in front of a cult image.

Mary Carruthers argues that many of the border illuminations of medieval manuscripts function as mnemonic aids, providing cues which help the reader to recall and memorize important liturgical texts.[65] It has been shown how borders featuring jewelled initials and phrases sometimes refer directly to the content of the text that they accompany, yet such explicit references are relatively few (Figs 77, 78, 82). Moreover, there are no recurring associations between the jewelled borders and the miniatures that they surround. For example, an identical image of St George fighting the dragon appears in three books of hours: BL Add. MS 35313 (f. 223v; Fig. 69), the *Seelengärtlein* (f. 250v; Fig. 84) and the *Rothschild Hours* (f. 220v; Fig. 85). However, jewels appear only in the borders of BL Add. MS 35313; the borders in the other two manuscripts feature *trompe-l'œil* flowers and Gothic tracery.

Thus the mnemonic character of these borders is not specifically related to a particular image or text. The jewelled border with its shimmering, rich colours and meticulous representation was used sparingly by illuminators; it is the combination of rarity and beauty that makes certain pages memorable. Only two jewelled borders feature on the 423 illuminated folios of the *Blumen-Stundenbuch*; because they appear amongst endless pages of flowers their visual impact is all the more striking.[66]

---

[64] Lightbrown, *Medieval European Jewellery*, 76–77. For a reproduction see A. Paolucci, ed., *Il Tesoro di Santa Maria All'Impruneta* (Florence, 1987), 6.

[65] M. Carruthers, *The Book of Memory. A Study of Memory in Medieval Culture* (Cambridge, 1992), especially 241–48.

[66] Brinkmann and König, *Das Blumen-Stundenbuch*, ff. 103v, 130.

Given the role that gems and jewellery played in worship in the late Middle Ages, their representation in devotional manuscripts might seem to be sanctioned purely by their religious associations. However, we must not forget their significance in secular life, indicating rank, loyalty and, most of all, wealth. In the medieval mind gems were imbued with both pious and profane associations, similar to the dual significance of books of hours, which were essentially devotional aids, but were also considered to be a required fashion accessory for the wealthy, the *haute couture* of the Middle Ages. Thus, jewellery, with its similar elitist connotations, was perfectly suited to representation in this art form, becoming part of the decorative aesthetic developed by the illuminators in Flanders in the late fifteenth and early sixteenth centuries.

Appendix

The data presented in this appendix reflect the manuscripts to which I have had access to date; thus it has a strong bias towards the collections of the British Library, London, the Bodleian Library, Oxford and the Österreichische Nationalbibliothek, Vienna. Of the 37 manuscripts included here, I have seen 27 in the original or in full facsimiles; these are indicated with an asterisk. The folios of the remaining ten manuscripts were located as single reproductions in a range of publications. As I have not examined these manuscripts at first hand, I am unable to state whether they have other folios which feature jewellery in their borders.

Name of Manuscript	Number	Folios w. jewelled borders
Austria		
Vienna, Österreichische Nationalbibliothek		
1. Book of Hours*	MS 1887	53v
2. *Hours of James IV of Scotland and Margaret Tudor**	MS 1987	16v, 43v, 44, 48v, 50, 55, 57, 70v, 99, 134v, 135, 149v, 150, 154v, 155, 183v, 189v, 199v, 200, 221v, 222, 228v, 229, 240, 241v
3. Book of Hours*	MS 1926	7v, 8, 50
4. Book of Hours*	MS 1979	13, 88
5. Book of Hours*	MS 1984	22, 23, 30v, 36, 114, 118v, 141v, 144, 172, 172v, 177, 179, 243v
6. *Seelengärtlein**	MS 2706	54, 215v, 223v, 236, 244v, 247, 256v, 257, 271v, 282, 293, 301, 319v, 320, 324, 339
7. Book of Hours*	MS Ser. n. 2600	42v
8. *Legend of St. Adrian**	MS Ser. n. 2619	3v
9. *Hours of Duke of Ferdinand of Austria**	MS Ser. n. 2624	52v, 53

Name of Manuscript	Number	Folios w. jewelled borders
10. *Rothschild Hours**	MS Ser. n. 2844	65v, 66, 80v, 84v, 85, 125, 197v, 209v, 210, 215, 221v, 222, 224v, 225, 234v, 235, 238v, 239
11. Book of Hours*	MS Ser. n. 13238	177

Belgium

Brussels, Bibliothèque Royale de Belgique

12. Book of Hours	MS II. 5941	95v

Germany

Berlin, Kupferstich Kabinett

13. Book of Hours	MS 78. B. 12	190v, 191, 338v

Cassel, Murhardsehe Bibliothek der Stadt Kassel und Landesbibliothek

14. *Hours of Johann Albrecht von Mecklenberg*	MS math. et art. 50	5, 9, 9v, 11, 14v, 33v

Darmstadt, Landesbibliothek

15. Book of Hours	MS 69	105v

Munich, Bayerische Staatsbibliothek

16. *Blumen Stundenbuch**	MS Clm. 23637	103v, 130
17. Book of Hours	MS 28346	45v, 78v, 197v

Italy

Rome, Vatican City, Bibliotheca Apostolica Vaticana

18. Book of Hours*	MS Ross. 94	33v, 34, 109v, 110, 119v, 120, 166v, 167

Name of Manuscript	Number	Folios w. jewelled borders
Venice, Bibliotheca Marciana		
19. *Grimani Breviary*	MS lat. 1, 99	514v, 579v, 635v, 706
The Netherlands		
(Formerly in Amsterdam, Bibliotheca Philosophica Hermetica; present whereabouts unknown.)		
20. *Hours of Albrecht of Brandenburg**	MS 40. Vol. 1	76, 156, 254
21. *Hours of Albrecht of Brandenburg**	MS 40. Vol. 2	7, 13v, 29, 65, 68, 70, 71, 78, 97
Sweden		
Stockholm, Kungl. Biblioteket		
22. Book of Hours	MS A227	69, 79
United Kingdom		
Cambridge, Fitzwilliam Museum		
23. Four Miniatures on Parchment*	Marlay Cutting Sp. 2–5	Sp. 5
24. Five Miniatures from a Book of Hours*	MS 294 a–e	294 e
London, British Library		
25. *Breviary of Queen Isabella of Castile*	Add. MS 18851	431
26. *Hours of Joanna of Castile**	Add. MS 18852	26v, 53, 53v, 54v, 58v, 61v, 74, 74v, 93v, 130, 131v, 140, 140v, 145v, 156v, 159, 174v, 184, 191, 195v, 206, 206v, 212, 212v, 217, 226, 226v, 228, 228v, 239, 243, 248v, 259, 274, 274v,

Name of Manuscript	Number	Folios w. jewelled borders
[26. *Hours of Joanna of Castile* continued...*]		277v, 281, 281v, 288v, 294v, 319, 320v, 327, 351v, 362, 362v, 370v, 394v, 395, 395v, 400, 400v, 406v, 416v, 421v
27. Book of Hours*	Add. MS 35313	10v, 11, 28v, 29, 44, 48v, 51, 95v, 96, 116, 117, 123, 136, 141v, 142v, 218v, 219, 223v, 224, 231v, 232, 235v, 236
28. Huth Hours*	Add. MS 38126	67
29. Hours of Joanna of Ghistelles*	Egerton MS 2125	143v

Oxford, Bodleian Library

30. Book of Hours*	Douce MS 8	348, 442v
31. Hours of Engelbert of Nassau*	Douce MSS 219–220	40
32. Hours and Benedictional of Philip II Convault*	Douce MS 223	32v
33. Book of Hours*	Douce MS 256	15, 86v, 101v, 131v, 177v, 178, 183v
34. Hours of Louis Quarre, Treasurer of the Golden Fleece*	Douce MS 311	29v

United States of America

Los Angeles, J. Paul Getty Museum

35. Hours of Albrecht of Brandenburg	MS Ludwig IX. 9	36v, 148

New York, Pierpont Morgan Library

36. Hours of Catherine of Cleves*	MSS M. 917, M. 945	p. 237, p. 300

Private Collections

37. Imhoff Hours		43, 154v, 331v

Figure 69. St George and the dragon. Book of Hours. London, British Library, Add. MS 35313, f. 223v. 237×152 mm.

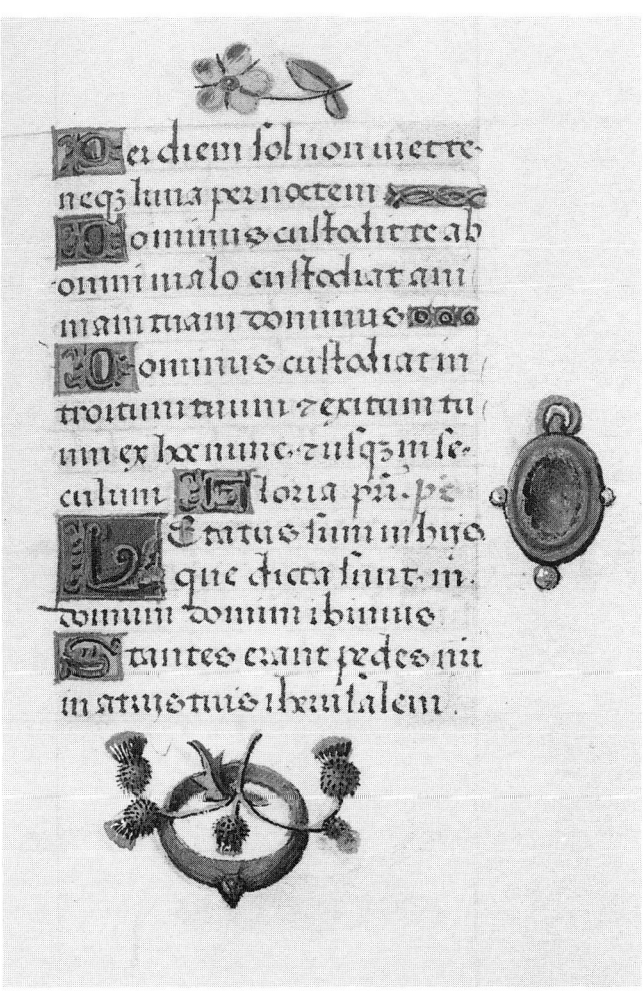

Figure 70. Border decoration. *Hours of Joanna of Castile*. London, British Library, Add. MS 18852, f. 243. 109×75 mm.

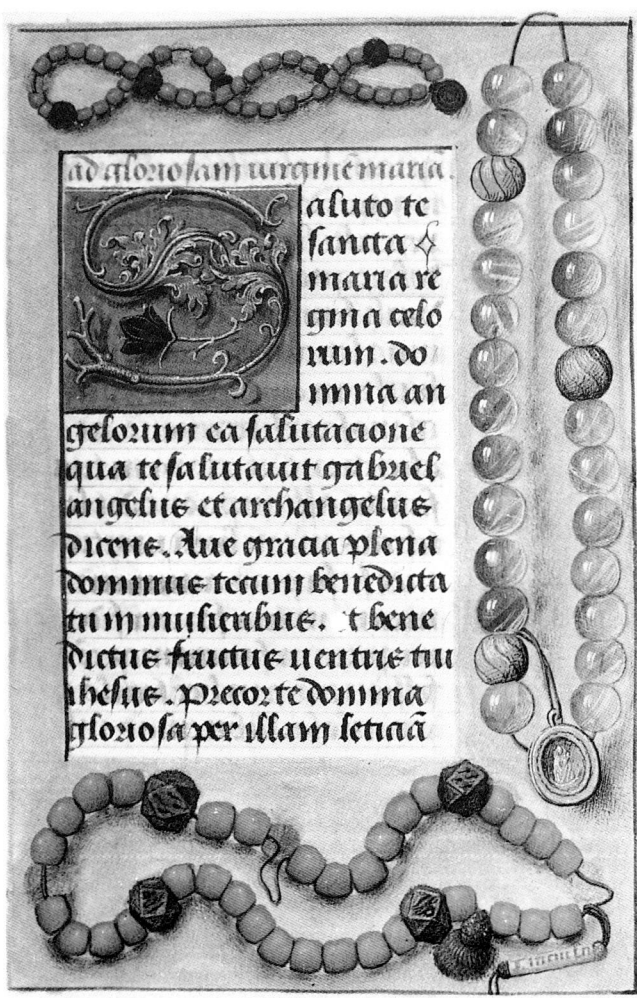

Figure 71. Border decoration. Book of Hours. Vienna, Österreichische Nationalbibliothek, MS 1979, f. 88. 131×90mm.

Figure 72. St Agnes. *Hours of Catherine of Cleves.* New York, Pierpont Morgan Library, MS M.917, p. 300. 192×130mm.

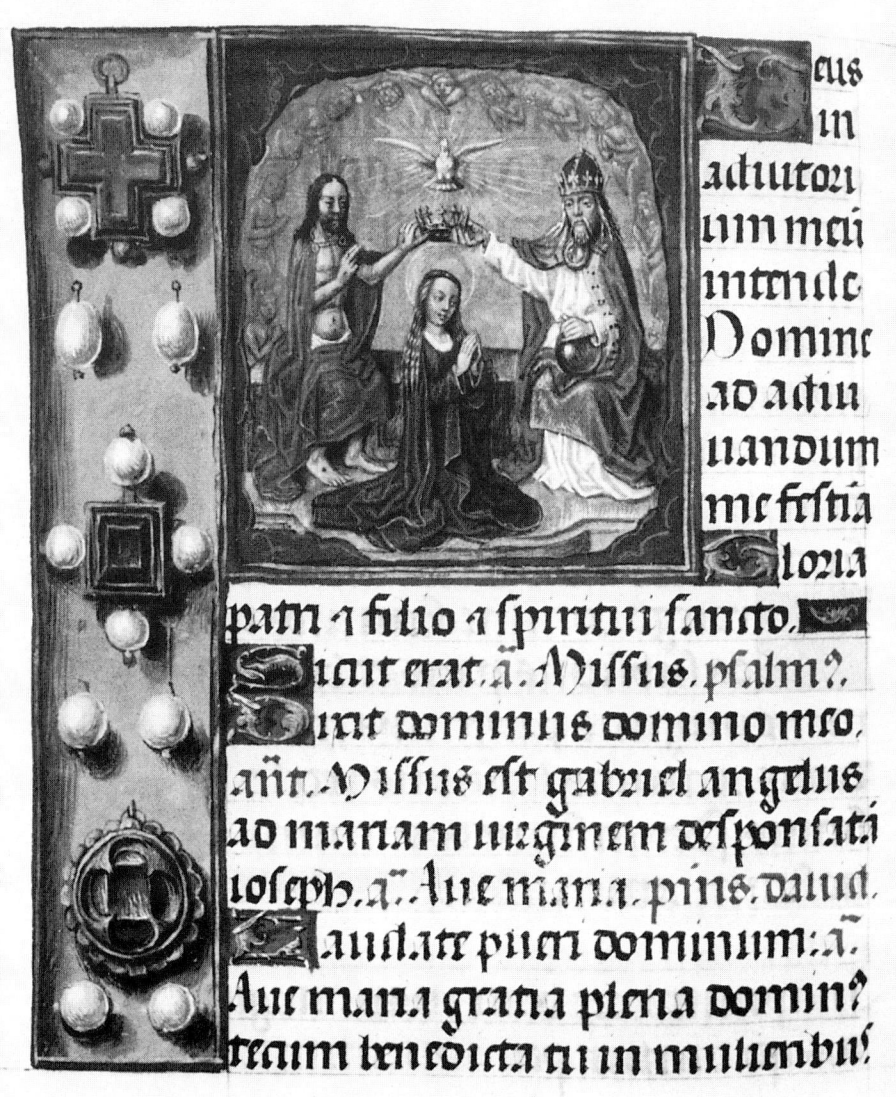

Figure 73. Coronation of the Virgin. Book of Hours. Oxford, Bodleian Library, MS Douce 256, f. 101v. 190×144 mm.

Figure 74. St Luke painting the Virgin. Book of Hours. Oxford, Bodleian Library, MS Douce 256, f. 15. 190×144 mm.

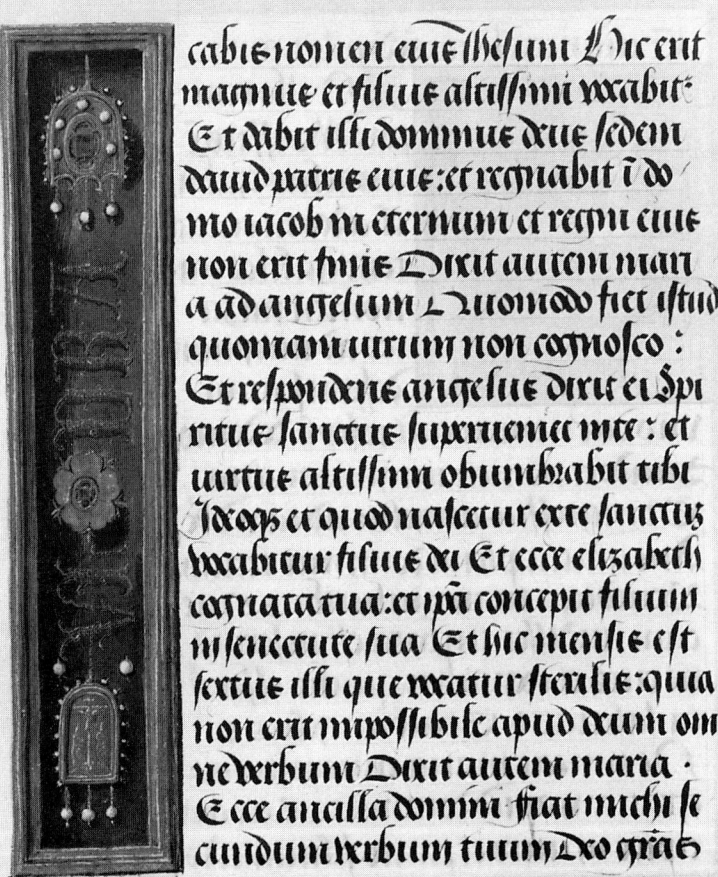

Figure 75. Border decoration. *Hours of James of Scotland*. Vienna, Österreichische Nationalbibliothek, MS 1897, f. 16v. 200×140 mm.

Figure 76. Last Supper. *Hours of Joanna of Ghistelles*. London, British Library, Egerton MS 2125, ff. 142v–143. 150×105 mm.

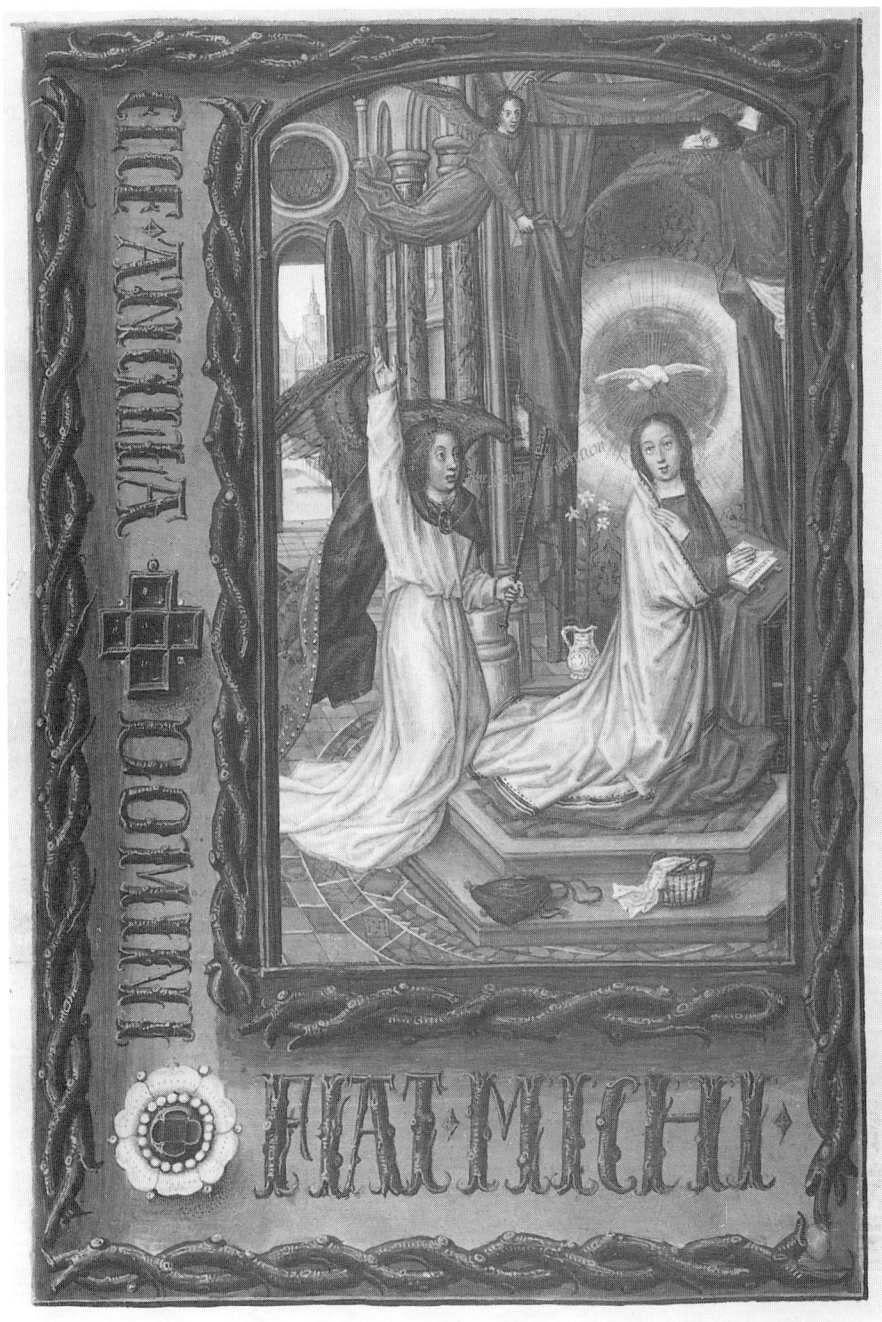

Figure 77. Annunciation. *Rothschild Hours*. Vienna, Österreichische Nationalbibliothek, MS Ser. n. 2844, f. 84v. 228×160mm.

Figure 78. Border decoration. *Rothschild Hours*. Vienna, Österreichische Nationalbibliothek, MS Ser. n. 2844, f. 85. 228×160 mm.

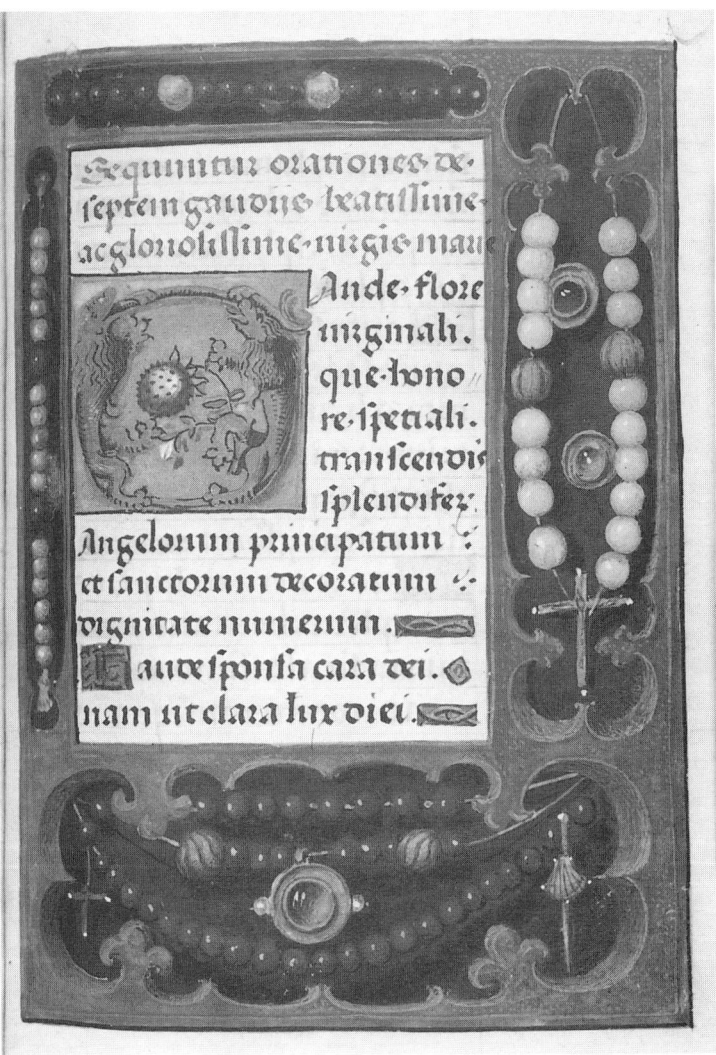

Figure 79. Border decoration. *Hours of Joanna of Castile*. London, British Library, Add. MS 18852, f. 319. 109×75mm.

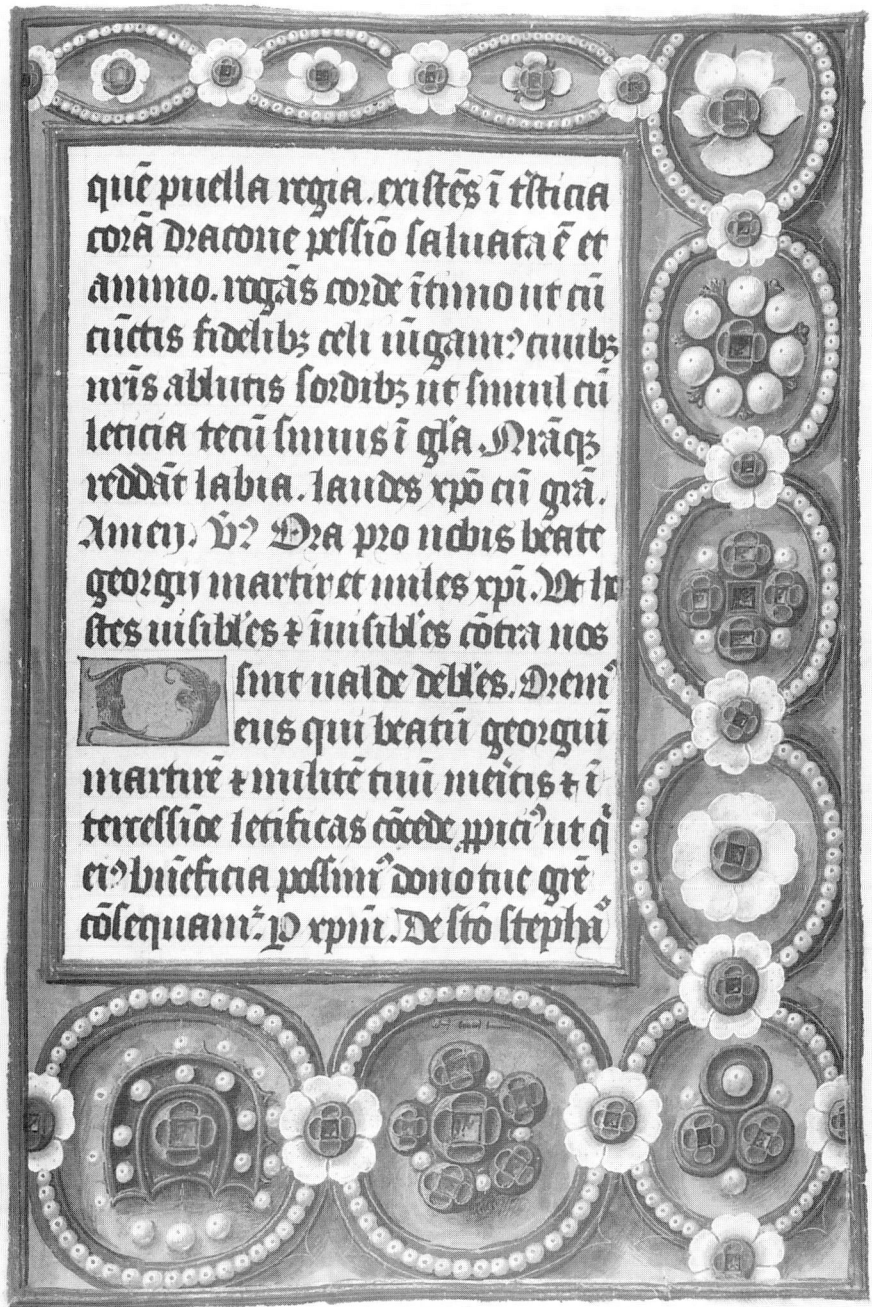

Figure 80. Border decoration. Book of Hours. London, British Library, Add. MS 35313, f. 224. 237×152 mm.

Figure 81. Resurrection. *Hours of James of Scotland*. Vienna, Österreichische Nationalbibliothek, MS 1897, f. 183v. 200×140mm.

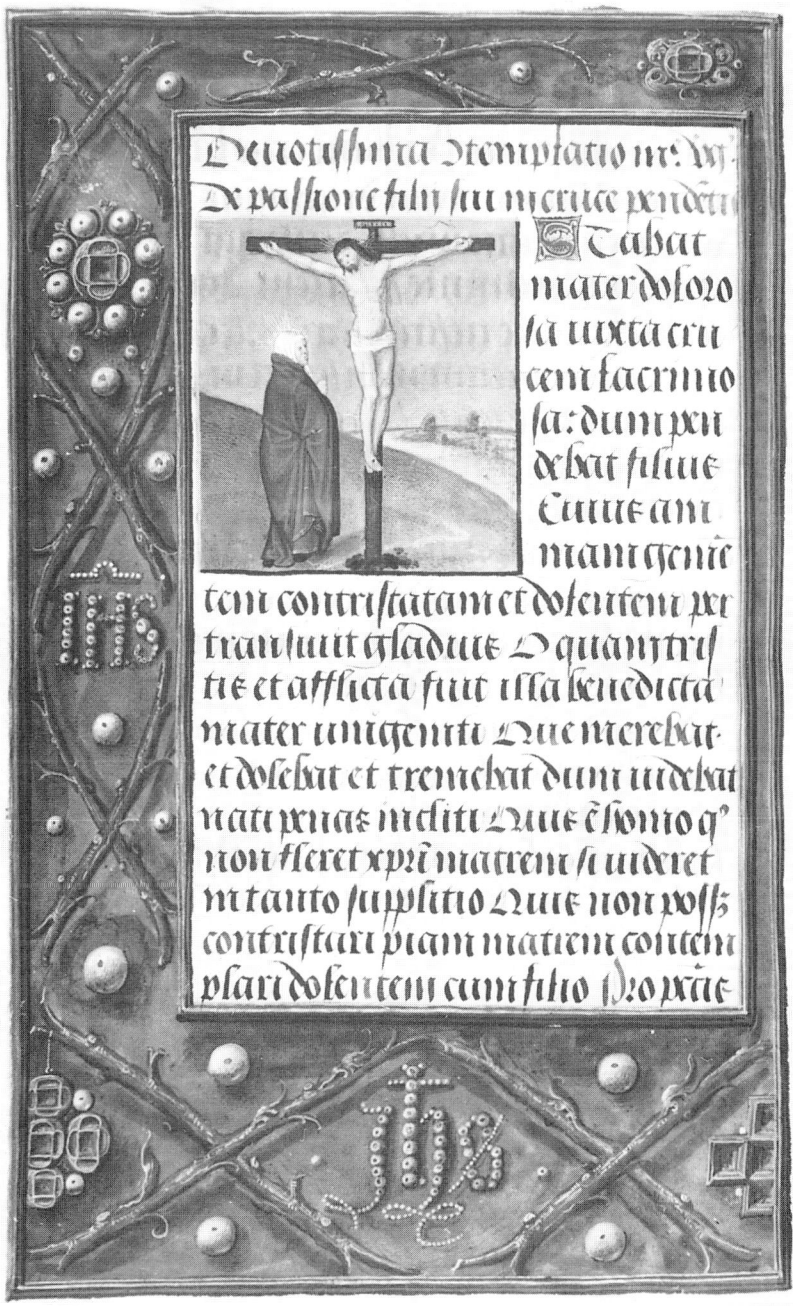

Figure 82. Crucifixion. *Hours of James of Scotland*. Vienna, Österreichische Nationalbibliothek, MS 1897, f. 241v. 200×140mm.

Figure 83. St George and the dragon. *Seelengärtlein*. Vienna, Österreichische Nationalbibliothek, MS 2706, f. 250v. 214×155 mm.

Figure 84. St George and the dragon. *Rothschild Hours*. Vienna, Österreichische Nationalbibliothek, MS Ser. n. 2844, f. 204. 222×160mm.

TEN

Devotional Objects in Book Format: Diptychs in the Collection of Margaret of Austria and her Family

Dagmar Eichberger

SMALL DEVOTIONAL DIPTYCHS FEATURE quite prominently in the private collections of members of the Burgundian–Hapsburgian dynasty from the late fourteenth to the early sixteenth centuries. This study explores the significance of this particular art object within the context of the development of private worship in the Late Middle Ages with special reference to Margaret of Austria and her great grandfather Duke Philip the Good.

In documentary sources of the fifteenth and sixteenth centuries diptychs are generally described in terms of their physical structure: 'a panel consisting of two pieces', 'a double panel', 'a panel with two leaves'.[1]

---

[1] Panel: 'Ungs tableaux de deux pieces'; from J. Labarte, ed., 'Inventaire du Mobilier de Charles V, Roi de France (1380)', in *Collection des Documents inédits sur l'histoire de France*, (Paris, 1879) 226; cited in D. Eichberger, *Bildkonzeption und Weltdeutung im New Yorker Diptychon des Jan van Eycks* (Wiesbaden, 1987) 117. There is a full list of the inventories referred to in abbreviated form in the footnotes in the Appendix below. Double panel: 'Double tableau de Nostre Dame, d'ung coust sainct Jehan et de l'aultre saincte Marguerite... X livres' 1535 (Le Glay (1839), 484). This entry refers to one of the diptychs by

Such descriptions make clear the distinction between the shape of the diptych and that of a single panel or a triptych.² Sometimes, however, diptychs are described in more evocative terms as 'panels made in the shape of books' or even more specifically as 'panels made in the shape of a book of hours'. In an inventory dating from 1521, for example, which lists objects inherited by Margaret of Austria from her father, Emperor Maximilian, one particular diptych is described as 'a small gold panel made in the shape of a book'.³ The same object is described in more detail in a later inventory as: 'a small rectangular gold panel, in the manner of a book of hours, which opens with hinges, on which are depicted Our Lady and Saint Louis, etc.'⁴ Another diptych in the same inventory is described as 'a small gold panel in the shape of a book of hours, with two enamelled images, one of Our Lady and the other of St Barbara . . .'.⁵ This particular paraphrase of the term 'diptych', likening it to a devotional prayer book, invites further enquiry.

The most apparent reason for the analogy between a double panel and an opened book of hours is their formal similarity: both objects are generally small in format and therefore portable; both can be opened and closed, and secured with clasps; and both sometimes contain full-length images on facing leaves. These general similarities have been discussed in some detail in relation to the Wilton Diptych in the National Gallery in

---

Michiel Sittow, which is described in more detail in the 1516 and 1523–4 inventories; see n. 3. Panel with two leaves: 'Ung tableau a double feullet.' The same object is described in 1516 as: 'Ung petit tableaul a double feullet de la main de Michiel, de l'ung des coustez de Nostre Dame . . . de l'autre coustez d'ung Sainct Jehan et de Saincte Marguerite, faiz a la semblence du prince d'Espaigne et de Madame' (Le Glay (1839), 481); and in 1523–4 as: 'Item, ung aultre petit de N(ost)re Dame d'ung costel et de sainct Jehan l'Evangeliste et de saincte Marguerite, tirez apres le vif du feu prince d'Espaigne, mary de Madame, aussy apres le vif de Mad. Dame' (Michelant (1871), 93).

² This terminology is used so consistently that the shape of only one object—listed in the 1523–4 inventory—is unclear: 'Item, ung aultre petit tableau de N(re) Dame en chief ou est la representation de l'empereur moderne et de Madam a genoux, adorant ladit ymaige, dessus ung blason aux armes d'Espaigne et de Bourgogne et quatre blasons es quatre coins' (Michelant (1871), 83–84).

³ 'Un petit tableau d'or, fait en forme de livre = 4 onces, 2 est, donne a Madame (l'archiduchesse Marguerite), porte ici pour la moitie de sa valeur = 40 livres, 17 sols, 6 derniers' (Finot (1895), 183).

⁴ 'Ung petit tableau d'or quarre en facon d'heures, que se ouvre a charnieres, ou quel sont une ymage de Notre-Dame et une ymage de sainct loys esmaillez. A l'entour des deux tableaux sont six grains de balay, quatre de saphiz et dix perles, entremeslee de fuillage, esmaille de vert, pesant . . . 4 onces 3 estrellins' [19/3/1531] (Voltelini (1890), IX, No. 80). Margaret bequeathed this to her nephew, King Charles V; see n. 32.

⁵ 'Une tablette d'or en facon d'heures, ou sont deux ymages esmartees, unde de Notre-Dame, et l'autre de saincte Barbe, et n'y a qu'ung fermeillet, l'autre est tumbe, pesant . . . 1 once 5 1/2 estrellins' [19/3/1531] (Voltelini (1890), IX, No. 82). This was also left to Charles V; see n. 32.

London (Figs 85–86), and the double page composition on pages 10–11 of the *Très Belles Heures de Notre Dame* (Brussels, Bibl. Royale, MSS 11060–1; Figs 87–88) both of which date from the last decade of the fourteenth century.[6] In these works the owners, Richard II and Jean de Berry respectively, are portrayed in the company of their patron saints on the left half of a double page or panel, at a respectful distance from the object of their devotion, the Virgin and Child, who face them on the other half.

These two types of objects, however, which were very popular with the aristocracy of the late medieval period,[7] have more in common than their purely formal qualities. While the role of the book of hours as an aid to personal prayer has long been recognized, Kermer argues that the diptychs listed in royal and ducal inventories also played an important part in the daily devotions performed by their owners.[8] His interpretation rests mainly on the analysis of written sources, but it can also be substantiated by reference to works of art. Two excellent examples are provided by works belonging to Philip the Good, Duke of Burgundy (1396–1467).

A miniature illustrating the *Traité sur l'oraison dominicale* (Brussels, Bibl. Royale, MS 9092, f. 9, *c*.1457; Fig. 89) demonstrates how diptych and private prayer book could function in tandem.[9] By contrast to the priest shown publicly celebrating Mass in front of a large triptych, the duke kneels apart in a secluded tent-like structure; an illuminated prayer book lies open on the *prie-dieu* before him and a small diptych hangs on the wall directly above it. This displays an image of the Virgin and a portrait, perhaps of Philip himself.

Another devotional object in the duke's collection combines text and image in unusual fashion (Vienna, ON MS 1800; Pl. 8 and Fig. 90). It consists of a prayer book surmounted by a small diptych in a wooden frame, showing two devotional images, the *Trinity* on the left and the *Coronation of the Virgin* on the right.[10] Both illuminated manuscript and diptych are

---

[6] See J. Dunkerton, S. Foister, *et al.*, *Giotto to Dürer, Early Renaissance Painting in the National Gallery* (New Haven & London, 1991), 136–39; and Eichberger, *Bildkonzeption* (1987), 42–43.

[7] King Charles V, for example, kept five diptychs in the study of his residence at St Germain-en-Laie: two painted double panels, two reliquary panels, and one ivory diptych. See Eichberger, *Bildkonzeption* (1987), 117.

[8] W. Kermer, *Studien zum Diptychon in der sakralen Malerei von den Anfangen bis zur Mitte des 16. Jahrhunderts* (Neunkirchen, 1969), 4.

[9] See L.M.J. Delaissé, *Middeleeuwse Miniatuuren van de Librije van Bourgondie tot het Handschriftenkabinet van de Koninklijke Bibliothek van Belgie* (Amsterdam, 1960), 172–75; and H. van Os *et al.*, translated M. Hoyle,*The Art of Devotion* (Princeton, 1994), 161.

[10] The diptych which is parchment on wood is dated *c*.1430; the manuscript: is *c*.1450. See O. Pächt, U. Jenni and D. Thoss, *Flämische Schule I*, (Vienna, 1983) 19-23; D. Thoss,

permanently linked together by a single leather binding and were obviously designed to be used in conjunction with each other, so that as the owner prayed from the book he could fix his gaze on the images of the diptych that represented the object of his devotion. Interestingly, the manuscript opens with an illustration of Philip praying with his son Charles the Bold, before an altar surmounted by an opened diptych (Pl. 8).

In this context, it should be noted that diptychs were not the only artefacts that imitated the format of the book. Occasionally, late medieval inventories mention small objects that take the concept of a picture book *en miniature* even further. A fifteenth-century Burgundian inventory itemizes a 'little book comprising eight leaves of gold and enamel, containing several histories such as the Annunciation, Nativity, Circumcision, and others from the life of our Lord'.[11] The selection and ordering of these scenes indicate that this metal artefact imitated a book of hours not just in form, but also in content, since the sequence, which starts with the Annunciation, Nativity and Circumcision, resembles that used conventionally to illustrate the Little Office of the Virgin.

Earlier devotional diptychs were frequently made from expensive materials such as enamelled gold or ivory and were mostly owned by important noble families; but the popularity of this format led to a dramatic increase in the production of painted diptychs in the course of the fifteenth century.[12] The idea of possessing a copy of a famous devotional icon combined with a life-like portrait of oneself became so fashionable that wider sections of the community, common burghers as well as nobility, commissioned these works from the leading artists of the day. In a diptych now in Antwerp, for example, Abbot Christiaan de Hondt is depicted praying in front of a well-known Marian image, a copy of *The Virgin in the Church* by Jan van Eyck (Figs 91–92).[13] What at first glance looks like a rendering of the Abbot's private bedroom is probably a conventionalized setting. A very similar composition is used for a diptych of almost identical dimensions, now in Ghent, which was commissioned

---

Flämische Buchmalerei, Handschriftenschätze aus dem Burgunderreich (Vienna, 1987) 27–28; and O. Mazal and D. Thoss, eds, *Das Buchaltärchen herzog Phillips des Guten von Burgund. Codex 1800 der Österreichischen Nationalbibliothek in Wien.* (Lucerne, 1991).

[11] Cited in R.W. Lightbown, *Medieval European Jewellery* (London, 1990), 217.

[12] For examples of devotional diptychs in ivory, see van Os, *Art of Devotion*, Pls 1 and 6.

[13] Antwerp, Koninklijk Museum voor Schone Kunsten, by the Master of 1499; each panel is 315x146 mm. See P. Vandenbroek, *Catalogus schilderkunst 14e en 15e eeux, Koninklijk Museum voor Schone Kunsten* (Antwerpen, 1985) 125–30; and P. Eeckhout, 'Les trois diptyques du Maitre 1499', *Bulletin-Musées royaux des beaux-arts de Belgique, Miscellanea Philippe Roberts-Jones* (1985–8), 49–62.

by Margaret of Austria, the regent of the Netherlands (Figs 93–94).[14] Margaret's *prie-dieu*, too, is placed in a domestic interior which includes a stately bed, a cupboard with a variety of vessels and a lit fire-place. The coat-of-arms on the mantelpiece and carpet clearly identify her as the dowager duchess of Savoy and regent of the Netherlands. While there are no grounds for assuming that either of these paintings portrays its owner's personal apartments accurately, it is nevertheless of interest that both the abbot and the archduchess are depicted performing their religious duties in the privacy of their home and not in a church. And although the similarity of the settings indicates the application of a standard formula, these representations nevertheless testify to contemporary religious practices such as the placing of a small devotional image next to the bed.[15] The Ghent diptych surfaced for sale on the French art market in 1971 and has not yet attracted much attention.[16] This small double panel is, nevertheless, of particular importance for the current discussion, since it is one of twelve devotional diptychs which can be linked to Margaret of Austria's patronage or to her collection. Most of these objects are now lost, and their appearance has largely to be reconstructed from detailed inventory descriptions which were kept for housekeeping purposes and clarification of ownership. The Ghent diptych, however, matches one of the inventory descriptions; the entry reads: 'Received after this inventory was made, a double panel; and one panel is (an image of) Our Lady dressed in blue, holding her child on the right, and on the other (panel) is Madame on her knees, adoring the said child.'[17]

---

[14] Ghent, Museum voor Schone Kunsten; each panel is 305x146 mm. Some art historians have attributed this second diptych also to the Master of 1499. Paul Vandenbroek, however, questions the quality of the Ghent diptych and points out that the left panel has been repainted almost completely. The right panel, which contains the portrait of Margaret of Austria, has been partially repainted (Vandenbroek, *Catalogus*, 127).

[15] The diptych in the de Hondt panel depicts a Virgin and Child and a Crucifixion. Margaret owned at least one picture for the head of a bed: 'Ung tableau d'or de bonne grandeur pour pendre a ung lict, ouquel est ung dieu de pitie avec Nostre-Dame et sainct Jehan, esmaillez d'azure, rouge et violet, et derriere est escript: Nate Jesu fili David miserer mei; pendant a une chainette et ung crochet, le tout d'or, pesant . . . 1 marc 1 once 13 1/2 estrellins' [9/3/1531] (Voltelini (1890), no. 91).

[16] See Eeckhout, 'Trois diptychs', 60; and Brussels, Palais des Beaux-Arts, *Albert Dürer aux Pays-Bas: son voyage (1520–21), son influence* (Brussels, 1977), 120.

[17] 'Receu puis cest inventoire fait ung double tableau; et l'ung est N(re) Dame habille de bleu, tenant son enffant droit, et en l'aultre Madame a genoux, adorant ledit enffant'. (Michelant (1871), 87). This entry states that the picture entered the collection after 1524; but if Margaret commissioned the work herself, it is unlikely that it was executed much before that date. The match with another entry suggested by F. Baudson in the exhibition catalogue is untenable, as is her suggestion that there may have been a third panel; see Brou, Musée de Brou, *Van Orley et les Artistes de la cour de Marguerite d'Autriche* (Brou, 1981), 54–55.

This late example of the most common type of devotional diptych showing the patron facing an image of the Virgin and Child maintains the spiritual power and meaning characteristic of the genre since its inception. Portrayed with prayer book and joined hands, symbols of steadfast devotion, Margaret entreats the Virgin Mary's intercession with her divine son, on behalf of herself and the whole human race.

In order to establish a precise historical context for a more detailed examination of the selection and display of such devotional images in Margaret of Austria's residence in Mechelen, it is appropriate to recall the basic facts of her life and the ways in which she expressed her piety throughout it.

Margaret was born in 1480, the daughter of Emperor Maximilian and Mary of Burgundy; she and her brother, Philip the Fair, were the sole heirs to the Burgundian–Hapsburgian dynasty, which was then attempting to dominate the political landscape of Europe.[18] Astutely arranged marriages formed an important role in the political strategy of the family.[19] This may explain why Margaret was betrothed three times and widowed twice before settling into a more regular lifestyle in the Netherlands, of which she was appointed regent in 1507.[20] While she exerted considerable power over the fate of the Netherlands during her rule (1507–15 and 1518–30), her official titles are a better indication of the wide sphere of her personal influence. They also point to the sources of the revenue on which she drew to finance her court and various projects. In 1523 Margaret's official titles were, 'Archiducesse d'Autriche et de Bourgoigne, ducesse de Savoye, contesse de Bourgoigne, de Charrolais, de Romont, de Baugey, de Villars, dame de Salins, de Malines, de Chastelchinon, de Noyer, de Chaulcins, de la Parriere, des pays de Bresse, de

---

[18] For the life of Margaret of Austria, see M. Bruchet, *Marguerite d'Autriche, Duchesse de Savoie* (Lille, 1927); G. De Boom, *Marguerite d'Autriche-Savoie et la Pre-Renaissance* (Brussels, 1935); and G. Königsberger, *Erzherzogin Margarethe im politischen Dienst ihres Vaters Kaiser Maximilian I, von 1506–1515* (Diss., Graz, 1980).

[19] The two diptychs of Philip the Fair (London, National Gallery) and Margaret of Austria (Vienna, Kunsthistorisches Museum), for example, were probably commissioned in relation to negotiations between the Spanish and the Hapsburgian families, which ultimately led to the double marriage of Margaret of Austria to Juan of Castille and Philip the Fair to Joanna of Castille; see *Porträtgalerie der Geschichte Österreichs von 1400 bis 1800, Katalog der Gemäldegalerie* (Vienna, 1976), 57–58.

[20] See M. Debae, Brussels, Bibliothèque Royale Albert 1er, *La Librairie de Marguerite d'Autriche* (Brussels, 1987), XIV–XV.

Vaulx, and de Faucigny'.[21] These villages, counties and duchies were the site of her active support of monasteries, churches, and hospitals.[22]

That Margaret's major activity as a patron of the arts was in the area of religious projects and commissions is by no means unusual. As recent studies of Isabella of Portugal, Isabella la Catolica, and Margaret of York have shown, this was the case with a number of noble women in late medieval society.[23] Examples drawn from three key areas of her patronage will help to indicate the nature and range of these religious interests.

After the death of her last husband, Duke Philibert of Savoy, in 1504, Margaret embarked on an unusually large and costly project, the building of the church and convent of Brou in her county of Bresse.[24] Undertaken in fulfilment of a pledge given by her mother-in-law, Marguerite de Bourbon, to build a memorial church as a token of gratitude for the recovery of her husband from a serious illness, it was a project to which Margaret had a deep personal commitment and one which she pursued with extraordinary persistence and even a grain of stubbornness, despite major financial and organizational difficulties. Both the church and associated Augustinian convent feature prominently in her last will.[25] Moreover, from the outset, the church, St Nicholas in Brou, was destined to become Margaret's burial site. It was not only built to contain her funerary monument, together with those of her late husband and her mother-in-law, but also to house a lavishly decorated private chapel for the archduchess. The church featured stained glass windows, choir-stalls and many other objects paid for by Margaret and her courtiers.[26]

---

[21] Lille, Archive du Nord, B 2312, no. 81524, cited in Bruchet, *Marguerite d'Autriche*, 57, n. 1.

[22] Perhaps the most telling document is her testament, drawn up in 1508 and only added to at the time of her approaching death in 1530; it is fully reproduced in J. Baux, *Histoire de l'Eglise de Brou* (Bourg-en-Bresse, 2nd ed., 1862) 345–67; see also De Boom, *Marguerite d'Autriche-Savoie*, 110–14.

[23] See W. Blockmans, 'The devotion of a lonely Duchess', in T. Kren, ed., *Margaret of York, Simon Marmion and 'The Visions of Tondal'* (Malibu, 1992) 29–46; N. Morgan, 'Texts of devotion and religious instruction associated with Margaret of York', in Kren, ed., *Margaret of York*, 63–76; and C. Lemaire, M. Henry and A. Rouzet, Brussels, Bibliothèque Royale Albert 1er, *Isabelle de Portugal, Duchesse de Bourgogne, 1397–1471* (Brussels, 1991).

[24] See J. Baux, *Histoire*, 24; and M Hörsch, 'Architektur unter Margarethe von Österreich, Regentin der Niederlande (1507–1530)', in *Verhandelingen van de Koninklijke Academie voor Weteschappen Letteren en Schone Kunsten*. jg. 56, 58 (1994), 1–236.

[25] Baux, *Histoire*, 349–54.

[26] M.-F. Poiret, *Le Monatere de Brou. Le chef-d'oeuvre d'une fille d'empereur* (Paris, 1994). A letter written by her secretary from Brou in 1512 refers to a secret walkway which led from Margaret's private apartments in the monastery across the choir-screen to her chapel situated behind her own funerary monument on the northern side of the church. (E. Tremayne, *The first Governess of the Netherlands, Margaret of Austria* (London, 1908), 299).

Her will and inventories indicate very clearly that Margaret saw the convent and the church of Brou as the final destination for many of the devotional objects in her private collection, especially relics and religious images.[27] Among the objects which were sent to Brou in 1532, for example, were an *Ecce Homo* image[28] and a *Vera Icon*.[29]

According to Margaret's will, five of the devotional diptychs in her collection were earmarked for the prior and religious of the convent in Brou, but only one of these, a very old painting with Passion scenes, was actually delivered there.[30] Contrary to her wishes, the other four entered the collection of her niece, Queen Mary of Hungary.[31]

---

[27] 'Item, donnons et legons a lesglise de nostre couvent de sainct Nyclas toutes les sainctes relicques que avons et aurons au jour de nostre dict trespas, tant de fust de saincte croix, du sainct suaire, ossemens de saincts et sainctes et tous aultres images de saincts et sainctes que avons et seront trouvees a nostre dict trespas et qui pourroyent servir a decourer icelluy nostre dict couvent, lesquelles voulant incontinant estre pourtees au dict couvent et que noz dicts exequuteurs sur noz dicts biens facent faire casses et reliquieres a leur bon advis pour mectre les dictes relicques' (Baux, *Histoire*, 352).

[28] 'Item, tabula in qua est depicta ymago ipsius Domini Nostri ad formam ECCE HOMO, que verba sunt pendentia in ejus collo et in alia manuum tenet flagellum et in altera harundinem, et fondus ejus est colore rubeo dipictus' [12/6/1532] (Bruchet, *Marguerite d'Autriche*, 429).

[29] 'Item, aliam tabulam in qua est caput quod fertur esse depictum ad veram effigiem Christi, et in duobus lateribus ejusdem tabule scriptum est litteris aureis, et est ipsa tabula vitro clausa et fermata' [12/6/1532] (Bruchet, *Marguerite d'Autriche*, 429).

[30] 'Item, ung aultre double tableau assez vieux, figure de Passion N(re) S(gr) et aultre mistere, donne a Madame par Mons(gr) le conte d'Hocstrate.' A remark on the margins reads: 'Delivre aux prieur et religieuse de Broux . . .' [1523–4] (Michelant (1871), 86). This is also confirmed by a list in Latin of objects received by the prior of Brou on 12 June 1532: 'Item, tabul antiquam in qua est dipicta Passio Christi cum aliis ministeriis' (Bruchet, *Marguerite d'Autriche*, 430). Other objects initially destined to go to Brou were still in the palace in Mechelen in 1535, when they were valued by Bernard van Orley, probably with the intention of giving the priory in Brou financial remuneration for the undelivered works: '. . . et fere extimation des tableaulx et pointures qui sont esdis cabinetz et librairie que Ma dite feue dame a legue en son cloistre de Brou les Bourg en Bresse, affin que si il plaisoit a la Royne, a qui appartiennent presentement les dis cabinetz et librairie retenir les dis tableaulx . . .' (Lille, Arch. Nord., B459, no. 22932, in Bruchet, *Marguerite d'Autriche*, 256). This list and accompanying evaluations were transcribed by Le Glay with the 1516 inventory fragments (Le Glay (1839), 483–84). See also Finot (1895), 212–13.

[31] The four diptychs are described in the inventories: 'Double tableau de Nostre Dame, d'ung coust sainct Jehan et de l'aultre saincte Marguerite . . . X livres' (Le Glay (1839), 483–84); 'Aultre double tableau; en l'ung est Nostre-Seigneur pendant en croix; en l'aultre l'histoire de sainct Gregoire . . . IIII livres' (Le Glay (1839), 484); 'Double petit tableau de Chipres; en l'ung est l'ascension Nostre Seigneur, et en l'aultre l'assumption Nostre Dame... XL livres' (Le Glay (1839), 483); and, 'Riche double tableau de Nostre-Dame, double par dehors de satin broche . . . C livres' (Le Glay (1839), 483). For Mary of Hungary, see B. van den Boogert, 'Macht en Pracht. Het Mecenat van Maria van Hongarije', in Utrecht, Rijksmuseum Het Catharijneconvent and S'Hertogenbosch, Noordbrabants Museum, '*Maria*

In addition to the largesse shown towards the men's convent in Brou, Margaret bestowed extensive patronage on a newly founded women's order, the so-called 'Annonciades'.[32] In 1517, shortly after its institution, she established a community in Anes, close to Bruges. In the late 1520s Margaret herself seriously considered giving up her position as regent of the Netherlands in order to retire into this order.[33] In addition to pledging many liturgical garments and objects to the foundation, she commissioned her court artist Bernard van Orley to paint a large altarpiece now in Brussels (Centre publique d'Aide Sociale) for the main altar of its church. The triptych shows the *Death and the Assumption of the Virgin* on its central panel.[34]

Another large altarpiece, with a representation of the Virgin Mary, was commissioned for the Sainte Chapelle of Chambery in Savoy.[35] Not long after Margaret's final departure from Savoy, this church became a focal point of her patronage because it possessed a relic of the Holy Shroud (now in Turin). This widely venerated relic, which had fallen into the hands of the dukes of Savoy in 1453, attracted visitors of the highest rank, including King Francis I, the Cardinal of Aragon, and Philip the Fair.[36] Margaret of Austria fostered the cult which developed around the Holy Shroud and expressed her own veneration for this precious relic by giving orders to her goldsmith, Lievin van Lathem, to make a gilded silver shrine to protect and embellish it.[37] This extraordinarily expensive object, which was delivered to the Sainte Chapelle in 1509, was not the only tribute paid to the relic by the archduchess. In addition to donating the shrine, she also commissioned van Orley to paint an image of the Holy

---

van Hongarije, Konigin tussen Keizers en Kunstenaars, 1505–1558 (Zwolle, 1993). Charles V also received two splendidly jewelled diptychs from his aunt. For their descriptions see nn. 6 and 7. These are listed, together with most of the precious jewels, in the 1535 inventory; but they do not appear in the inventories of 1516 and 1523–4, perhaps indicating that such valuable things were itemized separately from the rest of Margaret's posses-sions.

[32] A.-J. Wauters, 'Orley, Bernard van', in *Biographie Nationale de Belgique*, vol. XVI (1901), col. 261.

[33] Baux, *Histoire*, 106–10.

[34] See Wauters, 'Orley', cols 261–62 for payment to van Orley for 'un beau tableau ou il peinte et figuree la Remembrance de Marie morte, lequel la dicte dame a envoye au couvent des Sept Douleurs Notre-Dame a Bruges'.

[35] Bruchet, *Marguerite d'Autriche*, 371, Pl. XLIV.

[36] Bruchet, *Marguerite d'Autriche*, 140. It is now generally agreed that the shroud is a medieval forgery; see W.C. McCrone, 'The Shroud of Turin: Blood or artist's pigment', in *Acc. Chem. Res.* 23 (1990), 77–83; and London, British Museum, *Fake? The Art of Deception* (London, 1990), 284.

[37] Bruchet, *Marguerite d'Autriche*, 139. Liévin van Lathem is not identical with the Flemish painter and illuminator called Liéven van Lathem (*c.*1430–1493).

Shroud on white taffeta.[38] This she kept in a cupboard of the bedroom of her main residence, presumably so that she might have a memento of the relic near her.[39]

Such was the nature of Margaret's patronage towards the religious institutions of her realm. Let us now turn to the devotional objects commissioned or acquired for her permanent home, the Palais Savoy in Mechelen.

Soon after Margaret's return to the Netherlands in 1507, she established herself in Mechelen, where she had already spent some time in her childhood at the court of her close relative, Margaret of York, the third wife of her grandfather Charles the Bold. Following in her namesake's footsteps, she herself now ruled over a courtly household of more than 150 people.[40] Margaret's residence, which consisted of several older buildings and some new additions, had been built under the supervision of the Flemish architects Anthoon and Rombout Keldermans.[41] The suite of rooms which comprised her private apartments can be reconstructed from both civic records and the inventory of 1523–4.[42] Eight rooms, housing her private possessions, can be identified: chapel, library, the 'premiere chambre', followed by the adjoining 'riche cabinet', the 'seconde chambre a chemynee', followed by the 'petit cabinet', the 'cabinet empres le jardin', and a separate room to house treasures, such as jewels and other objects made from gold and silver.[43] The majority of her religious artworks—paintings, sculptures and decorative textiles—were housed in three of these rooms: the 'seconde chambre a chemynee' with the adjoining 'petit cabinet' and the 'cabinet empres le jardin'. No major works of religious art were kept in the chapel, the library, the 'premiere chambre', or the 'riche cabinet' at the time when the inventory was taken.

Of the eleven diptychs mentioned in the various inventories of Margaret's collection, eight can be associated with a specific location in the palace; three are listed without reference to a specific room.[44] In 1523, five

---

[38] Wauters, 'Orley', col. 261.

[39] 'Item, la pourtraiture du sainct Suaire de Nre Sgr, fete en toille' [1523–4] (Michelant (1871), 91).

[40] This figure is for the year 1525; see Bruchet, *Marguerite d'Autriche*, 71.

[41] See *Bouwen door de eeuwen heen, Inventaris van het cultuurbezit in Belgie, Architectuur, deel 9n: Stad Mechelen/Binnenstad* (Ghent, 1984), 262–69.

[42] J. Grootaers, 'Aspecten van het burgerlijk interieur te Mechelen c.1480–1530, Hof van Margareta-Hof van Cortenbach', in Mechelen, Stedelijk Museum, *De Habsburgs & Mechelen* (Mechelen, 1987), 39–47.

[43] Brussels, Algemeen Rijksarchief, Stadsrekening Mechelen, no. 412303 (1524/25), f. 201v: 'Inde camere vanden jouweelen . . . Item aen bancken daer men de cofferen metten jouweelen op stelt'.

[44] The Erard de la Marck diptych was added later to the inventory; the two gold metal diptychs bequeathed to Charles V, mentioned in note 33, appear only in the 1531

of the eight diptychs were kept in the 'seconde chambre a chemynee'; three others were in the adjoining 'petit cabinet'. These two rooms, which contain by far the greatest concentration of religious artworks in her apartments, were also the most private of Margaret's rooms, one being her bedroom, the other her study.[45]

Certain kinds or types of diptychs can be distinguished among this collection. Since devotional diptychs with donor portraits were so popular in fifteenth-century northern Europe,[46] it is not surprising that this type features prominently in Margaret's collection: she had five of them, four of which depicted members of her family. Reference has already been made to the diptych in Ghent showing Margaret at prayer before the Virgin and Child which entered her collection after 1523 (4s 94–95). One of the most valuable devotional portrait diptychs in her collec-tion represented her grandfather, Charles the Bold;[47] another double panel portrayed her grandmother, Isabella of Bourbon.[48] The double panel with the portrait of Charles the Bold, which had been valued at the considerable sum of '100 livres', is described in the inventory as a 'rich and very exquisite double panel' depicting our Lady and the Duke of Burgundy.[49] Charles was shown dressed in gold brocade and kneeling in front of the Virgin with a book of hours on the *prie-dieu* before him. The formula chosen for this diptych is clearly quite similar to that employed for the Ghent picture.

A fourth diptych of small dimensions is similar. Here Margaret and her first husband, Juan, the Prince of Spain, were depicted in the guise of

---

inventory, which clarifies inheritance and, unlike the standard housekeeping inventories, is not concerned with the location of the object.

[45] In some cases the main purpose of a room can be deduced from the heading used: e.g., 'librairie'. In others, this must be deduced from the list of contents and other clues. The 'seconde chambre a chemynee', for example, has some very personal belongings and is the only room that contains a bed. This, together with the fact that it had heating, makes it reasonable to assume that it was Margaret of Austria's bedroom.

[46] See J. Friedman, *The Half-Length Devotional Portrait Diptychs in the Netherlands* (Los Angeles, 1977); L. Campbell, *Renaissance Portrait: European Portrait Painting in the Fourteenth, Fifteenth and Sixteenth Centuries* (London, 1990); and P. Pieper, 'Ein Diptychon der Spätgotik als Andachtsbild', *Pantheon*, 50 (1992), 21–23.

[47] 'Item, ung riche et fort exquis double tableau de N(re) Dame, double par dehors de satin brochier, et Mons(gr) le duc Charles de Bourgogne painct en l'ung desdits fulletz, estans a genoux, habille de draps d'or a ung coussin de velour noir et une heure estant sur son siege devant luy, le bors dudit tableau garnie de velours vers, avec trois ferrures d'argent dore servant audit tableau' [1523–4] (Michelant (1871), 88).

[48] Le Glay (1839), 481: 'Ung petit tableaul d'une Nostre-Dame et de madame de Charorlois, de illuminure, mise en ung estuy ensemble' [1516].

[49] 'Riche double tableau de Nostre-Dame, double par dehors de satin broche . . . C livres' [1535] (Le Glay (1839), 483).

their respective patron saints, St Margaret and St John.⁵⁰ This work was executed by one of Margaret's favourite painters, Michiel Sittow, and was kept in the 'petit cabinet'.

Yet another diptych in her collection combined portraiture and devotional image. Right towards the end of her life Margaret received one or possibly two large diptychs showing her close political adviser, Cardinal Erard de la Marck, opposite the Virgin Mary and Christ Child.⁵¹ The diptychs were executed by her court painter Jan Vermeyen. A portrait painting in the Rijksmuseum in Amsterdam has been identified as one half of this work and another panel in Haarlem has been suggested as its companion-piece.⁵² Erard de la Marck was not only an influential political ally, he was also a financial backer of the Hapsburg family.⁵³ This interesting commission testifies to his importance as a personal adviser at Margaret's court, since it is the only diptych in her collection which portrays a high ranking courtier rather than a family member.

---

⁵⁰ This diptych is described three times in the inventories: 'Ung petit tableaul a double feullet de la main de Michiel, de l'ung des coustez de Nostre Dame ... de l'autre coustez d'ung Sainct Jehan et de Saincte Marguerite, faiz a la semblence du prince d'Espaigne et de Madame' [1516] (Le Glay (1839), 481); 'Item, ung aultre petit tableau de Nre Dame d'ung costel et de sainct Jehan l'Evangeliste et de saincte Marguerite, tirez apres le vif du feu prince d'Espaigne, mary de Madame, aussy apres le vif de Mad. Dame' [1523–4] (Michelant (1871), 93): and, 'Double tableau de Nostre Dame, d'ung couste sainct Jehan et de l'aultre saincte Marguerite ... X livres' [1535] (Le Glay (1839), 484). See J. Trzina, *Michel Sittow, Peintre revelais de l'Ecole brugeoise (1468–1525/6)* (Brussels, 1976), 90–91; and C.T. Eisler, 'The Sittow Assumption', in *Art News* 64 (1965), 34–37.

⁵¹ 'Ung tableau, painct d'ung couste d'une Nostre Dame et de l'autre du cardinal de Liege, fermant a deux fuilletz' [1531] (Zimerman (1885), CXXI); and, 'Deux tableaux receuz de M(e) Jehan, le paintre, semblables; en l'ung est N(re) Dame et en l'Aultre Mons(gr) de Liege' (Michelant (1871), 97). The wording of the latter entry, which occurs as a later addition among other portraits by Vermeyen, seems to indicate two diptychs; Horn, also, cites Vermeyen's request for payment outstanding on four panels: 'Ledit Jehan a fait et delivre a ma dite dame quatre grans tableaux assavoir: deux a la figure du cardinal de Liege et autres deux a l'ymage de Notre Dame; pour le bois, estoffes d'or, d'azur et autres... XXI' (H.J. Horn, *Jan Cornelisz Vermeyen, Painter of Charles V and his Conquest of Tunis: Paintings, Etchings, Drawings, Cartoons and Tapestries* (Doornspijk, 1989), I.61). It seems, therefore, that Margaret at some stage commissioned two sets of double panels from Vermeyen. Yet another diptych with similar iconography is recorded as having already been divided into two in the 1523-4 inventory: 'Item, ung double tableau dont l'un N(ot)re Dame et l'autre le cardinal de Liegne, laquelle N(ot)re Dame a este delivree audit couvent de Brou et le Cardinal demora decha' (Michelant (1871), 86). Since Vermeyen only entered Margaret's service c.1525, it is doubtful that this diptych was also made by him.

⁵² See J.P. Filedt Kok, W.Th. Kloek and W. Halsema-Kubes, Amsterdam, Rijksmuseum, *Kunst voor de Beeldenstorm, Noordnederlandse Kunst 1525–1580* (S'Gravenhage, 1986), no. 78; and *Maria van Hongarije*, no. 34 (322–23).

⁵³ See H. Lonchay, 'Erard de la Marck', in *Biographie Nationale de Belgique*, (1894–95), XIII, cols 497–542; and Horn, *Vermeyen*, 8, n. 52.

While devotional portrait diptychs were well represented in the collection in Mechelen, a similar number concentrated exclusively on religious subject-matter. Six of the eleven diptychs in Margaret's collection depicted either a selection of narrative scenes from the life of Christ and the Virgin, or a combination of individual saints. Two small diptychs made of enamelled gold and precious jewels, for example, showed an image of the Virgin and Child combined with a representation of St Louis and St Barbara respectively.[54]

Margaret received many religious objects as gifts from the Spanish royal family, from the time of her marriage to Juan of Castille in 1497 until she left Spain in 1499. Liturgical objects and tapestries with religious subject-matter were given to her by her parents-in-law, Isabella of Castille and Ferdinand of Aragon, both of whom were known for their conscientious observance of the strict devotional practices characteristic of Spanish lifestyle at the time.[55] Isabella, called 'La Catolica', was herself an active patron of the arts and it may be assumed that she left a lasting impression on the seventeen year old Margaret.[56] A shared interest with her Spanish connections in religious artefacts by Flemish artists is apparent in Margaret's acquisition of a fragmentary set of paintings formerly belonging to her mother-in-law. *The Temptation of Christ in the Desert* (Fig. 95) and *The Marriage Feast at Cana* (Fig. 96) by Juan de Flandes initially formed part of a set of forty-seven individual panels which had been commissioned by Isabella of Spain for a polyptych-altarpiece.[57] This project was not completed during Isabella's lifetime and the separate panels were sold off after her death in 1505. It seems that Margaret instructed her treasurer, Don Diego Flores, to purchase some of these on her behalf from Isabella's estate.[58] For reasons unknown, he acquired only thirty-two of the forty-seven panels; some of the other paintings were

---

[54] See nn. 6 and 7.

[55] 'Libro de las joyas de oro e plata, perlas y pedras y otras cosas de azienda de la camera de la muy alta y ecelente dona Margarita, princesa de Castilla, las quales se entregaron a su alteza en la cibdad de Granada en beynte e ocho dias de setienbre de nobenta e nueve anos en presencia de museur de Sanpique e museur de Bere, sus embaxadres, las qualas son las siguientes . . .', [28/9/1499], Granada (Inventory published by R. Beer in *Jahrbuch der kunsthistorischen Sammlungen des allerhöchsten Kaiserhauses*, 12 (1891), CX–CXXIII [Reg. 8347]).

[56] See F. Sanchez Canton, *Libros, Tapices y Cuadros que collecciono Isabel la Catolica* (Madrid, 1950).

[57] See E. Bermejo, *Juan de Flandes* (Madrid, 1962); J. Sanchez Canton, 'El retablo de la Reina Catolica', *Archivo Espagnol Arqueologia* 6 (1930), 97–133. Ch. L. Ishikawa, *The 'Retablo de la Reina Catolica' by Juan de Flandes and Michel Sittow* (Diss., Bryn Mawr College, 1989).

[58] Diego is described as 'conseiller, tresorier et receveur general de Madame l'Archiduchesse d'Autrice' [9/6/1514] (Finot (1895), 224). See M. Davies, *Les Primitifs Flamands, The National Gallery, London*, III (Brussels, 1970), 14–17.

purchased by the Marquesa de Denia. When the thirty-two paintings reached Mechelen, Margaret was faced with a fragmented collection of small but artistically very accomplished panels. The series contained scenes from the childhood, Passion and Resurrection of Christ, as well as several images depicting the life of the Virgin Mary. From their ensuing history it is clear that Margaret cherished these panels both for their quality as works of art and as a memento of the close dynastic ties between the Spanish and the Hapsburgian royal houses. She recognized their potential for use in her private devotions, and consequently set out to transform them into fully functional objects. By 1530, twenty-two of the paintings had been remounted to form two diptychs, a small one incorporating two panels and a larger one incorporating twenty.

For some twenty years after their acquisition, however, the majority of these pictures were kept as separate panels in a wooden box in Margaret's bedroom, occasionally being shown to interested visitors.[59] *The Ascension of Christ* (Fig. 97) and *The Assumption of the Virgin* (Fig. 98) by Michiel Sittow were the first to be redeployed. By 1516, they had been made into one small devotional diptych, set into a frame made of cypress wood. As a result, in inventories from 1516 and in 1523–4 it is listed under a separate entry as an independent object.[60] It is obvious from the various written descriptions that this newly created double panel was not permanently displayed on the walls of Margaret's private apartments, but was kept in a protective leather box inside a cupboard in her bedroom. Her intention to use these precious panels by Sittow and De Flandes as aids for her private devotion is borne out by the fact that she created not

---

[59] 'Trente petis tableaux, tous d'une grandeur, de la vye et passion de Nostre-Seigneur qui sont deans une layette de sapin ou y en avoit XXXII; mais les deux qui estoient faiz de la main de Michiel sont estez prins pour faire ung double tableaul, lequel est touche cy devant, et est enchassey de cipre; et sont l'assumpcion de Dieu et celle de Nostre-Dame. Nota qu'il fault quatres pieces pour l'accomplissement de la passion: ung Dieu qui porte la croix, ung autre cruciffie, ung dessendu de la croix et ung mis au sepulcre; qui sont IIII pieces; aussi il fault l'assumpcion de Nostre-Seigneur' [1516] (Le Glay (1839), 482). In 1521 Dürer recorded his visit in his diary as follows: 'Ich bin auch bey frau Margareth gewest und hab sie mein kayser sehen lassen und ir den schenken wollen. Aber do sie ein solchen mißfall darinnen hett, do führet ich ihn wieder weg. Und den freydag wis mir frau Margareth all jhr schön ding; darunter sahe ich bey 40 klainer täfelein von öhlfarben, der gleichen jch von reinigkeith und guth darzu nie gesehen hab . . .' (H. Ruppich, *Dürers schriftlicher Nachlaß* (Berlin, 1966–7), 199.

[60] 'Ung double tableaul de la main de Michiel de l'Assumcion de Nostre-Seigneur et de celle de Nostre-Dame; qui a une coustode couverte de cuyr' [1516] (Le Glay (1839), 481); 'Item, ung double tableau de bois de cypres, eng l'ung est portrait l'Assumption N(re) S(re) et en l'aultre l'Ascension de N(re) Dame, auquel tableau il y a deux ferrures d'argent' [1523–4] (Michelant (1871), 89); and 'Double petit tableau de Chipres; en l'ung est l'ascension Nostre Seigneur, et en l'aultre l'assumption Nostre Dame . . . XL livres' [1535] (Le Glay (1839), 483).

just the small diptych with the *Ascension* and the *Assumption* but also a second one of much larger proportions. Some time after 1526 twenty paintings from the same series were mounted into a diptych with an ornate gilded silver frame, which carried Margaret's enamelled coat of arms, angels, and ornaments on it. This work which seems to have involved incorporating twenty paintings into two large 'super-panels' was further embellished when the individual panels were reset into an ornate silver frame some time after 1526. This large and luxurious diptych was later given a place of honour in the 'riche cabinet' which probably served as Margaret's main reception room; it was located next to the portrait gallery.[61]

Whereas the small diptych by Sittow was kept in a cupboard, Margaret chose to display the majority of the religious paintings on the walls of her bedroom, the so-called 'seconde chambre a chemynee' and the small study or 'petit cabinet'—it should be recalled that diptychs comprised only a small part of her collection; in all, she kept thirty-three art works with religious subject matter in her bedroom.[62] The walls of both rooms were covered with green taffeta and in the larger room, the 'seconde chambre a chemynee', sixteen small and large curtains of the same material functioned as covers for some of the paintings.[63] In addition to the Sittow paintings, other particularly valuable artworks, such as the diptych of Charles the Bold, were kept in the cupboard. The written sources indicate that the larger devotional paintings were generally displayed on the bedroom walls. One of the diptychs listed in this category was a painting which had been given to Margaret by Antoine de Lalaing, the Count of Hoogstraten. It represented various scenes from the Passion of Christ and is described as being 'assez vieux'.[64]

Twelve religious art works are listed as being housed in the adjoining 'petit cabinet'; these include several small sculptures of saints, one triptych and two diptychs.[65] Most of these objects were small in scale, including the diptychs such as the double panel depicting Margaret and Juan mentioned earlier.[66] The other diptych in this room juxtaposed *The*

---

[61] The mounted diptych measured approximately 880x990 mm.

[62] Michelant (1871), 74–91.

[63] 'Item, ladite chambre a chemynee toute tendue de taffetas verd, avec XVI courtines de mesmes taffetas, que grandes que petites, servans a la couverture desdites painctures et aultres choses estans en ladite chambre; le tout double de boucran noir, reserve lesdites courtines' [1523–4] (Michelant (1871), 87); 'Item, ledit petit cabinet tout tenduz de taffetaf vert, double de boucran noir' (Michelant (1871), 97).

[64] See n. 32.

[65] Michelant (1871), 91–97; this count does not include the later additions to the inventory, starting with the 'Jesus taille en marbre'.

[66] See n. 3.

Crucifixion of Christ with *The Mass of Saint Gregory* and is listed as a work by Rogier van der Weyden.[67]

The contents of these two rooms, when compared with the rest of her private apartments, suggest that Margaret considered the bedroom and study to be the most suitable location for the display of her religious art works. It comes as a surprise that her private chapel seems to have been decorated only with a large gold-metal cross and some liturgical furniture and textiles. In a recent article, Guy Delmarcel suggests that a series of square-shaped Passion tapestries and an accompanying *ciel* were commissioned to decorate Margaret's court chapel.[68]

No altarpiece or religious panel painting of any sort is recorded in the inventory drawn up in 1523–4, although the list of contents and the description of the chapel interior clearly indicate that Mass was celebrated there.[69] Two missals and three book of hours, for example, were housed in the chapel.[70] It is of particular interest for the study of private devotional practice that book of hours were kept in various parts of the palace. In all, Margaret of Austria possessed at least twelve such prayer books, which were variously housed in the chapel, library, and study.

Three book of hours with 'illuminations and historiated initials' are mentioned among the small number of books kept in the 'petit cabinet'.[71] That Margaret actually used these prayer books in her study or the neighbouring bedroom is suggested by another entry in the same section of the inventory. This describes a small ivory casket with silver bookmarks kept there 'to be put into the Hours'.[72] Closer study of the contents

---

[67] It is described three times in the inventories: 'Ung petit tableau d'ung cruxefix et d'ung Sainct-Gregoire. Fait de la main de Rogier' [1516] (Le Glay (1839), 481); 'Item, ung aultre double tableau; en l'ung est N(re) S(gr) pendant en croix et N(re) Dame embrassant le pied de la croix, et en l'aultre, l'histoire de lanesse Mons(gr) sainct Gregoire' [1523] (Michelant (1871), 93); and, 'Aultre double tableau; en l'ung est Nostre-Seigneur pendant en croix; en l'aultre l'histoire de sainct Gregoire . . . III livres' [1535] (Le Glay (1839), 484). See n. 33.

[68] G. Delmarcel, 'De Passietapijten van Margarets van Ostenrijk (c.1518-1524). Nieuwe Gegevens en Documenten', in *Revue Belge d'Archeologie et d'Histoire de l'Art* 61 (1992), 147.

[69] Michelant (1871), 11–16.

[70] Michelant (1871), 15.

[71] Three extant book of hours have been identified with Margaret of Austria: Vienna, ON MS 1862; see Debae, *Librairie* cat. 37, 129–32 and Thoss, *Flämische Buchmalerei*, 107–108; Vienna, ON MS 1858 (*Croy Hours*); see F. Unterkircher, *European Illustrated Manuscripts in the Austrian Library* (London, 1967), 235–38; and London, BL Add. MS 34294 (*Bona Sforza Hours*); see T. Kren, ed., *Renaissance Painting in Manuscripts, Treasures from the British Library* (New York, 1983), 113–14; and J. Duverger, 'Gerard Holrenbault (1465–1540) hofschilder van Margareta van Oostenrijk', in *Kunst, Maandblad voor oude en jonge Kunst* 4 (1930), 81–90.

[72] 'Item, ung petit coffret d'ivoire auquel il y a plusieurs legieres enseignes d'argent, a mettre dedans Heures' [1523–4] (Michelant (1871), 94).

of the 'seconde chambre a chemynee' reveals that this room was furnished not only with a bed, a table, chairs, chests and a writing desk, but also with a kind of altar. The first three entries for the 'seconde chambre a chemynee' list a complete set of altar hangings comprising a baldachin, a wall covering and an altar frontal, each made of gold brocade and blue velvet.[73] A cushion of the same material is also mentioned, probably for Margaret to kneel on during prayer. The accounts of the city of Mechelen tell us that in 1518–9 the carpenter Gheerden van den Veckene made a small footstool for Margaret's bedroom, 'for my Lady *to kneel upon*'.[74] The existence of an altar-like structure in Margaret's apartments indicates that private worship was carried out in various venues and in different ways. The decoration of the 'seconde chambre a chemynee' and the 'petit cabinet' with a large number of religious art works is further indication that the Regent frequently performed her devotions in the seclusion of her own bedroom or study.[75]

The study of Margaret of Austria's inventories and related sources thus provides an insight into the spiritual life of this sixteenth-century ruler, showing that as well as her political and family responsibilities, she was consistently concerned with religious matters. This concern embraced not only the foundation and endowment of churches and religious institutions and the establishing of specific commemorative ties with such places on behalf of herself and her family; it also involved, in addition to frequenting places of public worship, the carrying out of devotional exercises within the privacy of her own apartments. The diptychs in her

---

[73] As with the chapel, the altar can only be identified from descriptions of its decoration: 'Premier, ung petit docelet de drapt d'or rez, bandez sur les coustures de velours bleu, en maniere de losaigne a semlable M par dessus, contenant de longeur, deux aulnes et III carties et de deux drapts d'or de large; les goutieres de mesmes, doublee de satin bleu fraigees de fil d'or, soie noire et blanche, avec le ciel dudit docelet qu'est de damas jaulne, contenant de longeur I aulne et demy cartie eschars et de la largeur II aulnes' [1523–4]; 'Item, ung petit devant d'haustel ou frontal, de mesmes drapt d'or audit docelet et bande aussi de mesme, frange de fil d'or, soie blanche et verde, contenant de longeur une aulne demie et deux drapts d'or de large'; 'Item, ung petit coussin de drapt d'or trait double de velours vert' (Michelant (1871), 74).

[74] Brussels, Algemeen Rijksarchief, *Stadsrekening Mechelen*, no. 41297, f. 212v.

[75] While the altar in Margaret's bedroom can only be reconstructed from the furnishings listed in the inventories of her private apartments, an unequivocal remark, relating to another room in the same palace, can be found in the account books of the city of Mechelen. Two records pertaining to the financial year 1529–30 refer to an altar in the apartment of Monsieur de Rosimbos, her close adviser and 'Premier Maître d'Hotel'. Again, Gheerden van den Veekene was paid for the carpentry work, this time on an altar, which was used for celebrating Mass; see Brussels, Algemeen Rijksarchief, *Stadsrekening Mechelen*, no. 41308, f. 203: 'Item van een autaer daermen misse op doet in de camere van mynen heere van Rosimboz', and also f. 218v. I wish to thank Dr Wim Huesken for transcribing these records for me.

collection together with evidence, both visual and literary, about those belonging to her grandfather Philip the Good, demonstrate how these small double panels, which often included an image of the donor as well as a religious subject, were associated with the private domain. Their description as 'objects in the shape of a book' is expressive of the related functions of the diptych and the personal prayer book or book of hours in late medieval devotional practice.[76]

---

[76] I gratefully acknowledge the financial assistance of the Australian Research Council and the contribution of my research assistant Lisa Beaven to the first draft of this paper. I also thank Anne van Buren for her useful comments on a later version of this paper.

Appendix

The following are the reference works mentioned in footnote 1; they are cited in abbreviated form throughout the paper.

ZIMERMAN (1885): 'Inventoire des parties de meubles estans es cabinetz de Madame en sa ville de Malines, estans a la garde et charge de Estienne Luillier, varlet-de-chambre de ma dite dame, lequel en doit respondre a Richard Contault, garde-joyault de ma dite dame, et le dit Contault en tenir compte a icelle ma dite dame' (Vienna, Habsburg-Lothringisches Familienarchiv, Familienurkunden no. 1174 (1524, April 20), published by H. Zimerman, in *Jahrbuch der kunsthistorischen Sammlungen des allerhöchsten Kaiserhauses* 3 (1885), XCIII–CXXIII.

MICHELANT (1871): 'Inventaire des vaisselles, joyaux, tapisseries, peintures, manuscrits, etc. de Marguerite d'Autriche, régente et gouvernante des Pays-Bas, dressé en son palais de Malines, le 9 juillet 1523' (Paris, BN, no. 128 des Cinq Cents de Colbert), published by H. Michelant in *Academie Royale des Sciences des Lettres et des Beaux-Arts de Belgique, Bulletin* 3 ser. 12.2 (1871), 3–75 and 83–136.

LE GLAY (1839): Different fragments of an inventory of books, art objects and textiles, drawn up in 1516 in Mechelen (Lille, Archives Départementales du Nord, B.3509/3510) published by A. Le Glay, *Correspondance de l'Empereur Maximilien Ier et de Marguerite d'Autriche, sa fille, gouvernante des Pays-Bas de 1507 à 1519, publiée d'après les manuscripts originaux* (Paris, 1839), II, 468–77.

FINOT (1895): The fragments transcribed by Le Glay were published in a more accurate form by J. Finot, 'Fragment d'un inventaire de tableaux et d'objecs d'art', in *Inventaire sommaire des archives departementales du Nord, anterieures à 1790* (Lille, 1895), Series B, VIII.208–12.

VOLTELINI (1890): List of objects which Charles V inherited from Margaret of Austria on 19/3/1531, published by H. von Voltelini, 'Urkunden und Regesten aus dem K.u.K. Haus, Hof- und Staatsarchiv', in *Jahrbuch der kunsthistorischen Sammlungen des allerhöchsten Kaiserhauses* 11 (1890), Reg. 6286, V–XII.

VOLTELINI (1892): 'La troisième des meillieurs et plus riches baghues, delaissées part la dit feu seigneur empereur, avecq une autre bague qui choisirons a nostre plaisir et discretion pour avoir de tant meillieure souvenance s'icelluy feust seigneur (Maximilian) et de nous' (Brussels, 18 September 1520), published by Hans von Voltelini, 'Urkunden und Regesten aus dem K.u.K. Haus,-Hof- und Staatsarchiv', in *Jahrbuch der kunsthistorischen Sammlungen des allerhöchsten Kaiserhauses* 13 (1892), Reg. 8649, XXVIII.

Figure 85. King Richard II praying to the Virgin and Child (left panel). *Wilton Diptych*. The National Gallery, London. 475×292 mm.

Figure 86. King Richard II praying to the Virgin and Child (right panel). *Wilton Diptych*. The National Gallery, London. 475×292 mm.

Figure 87. Jean, Duc de Berry, praying to the Virgin and Child (left page). *Très Belles Heures*. Brussels, Bibliothèque Royale, MS 11060–11061, p. 10. 275×185 mm.

Figure 88. Jean, Duc de Berry, praying to the Virgin and Child (right page). *Très Belles Heures*. Brussels, Bibliothèque Royale, MS 11060–11061, p. 11. 275×185 mm.

Figure 89. Philip the Good in his private prayer tent. *Traité sur l'oraison dominicale*. Brussels, Bibliothèque Royale, MS 9092, f. 9. 400×290 mm.

Figure 90. Philip the Good praying to the Virgin. Diptych and book. Vienna, Österreichische Nationalbibliothek, MS 1800, ff. 13v–14. 185×130 mm (page size).

Figure 91. Master of 1499. *Virgin in the Church* (left panel). Antwerp, Koninklijk Museum voor Schone Kunsten. 310×145 mm.

Figure 92. Master of 1499. *Christiaan de Hondt praying* (right panel). Antwerp, Koninklijk Museum voor Schone Kunsten. 310×145 mm.

Figure 93. Anonymous Master. *Virgin and Child* (left panel).
Ghent, Museum voor Schone Kunsten. 305×146mm.

Figure 94. Anonymous Master. *Margaret of Austria praying* (right panel). Ghent, Museum voor Schone Kunsten. 305×146 mm.

Figure 95. Juan de Flandes. *The Temptation of Christ*. Washington, National Gallery of Art, Ailsa Mellon Bruce Fund. 210×155mm.

Figure 96. Juan de Flandes. *The Marriage Feast at Cana*. New York, Metropolitan Museum of Art, The Jack and Belle Linsky Collection. 210×155mm.

Figure 97. Michiel Sittow. *The Ascension of Christ*. Collection of the Earl of Yarborough. 210×155 mm.

Figure 98. Michiel Sittow. *The Assumption of the Virgin*. Washington, National Gallery of Art, Ailsa Mellon Bruce Fund. 210×155mm.

CONTRIBUTORS

KATE CHALLIS, a doctoral student at the University of Melbourne, is researching late fifteenth- and early sixteenth-century Flemish Book Illumination with special reference to the work and patrons of Gerard Horenbout.

DAGMAR EICHBERGER, formerly of the Department of Fine Arts, the University of Melbourne, is a senior research fellow at the University of Saarlandes, Saarbrücken. Her publications include *Jan van Eyck als Erzähler* (with H. Belting; Worms, 1983); and *Bildkonzeption und Weltdeutung in New Yorker Diptychon des Jan van Eyck* (Wiesbaden, 1987). She is currently researching the artistic patronage of Margaret of Austria.

HILARY MADDOCKS teaches art history at La Trobe University, Melbourne. Her doctoral thesis was on the illumination of Jean de Vignay's French translation of the *Legenda Aurea*. She is at present researching book illustration and illumination in France *c*.1500.

MARGARET M. MANION is professor emeritus at the University of Melbourne. Her publications on medieval book illumination include: *The Wharncliffe Hours* (London, 1981); *Medieval and Renaissance Illuminated Manuscripts in Australian Collections* (with V.F. Vines; London, 1984); *Medieval and Renaissance Manuscripts in New Zealand Collections* (with V.F. Vines and C. de Hamel; London, 1989); and *Medieval Texts and Images* (edited with B.J. Muir; Sydney and New York, 1991). She is currently researching lay and religious female patronage and the art of the medieval book.

BERNARD J. MUIR, a Reader at the University of Melbourne, specializes in medieval English and Latin language and literature. His publications include: *A Pre-Conquest English Prayerbook* (Bury St Edmunds, 1988); *The Exeter Anthology of Old English Poetry* (Exeter, 1994); *Medieval Texts and Images* (edited with M.M. Manion; Sydney and New York, 1991); and *The Life of St Wilfrid by Edmer of Canterbury* (with A. Turner; forthcoming, Exeter 1998). He is currently developing DUCTUS, an online program for teaching codicology and paleography.

JOAN NAUGHTON is a research fellow in the Department of Fine Arts, University of Melbourne. The subject of her doctoral thesis was the manuscripts from Saint-Louis de Poissy, a medieval royal foundation for Dominican nuns. In collaboration with M.M. Manion, she is currently investigating the role of patronage and the art of the medieval book, with special reference to female religious.

JOHN STINSON, senior lecturer in musicology at La Trobe University (Melbourne), has carried out extensive research on the history and performance of medieval chant. His work includes the development of the SCRIBE Database which has enabled the details of music, text, decoration in a comprehensive set of fourteenth century Italian Dominican choir-books to be searched and plotted electronically. He is currently researching the liturgical history of San Lorenzo, Florence.

BRONWYN C. STOCKS teaches Italian Medieval and Renaissance art history at the University of Melbourne. She has recently completed her doctorate at Melbourne on text and image in the early Italian book of hours.

VERA F. VINES is an associate of the Department of Fine Arts, University of Melbourne. Her research centres on late medieval French and Netherlandish manuscript illumination and panel painting. She is co-author with M.M. Manion of *Medieval and Renaissance Illuminated Manuscripts in Australian Collections* (London, 1984) and co-author with M.M. Manion and C. de Hamel of *Medieval and Renaissance Manuscripts In New Zealand Collections* (London, 1989).

INDEX

Named manuscripts are included in the index proper (e.g. *Arenberg Gospels*). All manuscripts cited in the body of the text are listed alphabetically by location in a separate section at the end of the index.

Aaron...233
Abel...232
Abgarus...16
Abraham...29, 231
acorn...259–62
Adam...29
Adelaide Hours...4, 113, 116–29
Adoration of the Christ child...295
Adoration of the Shepherds...263
Adoro te...16
Advent...74, 83, 227, 230, 235–37
Aelsinus...113
Æthelberht (St)...17
Æthelred (King)...18
Æthelstan (King)...17–18
Æthelwold (Bishop)...18
Agnes of France...23
Alcuin...13
Aldhelm...17
All Saints...77, 205–06
allegory...230, 232
altar...306
altarpiece...231–32, 235, 266, 299, 303, 306
Andrew...80
Anes (near Bruges), 'Annonciades' nunnery...299
angel(s)...29, 39, 80–81, 85, 155, 232, 235
Anglo-Saxon...9–19
Annas...120
Anne (St)...227–28, 230, 261
Anne of Brittany...228–29
Annunciation...77, 83, 235–36, 258, 265, 294
Annunciation to the Shepherds...266
Antidius (St)...200
antiphon(s)...28, 36, 71, 85, 114, 118, 120, 122, 126–27, 165–66, 171, 173, 196, 236–37

antiphonal...2, 9, 70–92, 158–60, 165, 168–69, 172
Antoine de Lalaing (Count of Hoogstraten)...305
Apocalypse...267
Apollonia (St)...36
Apostles...29, 31, 76, 157, 231
Apostolic Constitutions...111
Arenberg Gospels...10
Arouca, Sts Peter and Paul (Cistercian monastery)...172
Arras, monastery of Saint-Vaast...174
Arrest of Christ...37
Ascendit Christus super coelos...171–72, 174
Ascension of Christ...75–76, 203, 304–05
Ash Wednesday...230
Aspremont psalter-hours...32
Assisi, S. Francesco...154–56, 160
Assumption of the Virgin...2, 31, 77, 83, 153–61, 163–75, 263, 299, 304–05
atelier (see also workshop)...5, 37, 195–96, 207
Aubert, David...255
Auckland Public Library...2, 198
auctoritas...14
Augustine (St)...2, 12, 14, 158
Avril, François...71, 85, 197–98

badge (incl. pilgrim)...253, 266
banderole...232–33
baptism...126
Baptism of Christ...29, 83
baptismal order...9
Barbara (St)...292, 303
Barbieri, Filippo O.P.: *Discordantiae nonnullae*......233–34
Barcelona, Dominican priory...90

Barnwell, St Giles (Augustinian Abbey)...172
Bartholomew (St)...80
bas-de-page...25
beguines...84
Belleville Breviary...3, 33, 37, 87–89
Benedicite...19
Benedict of Nursia (St)...10
Benedictine...18, 38, 165
Benedictine Rule...10, 76, 165
Benedictional of Saint Æthelwold...10
Bernard Gui O.P....72
Bernard of Clairvaux (St)...169
Besançon...2–5, 195–209
Besançon, Cathedrals and churches...196, 201, 203–09
Betrayal of Christ...115–19
Betrothal of Christ...159–61
binding...88
Black Death...69, 71
Black Prince...68
Blanche de France...86
Blanche of Burgundy...3, 21, 23, 25, 31–32, 40
Blumen-Stundenbuch...257, 263, 268
Bologna...123–26
Bonaventure (St)...39, 113, 115, 267
Boniface VIII (Pope)...76
Bonne of Luxembourg...3, 25, 38–39
Book of Cerne...12–19
Book of Nunnaminster...12–19
book(s) of hours...1–6, 11–12, 16, 19, 26, 32–33, 36, 111–29, 196, 198, 207, 231, 235, 256–66, 258, 292–93, 301, 306, 308
bookmarks...306
border(s)...5–6, 23–25, 74, 86–87, 208, 226, 230, 232, 235–36, 253–69
branch(es)...259–60, 262, 264–65
Brescia...80
breviary...1, 3, 11–12, 26–29, 31, 36, 70–92, 114–15, 120, 126
brooch...257, 259, 261–62, 264, 266–67
Brou, church and Augustinian priory...297–99
Bruges...5, 254–56
Burgundy(-ian)...197–99, 255, 294
(Burgundian-)Hapsburgian dynasty...6, 291, 296, 302, 304
Busleyden, François de (archbishop of Besançon)...207

Caiaphas...120
calendar...11–12, 15–18, 22, 24–27, 31–32, 37, 70, 87–88, 115, 196, 207, 228–29, 236
Calvary...32
Cambrai Cathedral...174
canonical hours (incl. matins, lauds, etc)...11, 19, 27–30, 35–36, 73, 84–85, 89, 111–29, 160, 165–66, 171, 173, 236
Canterbury...15,
canticles...11–12, 15–16, 114, 126, 171
Capitella...18
Carolingian...13, 16, 202
casket...306
Cavalca, Domenico O.P....30
Celtic...17–18
Celtic Capitella...18
Charlemagne...13
Charles V (King of France)...23, 37, 39
Charles VI (King of France)...23–24
Charles VIII (King of France)...228–29, 238
Charles the Bold (Duke of Burgundy)...294, 300–1, 305
charts, computational...17
chef d'atelier...5
Chiusi...117
choir-book(s)...1–3, 67–92, 153–61, 163–75
Christ...6, 14–15, 19, 27–28, 31, 33–34, 38, 75–76, 80, 82–83, 85, 111–13, 115–29, 155–61, 166, 231, 233, 235, 236, 294, 303–4
Christ Carrying the Cross...115, 117, 121–22, 232
Christ before Pilate...115, 117, 119–21
Christ in Majesty (*Maestà, Maiestas*)...82, 154, 199, 229, 232
Christmas...203, 230, 232–33, 236
Church Fathers...29, 126, 158–59, 232
Churc (*mater ecclesiae*)...159, 231
Cimabue...155–59, 161
Circumcision...294
Cistercian(s)...166, 169–74
Clement IV (Pope)...171
Clement V (Pope)...67
Clement VI (Pope)...68
Codex Hartker...165–66
Coëtivy, Katherine de...236
Columba (St)...18
Common of Saints (*communale*)...11, 27, 230, 237

compassion, *compassio*...112, 113, 117–19, 122, 125, 127–28
Compiègne Antiphonal...165
Confiteor...19
Confraternity of St John the Evangelist...225
Coronation of the Virgin...83, 161, 293
coronation *ordo*...78
coronation robes, insignia...78–80
Corpus Christi...84–85, 231
Cotton Troper...10
Council of Trent...166
Credo, Creed...15–16, 18
Creed, Athanasian...19
cross...116, 121–25, 235, 237, 306
cross, veneration of the...19
crown of thorns...203, 228
crucifix...259
Crucifixion...82, 115–17, 122, 126–28, 199, 207, 229, 231–32, 237, 265, 295, 306
cursus...165–66, 172

David (King, biblical)...73, 120
de Hondt, Christiaan (Abbot)...294–95
dedication ceremony...68, 70–71, 196, 201–3, 206, 228
Delisle, Leopold...24
Denia, Marquesa de...304
Denis (St)...77, 229
Deposition from the Cross...116–17, 123, 126 28, 155
devotion, private or personal...10, 13–19, 21–40, 87, 89, 230, 291–308
devotional books, manuscripts...196, 253–69
devotional paintings, images...291–308
Dijon...31
diptych...6, 291–96, 300–05, 307–08
disciples...232
Divine Office...2, 11, 26–27, 31, 35, 69–70, 88, 90, 160, 163–75
Dominic (St)...71, 77, 80–81, 88, 92
Dominican(s)...2–3, 31, 33, 36, 67–92, 153–61, 163–74
Dominican Chapters General...171
Dominican nuns...67–92
Dominican Rule, Constitutions...89
Dominican saints...74–75, 85
Dormition (death) of the Virgin...83, 157–59, 299

drawing...115
Dunstan (Bishop, St)...17–18
Durand de Champagne, O.F.M...40
Durrieu, Paul...24, 26, 30, 225–26, 228, 254

Eadui Gospels...10
Easter...203–5, 230, 232
Easter Sunday...74, 76
Ecce homo...297
Ecclesiasticus...166
Ecgbert, Archbishop of York...9
Edmund (King)...18
Edward (King)...18
Edward III (King)...68
Edward of Savoy...23
effigies, royal...79
Egerton Master...196
Eleven Thousand Virgins...77
Eligius...229
engraving(s)...225
Entombment of Christ...116–17, 127–28, 232
Epiphany...200, 203
episcopal insignia...4
Erard de la Marck (Cardinal)...302
Eucharist...4, 126, 231
Eustace (St)...230
Evangelists...232
Eve...126
Evreux, Dominican priory...85
Exaltata es, sancta Dei genetrix...173
Exeter...15
Exultet...2, 204–6

Fécamp...78
Ferdinand II (Archduke)...258
Ferdinand of Aragon...303
Five Joys of the Virgin...26
Flagellation of Christ...115–17, 121
Flemish...81, 207, 253–69, 300
fleur-de-lys...78, 228
Fleury prayer book...13
Flight into Egypt...263
flowers...253, 257, 259–64, 266, 268
Fra Angelico...81
frame (architectural, wooden, etc)...231–32, 235, 237, 258, 262–66
Franche-Comté...196, 198–99
Francis (St)...114

Franciscan(s)...31, 33, 36, 39–40, 79, 87, 115, 154, 157, 166, 173
François I (King of France)...234, 299
frontispiece...235

Gabriel (Archangel)...235–36, 265
Galba prayer book...13–19
gems...255, 259, 267–68
Geneviève (St)...229–30
Genoa ...114
George (St) and the Dragon...268
Gerard David: *Justice of Cambyses: Arrest of the Judge Sisamnes*...265
Germania, Dominican Province of...81
Germanus of Auxerre (St)...229
Germanus of Paris (St)...229–30
Ghent-Bruges School...254, 266–67
Ghent...5, 254, 256
Giotto...117
girdle...263
Gloria...15–16, 18
gloss...15, 18
God...231, 235, 267
Golgotha...127
Good Friday...19
Gospels...15–16, 33, 119, 124–26, 155, 166, 258
gradual(-prosar)...2, 70–92, 168
gradual psalms...26, 35
Grandes Heures of Jean de Berry...29
Gréban, Arnoul...235
Gregory I (Pope, St)...12, 29, 166, 306
Grimani Breviary...261, 263–64
grisaille...25
Guido d'Arezzo...168
Guillaume de Saint-Pathus: *Vie et Miracles de saint Louis*...78–80

Harley fragment...12–19
Harrowing of Hell...15
heraldic arms...4, 23–25, 34, 37, 88, 199, 207, 227–28, 295
Herod...120
Hodie Maria Virgo coelos ascendit...174
Holy Saturday...204–5
Holy Shroud...299–300
Holy Spirit...29–31, 76, 204, 206, 231, 235
Honorius (Pope)...89

Hours (Little Office) of the Virgin...11, 19, 23, 26–27, 33, 35, 37, 112, 196, 235–36, 258, 294
Hours of St Louis of Marseilles...27
Hours of St Mary Magdalen...27
Hours of the Angels...27–28, 34
Hours of the Trinity...27–28, 33, 39
Hours of Albrecht of Brandenburg...257, 263, 264, 265–66
Hours of Catherine of Cleves...256–57
Hours of Engelbert of Nassau...261–62
Hours of Ferdinand of Austria...260
Hours of James of Scotland...258–61, 263–65
Hours of Jeanne d'Evreux...30, 34, 78–80, 85
Hours of Jeanne of Navarre...21–40, 78, 85
Hours of Joanna of Castile...257, 263
Hours of Joanna of Ghistelles...260
Hours of Johann Albrecht of Mecklenburg...265–66
Hours of Louis de Laval...234
Hours of Philip II Convault...263
Hugues de Salins...202, 204–6
humanism...234–35
Humbert of Romans O.P....89, 170–71, 174
Hundred Years' War...68, 71, 196
Huth Hours...261
hymn(s)...11, 15–16, 18, 28, 114, 116, 118–21, 123, 125–28, 165

Ile-de-France...83
illusionism (*trompe-l'œil*)...254–56, 264, 268
initials, historiated...23–24, 27, 74, 82–83, 86, 154, 160, 227, 230, 306
initials, ornamented or decorated...23–24, 73–74, 83, 87, 116, 154, 208, 226, 230
Innocent (Pope)...89
Irish Liber Hymnorum...18
Isabella of Bourbon...301
Isabella of Castile...303
Isabella of Portugal...297
Isaiah...29, 83, 118, 122

Jacques de Besançon...225–26
James (King of Scotland)...265
Jean de Venette...71
Jean duc de Berry...23–25, 39, 88, 293
Jean Flamel...23
Jean le Bon (King of France)...25, 31

Jean le Noir...23, 25, 33, 39, 85
Jean Pucelle (and atelier)...21–23, 25, 33, 36–37, 71, 74, 78, 85–87
Jeanne d'Artois et Bourgogne...87
Jeanne d'Evreux...27, 30, 36, 79–80
Jeanne de Belleville...87–88
Jeanne de Bourbon...23, 37
Jeanne I of Navarre...39
Jeanne II of Navarre...3, 25, 34, 37, 39
Jeanne of Savoy...36
Jeremiah...118, 120
Jerome (St)...12
Jerusalem, Heavenly...267
jewel(s), jewelled...5–6, 253–69, 303
John of Afflighem: *De musica*...168–69
John the Baptist (St)...30–31, 75, 83–84
John the Evangelist (St)...31, 127, 155–56, 201, 205–6, 231, 301
John XXII (Pope)...113
Joseph of Arimathea...127
Joyenval, Premonstratensian Abbey...82
Juan de Flandes: *Temptation of Christ in the Desert*...303–4
Juan de Flandes: *The Marriage Feast at Cana*...303–4
Juan of Castille...301, 303, 305
Judas...117

Katherine (St)...77
Katharina de Radegge....81
Keldermans, Anthoon and Rombout...300
Kunigunde (Benedictine abbess)...38

Lactantius: *Divinarum Institutionum*...233–34
Lamentation of Christ...155
Last Supper...85, 155, 231
Laurence (St)...80, 205–6
lectionary...9, 81
Legend of St Adrian...262
Leo IX (Pope)...202
lesson(s)...80, 83–84, 88, 114, 118–19, 128, 160, 165
libelli precum...13, 16
library...208
Liédet, Loyset...255
Liège...84
lily...228, 266
litany...11–12, 14–16, 18, 26, 33, 196
literacy, in Latin...72, 89

liturgical book(s), manuscript(s)...67–92, 195–209, 225–26, 229
liturgical chant...163–74, 206
liturgy...14, 17, 26–27, 71, 75–77, 88–89, 163–74, 200, 202, 205, 229, 238
Longchamp, Franciscan nunnery...86
Longinus...116, 124–25
Louis IX (King of France, St)...23, 30, 34, 68, 71–72, 74–75, 77–80, 91, 292, 303
Louis X (King of France)...25, 82
Louis XI (King of France)...199, 236
Louis of Marseille (or Toulouse, St)...31, 34
lux (light)...267

Maître François...226, 231, 236
Maître Honoré...86
Malmesbury...17
Man of Sorrows...116
manuscript production...91–92, 196–205
Marcel...229
Marches region...114
Margaret (St)...34, 302
Margaret of Austria...6, 291–92, 294–308
—inventories of...291–92, 295, 298, 302, 307
Margaret of Burgundy...25
Margaret of Provence...37, 91
Margaret of York...297, 300
Margaret Tudor...265
marginal ornamentation...23–25, 74, 87, 232, 253–69
Marguerite de Bourbon...297
Marie de Clermont....68, 91
Marie de France...88
Marie Jouvenal des Ursins...88
Marino da Perugia...154
Martial (St)...70–71
Martin (St)...77
martyrology...9, 76
Mary (see also Virgin), Marian...6, 27–28, 31, 75, 77, 126–27, 155–61, 294
Mary Magdalen (St)...31, 76–77, 124, 261
Mary of Burgundy...296
Mary of Hungary...297
Mass (incl. canon, etc)...2, 4, 26, 29, 35, 67, 70, 82–85, 90, 164, 168, 199, 202, 227–31, 233, 237, 293, 306
Master of Jacques de Besançon...5, 225–26, 230, 235–38

Master of Jean Rolin...226
Master of Mary of Burgundy...254
Master of Morgan MS. M.293...197–98
mathematical acoustics...168
Maundy Thursday...230
Maximilian (Emperor)...292, 296
Mazerolles, Philippe de...255
Mechelen...296, 299, 303, 306
Meeting of the Three Kings...200
melody...167–73, 205
Mercia...15,
miniature(s)...23–25, 27, 33, 38, 74, 87, 199–202, 206–7, 225–26, 228, 230–31, 236, 254–55, 258, 260, 262–63, 265, 268
Miroir des Dames...40
Miroir des Princes...40
missal...1, 3–5, 9, 69–92, 198–208, 225–38, 306
missionaries...17
mnemonic...265, 268
mode (Gregorian)...168–70, 172
monasticism...10, 14, 18
monochord...168
Montargis, Dominican nunnery...68
Mosan Master: *Norfolk triptych*...266
mourning...126
musical intervals...168
musical notation...74, 166–68, 172–73, 204, 206
musical pitch...167–68, 173
musical theory...168–69
myrtle...232

narrative...230, 232, 268
Nativity of Christ...85, 233, 294
Nativity of the Virgin...77, 227–28, 230
Netherlands(-ish)...5, 197, 200, 294–96, 300
Neufchâtel, Antoine de (bishop of Toul)...207
Neufchâtel, Charles de (archbishop of Besançon)...4, 198–200, 202–3, 205–7
Nicholas (St)...203, 206
Notre-Dame, Paris...5, 82, 228–29, 236

O antiphons...236–37
Office(s)...2–4, 22, 26–29, 31, 33, 35, 76, 114, 154, 156, 158–60, 164–66, 168, 174, 236, 258, 260

Office (Hours) of St John the Baptist...27–28, 30, 39, 83–84
Office (Hours) of St John the Evangelist...27, 225–26
Office (Hours) of St Louis, King of France...27, 30, 33–34, 78, 88
Office (Hours) of the Cross...4, 26, 28, 32–33, 112–14
Office (Hours) of the Holy Spirit...26, 28–29, 33
Office (Hours) of the Passion...2, 4, 23, 26, 28, 111–29
Office (Vigils) of the Dead...11, 19, 26, 36, 115, 196
Office of St Dominic...80, 88
Olivier de Clisson...87
Order of St Michael...228
ordination books...9
Orpheus...30
Orsini (Cardinal)...23
Our Lady of Impruneta...267

painting, fresco...39, 81, 124, 154–56, 159, 161, 234
painting, panel...5–6, 124, 154–55, 255, 292–308
Paris...3, 5, 21, 37, 67–69, 71–72, 77–82, 85–87, 89, 195 –97, 225–26, 228, 235–36
Passion...2, 4, 15–16, 28, 31, 33, 37–38, 111–12, 114, 235, 237
Passion cycle...115–29, 232, 298, 304–6
Passion plays...124, 235
Pater Noster...15, 18
patriarchs...232
patron(age)...4, 6–7, 198, 204, 227–29, 231, 234–35, 238, 255, 266, 291–308
Paul (St)...29, 80, 89
pearl...259–66
penitential psalms...11, 16, 26, 33, 35
Pentecost...2, 29, 75–76, 203–06, 231
Perugia(n)...153–55, 160, 166, 171, 174
Perugia, Bibl. Comunale Augusta...2, 153
Perugia, S. Domenico (Dominican priory)...153–54, 160–61, 164
Peter (St)...29, 80, 89
Peter Martyr O.P. (St)...26, 71, 76, 80, 171
Petites Heures of Jean de Berry...28–30, 39
Philibert (Duke of Savoy)...297
Philip the Fair...296, 299

Philip the Good (Duke of Burgundy)...199, 291, 293–94, 306
Philippe IV le Bel (King of France)...67, 72, 79, 82, 87
Philippe V (King of France)...87
Philippe VI de Valois (King of France)...25, 31, 34, 67
Philippe, Comte d'Evreux...25
pietà...126
Pisa, Campo Santo...39
placard, billboard...235
Plummer, John...196–98, 207
poems, abecedary, alphabetical...16, 18
Poissy, St Louis de (Dominican nunnery)...2–3, 67–92
pontifical...207
Pontius Pilate...111, 119–21
Poor Clares...31, 37
Portiforium of Wulstan...18
portrait(s)...293–96, 301–3, 305
Portsmouth Cathedral, Episcopal Library of...24
Prague...38
prayer(s)...10–19, 21–22, 25–26, 28, 32–36, 38–40, 112, 114, 116, 119–21, 125–26, 127, 260–61, 294, 301
prayer book(s)...1–5, 10–19, 22, 24–26, 30, 32, 34–35, 40, 256, 267, 292–93, 296, 306, 308
Premonstratensians...173
Procès de Paradis...235–36
procession(s)...203
processional...76, 174
Proper of Saints (*sanctorale*)...11, 27, 74–75, 199, 201, 229–30, 237
Proper of Time (*temporale*)...11, 74–75, 86, 199, 230, 237
prophets...232
Provence...200
psalm(s)...10, 11, 14, 26, 28, 32, 35, 75, 90, 114, 117–18, 120, 122, 124–28, 165, 235
psalm-tones...173
psalter...3, 9–12, 22, 25–26, 35, 38–39, 73, 81, 86–87, 231
psalter-hours...12, 21–23, 26
psalter-processional...73, 76, 84
Psalter of Bonne of Luxembourg...21–40
Psalter of St Jerome...35
psaltery...170

Pseudo-Bede: *De meditatione Passionis Christi*...112
Pseudo-Bernard: *Liber de Passione Christi*...112
Pseudo-Bonaventure: *Meditations on the Life of Christ*...112–13, 120, 123–24
Purification of the Virgin...77

quatrefoils...22–23, 25, 123

Raymond of Peñafort O.P....76
reform, liturgical...170–71, 174
reform, religious...18, 75
Regensburg, Dominican nunnery...81
Regina mundi hodie de seculo...174
Registre des ordonnances de l'hôtel du roi...78
Regularis Concordia...16, 18–19
relics, reliquary...201–03, 205–06, 228–29, 298–300
Resurrection of Christ...127–28, 232, 304
Richard II (King of England)...293
Robert II (Duke of Burgundy)...23
Rolin, Jean (Cardinal)...227
Rome, S. Maria in Trastevere...155
rosary...257, 259, 261–63, 266–67
Rothschild Hours...260, 263–65, 268
Rouen, Archbishop of...68
Royal prayer book...12–19
rubrics...12, 14, 35–36, 205, 229–30

Saint-Benoît-sur-Loire...13
Saint-Denis (abbey)...78–80, 229, 267
Saint-Jacques, Paris (Dominican priory)...91–92
Saint-Maximin, Dominican priory...76
Saint-Père de Chartres...79
Sainte Chapelle (Chambery)...299
Sainte Chapelle (Paris)...31, 38, 78, 228–29
saints (incl. martyrs, confessors, virgins, etc)...31, 77, 205, 230, 263, 303
Saluces Hours...197
Saluces Master...197–98, 207
salvation...232
Salve regina...76
San Marco, Florence (Dominican priory)...81

Sankt Katherinenthal (Dominican nunnery)...81
Sarum...172
Saul...120
Savoy(ard)...197–99, 207–8, 295, 299
Savoy Hours...21–40
Schloß Ambras, Kunstkammer...258
Scrovegni Chapel...117
sculpture...79–80, 83, 232
Sebastian (St)...71
Seelengärtlein...261–63, 265, 268
Sens, Archbishop of...67
Servatus (St)...70
sibyl(s)...232–34
sin(s)...18, 236
Sittow, Michiel...292, 302, 304–5
Six Degrees of Charity...39
Solomon...159–60
Song of Songs...156, 158–61, 166, 174
soul(s)...18, 39, 83, 118, 120, 125, 127, 161, 227
Speculum dominarum...39
Stabat Mater...265
stained glass...77–79, 297
statue...79
Stephen (St)...80, 201–3, 205–6, 229
suffrages...11, 22, 26–27, 31–34, 261
Suger (Abbot of Saint-Denis)...267
sun and moon...232
Supplicationes Variae...114–15

tapestry...306
textual inscriptions...265, 268
theatre...235
theotokos...159
Thomas Aquinas (St)...29, 71, 84, 267
Toul...207
Traité sur l'oraison dominicale...293
Très Belles Heures de Notre Dame...293
Treviso...120
Trinity...29–30, 75, 231, 235, 293
triptych...292–93
Turin, National Library of...24

Udalric (St)...113
Umbria(n)...154–55
Utrecht...255

van der Weyden, Rogier: *Crucifixion of Christ*...306

van der Weyden, Rogier: *Mass of Saint Gregory*...306
van Eyck, Jan: *Ghent Altarpiece*...255
van Eyck, Jan: *Virgin in the Church*...294
van Laethen, Lieven (painter)...255
van Lathen, Liéven (goldsmith)...300
van Orley, Bernard...299
Vera Icon...297
Vermeyen, Jan...302
vernacular...18, 25, 33, 35, 39–40, 87, 156, 236
verse, versicle (and responsory)...36, 114, 118, 120, 122, 126, 128, 158, 160, 165–66, 173–74, 196
Vézelay...76
Vidi speciosam quasi columbam...166, 173
Vincennes...37
Vincent (St)...70
Virgin, Our Lady (see also Mary)...11, 33–35, 38, 76–77, 80, 83, 85, 112, 122, 124–27, 155–60, 166, 227, 231, 233, 235–37, 258, 292–93, 296, 301, 303–4
Virgin and Child...34, 37, 155, 228, 293, 295–96, 301–3
Virgin enthroned...155, 157
Virgin, St Luke painting the...258
virtues (incl. justice, faith, etc)...232, 235
Voragine, Jacopo da O.P.: *Golden Legend*...156–58, 160, 236–37
Vrelant, Willem...255

Wearmouth and Jarrow...17
Wilton Diptych...292
Winchester...16
woodcut...234
Worcester...15
Worcester Cathedral...172
workshop (see also atelier)...196, 206–8, 225–28, 230–32, 235–36, 238
wounds of Christ...38–39, 123, 125–26

Yolande of Flanders...36
York...17
Yves (St)...71

Manuscripts by location:

Adelaide
State Library of South Australia
(no shelfmark)...116–29
Amsterdam
Bibl. Philosophica Hermetica
40...257, 263, 265–66
Arras
Bibl. Mun.
465...174
Auckland
City Central Library, Special Collection
Med. G138-39...198–208
Basle
A.VII.3...18
Besançon
Bibl. mun.
72...204
75...205
76...205, 207
77...205, 207
115–17...207
127...207
157...207
Boston
Public Library
qMed. 131...114–16, 119
Brussels
Bibliothèque Royale
139...84
9092...293
11060–1...293
Cambrai
Bibliothèque Municipale
C 38...174
Cambridge
Corpus Christi College
391...15
Fitzwilliam Museum
294e...263
Marley Cutting Sp. 5...263
University Library
Ll.I.10...12–19
Mm.ii.9...172
Cassel
Murhandsehe Bibliothek
4^0 math. et art. 50...265–66

Chantilly
Musée Condé
51...36
1887...79
Chartres
Bibliothèque municipale
581...85
Darmstadt,
Landesbibliothek
69...262
Florence
Bibl. Laurenziana
Plut. XXV. 3...114
Hanover
Kestner Museum
WM xxia 36...10
Ivrea
Biblioteca Capitolare
CVI...174
Lisbon
Gulbenkian Collection
f. 13...236
London
British Library
Add. 15265...120, 122
Add. 18852...257, 263
Add. 23935...89, 171, 174
Add. 27697...197
Add. 30072...81
Add. 34247...123, 126
Add. 35313...261–65, 268
Add. 38126...261
Add. 49598...10
Add. 54180...86
Arundel 155...15
Cotton Caligula A.XIV...10
Cotton Galba A.XIV...13–19
Cotton Nero A.II...13–19
Egerton 2125...260
Egerton 3037...70–92
Harl. 863...15
Harl. 2965...12–19
Harl. 7633...12–19
Royal 2.A.XX...12–19
Yates Thompson 27...36
private collection...70–92
Sotheby's
9 December 1974, lot 60...73
7 December 1982, lot 70...81
22 June 1993, lot 99...209

20 June 1995, lot 90...209
Los Angeles
  J. Paul Getty Museum
    Ludwig IX. 91...264
Melbourne
  National Gallery of Victoria
    Felton 1...236
  State Library of Victoria
    *096 1/R66A...71–92, 171, 174
Munich
  Bayerische Staatsbibliothek
    Clm. 10170...89
    Clm. 23637...257, 263, 268
New Haven
  Yale University, Beinecke Rare Book and Manuscript Library
    390...21–40
New York
  Metropolitan Museum of Art, Cloisters Collection
    (54.1.2)...27, 78, 85
    (69.86)....21–40
  Morgan M.28...197, 199–200, 207
  Morgan M.73...235
  Morgan M.196...197
  Morgan M.293...196–97
  Morgan M.869...10
  Morgan M. 917...256–57
  Public Library
    41...207
  Union Theological Seminary, Bourke Library
    DeR 52...73
Orléans
  Bibliothèque Municipale
    116...13
Oxford
  Bodleian Library
    Douce 8...259
    Douce 51...266
    Douce 223...263
    Douce 256...258–59
    Douce 219-20...261–62
    liturg. Canon 43...236
    Rawl. liturg. e2...84
  Keble College
    49...81
Paris
  Archives Nationales
    JJ 2...90
    JJ 57...78
  Bibliothèque de l'Arsenal
    107...70–92
    602–603...70–92
  Bibliothèque Mazarine
    410...237
    412...5, 225–28, 230–38
    461...225, 234
  Bibliothèque Nationale
    fr. 244–45...236–37
    fr. 5716...78
    lat. 919...29
    lat. 920...234
    lat. 10483-4...87–89
    n.a. lat. 3145...21–40, 78, 85
  Musée Jacquemart André
    1...36
Perugia
  Biblioteca Comunale Augusta
    2785...154–61
Philadelphia
  Museum of Art
    45-65-7...71–92
Prague
  Narodni Gallery
    K.36879...237
Rome
  Dominican archives
    XIV L 1...172, 174
Vatican City
  Biblioteca Apostolica
    Urb. lat. 603...86
    lat. 10.000...115
    Ross. 94...257, 262
Venice
  Biblioteca Marciana
    lat. 1, 99...261, 263–64
Vienna
  Österreichische Nationalbibliothek
    1800...293
    1887...266
    1897...258–61, 263–65
    1979...257–58
    1984...257
    2706...261–63, 265, 268
    Ser. n. 2600...264
    Ser. n. 2619...262
    Ser. n. 2624...260
    Ser. n. 2884...260, 263–65, 268
    Ser. n. 13238...261, 264

Waddesdon Manor
  2…73, 76, 84
Worcester
  Cathedral Chapter Library
    F. 160…172
Zürich
  Schweizerisches Landesmuseum
    LM 26117…81